A
Russian
Merchant's
Tale

Indiana-Michigan Series in
Russian and East European Studies

Alexander Rabinowitch and William G. Rosenberg,
editors

A Russian Merchant's Tale

THE LIFE AND ADVENTURES OF
IVAN ALEKSEEVICH TOLCHËNOV,
BASED ON HIS DIARY

David L. Ransel

INDIANA UNIVERSITY PRESS

Bloomington and Indianapolis

This book is a publication of

Indiana University Press
601 North Morton Street
Bloomington, IN 47404-3797 USA

http://iupress.indiana.edu

Telephone orders   800-842-6796
Fax orders   812-855-7931
Orders by e-mail   iuporder@indiana.edu

The paper used in this publication meets the minimum requirements
of American National Standard for Information Sciences—
Permanence of Paper for Printed Library Materials, ANSI Z39.48-1984.

Manufactured in the United States of America

Ransel, David L.
A Russian merchant's tale : the life and adventures of Ivan Alekseevich Tolchënov,
based on his diary / David L. Ransel.
p. cm. — (Indiana-Michigan Series in Russian and East European Studies)
Includes bibliographical references and index.
ISBN 978-0-253-35236-1 (cloth : alk. paper) — ISBN 978-0-253-22020-2 (pbk. : alk. paper)
1. Tolchenov, Ivan Alekseevich, b. 1754. 2. Merchants—Russia (Federation)—Moscow (Oblast)—
Biography. 3. Merchants—Russia (Federation)—Moscow (Oblast)—Social conditions—
18th century. 4. Business enterprises—Russia (Federation)—Moscow (Oblast)—History—
18th century. 5. Moscow (Russia : Oblast)—Commerce—History—18th century.
6. Moscow (Russia : Oblast)—Biography. I. Title.
HF3630.2.Z8M677 2009
381.092—dc22
[B]
2008023839

1   2   3   4   5   14   13   12   11   10   09

To Firuz Kazemzadeh and Marc Raeff
with thanks for the good start

Contents

Acknowledgments

I first want to thank the Swedish historian Claes Peterson, who introduced me to the diary of Ivan Tolchënov and furnished a copy of the portion of it printed by Soviet scholars in the early 1970s. The Russian historian Boris Nikolaevich Mironov was also helpful in obtaining additional materials and giving references to sources. Leonid Romanovich Vaintraub provided a great deal of assistance and advice when I began to do archival work, and he went with me to Dmitrov and the surrounding district on several occasions to show me surviving architectural monuments from the time in which the figures in this book were alive. He and Irina Piatiletova of Vesti Press in Dmitrov helped me to gain entrance into and to photograph the interior of the Tolchënov house. Galina Nikolaevna Ul'ianova shared with me her knowledge of Russian commercial elites and their charitable practices. I also want to acknowledge the patience and assistance of the staffs of the Russian State Archive of Ancient Acts, the Central Historical Archive of Moscow, and the Archive and Museum of the Dmitrov District, and the Slavic bibliographers at Indiana University's Wells Library and those at the Helsinki University Library's Slavonic Division.

My colleagues at Indiana University, Nina Perlina, Dodona Kiziria, Michael Alexeev, Galina McClaws, Jerzy Kolodziej, Larisa Privalskaia, Henry Cooper, and Ronald Feldstein patiently responded to my questions about Russian usage and Orthodox religious practices. John T. Alexander of the University of Kansas read through much of the first draft and saved me from a number of mistakes. Daniel Kaiser of Grinnell College and Alexander M. Martin of Notre Dame University went through the entire manuscript and offered many helpful suggestions for improvement. Dale Peterson of Amherst College and Laura Engelstein of Yale University provided helpful interpretive suggestions at an early stage of the work. I am also indebted to Willard Sunderland of the University of Cincinnati, Gregory Freeze of Brandeis University, and the participants of the Midwest Historians of Russia Workshop for useful observations and bibliography materials. Irina Piatiletova and Leonid Vaintraub kindly allowed me to reproduce photographs taken by them, on page 87, and pages 110 and 111, respectively. Janet Rabinowitch, director of Indiana University Press, offered helpful suggestions for shaping the introduction, and Candace McNulty did sensitive copyediting.

Financial assistance for research and travel was provided by Indiana University. A fellowship from the International Research and Exchanges Board (IREX) in spring of 1999 allowed me to launch my initial archival investigations. I am also grateful to the Bogliasco Foundation Inc. for a fellowship at its Liguria Center for the Study of Arts and Letters near Genoa in the spring of 2007 that gave me uninterrupted time to finish the manuscript.

Introduction

On March 16, 1797, in the city of Dmitrov, 80 kilometers north of Moscow, Ivan Alekseevich Tolchënov, a Russian merchant, together with his family and its servants, loaded their worldly goods onto wagons in final preparation for a permanent move to Moscow. Just after the midday dinner hour, Ivan's wife, children, and servants left with the family's belongings. The following day, Ivan himself said his farewells to two close family members and a physician friend, and he too departed for Moscow in the company of a cousin. The Tolchënovs were leaving behind a large, elegant townhouse, the first masonry residence ever constructed in the city. The property on which the home stood was resplendent with orchards, gardens, orangeries and fish ponds. This marvelous urban estate, the envy of everyone in the city, had been lost. Ivan had dissipated his family's fortune and gone deep into debt by failing to attend to business and living beyond his means. And this was not the end of his troubles. Creditors hounded him in Moscow until he was arrested temporarily and forced to account for the many tricks he had used to evade payment by stringing his creditors along and shielding his assets. In Moscow he found employment, but life had to be lived in much reduced circumstances.

This story is not unusual. The life of a merchant in early modern Russia was risky, and many commercial families suffered bankruptcy and the loss of their property and privileges. Unfortunately, we know very little about how these failures occurred and almost nothing about the inner life of merchant families in this period. In the case just described, however, Ivan Tolchënov (pronounced Tal-CHO-naff, the Russian letter ë always being stressed and voiced as o or yo) did something altogether out of the ordinary. He kept a diary—and not just a brief record of major events in his town or a count of births and deaths in the family. Records of that sort have been found for a few other merchants in late eighteenth-century Russia and are not especially revealing.[1] In contrast, Ivan Tolchënov produced a document of unmatched length and interest. Ivan began writing his diary in 1769 and continued faithfully recording his experiences almost daily for more than forty years. In this rare account we learn about his education and training, family dynamics, commerce, philanthropy, personal achievements and losses, and also much about the life of his city, the surrounding country estates, and the city of Moscow. He kept track of the rituals and rhythms of daily life, structures of the days and seasons, the quality of agricultural output and the conditions of its transport, while also recording family events and social contacts with a wide array of people from lords to laborers. What is missing most often is the content of his personal and business relations; that is, the diarist did not report conversations or even topics of conversations. Accordingly, much of the story can be understood only when supplemented by research in documentary and printed sources in the archives and libraries of the city of Moscow and Moscow province. My objective has been to combine the diary and these additional materials to form a picture that takes us beyond the stereotypical understanding we have long had of merchant community and family life as exclusively static, benighted, and self-enclosed.

One of the diary's strengths is its record of contacts across the social hierarchy. Some years ago, Michael Confino challenged historians to study Russia as an integrated social body and not as a collection of isolated groups.[2] Yet because Russia was ruled as a collection of socially specific groups and archives were accordingly organized and preserved by institution and social position, scholars have found it difficult to integrate and analyze the interactions between people of different social statuses. The observable interactions, when they go beyond a single ministry, party, or social estate, are usually two-sided. Scholars examine petitions from subordinates to superiors or look at court cases that pitted a person of one social estate against a person of another. But these limited and usually conflictual documents tell less about what held Russian society together than about points of stress and possible rupture. A source like Ivan Tolchënov's diary offers a way around the barriers posed by this structure of preserved knowledge. The diary shows Ivan in frequent contact with people of four social spheres: his merchant colleagues, the local nobility, state officials, and the clergy at all ranks save for the very highest such as metropolitans (although Ivan once enjoyed an hour-long personal visit with the illustrious Metropolitan Platon Levshin). Ivan's family even owned serfs, who were members of its large household. The family lived in close, daily contact with people from every social level. The diary therefore constitutes an unusual record of the attachments of an individual and his family to the broader collective and, indeed, delineates the boundaries of the collective and reveals the expectations and demands of its various actors. This evidence, in turn, allows us to understand and analyze the shared cultural and social practices that held Russia together and gave meaning to its collective life.

Equally important, the diary allows us to follow what may have been a frequent aspiration of Russian merchants, the desire to associate with the nobility and, if possible, to share in the privileges and the security of person and place that only the nobility enjoyed. The life of a merchant anywhere is seldom secure. In imperial Russia it was exceptionally unstable. Vertical mobility was high, and few families were able to sustain their position in the first rank of merchants for more than a generation or two.[3] The only guarantee against falling into the degraded, soul-tax paying population was to rise into the nobility. A number of families did succeed in this aspiration in the eighteenth century when social categories were less rigid than they later became. By the time Ivan Tolchënov rose to local prominence, Russian elites were becoming anxious about the stability of social identities, and the government began erecting barriers to the transgression of social boundaries. Ivan was nonetheless able to transcend his ascribed position in some respects. He adopted the tastes, style of life, and the habits of his friends and acquaintances in the nobility. He started out his adult life as a wealthy grain merchant and magistracy councilor, and later became mayor of his hometown of Dmitrov. He spent time with the local nobility, the clergy, and government officials and outdid some of them in his expenditures on his elegant townhouse with its orangeries, gardens, and fish ponds. He attended the theater, purchased books and scientific instruments, and joined an exclusive club. Like wealthy members of the Russian nobility and other merchants of his rank, Ivan eagerly joined the new consumer economy of the eighteenth century, and his life demonstrates the central role that style, taste, and impressive self-presentation played in defining and maintaining social status. Ivan's self-fashioning was sufficiently effective that even after business failures propelled him down the social ladder, he was able to reclaim elements of the self-identity he had earlier created and continue to gain entrée to some important events and persons in Moscow and St. Petersburg.

MICROHISTORY

In choosing this subject, I hoped to gain the insights offered by the microhistorical research method. The Italian scholars who developed this approach in the 1970s and 1980s took their inspiration, interestingly enough, from a Russian source: Tolstoy's theory of history in *War and Peace*. Tolstoy called attention to the unpredictable and contingent character of historical events. The Italians were reacting against the traditional grand narratives and also against the new "serial" methods associated with quantification and the Annales school.[4] Both of these stances shared the functionalist practice of taking a series of observations and imposing on them a constructed order or regularity. By experimenting with observations on a radically reduced scale, the Italian practitioners of microhistory discovered that the interpretations built on the macrohistorical or serial methods obscured, or even remained altogether blind to, relationships that were essential to an understanding of the social order. To take one example, what historians working on the macro level thought to be a modern "depersonalized" market in land turned out on closer inspection to be a land exchange in which prices were set by kinship bonds. One of the key problems in microhistory is, accordingly, the degree of fit between macro and micro observations. The photography critic and historical theorist Siegfried Kracauer, using an analogy from film, adopted a highly pessimistic stance on this question, contending that no necessary correlation existed, but microhistorians usually understand the relationship between a wide angle of vision and a tightly focused observation to be problematic rather than ultimately incommensurable.[5]

Microhistorians seek to craft a narrative account of their subject, but they often insert themselves, like ethnologists, into the account. As Giovanni Levi and Carlo Ginzburg have explained, the narrative of microhistory exposes the ambiguities and gaps in the evidence and incorporates into the narrative an account of the research process itself, including the formulation of hypotheses and the working through of interpretive strategies.[6] In other words, instead of closing off the generative potential of the evidence by clamping it into a given design, the method explores the latitude actors enjoy for making choices contrary to the normative reality or hegemonic discourse of their time and can therefore reveal what is unseen in observations at a macro level.

A PLEBEIAN DIARY AS A SOURCE

In seeking to use an eighteenth-century diary as a source of information about the personal and family life of a merchant, I thought that some knowledge of the writing as a literary form would be helpful. I looked at Andrei Tartakovksii's classifications of Russian memoirs and diaries from this period, but so far as diaries were concerned, his spacious categorizations did not offer much instruction in how to situate and unpack such a source. Like literary analysts elsewhere, Tartakovskii was not especially interested in diaries before they became the work of educated men of affairs or creative artists and therefore displayed the qualities that literary scholars understandably most enjoy describing and comparing.[7]

A look outside the field of Russian studies showed the same thing. Literature specialists considered diaries a kind of bastard genre of little intrinsic interest before they became conscious literary productions intended for publication. The Goethe specialist Peter Boerner, who tried to give a systematic account of diaries, found the task difficult because the form varied in literary quality from very high to very low and offered no rules about what might be true or false.[8] The editors of a recent book of essays on the diary argued that the diary is "an uncertain genre uneasily balanced between literary and historical writing, between spontaneity of reportage and the reflectiveness of the crafted text, between selfhood and events, between subjectivity and objectivity, between the private and the public, . . . [it] constantly disturbs attempts to summarise its characteristics within formalized boundaries. The diary is a misfit form of writing, inhabiting the frontiers between many neighbouring domains, often belonging simultaneously to several 'genres' or 'species' and thus being condemned to exclusion from both at once."[9] So, historians working with diaries cannot expect genre analysis to give much of a guide to interpretive strategies. The specialists on literary analysis themselves seem to be either dismayed or confused by this cultural product.

The diary does nevertheless have a history, and it is in its history that much of the difficulty of analysis of diaries as a genre resides. Each scholar who considers a diary of a particular era is inclined to invest it with meaning derived from a broader understanding of the values that are thought to characterize that particular era. If we set aside some classical antecedents and East Asian examples, the diary did not exist before the fifteenth century, and its appearance is usually ascribed to the development of an articulated individual self-consciousness associated with the European Renaissance. In this view, the diary is a sign of what is understood as the central truth of the Renaissance. Considering this origin, it is interesting to observe that diary-keeping grew rapidly in the seventeenth and eighteenth centuries among pietists—in other words, people who were reacting against Renaissance humanism. Pietists nevertheless shared with the people of the Renaissance a concern with the individual. In the case of the pietists, this concern stressed not individual expression so much as individual responsibility and individual salvation.

Historians locate the usual starting point and model for the diary in personal or household account books.[10] In the hands of the Puritans in England and the Moravian Brethren in Germany in the seventeenth and eighteenth centuries, account books became records of an individual's successes and failures in meeting the moral standards of these religions. In their daily entries, diarists sought to dissect their inner selves with the aim of improving themselves and justifying their position as members of the elect. This was the dawn of the age of science, and so analysts want to understand these literary efforts as reflective of a scientific outlook. Jürgen Schlaeger, for example, framed this attitude in a metaphor suitable to the scientific age in which these pietists lived when he wrote that they explored the inner self "through a medium that allows meticulous procedures, careful observation, faithful documentation and critical self-reflexivity." Despite this gesture to the age of science, he may have been closer to understanding their efforts when he later noted that they turned themselves into texts to which they could return again and again to assess their behavior and guide it along the proper path to salvation.[11]

The French scholar Béatrice Didier pursued the connection between the diary, Protestantism, and business accounting in the seventeenth and eighteenth centuries. If this was the age of science, it was also the age of the rise of the middle classes, and so Didier wrote that we should view the diary as a quintessential sign of bourgeois civilization; it translated the personal into a business account. Like the archetypical diary of Samuel Pepys, composed during the 1660s, this daily record-keeping often inscribed money and business matters but also spilled over into an accounting of love, work, and friendships. Didier claimed that the diary functioned as a number of capitalist devices. It served as a balance sheet that calculated moral failures and successes. It also worked as a savings account on which one could draw for memories untarnished by the passage of time. "Lost times will be less squandered because their passing will have been committed to the diary."[12] As a practice, the diary had parallels in the life of a bureaucrat of the state administrations that were forming in early modern Europe. "The attitude of the diarist in this account-keeping is that of an official. . . . The diary quickly becomes a kind of daily obligation, altogether comparable to the daily output reports of an office worker."[13] Indeed, some famous diarists were officials who seemed to be extending bureaucratic logs to cover personal matters, for example, Samuel Pepys, the English naval administrator of the seventeenth century, and Aleksandr Khrapovitskii, the personal secretary of Catherine the Great in Russia a century later. Looking ahead to more recent times, Didier also considered the diary an extension of a childhood religious practice of daily bedtime prayer, a means of putting a messy world into order at the end of each day. The loss of religious belief in adulthood is compensated for by a continuation of this practice in the form of a diary reckoning. In short, for Didier the diary appeared at a convergence of capitalism, individualism, and Christianity.[14]

The idea that the diary compensates for something lost in childhood was picked up in a slightly different way by the inventive and indefatigable researcher of autobiographic writings, Philippe Lejeune. He noted that diary writing grew in importance at just the time, the late eighteenth and nineteenth centuries, that Philippe Ariès located the emergence in professional and popular thinking of a life stage between childhood and adulthood, a period of adolescence.[15] Lejeune's own researches in recent decades have demonstrated that teenagers comprise the largest number of diary writers and that they use diaries to work out their sense of who they are becoming.[16] Lejeune contended that the development of diary-keeping in earlier times should therefore be understood in relationship to the appearance of this new life stage.[17] In other words, if we can extend Lejeune's idea, the diary was a sign that individual self-consciousness had reached a point that more and more Europeans felt a need to take time between childhood and adulthood to work through on paper a personal identity crisis before they could move on and fully engage their adult roles. So, now the diary is made to satisfy our need to explain a twentieth-century concern with the psychological development of youth. Young diary keepers were involved in the reflexive project of the self that Anthony Giddens claimed is an inescapable aspect of modern life.[18]

As a literary form, then, the diary can serve a variety of ends and be interpreted in a number of different ways. It is an almost empty vessel or, perhaps better, an adaptable tool, at the disposal of its user for the purposes at hand. Its interpreters can fill it with whatever meaning they find appropriate to the age they are studying.

What about the Russian diary? One of the first things I learned when I shifted my attention to Russian diaries was that the form was borrowed from the West and, like many other Western imports, it first appeared in Russia during the reign of Peter I. Not surprisingly, the first Russian word for diary, *iurnal*, was a borrowing from the Dutch *Journaal*. By 1720 the French articulation *zhurnal* came into use, and it remained the designation for a daily account through the century and beyond. The most common modern word for diary, the calque *dnevnik*, did not enter the vocabulary until late in the eighteenth century.[19] The earliest uses of the journal in Russian are associated with military operations on land and on sea, a log of movements and events. With a few exceptions, such as the travel journals of Pëtr Tolstoi and Boris Kurakin, writers only later developed this form as the record of personal actions and impressions that we associate with the modern diary.

The term zhurnal could also be used to designate "a book of householder, accounting, or commercial notes," as in "keeping a journal of revenue and expenditures."[20] This type of record in a somewhat expanded definition was described in a book for merchants published in Russia in 1768. There the author compared a "memoir or daily book" and a "journal," which he saw as similar in form to a bookkeeping record but containing more thorough descriptions of sales, purchases, contracts, and daily business activities.[21] Since this work appeared in St. Petersburg in the very year that Ivan Tolchënov was studying there, it is tempting to think that it may have been the genesis of his interest in making a daily record of his life. However, the full title that Ivan eventually used for his dairy, "A Journal or Notes on the Life and Adventures of I. A. Tolchënov," was most likely borrowed from a Russian translation of Daniel Defoe's famous work, *The Life and Strange Surprising Adventures of Robinson Crusoe*, or one of its many imitations in eighteenth-century Russia.[22]

The number of Russian diaries before the nineteenth century, at least the number of those that have been preserved, was not large. The historian Pëtr Zaionchkovskii's compilation of diaries and memoirs before 1800 lists 867, and of these, according to Orest Pelech, only 82 "fitted a strict definition of diaries as distinct from autobiographies, memoirs and some travelogues." A mere six of these 82 were composed before 1700, and only 25 before 1750. The large majority were written in the second half of the century. Borrowing a phrase from Emil

Cioran, Pelech observes that this emergence of "[d]iary-keeping, the writing of memoirs and autobiographies—all are testimony to Russians' 'fall into time,' to their self-discovery as actors on the stage of history—a stage not only with a past, but also with a future. . . . Before 1700, this kind of historicist self-consciousness was absent among Russians of all classes."[23]

At first, classes other than the nobility hardly mattered. Until the late 1700s journals and memoirs were produced in Russia almost exclusively by members of the nobility and, as such, they functioned symbolically as a sign of elite status and perhaps also as a sign of leisure, even if nobles in the first half of the eighteenth century could scarcely be considered a leisured class.[24] Tolstoi and Kurakin, for example, kept their travel journals in large part to prove that they were doing the work that Peter I had demanded of them during their stays in Europe. Nevertheless, as a rule, such writing was confined to the nobility. Social position as distinct from literacy was the issue, for many merchants were literate and could well have kept diaries if they had known about the practice and considered it useful or appealing. Yet scarcely any merchants' diaries from the eighteenth century have come to light. Besides the Tolchënov journal, the few others that have been preserved are brief and refer primarily to well-known national events and the weather. Our opportunity for a glimpse into the daily and intimate life of a Russian merchant in the eighteenth century may rest largely on this one source. What can be done with it?

The ways that historians use diaries are principally two. First and most commonly, they draw passages or specific incidents from diaries to illuminate the larger issues under discussion or analysis. These are usually references to national or international events, that is "historical" actions, and historians deploy diary passages to support their interpretation of how people were reacting to the events in question. The famous eighteenth-century Russian retrospective diary of Andrei Bolotov is often used in this way.[25]

A second approach is to publish a diary in whole or in part with more or less detailed editing. Recent examples of Russian diaries translated into English with introductory contextualization and careful editing are *The Travel Diary of Peter Tolstoi*, by Max Okenfuss, and *Time of Troubles: The Diary of Iurii Vladimirovich Got'e* by Terrence Emmons.[26] These valuable undertakings provide rich source material on the periods they cover and a wealth of contextual information in their notes and introductions.

Much less common is another method: the use of a diary as the basis for a community study. To my knowledge this device has not yet been used by historians of Russia. A few examples of this approach can be found elsewhere. Arne Jarrick developed a picture of artisan life in eighteenth-century Stockholm on the basis of Johan Hjerpe's journal and, most famously, Laurel Thatcher Ulrich in *A Midwife's Tale* not only brought alive Martha Ballard, the diarist, but thoughtfully contextualized Ballard's diary notes to recreate the life of an entire community of late eighteenth-century Maine (and won six national book prizes for her effort).[27] Ulrich's work inspired me to try something similar with the Russian merchant diary. Its author, like the midwife of Ulrich's story, was a provincial who occupied an intermediate social position and lived in the late eighteenth and early nineteenth centuries.

A historian who decides to do an exegesis of a plebeian diary, to bring to life an individual as part of a community and the larger world that impinges upon it, runs into a series of choices that do not face a writer who is merely mining the diary for a few illustrative quotations. The most obvious issue is what to make of the bulk of a diary's contents, which include listings of mundane tasks, the comings and goings of everyday life. Diary entries by ordinary people are not the record of History (with a capital H). For just that reason researchers often pass by the plebeian diaries of the early modern period, seeing them as merely the same dull insignificant jottings day after day. As Laurel Ulrich pointed out, however, the dull dailiness may constitute this source's principal value. If a plebeian diary facilitates close study of community, showing how people normally spent their time and money, it can be used to test the observations that inform the grand narrative. As mentioned earlier, by radically reducing the scale of observation, it is possible to see social dynamics that not only do not appear in the larger picture but that may even be at odds with it.

To read the life of a family or community from the evidence of a diary, a scholar has to challenge received notions of what is historically and experientially important. To achieve such a shift in valuation of everyday life as against actions of national and international prominence requires a narrative powerful enough to offer insight into the lives of ordinary people that balances, modifies, or extends the established grand narrative in instructive ways. In other words, it has to do what the best examples of microhistorical analysis achieve. Laurel Ulrich accomplished this by making visible and comprehensible the key role that women played in weaving Martha Ballard's Maine community together, the extensive rather than intensive ties that women maintained to this end, and the daily engagement of women not only in the social relations of the community but in its business, medical, and political practices.

My objective is to do something similar for the provincial life of central Russia in the same period. In this case the subject is a man, and the source tracks primarily his interactions with other men. The goal is to make visible the multifaceted role that a merchant could play in the larger community of which he was a part, including the entire range of the social hierarchy. But women also appear in the story. I have long been interested in the role of women in Russian life and have sought to draw from the diary and other sources what information I could about women who came within the orbit of Ivan Tolchënov's life.

QUESTIONS OF THE SELF

Because diaries are associated with the emergence of an articulated individual self-consciousness (individualism) in early modern Europe, they are also a natural source for considering questions of identity. The largely first-person rendering of Ivan Tolchënov's diary supports the notion of individual consciousness, as does its evidence of the author's desire to stand out from the crowd and to display his interests and tastes as signs of his identification with particular social milieu and style of life. At the same time, the diary constitutes a record of Ivan's connectedness, his bonds to family, church, and the other communities in which he fashions his personal identity.[28] Another seeming paradox distinguishes Ivan's self-presentation: while obviously fascinated with the rationalist and materialist devices of the new culture such as clocks, telescopes, and greenhouses, he deployed these devices not so much for business purposes as for symbolic and aesthetic effect. Likewise, his embrace of Enlightenment-era material and cultural elements failed to shake his commitment to traditional Orthodox Christianity and its Russian cultural expression, including a belief in miracle-working icons.

In modern adolescent diaries questions of identity are often the main focus, but even in the laconic journals of ordinary people of the early modern era, like Ivan's, we can observe the author constructing and trying out a "self" to inhabit the space allowed within prescribed social boundaries. A measure of these boundaries can often be found within the source itself by noting the transgressions that occur and the social or psychological sanctions that the diarist suffers. These boundaries can then be checked against the legal or other more general prescriptions that appear in the grand narrative of the period and thus yield a measure of the distance between prescribed and actual behavior.

To use the language of the "self" is to draw on what has become the most recent expression of the tension between the determining power of discourse and the possible scope for individual agency. Here we are looking at an updated version of the issues of individualism and the community. In historical studies this terrain was first mapped by Jakob Burkhardt, who identified the Renaissance as the time when individuals were able to separate their identity from the community. Other historians have since argued about whether the emergence of an individual self-consciousness came earlier or later. In anthropology, Clifford Geertz established a dichotomy not between the past and a later emergence of the self but between Western ego-centric cultures and the rest of the world that lived in socio-centric communities. Neither of these formulations escaped vigorous assaults by scholars who argued convincingly that however far back in history one went, cases of individuals standing against the community could be found, the story of Socrates being an obvious example, and that non-Western societies provided room for individual agency as well as community. In every case, it was simply a matter of degree. The Russian picture has long offered a combination of formulae in accordance with the division in Russian thought between society and the common people (*narod*). Russian thinkers ascribed emergence of the individual consciousness and the self to the educated elites and denied this attribute to the common people, who were thought to reside in a communitarian realm devoid of space for individual self-expression.

The theoretical approach that may best illuminate the expression of the self in this merchant's tale is a combination of the concepts of *habitus* and reflexivity. The concept of *habitus* as worked out by Pierre Bourdieu and his disciples refers to the set of behaviors and responses habituated in a person as he or she moves through the given "fields" of life. A field is defined as an obligatorily bounded arena of experience and "a relational configuration endowed with a specific gravity which it imposes on all the objects and agents that enter it."[29] People move through fields defined by their social position and become habituated to the requirements of them more or less unconsciously. The use of an anthropological concept that is based in body language, tone of voice, speech patterns, and the like has its limitations when treating a historical subject known mainly through a diary, but it may be helpful in reminding us that the socially stratified Russian society of the eighteenth century defined as appropriate for particular social positions dress, housing, conveyances, and manners, which, when not monitored legally by sumptuary laws, were inculcated through education, training, and observation—as well as by challenges from those offended or threatened by transgressions in what was a highly honor-conscious social arena. Another difficulty is the essential determinacy of habitus. Because it is unconsciously formed and enacted instinctively, the concept does not readily allow for the play of conscious agency.[30]

The self is not passively constructed, a mere product of external forces. If we want to understand the choices of our subject as at least in part conscious decisions to change his life and move into circles (fields) to which he was not habituated by early life and training, we need to be able to include in our analysis elements of reflexivity. And, indeed, the diary of Ivan Tolchënov in some respects served its author as an instrument of reflexivity, a record of the reordering of his life in response to his experiences. Reflexivity in this sense is the process of receiving and responding to feedback from fields into which a person has not been habituated by upbringing and training, an activity in which the responses reshape his or her established, habitual behavioral repertory. This process can be seen in one form in Ivan's terse daily entries, where he recorded almost exclusively his visits and visitors, attendance at church, work, civic activities, and travels. His choice to spend time at this or that place, or to seek out this or that person, signaled the relationship between his experiences and his changing aspirations. His journal provided the means for sorting out and ordering the events of his life and in that sense was a reflexive narrative construction. As the philosopher Charles Taylor wrote, "a basic condition of making sense of ourselves" is that "we grasp our lives in a *narrative*." In other words, Taylor continued, "to have a sense of who we are, we have to have a notion of how we have become and where we are going."[31] Or, to borrow Giddens's language, Ivan was demonstrating a "capacity to keep a particular narrative going," which is a key to self-identity.[32] But it is in another portion of Ivan's journal that we find the kind of clearly articulated reflexivity that we more commonly refer to as introspection. In 1790 Ivan began to transcribe his earlier daily entries into impressive leather-bound volumes, eventually three in all. As he did this transcription, he appended at the end of each year a summary of his commercial activity, a survey of the weather for the year, a list of people who had died, and occasionally some additional information on events in his town. In these year-end summaries he would sometimes also comment on his behavior and his state of mind during the year in question. In other words, in these interpolations he became a biographer of his earlier diary-keeping self and was able to express a reflexive awareness of his changing circumstances and assess his means of adjusting to them. These summaries include some of the most powerful and revealing testimony in the diary.

It is at these points that we can also see the growth of Ivan's writing style. When he stopped to ponder and comment on his earlier daily jottings, his writing rose to a literary level, revealing the influence of his reading in the popular texts of the period. Although Ivan did not report on his reading, and we know only that he claimed to be an avid reader and that he visited bookstores when he was in Moscow and Petersburg, the year-end summaries that he began writing in the 1790s exhibit obvious influences of the sentimentalist and moralistic texts of the age. The daily notes on the pilgrimages that he and his wife took after the turn of the century show the same maturation of his writing. His descriptions of the places they visited are fuller and more vivid than those he penned during journeys earlier in his life. We see in the later descriptions touches that suggest he had been reading the traveler accounts that were published in large numbers in Russia in the late eighteenth and early nineteenth centuries. A more literary style also appears at a few places earlier in the daily entries. These passages, some quite long, look very much like interpolations that Ivan later inserted as he was transcribing his daily entries into the three leather-bound volumes from their original placement in what may have been account books or almanacs. The interpolations appear after especially important personal losses and stand out textually and stylistically from the usual entries.

To return to the question of habitus and reflexivity, the problem with using these otherwise fruitful and well-established frameworks is that in their "thick" forms, they are incompatible. Because habitus is formed unconsciously and enacted instinctively, it would not very well accommodate the reflexive awareness that sociologists associate with the modern person, who can discern opportunities for altering his or her situation or identity and, if in command of sufficient resources, act to make changes. Even so, sociologists have recently been suggesting combinations of the two concepts that could be helpful. One option is that a person might remain within his prescribed and habituated field but be able to create a sense of himself as a person with greater value than is normally accorded people of his status. Another opening for reflexivity can even be found in less studied areas of Pierre Bourdieu's own work, particularly where he mentions the effects of crises or rapid change, "fateful moments" in Giddens' conceptual scheme, in which people suddenly find themselves between fields or shifted into a new field. Habitus, in other words, may be temporarily destabilized and open a space for reflexive awareness of new opportunities.

This way of looking at habitus and reflexivity has appeal for historians, especially when they are narrating the story of a rapidly changing society of the kind we observe in Russia of the late eighteenth century, and it is the approach I will be using most often in this book. Indeed, in the life of Ivan Tolchënov we can see both of the circumstances just mentioned. While remaining within his social position, he strove to create for himself a valued place above the norm accorded to his position. He also found himself in situations of crisis that shifted him outside his field of habituated practice and heightened his reflexive awareness and need to reorient himself and reclaim a new sense of self. We might say that Ivan was engaged in a "thin" reflexive project. He was finding new definitions of what it was to be a Russian merchant. He could be a man of taste, of culture, a consumer of the latest fashionable products and lifestyle symbols, he could be a man of civic action, a friend of the well-born; but he was also well habituated to his inherited cultural practices and continually fell back on them when he suffered the anxieties of displacement from a particular social position, whether it was he who had been edging toward a new status or outside forces that were pressing him back into the condition for which he had been destined.

REPRESENTATIVENESS

When I first visited the city of Dmitrov, got acquainted with the curator of the local museum, Romual'd Khokhlov (now deceased), and told him that I was interested in doing a study of Ivan Tolchënov, his reaction surprised me. While willing to be helpful, he did not think that Tolchënov was a worthy subject because he was not, according to Khokhlov, typical and was in fact "a freak of nature."[33] True enough, the very fact that Ivan kept a diary for forty-some years set him apart from his peers. But it is hard to find other characteristics of his behavior that would make him different, let alone freakishly different, from many other men of his time and place. His community of peers considered him worthy to represent them and their interests in a variety of forums. Even before he was elected to an official position in his city, he was asked to serve as an envoy on behalf of the city to high officials in Moscow. Subsequently, he was elected again and again to positions of responsibility and also put in charge of local charitable projects. He easily won the trust of highly placed persons not only in his city and district but also in adjoining administrative districts and in Moscow province. Someone who was odd or out of place could not have attained the positions or moved in the circles that he did.

Moreover, many of his avocations and personal projects such as theatergoing, the construction of gardens and orangeries, and a new home were by no means unusual for merchants of his level of wealth and education.[34] We encounter a number of these merchants in the diary itself, as Ivan visited their gardens and greenhouses, went to the theater with them, and attended masquerades and other festive events at which people of various social strata mingled. They also appear in other sources. In a recent study based on a limited sample of Moscow merchants, Ol'ga Fomina found that scores of them possessed urban estates and gardens of the type Ivan developed in Dmitrov.[35] What is more, such people did not reside solely in the big cities. Nikolai Chechulin, in his prerevolutionary survey of Russian eighteenth-century provincial life based on memoirs of the time, noted that in the provinces merchants could be found who "were knowledgeable and even well educated, people with whom nobles did not consider it embarrassing or unpleasant to be acquainted. The children of merchants and lesser townspeople were going to school in fairly large numbers, attending special schools and schools that sometimes were quite good."[36] Such persons formed an emergent upper echelon of commercial families, people who had fought for and acquired in the course of the eighteenth century privileges and exemptions that endowed them with the standing and mentality of a true social estate.

The difficulties that later generations had in seeing this were two. First, the merchant estate grew in size rapidly in the nineteenth century and was continually being entered and replenished by members of the peasantry, whose dress and manners lent a less refined aspect to the estate as a whole. Second, the view most educated Russians later received of the merchants of imperial Russia was shaped by the literary representations of the intelligentsia, who for a variety of reasons regarded the commercial groups of their own nation with contempt. One of the most influential writers was the playwright Aleksandr Ostrovskii, who grew up in Moscow's merchant quarter the son of a minor official. Though little known outside of Russia, Ostrovskii's many plays "provide, along with Shakespeare, the bulk of the classical repertoire of the Russian stage,"[37] and his stereotyped portrayals of habitually dishonest traders, tyrannical merchant fathers, and dowerless merchant daughters sold to the highest bidder left an indelible mark on Russian consciousness. Virtually every educated Russian with whom I discussed this project immediately assured me that he or she had read Ostrovskii and knew about merchants. Ostrovskii's characters likewise formed the basis for the enormously influential essay by the literary critic Nikolai Dobroliubov, "The Dark Kingdom," which caricatured merchant life as brutal, self-enclosed, and bigoted. The admonition expressed nearly a century ago by the Russian historian V. N. Storozhev that it is not only unscholarly but "naïve beyond belief" to judge the culture of merchants by intelligentsia stereotypes seems to have been lost on most Russians, including the former Dmitrov museum curator Romual'd Khokhlov.[38] I hope that my tale will help in some measure to modify this view by illuminating the position of a Russian merchant typical of the educated people of his station who were acquiring an estate consciousness, living a cultivated life, and unabashedly seeking recognition of their contributions to society and state.

PROVENANCE AND APPEARANCE OF THE DIARY

The diary of Ivan Tolchënov resides in three leather-bound volumes in the archives of the Library of the Russian Academy of Sciences in St. Petersburg. According to A. I. Kopanev, who in the 1970s composed a short essay about its form, the manuscript came to the archive sometime in the nineteenth century.[39] In my own work on it, I noticed that an archivist had apparently inspected it in the early 1930s. Inside the back cover of the first volume is a note in ink, reading "Altogether one hundred and eighty-six (186) folios. 8/VI 1933, E. Shipova." The three volumes are the same format. The size is roughly eighteen centimeters from top to bottom and fifteen centimeters across. The first page of the first volume reads "Zhurnal, part 1" and on the back side of this first page the author has written that "this book was started as a clean copy on August 30, 1790." Then on the opposing page the diary begins with the full title: *Zhurnal ili Zapiska Zhizni i Prikliuchenii I. A. Tolchënova* (A Journal or Notes on the Life and Adventures of I. A. Tolchënov). This first volume runs to 369 pages in the author's pagination. Part 2 begins with a note on the inside first page, reading: "This book was begun on September 13, 1796, and completed on December 23, 1804." At the very end of this volume the author appended a list of the sixteen children born to him and his wife and included her name, along with his own, at the head of the list. This second volume also runs to 369 pages and carries a note from 1933 similar to the one in the first volume. The third volume has, behind the first page and opposite the title page in the author's hand, the phrase: "This book was started on December 27, 1804." Because the record of the author's life, though not his actual life, was cut short in 1812, the third volume is not filled out. It runs to only 330 pages. The rest is blank, including an entire signature of paper.

The first two volumes are bound in red leather with gold trim. The gold embossing on the first volume is less ornate than on the second. The second volume has much wider gold trim on the front and back and includes urns, large leaves, and even a house and tower scene. The first two volumes also have gold-edged paper, which was not used for the third volume. The third volume is altogether less impressive looking. It is done in brown leather and embossed front and back, not with gold but in a darker brown to black colored pressing. The first two volumes have colored paper inside the cover, the third merely white paper.[40]

The handwriting of the source is uniform throughout and is characterized by small rounded letters, each separate from the next. In other words, it has nothing in common with chancery hand of the day and seems to confirm the author's own admission that he failed as a child to master proper penmanship.

NOTE ON LANGUAGE

I have followed the standard Library of Congress form of transliterating Russian words and names into Latin letters, omitting the ligatures and the symbol for soft sign (') at the end of words (so as to avoid confusion with the English possessive form). The final soft signs have, however, been included in the bibliographic entries. I have tried to anglicize names of institutions, churches, and icons to make Russian life more accessible to readers without a command of the Russian language. In the case of some palaces and monasteries, I left the names in their Russian adjectival forms, either because I could not think of an equivalent English name or because the Russian name was generally well known and searchable on standard maps and reference guides.

Dates are all according the Julian calendar that was in effect in imperial Russia. It ran eleven days behind the Gregorian calendar in the eighteenth century and twelve days behind it in the nineteenth century.

Maps

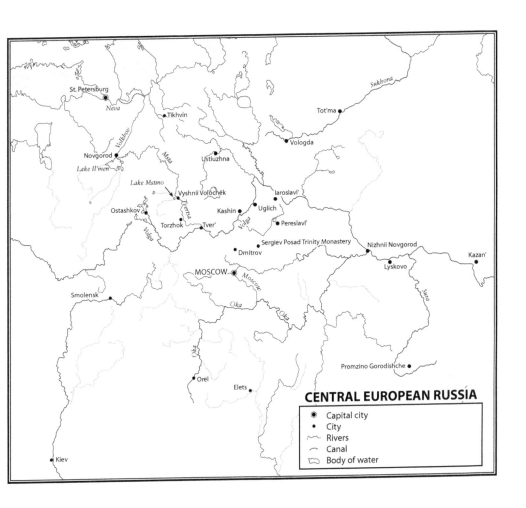

St. Petersburg

Neva

Sukhona

Tot'ma

Tikhvin

Volkhov

Vologda

Novgorod

Msta

Ustiuzhna

Lake Il'men

Lake Mstino

Vyshnii Volochek

Iaroslavl'

Tvertsa

Kashin

Uglich

Ostashkov

Volga

Torzhok

Tver'

Volga

Pereslavl'

Sergiev Posad Trinity Monastery

Nizhnii Novgorod

Dmitrov

Kazan'

Lyskovo

MOSCOW

Moscow

Sura

Smolensk

Oka

Oka

Oka

Promzino Gorodishche

Orël

Elets

CENTRAL EUROPEAN RUSSIA

- ◉ Capital city
- • City
- 〜 Rivers
- ⌒ Canal
- ⌒ Body of water

Kiev

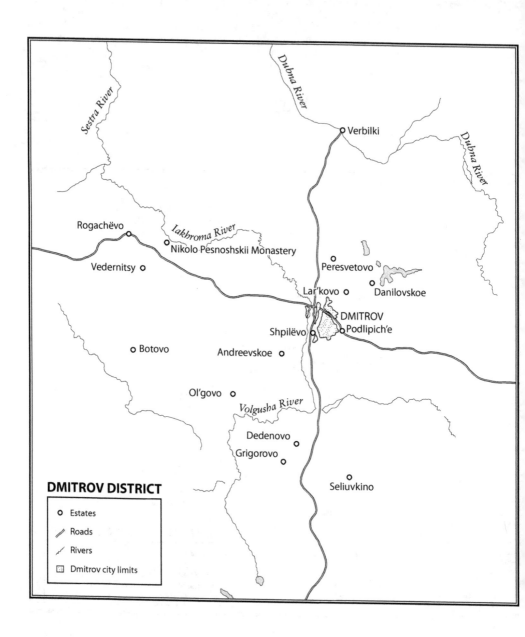

Sestra River

Dubna River

Dubna River

Iakhroma River

Verbilki

Rogachëvo

Nikolo-Pesnoshskii Monastery

Vedernitsy

Peresvetovo

Danilovskoe

Lar'kovo

DMITROV

Shpilëvo

Podlipich'e

Botovo

Andreevskoe

Ol'govo

Volgusha River

Dedenovo

Grigorovo

Seliuvkino

DMITROV DISTRICT

o Estates

Roads

Rivers

Dmitrov city limits

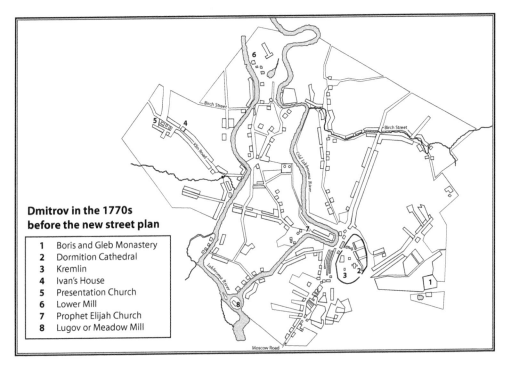

Dmitrov in the 1770s before the new street plan

1 Boris and Gleb Monastery
2 Dormition Cathedral
3 Kremlin
4 Ivan's House
5 Presentation Church
6 Lower Mill
7 Prophet Elijah Church
8 Lugov or Meadow Mill

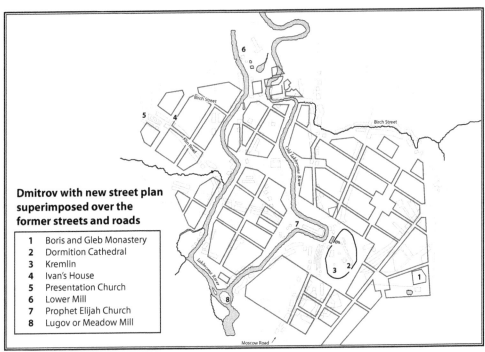

Dmitrov with new street plan superimposed over the former streets and roads

1 Boris and Gleb Monastery
2 Dormition Cathedral
3 Kremlin
4 Ivan's House
5 Presentation Church
6 Lower Mill
7 Prophet Elijah Church
8 Lugov or Meadow Mill

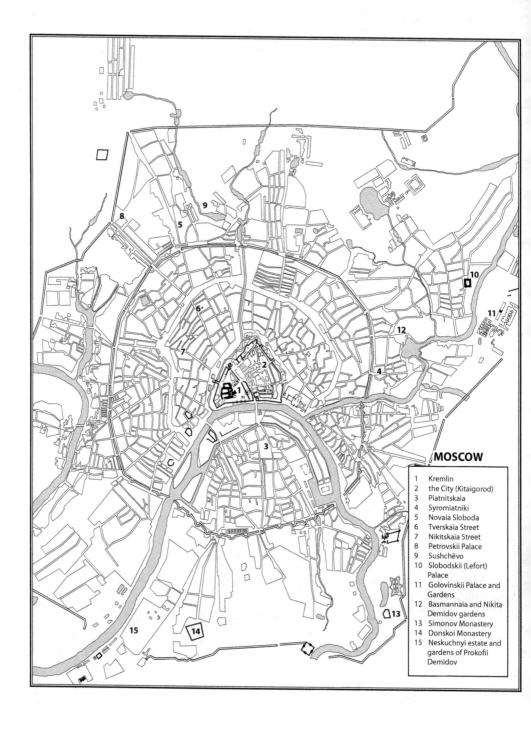

MOSCOW

1 Kremlin
2 the City (Kitaigorod)
3 Piatnitskaia
4 Syromiatniki
5 Novaia Sloboda
6 Tverskaia Street
7 Nikitskaia Street
8 Petrovskii Palace
9 Sushchëvo
10 Slobodskii (Lefort)
   Palace
11 Golovinskii Palace and
   Gardens
12 Basmannaia and Nikita
   Demidov gardens
13 Simonov Monastery
14 Donskoi Monastery
15 Neskuchnyi estate and
   gardens of Prokofii
   Demidov

A
Russian
Merchant's
Tale

1

The Setting, Education, Youth, and Marriage

Ivan Tolchënov was born and grew up in Dmitrov, a city 80 kilometers north of Moscow. Ancient by Russian standards, Dmitrov was founded in the twelfth century. It played a role in early Russian princely politics and twice suffered destruction by the Mongol-Tatar invaders of the thirteenth century. The town nevertheless survived Mongol rule, and when trade with England and Holland opened through the White Sea port of Arkhangel'sk in the late fifteenth and sixteenth centuries, Dmitrov shared in the renewed prosperity that this commerce brought to towns north of Moscow. Of all the cities connected to the northern waterways Dmitrov was the closest to Moscow. It was in this period of economic growth that two of Dmitrov's most impressive cultural monuments were built: the Boris and Gleb Monastery and the Dormition Cathedral, both of which figured importantly in the life of Ivan Tolchënov and his family.[1]

Dmitrov's prosperity was undermined for a time by a shift of trade routes to the northeast through Iaroslavl and Vologda and the disruptions of Ivan the Terrible's reign, which drained Dmitrov's commerce and shrank its population. The Time of Troubles soon after caused further losses of trade and population, so that by the middle of the seventeenth century, after conditions had improved somewhat, the city counted only 242 homes (*dvory*, i.e., homes with their adjacent outbuildings and lands) and a population of 1,300. Thereafter, investments by the tsarist court in local meadows and fishing ponds slowly rebuilt the economy of Dmitrov. By 1705 the population reached 2,000.[2] At this time, an event of major importance for Dmitrov took place. Tsar Peter I decided to move his seat of government to the Baltic seacoast and began construction of the new capital city of St. Petersburg. This decision contributed to renewed prosperity for Dmitrov. The tsar recruited artisans and traders from the city for work in the new capital. The redirection of trade routes to the north and northwest likewise boosted Dmitrov's commerce.[3] Until this time its trade had been primarily in market gardening and small manufacturing sales locally and south to Moscow. Now it broadened to include a varied and growing proto-industrial base. When the German-born historian and member of the Russian Academy of Sciences Gerhard Friedrich Miller visited Dmitrov in 1779, he found it a lively commercial and artisanal center with a number of small manufactories in the surrounding countryside. The most recent census (1763) had counted a population approaching 3,000 persons (male and female) residing in 611 households. The commercial elite comprised about 200 merchants. Another nearly 1,100 male citizens, artisans and workers of various sorts, made up the rest of the population (not counting clergy, nobles, and government officials).[4] Of the fourteen district cities of Moscow province in 1787, Dmitrov ranked fifth in population and number of homes and fourth in the amount of commercial capital.[5]

Dmitrov lies on the northern slope of heights that run north and west of Moscow. The Iakhroma River flows out of these heights and northward through Dmitrov on its way toward the great commercial artery of the Volga River, which in the eighteenth century it reached just upriver from the town of Kimry via the Sestra and Dubna Rivers. The Iakhroma snaked through Dmitrov, which straddled the river. An ancient earthen fortress wall in the shape of an oval marked the center of the town. This impressive wall (which still stands today) stretched 6.4 meters high, and half of it was made more impregnable by a trench 2 meters deep. In early times, it was topped by a parapet and nine towers. On the east, the fortress stood at the foot of a sharply rising hill; the western side ended in a swampy area bordering the river. Dominating the walled city was the magnificent Dormition Cathedral, the seat of the bishop when one served in Dmitrov (for much of the eighteenth century the city either shared a bishop or belonged to the bishopric of Pereslavl-Zaleskii). In the square fronting the cathedral and in the adjoining market square stood a number of government buildings, including the ecclesiastical administration, district courts, the police administration and state financial offices, the city government and salt storage barns.[6] The Boris and Gleb Monastery with its masonry wall occupied a large space just to the southeast of the ancient fortress.

The citizens of Dmitrov took pride in the quality of its homegrown onions and garlic, which were mostly consumed locally, and its apples, which were harvested in great numbers and carted south for sale in Moscow. The city was known for its many orchards, and Ivan frequently reported in his journal on the size and quality of the year's apple harvest.[7] Merchants purchased about

Earthen fortress wall (kremlin) and Dormition Cathedral in Dmitrov.

Sts. Boris and Gleb Monastery in Dmitrov.

1,000 cattle each year, from which the local slaughterhouse prepared fresh and salted meat and tallow for sale in the surrounding region. At the time of Miller's visit, Dmitrov boasted 132 shops that sold a large variety of cloth products brought up from Moscow, plus "glassware, fruits, honey, wax, wax and tallow candles, various iron products and copperware, foods, flour," and other things. "They even sell wine and English beer," Miller added, "which is not surprising since it is well known that the consumption of such things extends even to the farthest reaches of Siberia."[8]

Artisanal manufactures were active. Five tanneries furnished leather products to the city and surrounding area, including Moscow. A ceramics workshop produced tiles for regional sale. Cloth was woven in eight households, while another stamped out prints on cloth, and three produced gold or silver braiding for uniforms or other decorative purposes. Two larger cloth factories and a crepe manufacturer operated in the nearby countryside. Most impressive was a large china factory founded in 1766 by an Englishman, Franz Gardner. Miller made a special trip to this factory, which lay about 25 kilometers to the north off the road to Kashin in a set of villages known as Verbilki. The quality of Gardner's china was already well known and appreciated by Russian elites. He had made a large table service for the tsarist court with such skill that it led to additional orders. Each knightly decoration given at the court required a special table service with the appropriate insignia, and Gardner was winning this business. Rightly so, according to Miller, who contended that, except for the exquisite china of Saxony, Gardner's wares were comparable to the best in foreign countries.[9]

The greatest source of wealth for the commercial leaders of Dmitrov was the grain trade to Petersburg. In the late eighteenth century, Dmitrov merchants were among the largest purveyors of grain to the northern capital, a trade based on purchases to the east and south along the Volga and its tributaries, supplemented by local purchases from peasant traders and large landlords like the Golitsyns and Saltykovs. A portion of the purchased grain was then stored and ground into flour in the Dmitrov area before being moved, together with unprocessed grain, by barge and overland to Petersburg for sale. Although the Iakhroma River at Dmitrov was too shallow to host commercial river boats, Dmitrov merchants operated their Volga commerce out of the nearby Rogachëvo wharf, twenty-five kilometers from the city at the confluence of the Iakhroma and Sestra Rivers. They also leased mills on navigable tributaries of the Volga for easier access. Miller in 1779 noted that Dmitrov merchants bought 30,000 sacks (or about 5,000 tons) of grain annually and ground over 162 tons of rye and barley in five mills that dotted the region.[10] It was principally this grain trade that furnished the wealth of Ivan Tolchënov's family.

IVAN'S FAMILY

I came into the world in the city of Dmitrov in the year 7263 from the beginning of time, that is 1754 from the birth of Christ our Savior, on Saturday the 15th of October before the start of the day at the very ringing of the bells for matins, and was named for St. Ioann Ryl'skii, whose name day is celebrated on the 19th of that month. My parents were Aleksei Il'ich Tolchënov, a merchant of the city of Dmitrov, at that time known as a first-rank merchant, and Fedos'ia Fëdorovna, daughter of another first-rank merchant, Fëdor Kirilovich Makarov. At my baptism the godparents were my maternal grandfather, Fëdor Kirilovich, and my paternal grandmother, Dar'ia Egor'evna. My father had his own parents: Il'ia Borisovich and Dar'ia Egor'evna, and his brothers, my uncles: Ivan, Pëtr, Mikhaila and Dmitrii Il'ichi, and with their agreement, my father was registered to the household of Fëdor Kirilovich Makarov as son-in-law and married to my mother on April 29, 1750. My mother had her parents: Fëdor Kirilovich and Marfa Matveevna, whose maiden name was Mosharova.[11]

Members of the Tolchënov family had been commercially active in Dmitrov from at least the early years of the seventeenth century.[12] The brief genealogy above that Ivan placed at the beginning of his journal shows (by virtue of the patronymic) that he understood the history of his family at a minimum as far back as his great-grandfather Boris Tolchënov, the progenitor of Ivan's branch of the family. Boris was born about 1658 and produced six sons who survived into the eighteenth century and left progeny of their own. The line leading to the diarist went through Il'ia Borisovich (born 1698), grandfather of the diarist. It was this grandfather and his sons (including the father of the diarist) who prospered from the grain trade. Il'ia Borisovich amassed considerable capital, enough to rise to the "first guild" of merchants. Not to be confused with West European artisanal corporations, the Russian guilds (*gil'dii*) were introduced in the legislation of Peter I as a device for differentiating the urban population by wealth and tax-paying capacity. Russian officials initiated this guild system in Moscow in 1724 and then gradually extended it to other towns; they divided merchants into three "guilds" in accordance with their declared capital. Merchants paid one percent of their declared capital in tax and enjoyed an ascending number of privileges and exemptions the higher their capital placed them on the guild ladder.[13] First guild merchants were also known as first-rank (*pervostateinye*), and this is the term that Ivan Tolchënov used to describe his father and grandfather.

Because the status of a merchant depended solely on his current capital declaration and corresponding tax payments, his position, privileges, and exemptions might change from year to year. This issue could become acute at the death of a wealthy merchant and the division of his assets among his heirs. Russians practiced partible inheritance, or the roughly equal division of property among male heirs (and even some provision for females). Il'ia Borisovich Tolchënov had produced five surviving sons among whom his capital had to be divided. The result was that none of the sons could, on the basis of their father's bequest, muster resources sufficient to register higher than the second merchant guild. This deeply rooted practice of partible inheritance in Russia was a key element in the high rates of vertical mobility among Russian propertied families, whether of the merchant community or the nobility.[14] Such chance occurrences as the sex and number of surviving children could make a large difference in the opportunities for the next generation, as we see in this line of Tolchënovs.

Other practices could counteract some of the effects of partible inheritance. One of these was the "adoption" of an in-marrying son-in-law (or *priëmysh*) in families with no son. This practice worked to the advantage of the diarist's father, Aleksei Il'ich Tolchënov, who was able to marry into the family of the wealthy first-guild merchant Fëdor Kirilovich Makarov and to move directly into the home of his new wife and father-in-law (contrary to the normal Russian practice of patrilocal residence of newly married couples). The marriage enabled Aleksei Il'ich to retain the first-guild privileges he had enjoyed as an unmarried member of his father's household. The archives contain two "amicable protocols" (*poliubovnye zapisi*) concerning this arrangement. The first, dated 1750 and evidently a portion of the marriage contract, declared the new son-in-law Aleksei Il'ich and his wife the owners of all of Makarov's movable and immovable property, even while he was still alive.[15] The second protocol, drawn up in 1763, took back some of what the earlier one granted. This time Aleksei Il'ich was given permanent ownership of two homes in Dmitrov, plus a tannery, a brewery, and a number of shop stalls and spaces for others. He retained the family capital, but now, instead of it being designated as his property, it was merely under his supervision. "Aleksei may keep this capital forever for commercial dealings," Makarov instructed, "but each year he must give an account of the profit made on my capital, apart from his own, and put that profit to uses that I shall determine."[16]

This change was occasioned by another family event and a troubling one at that, for it threatened the stability of the Makarov-Tolchënov alliance. The diarist disclosed the details when he reported on the death in 1763 of his maternal grandmother, the wife of Fëdor Kirilovich Makarov. "On July 22 at the setting of the sun, my grandmother Marfa Matveevna died and on the 28th was buried in the west end of the nave of the Presentation Church then under construction. In this same year, on September 22, my grandfather Fëdor Kirilovich married a second time, wedding Fedos'ia Mikhailovna, the daughter of the priest Mikhail Artemonovich of Prokov village in Kashin district, and he did this secretly without telling either my parents or other relatives. This inflicted terrible pain, especially on my mother, but it did not irreparably destroy accord in the family."[17] In other words, within two months of the death of his first wife, this fifty-two-year-old grandfather had brought home a new twenty-eight-year-old wife,[18] a stepmother younger than her stepchildren (who already had children of their own). The new family contract was evidently intended to provide in some fashion for this new member of the family and her possible progeny. Two years later, Fedos'ia Mikhailovna gave birth to a son, Andrei Fëdorovich, who after the death of his father became a member of the Tolchënov household and the underage charge of the diarist's father and later of the diarist himself, his step-nephew. Fëdor Kirilovich Makarov died in 1771, and the bulk of his capital seems to have remained under the supervision of his son-in-law Aleksei Il'ich Tolchënov. Later references make clear, however, that a sizable portion of this legacy remained legally separate, designated as the "Makarov capital," and eventually had to be transferred to Andrei Fëdorovich at his majority. It was at that time, the year 1788, when the diarist could least afford it, that he had to turn over to his step-uncle this trust of 11,000 rubles, a small fortune.

The diarist's father, Aleksei Il'ich, was an energetic and successful businessman and a person of considerable stature among the local elite. Not only was he the mayor and richest merchant in Dmitrov;[19] he was also elected by his peers to represent the Dmitrov townspeople at the Commission on Laws of 1767–1768, an assembly of representatives from throughout Russia convened by Empress Catherine II for the purpose of producing a new legal code. The diary of his son offers many examples of Aleksei Il'ich's tireless activity on behalf of his firm, listing the frequent rounds he made of his mills and daily engagement with affairs. He was quick to seize an opportunity for profit, as can be seen from his response to the news in late September 1774 of famine threatening regions of the Middle Volga and Ukraine. His son, the diarist Ivan, wrote: "Having learned of the sharp rise in prices in the southeast and Ukrainian areas due to the small harvest, father sent me [north] on September 30 together with [his agent] Afanasii Popov to Sosninsk wharf for the purchase of rye flour. On the Volkhov River and in Ladoga large numbers of grain barges were at a standstill because of low water, and some merchants were selling cheap due to low prices." However, the news of the famine in the south traveled faster than Ivan Tolchënov and Afanasii Popov could gallop. When they arrived at the northern Volga wharves, they found that "all the merchants, having heard about the price rises in the south, were wary of selling cheap."[20] Even Ivan's dash farther north to Ladoga with his uncle, Dmitrii Il'ich, failed to capitalize on the price rise. Although this venture did not pan out, the action was typical of the spirit that made Aleksei Il'ich's enterprises prosper.

He also cooperated with his less wealthy brothers in the grain business, employing them as agents and managers of mills, thus strengthening both the firm and the extended family. Although his brothers each enjoyed second-guild status with declared capital of at least 5,000 rubles, they could not individually command the credit and resources to support a large long-distance grain trading operation, which required heavy investments in the purchase of grain and barges, the hiring of boats, storage barns, pilots, and haulers, and the leasing of mills. Accordingly, they pooled their resources for their own trade and also worked with their wealthier brother as managers.

An unanswered question about Aleksei Il'ich's business success concerns the tannery, brewery, and shop stalls that he acquired from his father-in-law in the second amicable protocol. One historian accused him of not giving attention to these inherited assets.[21] But it is far from clear that he actually retained control of them; the local records do not indicate his possession. Aleksei Il'ich may well have turned the tannery and brewery over to a nephew of Fëdor Makarov who had been placed under Makarov's protection; this nephew, Ivan Alekseevich Makarov, later accumulated a substantial capital from such enterprises and moved to Moscow to become inscribed as an "distinguished citizen" (*imenityi grazhdanin*), a status requiring a 50,000 ruble capital. Or, possibly, Aleksei Il'ich sold off the tannery and brewery in order to concentrate on the lucrative grain trade (and no doubt leased the shop stalls at a good profit, as was customary).[22] Whatever may have happened to these other businesses, Aleksei Il'ich proved himself a success in the risky and highly competitive grain trade, turning over to his son on his death a substantial capital.

It was this family and its deep roots in the community, stretching back to the early seventeenth century, that provided the grounding for the diarist Ivan Tolchënov's social identity. For several generations his family had been among the most prosperous and prominent in Dmitrov. They had not only been successful traders but also occupied leading positions in the city administration. Young Ivan took pride in coming from his town's two most prominent merchant families. As he wrote proudly at the start of his diary, in the passage excepted at the head of this section, both his parents came from the "first-rank merchants." His father even enjoyed a modicum of national recognition, having served as a deputy to the Commission on Laws, and Ivan several times mentioned this distinction, which added to the family's luster. A deputy enjoyed a number of life-long privileges and exemptions, and in legal documents his father was forever after referred to as "First-Rank Merchant and Deputy," a social distinction that was in some measure shared by his entire family, including Ivan.

Another sign of Ivan's social station was his care and upbringing by a serf nanny. Although the right to own serfs had been restricted to nobles from the mid-eighteenth century onward, some wealthy merchants continued to be able through a number of stratagems to retain, and even buy and sell, household serfs, and the Tolchënovs enjoyed the services of a number of them. In this respect, Ivan's family was exceptional. Ol'ga Fomina in her study of Moscow merchants in this period found only a handful of families in her sample that owned serfs. Likewise, Irina Kusova in her book on merchants in the city of Riazan found that in 1782 only 6 out of 164 merchant families possessed house-hold serfs.[23] Ivan did not mention his serf nanny in his early diary entries. Apart from his birth, he wrote nothing about his childhood before his education began at age five. We learn about her much later at the time of her death in 1791, when Ivan recorded in his daily entry for October 5 that "we buried my nanny Akilina Kiril'evna in the churchyard on the hill and then hosted a dinner for the priests of the parish and some relatives." In his later summary of the year, he added that "at 9 am on October 2, my nanny Akilina Kiril'evna died; she had been purchased by my grandfather and had served us faithfully and attentively."[24]

Ivan grew up well cared for and habituated to the privilege and recognition that belonged to the two wealthiest and politically powerful merchant families in his city, the Makarovs of his mother's side and the Tolchënovs of his father's. This should not, however, imply that he had an easy life beyond the first few years when he was attended by his nanny and other household servants and lived in the spacious family home of his Makarov grandparents. The male children of merchants, like nearly all Russians in the eighteenth century, began their working life early, and the work of a grain trader was dangerous and demanding.

IVAN'S EDUCATION AND TRAINING

At age five I was first taught Russian grammar, and I can say that I was a good student, enjoyed learning, and worked hard. Even though I was studying at home without the guidance of a real teacher and was almost self-taught, in less than a year I was able to read any kind of printed text without difficulty. After that I learned to write, but I have to confess that, not having had an instructor, I did not succeed in mastering good penmanship.[25]

Formal education for merchant children in the provinces was unknown at the time of Ivan's childhood. Public and private schools of any kind scarcely existed outside the major cities, and, indeed, many merchants questioned the value of a school education for their children even when it was available. Empress Catherine II, whose long reign began in 1762 at the time Ivan was seven years old, sought to promote the education of the nobles and urban dwellers. Among her efforts was the establishment of a Commercial School in Moscow in 1772 on the plan of her educational adviser, Ivan Betskoi, whose schools sought to give students a well-rounded general and "enlightened" education. Although the government circulated information about the school and even offered scholarships to sons of merchants (this offer was received in Dmitrov early in 1773), officials were dismayed to find that very few merchant families cared to send their sons to the school.[26] The proportion of merchant sons at the school never exceeded one-third, and the classes were filled mainly by students from the "people of various ranks."[27] Merchant families understood that their sons had to know the rudiments of reading, writing and arithmetic in order to succeed in commerce, but some merchant fathers worried about giving their children a more elaborate schooling lest they acquire pretensions and tastes that would alienate them from their social roots and family business and prompt them to seek employment in government service or other fields.[28]

These attitudes were beginning to change during the reign of Catherine II. A few prominent merchant families began to provide formal education to their children, and the results could be seen and heard by early in the next century when, according to the essayist P. F. Vistengof, merchant sons could be heard spouting French phrases on the streets of Moscow.[29] In fact, Ivan himself, when he grew up and had children of his own, sent his first-born son to an expensive private school in Moscow that taught foreign languages. But these signs of change were not typical of commercial people as a whole early in Catherine's reign, despite some remarkable exceptions such as the merchants of Arkhangel'sk, who as early as 1764 were arguing strongly for state-sponsored educational institutions for children of townspeople.[30] More typically, only about 5 percent of the statements of local need (*nakazy*) submitted by merchants to the Commission on Laws in 1767 included requests for improved cultural facilities and schools for town dwellers. Many merchants believed that too great an interest in books was an indulgence that would keep their sons from "real learning." Real learning, in their view, had to be acquired by experience, by working in the family trade itself.[31] Ivan's father was from this old school. He had achieved success with a modicum of education, and he saw no need to provide more than the basics for Ivan.

As early as 1764, eight years before the founding of the Commercial School in Moscow, the government dangled in front of local town elites the encouragement and opportunity to send merchant sons abroad to learn about commerce. An edict sent by the empress on behalf of the Commission on Commerce on April 19 of that year mentioned that Peter the Great had urged his subjects to send their sons abroad for similar training. The government was now asking if local magistracies would like to send sons, "heirs or relatives to a commercial office abroad for a few years to learn the theory and practice of business in the port cities of England, Holland, and other countries." The government also expected them to learn the languages of the countries in which they were interning. If this idea appealed to the merchants, the edict stated, the government would be much in favor, and the edict asked for detailed information on those interested, on costs, possible countries of study and the like. In response, the Dmitrov magistracy promptly sent a letter expressing its lack of interest in the project. In a reply signed by the diarist's father Aleksei Tolchënov and two other members of the magistracy, the Dmitrov leaders declined to send any of their children, relatives, or heirs abroad for study.[32]

Despite their wariness about formal education for their children (let alone internships in foreign countries) many merchants, just like Ivan's father, made sure that their sons acquired the rudiments. Contrary to the typical portrait of commercial people in Russian literature, a substantial portion of merchants in eighteenth-century Russia had mastered basic literacy, and some boasted substantial personal libraries as early as the 1730s.[33] An ethnographer of early Russian town life pointed out some years ago that urban literacy was probably higher proportionally in medieval and early modern Russia than it was during the later period of rapid migration of peasants to the cities.[34] Evidence from urban elections and other sources indicate that in the first half of the eighteenth century, a large majority of first-guild merchants were literate, while at the lower end of the urban social scale as much as 15–20 percent of men could write.[35] A source from early in the second half of the eighteenth century confirms this observation. The results of a questionnaire sent from the Commission on Commerce in 1764 to merchants in thirty-seven provincial towns indicated that among the "best merchants" of that time literacy was very high indeed, if we can take the ability to sign one's name as proof of literacy. In one-quarter of these small towns literacy among the leading merchants was virtually 100 percent, and in three-quarters of the towns at least 60 percent.[36] In the Siberian city of Eniseisk in 1776, 74 percent of the guild merchants were literate.[37] Although this level of literacy might seem improbably high, it is not surprising if one considers that reference is made here to the men who bore responsibility for staffing the local organs of self-government, the magistracy, and other city offices. The central government insisted that such people command literacy and in a number of cases refused to accept illiterate officers on town magistracies even when they were elected by a large majority of their peers.[38] Apart from the requirements of official position, leading merchants had to conduct a large volume of paperwork in their own private commerce, such as contracts, receipts, attestations, and bills of exchange, and could scarcely have done so when illiterate.[39] Indeed, books and manuals of commerce, letter-writers, and form books were appearing in ever greater numbers to serve a growing market of literate business people.[40]

Like most merchant sons of his time, Ivan Tolchënov got his education at home. In the diary excerpt at the head of this section, he wrote that his lessons started at age five and that he enjoyed learning and quickly acquired the ability to read every type of printed text. He also admitted to poor penmanship, and anyone who has had to decipher the diary text in the original could well wish that Ivan had been more diligent in this aspect of his studies. In mathematics his father was the instructor, teaching Ivan arithmetic and algebraic functions "up to the rule of three" (the method of finding a fourth term in a proportion when three terms are given).

Ivan wrote nothing about his religious training. Possibly in a merchant household, saturated as it was by religious symbols and practices, this aspect of upbringing was taken for granted. Or he may have neglected to report on it because in this pre-Freudian age Ivan, like other memoirists, had not yet learned to conceive of childhood as a key formative stage of growth and therefore said little about it. But it is more likely that lessons in catechism did not figure in Ivan's training at all. We know, for example, that Ivan's own son proved deficient in this knowledge when he was later tested at school. Although Russian church leaders had begun in the mid-eighteenth century to encourage the teaching of catechism, they were still struggling at that time to educate their own personnel. They enjoyed little success with the laity until well into the next century, and then only among the nobility and wealthy city people.[41] Before the advent of formal instruction in elementary schools, families would have had to engage a local cleric to teach their children catechism, and it seems few did so.

Home study did not last long. For most merchant sons at this time home study took place between the ages of five and ten. After age ten, their practical on-the-job training began.[42] A merchant had to be a traveler, and so an important part of Ivan's education was learning firsthand about the places where he would later be working. In August 1765, two months short of his eleventh birthday, his father took him on his first long business trip. They rode by land north to St. Petersburg, and Ivan got acquainted with the sights of the imperial capital, including the Aleksandr Nevskii Monastery, Kazan Cathedral, the Winter Palace, and the great marketplace for overseas commerce at the eastern end of Vasilevskii Island. A year and a half later, Ivan followed his parents to Moscow, the great commercial hub of central Russia, where he lived for several months while his father represented Dmitrov at the Commission on Laws. This basic learning and the experience of working and traveling with his father was exactly the kind of education that was described as the norm by the enlightened eighteenth-century writer on commerce, the Arkhangel'sk merchant and official Aleksandr Fomin.[43]

January of the following year, 1768, the deputies were released and told to reconvene two months later in Petersburg for continuation of the Commission on Laws. At this time, an event of symbolic importance for Ivan took place, a pilgrimage that may have been intended to tie him to family traditions and signal his entry into young adulthood and his ability to shoulder responsibilities in the family firm. The pilgrimage took Ivan and his mother and father north to the ancient Volga city of Iaroslavl to pray before a miracle-working icon that was thought to have cured, among others, Tsar Ivan IV (the Terrible). The diarist first refers to the icon as the "Tolskaia" Madonna, and at another point as the "Tolchskaia" Madonna, associated with the "Tolchskii" monastery in Iaroslavl, which the Tolchënov family may have recognized as having a special relationship to them, perhaps through the correspondence of names.[44] Nearly all Russians of Ivan's time believed in the power of miracle-working icons. Some were of nationwide significance. But families and communities had particular favorites that bore a special relationship to them and a history of healing power. Miracle-working icons were an active force in Ivan's life and self-identity. Icons of both local and national significance were thought to have played a role in saving Ivan during two acute health crises.

At the time of this pilgrimage Ivan was thirteen years old. Two decades later when his own first son was the same age, Ivan took him, along with Ivan's wife, other children, young step-uncle and ward, and his wife's parents, on a similar pilgrimage to Iaroslavl, where they inspected the bustling shops of this major Volga port, attended mass, and prayed to the "pious" medieval princes of the city at the Monastery of Our Savior in what seems to have been a family rite of passage into young adulthood for the eldest son.[45]

It is worth noting here the continuing importance of pilgrimages in the life of Russians from paupers to princes. Empress Catherine a few years earlier in connection with her coronation trip to Moscow, in imitation of her subjects, traversed the same route to Iaroslavl that Ivan and his family took on the two occasions just mentioned. In Ivan's diary we encounter frequent references to pilgrimages by his family and many others, including the families of highly placed government officials. Despite the advent of the European Enlightenment in Russia, the new learning did not displace long-established devotional practices, even among the educated elite. Indeed, later in his life Ivan will for a time allocate a major portion of his time and resources to pilgrimages in gratitude for the restoration of his health.

The first trip to Iaroslavl by Ivan in 1768 marked the beginning of his practical training or apprenticeship in the family grain trade. As mentioned earlier, this business and the rise in the wealth of the Tolchënov family in the eighteenth century were closely connected to the founding of Petersburg. When Peter the Great founded his new capital on the shores of the Gulf of Finland in 1704, he gave a powerful impetus to commerce. Sited for easy access to Europe, Petersburg was not well positioned to supply itself with the necessities of life. The surrounding area was swampy and cold, unable to produce adequate grain or fuel to feed and warm the rapidly growing population of a major metropolis. Grain, in particular, had to be brought north to the new capital from distant centers of production in the south of Russia and in the east far down the Volga River and its tributaries. Since these waterways ran south, they had to be linked to the northern rivers running to Petersburg by portages and canals. Peter the Great had begun to build the needed connections in his own time, hiring an engineering firm to join a tributary of the Volga, the Tvertsa River, to the northern waterways through a canal at the continental divide at Vyshnii Volochëk. Although on the map the waterways appear to line up neatly and provide broad avenues for commerce, the journey itself in the eighteenth century was arduous and risky for commercial shipments and the persons accompanying them. Before improvements were introduced in the next century, the route from Vyshnii Volochëk down the Valdai Hills resembled at points the whitewater rafting of today, but in heavily loaded, rigid vessels, difficult to maneuver. It is in travels along these waterways that young grain merchants in eighteenth-century Russia learned their trade.

This was where Ivan began his practical training. In the spring of 1768, following the pilgrimage to Iaroslavl and when Ivan was still only thirteen years old, his father sent him to work on the grain traffic through the northern waterways under the supervision of one of the family's agents. His father and mother were then in Petersburg for his father's participation in the second session of the Commission on Laws. Ivan first helped to load the barges on the Tvertsa River and then followed them north through the canals and rivers until he reached the city of Novgorod in early May. There he received a message that cut short his work. "I found a letter from my father, ordering me to hasten by land to Petersburg. I arrived on May 13 and learned of an event that was more than I could bear."[46] The event was the death of his mother. She had died that week from tuberculosis. Though emotionally difficult, the death was perhaps not entirely unexpected, as Ivan's mother had suffered many personal blows, especially the loss of nearly all her children. Of her nine births, only Ivan survived early childhood. Ivan recorded in the diary that her last birth occurred just five months before her death. "My sister, Anna Alekseevna, was born on December 1, 1767, and to my parents' great sorrow died the same day unbaptized, and from that day forward my mother began to suffer the illness that turned into the tuberculosis that ended her life."[47] The burial of Ivan's mother attested to the wealth and prominence of the Tolchënov family at this time. She was interred in Petersburg's elite cemetery, the Aleksandr Nevskii Monastery churchyard. The archbishop conducted the ceremony.[48]

This event and his father's need to remain in Petersburg for the Commission on Laws postponed Ivan's practical training and extended his formal education. His father arranged for him to study through the spring and summer under the supervision of a monk and dean (*prefekt*) of the Petersburg seminary, a rare opportunity for the son of a provincial merchant. This experience exerted a powerful and even defining influence on Ivan's life. It was at this time, he reported, that "my eagerness for reading began to grow, and I began to occupy myself with books." Ivan remained an avid reader the rest of his life. More important, he now became a writer as well. Soon after his studies in Petersburg he began jotting down the notes that would form his journal and the story of his life. Undoubtedly, he found the model for his journal among the books he was reading at this time. But the stimulus to write must have come from a new consciousness of himself as a young man destined for a more expansive life than that of a typical provincial merchant. He aspired to a life worth recording in detail. Was it his father's position as a deputy to the Commission on Laws that made the difference? Was it the death of his mother and his position as the sole surviving child of his parents' marriage that allowed him to believe that his life was exceptional and deserving of a detailed daily record?

IVAN'S APPRENTICESHIP CONTINUES

[1769] November 24th I rode with my father to Moscow, and from there we con-tinued to Orël for the purchase of grain and arrived safely on December 3rd. My father remained in Orël until the 22nd and on that day started home, and I stayed [under the guidance of] Afanasii Popov.

1770.

March 8th the Oka [River] at Orël broke up, and starting on the 10th the load-ing began. I don't recall which day we started moving in the grain boats. How-ever, after going about 40 verstas[49] we stopped for 12 days because of low water that was caused by a severe cold snap. Later when it again became warm and water started to flow, we sailed farther.

April 4th was Holy Easter Day. I attended matins and mass in the village of Nikitino, 15 verstas upriver from Belev, and there we broke our fast. We stayed overnight near Belev. 8th we sailed to the city of Kaluga.

12th we reached the confluence of the Moscow River safely near Shchurovo and on the next day I left for home, leaving Afanasii Popov with the boats.[50]

Moving grain and flour through the northern waterways was just one side of the family's trade. Ivan also had to learn how to find, purchase, and transport grain to the family's flour mills for processing. In late November 1769, at age 15, he was introduced to this aspect of the business. His family's firm purchased some of their grain in its home district of Dmitrov, but the largest consign-ments came from the lower reaches of the great rivers to the south and east, and purchasing occupied much of each winter. Trips took them as far east as Kazan and as far south as Promzino Gorodishche on the Sura River, a port at that time in Simbirsk province.[51] In this winter of 1769–1770 when Ivan first participated, his father decided not to make his usual purchases at the Volga port of Lyskovo below Nizhnii Novgorod because of high prices there through the winter.[52] Instead, he and his agents went south to Orël on the Oka River and southeast down the Volga and Sura rivers to make purchases at other grain ports. In the diary excerpt at the head of this section, Ivan related that he accompanied his father on this trip to the city of Orël, where (as we know from another report) they purchased large allotments of wheat, buckwheat, and rye. His father then left to conduct business in Moscow, while young Ivan stayed on with a family agent. In March, they supervised the loading of grain onto large vessels known as *strugi* and moved them down river toward the Volga. The transport of grain from the south early in the year faced problems of unpredictable weather, and on this trip Ivan had traveled scarcely 40 kilometers downstream when a cold snap stopped the flow of melt water into the river and stranded the boats for two weeks. Once the weather warmed and the boats could again move, Ivan sailed with them to the juncture of the Oka and Moscow rivers, where he disembarked and rode north overland to assist with the barge traffic through the northern canals, again with an agent from the family business. This time he stayed with the barge traffic all the way to Petersburg—and not without incident. In the rapids of the Neva River a short distance from the city, two barges in his group collided in fog with a stranded waterboat and sank. Though distressing, such incidents were far from unusual or unexpected. Indeed, it was rare that all the firm's boats and barges arrived undamaged; the many rapids, shallows, sandbars, and dilapidated locks along the waterway claimed a share of each year's transport.

A closer look at this lengthy waterway reveals that it carried at this time 2,400–3,000 vessels each year from central Russia to the northern capital. The traffic passed through the waterway in three large caravans, one each in the spring, summer, and fall. At the high point in the system, the continental divide at Vyshnii Volochëk, the main problem, apart from deteriorating wooden canal walls and locks, was water flow. Spring runoff provided more than enough water for the first barge caravan that moved out in April, but flows for the summer and autumn caravans were much less reliable. Because of insufficient reservoir capacity, low water levels often brought the boats and barges to a halt. The greatest danger was on the Msta River, which was punctuated by stretches of white water, the most treacherous being the Borovichi rapids, where boats had to pass through eighteen kilometers of turbulent and rock-strewn river. In the 1760s the office in charge of these rapids floated logs attached to mooring lines to guide boats through the rough waters and keep them from smashing into the rocky shoreline, but accidents were frequent as barges broke apart on stones or ran aground. Villagers who lived along the route made good money mounting rescue and repair operations on damaged vessels, a business so profitable that a Senate commission looking into the matter believed that the villagers were replacing obstacles removed from the stream in order to increase their opportunities for earnings.[53]

When the barge caravans exited the Msta into Lake Ilmen, they encountered additional hazards. Not only was Lake Ilmen shallow and silty, putting vessels at risk of stranding, but the open waters of the lake also exposed the boats to high winds and unpredictable storms. The lake bottom became the final resting place of countless water craft. The boats that made it across Lake Ilmen then entered the Volkhov River. More placid than the Msta, the Volkhov nevertheless contained a number of rapids, the worst requiring portages, except during high water flow in the spring. Merchants appealed again and again for the authorities to clear the rapids, but no lasting solution was found until late in the century when the government began building canals in the stream bed through the rapids, a project only completed well after the turn of the century. After navigating the Volkhov, the barges ended their journey by turning into the Ladoga canal and following it to the Neva River and from there into the northern capital. The reason for the Ladoga canal was the turbulence of Lake Ladoga itself. Early in the century, the barges had used the lake route, but so many of them sank that the government soon realized the need to dig a canal along the south shore of the lake.

The condition of the waterway from Vyshnii Volochëk to Petersburg had another unfortunate feature: goods moved almost exclusively in one direction. The difficulties and expense of transporting goods downstream from central Russia to Petersburg were compounded in moving goods back up the shallow and rocky water courses. Indeed, shipments from Petersburg back up the waterway were so unprofitable that nearly all the boats and barges entering the city were broken up at their destination and sold for firewood. This practice brought complaints from people in central Russia about deforestation along the waterway and the increasing cost of wood locally. The government responded to these complaints in the 1780s with an inducement to merchants to run their barges back upstream. The authorities offered a dividend of 50 rubles for each boat taken back to the Borovichi rapids. But the offer proved inadequate, for it cost at least 200 rubles to haul a barge back to Novgorod, which was still some distance from the Borovichi rapids, whereas a trader could purchase a barge at Novgorod for 80–100 rubles.[54]

Ivan spent much of 1770 in Petersburg selling the previous year's consignments of flour and grain. In January of 1771 he returned home and was able to stay there until May when he resumed his education on the waterway, starting again at Vyshnii Volochëk and riding the family's grain barges down to Petersburg. At age sixteen he now had his first opportunity to run the barges down from Novgorod to the northern capital by himself. An agent of the family firm accompanied Ivan through the more hazardous segments of the waterway above Novgorod, but from there Ivan took charge and guided the family's boats into Petersburg, this time without incident. Even so, the firm suffered losses because of difficulties in fulfilling a contract with the military for the delivery of 10,000 sacks of flour. The Tolchënovs and other grain merchants did a portion of their business on government contracts at prices negotiated ahead of time. In this year Ivan's father was unable to purchase in central Russia the full 10,000 sack consignment he had contracted for with the government, and Ivan had to buy 2,000 sacks of milled wheat at high prices in the Ladoga Canal to complete the order, which according to Ivan "caused no small financial loss."[55] This story makes clear that even when large government contracts were available, the long-distance grain trade could be a risky business.

Although Ivan did not offer a reason for his father's inability to purchase the needed grain in central Russia in 1771, the reason may have been the bubonic plague. Moscow and the surrounding region had been hit by the last great plague epidemic in Europe, which started late in 1770, receded and then came back with devastating effect in the late summer and fall of the following year. The scourge carried away a quarter of Moscow's population in a short time and led to riots against the authorities, including the brutal murder of the archbishop by a mob enraged at his prohibitions of religious assemblies (intended to reduce the spread of the disease).

It was in August of this year that Ivan's maternal grandfather, the wealthy first-guild merchant Fëdor Makarov, died. He took sick while staying at the family's northern mill in Kashin district of Tver province, about 200 kilometers north of Moscow, and died as Ivan and his father were bringing him home down the Sestra River. Although Ivan failed to record the cause of Makarov's death, it was probably not the plague because of the distance of the Kashin mill from Moscow and the fact that Ivan's parents retreated to the same northern mill in the next months when the plague became most virulent.[56] Ivan spent the worst plague months in Dmitrov, and he recorded in his diary the flight from Moscow of many of the terrified common people, "who began to scatter to nearby towns and villages and some of them were themselves already infected, while others carried off clothing and other things impregnated with the deadly poison, and so the infection multiplied across many towns and villages, and the villages that lie close to Moscow in particular lost more than half their inhabitants." Ivan wrote that the scourge also reached Dmitrov, and he described the methods used by the townspeople to ward off what he called the righteous anger of the Creator. "They performed frequent religious processions on Sundays, departing from each church and going around the parish, and three processions were performed that circled the entire city."[57] As it happened, only about forty persons in Dmitrov died of plague. Ivan consoled himself with the thought that the dead were people who had received personal goods or visitors from Moscow without taking the proper precautions. He must have been referring to quarantining and fumigation, the methods then in use to contain the spread of the disease. People of this time did not understand the rat-flea vector of the plague infection, but they did know through observation that the plague moved from one locale to another, and the government accordingly devised measures to keep persons and goods from moving freely from plague-infested regions.[58]

The government precautions against spread of the plague hindered the grain business for a time. The following year, wheat purchases from the Moscow area had to be loaded at unfamiliar points and travel a circuitous route north because they were not allowed into the usual port cities of Tver and Gorodno. Farther up the route Ivan, who was again accompanying the family barges north, was held up for many days in the Volkhov River, waiting out a quarantine that was designed to protect Petersburg. Fear of the plague also caused trouble for sales. When the grain shipments finally reached Petersburg, buyers did not want the rye flour Ivan and his men had hauled from Moscow; they suspected that it contained plague contamination. Fortunately for the Tolchënovs, they had also made large purchases farther east in Lyskovo, and sales of this grain from beyond the most deadly plague areas were brisk.[59]

MARRIAGE

[1773] January 6th With the approbation and inducement of my father, I decided to marry.

9th We rode to Moscow to arrange the matter.

14th I viewed the young woman, the daughter of the merchant Aleksei Ivanovich Osorgin in Kozhevniki, who was determined by heavenly fate to be my spouse.

17th The agreement [between the father of the bride and the father of the groom] was negotiated.

20th We went back for a time to Dmitrov.

22nd We returned to Moscow.

24th The final compact was signed.

[The wedding took place three days later.][60]

Marriage marked a major turning point in Ivan's personal life and identity. In January his father arranged a marriage for him with the daughter of a merchant family from Moscow. Moscow provided a much larger and more advantageous marriage market than did provincial towns. Moscow was a powerful magnet for business from these other towns as well. The wealthiest and most ambitious of the merchant houses in the provincial cities were gradually relocating to Moscow during this period, and marriage to a Moscow family was a useful step in that direction because of the importance of kinship networks to the success of any endeavor in Russia. Indeed, Ivan's father had himself married a woman of a Moscow merchant family in 1769 following the death of his first wife, the daughter of Fëdor Makarov. This new wife, Mavra Kholshchevnikova, and her family may well have been helpful in finding the young Moscow woman chosen for Ivan, Anna Alekseevna Osorgina. The Kholshchevnikovs hosted the wedding banquet at their home.[61]

All indications are that Ivan first saw his future wife and lifelong companion only a week before the wedding. It was then that his father introduced him to the young woman and opened negotiations with her family. Ivan's notes express satisfaction with the process. This young woman, he wrote in the diary excerpt above, "was determined by heavenly fate to be my spouse."[62] His reaction is scarcely surprising. The thought that a merchant son or daughter might play an active role in the selection of a spouse would have been rare at that time, or even much later, to judge by the comments of a nineteenth-century merchant in regard to his parents' marriage in 1824, a half century later than Ivan's. "Could there really be any discussion in merchant life of that time about the necessity for closeness, feelings of the heart, mutual attraction, or love? Of course not. It was one of those marriages that was arranged by the older generation almost without regard for the wishes of the fiancée. The older generation had no qualms about taking full responsibility for the consequences, be they happiness or misfortune, that might arise." This commentator, writing late in the nineteenth century, was by no means critical of this method. He added that merchant families lived less openly in those days and young people could not get acquainted and learn about one another's families. Matchmakers who knew the internal life of the families in question were needed.[63]

It should be kept in mind that this way of forming unions was scarcely confined to the merchant community. Memoirs and ethnographic studies reveal that arranged marriages were customary for all social orders. Marriages of merchants and nobles involved economic and personal commitments between families that required detailed definition. We have seen this in the case of the marriage of Ivan's father and its meticulous contractual arrangements in regard to dividing the wealth of his father-in-law between the Tolchënov and Makarov families. As the references to the negotiations and compact associated with Ivan's own marriage to Anna Osorgina demonstrate, Ivan's marriage too implied an economic alliance between families. It was unusual only in that he married relatively young. He was eighteen and his bride seventeen at the time of the wedding. Most merchant sons were not in a strong enough financial position to make an advantageous match at a young age. They had to spend some years acquiring the necessary assets for a good match.[64] The business success of the Tolchënov family and Ivan's position as the sole surviving child gave his marriage proposal exceptional appeal and allowed this young provincial to succeed in the prestigious Moscow marriage market.

About the wedding itself, Ivan left only a sketchy description. He noted that "on January 27th the sacrament of marriage took place in the Church of the Kazan Madonna in Sushchëvo" (a village on the north side of Moscow that had been incorporated into the city in the seventeenth century).[65] "The wedding banquet," he added, "was held in the home of my father's father-in-law, Pëtr Demitrevich Kholshchevnikov. The next day we hosted a supper. On the 29th we did the same. On the 30th the final dinner (*otvodnyi stol*) took place at my father-in-law's. On February first, we left for Dmitrov together with my father-in-law and mother-in-law and several other new relatives." Back home the round of dinners continued, in this case to introduce the bride and the new in-laws to Ivan's relatives in Dmitrov and even to the neighbors, for whom a special separate dinner was hosted. Then on February 6 Ivan and Anna returned to Moscow with her family to celebrate the Maslenitsa holiday (Shrovetide) in the big city.[66] This lengthy round of socializing underlines the importance to Russians of reinforcing the economic contract of the marriage with strong personal links backed up by community understanding and acceptance.

While it is clear that Ivan's wedding involved plenty of mutual hosting and dining during an almost two-week period, he did not give us enough detail to judge if this merchant wedding was similar to the provincial weddings of this period described by the famous memoirist Andrei Bolotov, who wrote:

> Merchant weddings were very expensive, and everyone acted stupid and silly. A lot of drinking went on. The grandest banquet took place on the second day—the princely dinner. All the most prominent men of the town came for it together with their wives. The gathering continued for the whole day, and everyone was served tea, punch, and vodka. A huge amount of drink was provided. Then the gift giving began. All the guests received scarves. An entire trunk full of them was available. . . . Dinner did not begin until about 9 in the evening . . . and they eat, drink, dance, jump around and carry on all night long. If there is music, they play Russian dances.[67]

When Ivan eventually became head of his household, he himself arranged marriages and hosted weddings, and his records of these events will sketch in some further details of this rite of passage among merchants.

Unfortunately, one aspect of the wedding and marriage experience that Ivan Tolchënov's diary fails to convey is the voice of the bride or the people who were guiding her. Ivan's manner of speaking about the choice of Anna as his wife and information we learn from later diary entries make clear that he was not only satisfied with Anna but grew to love and respect her. Similarly, nothing in the diary indicates that Anna ever gave Ivan cause to complain about her behavior. We can probably assume therefore that Anna received and followed the kind of advice that other brides of the time reported having received. A good example is found in the memoirs of the noblewoman Anna Labzina, who married about the same time as Ivan and Anna. Her mother warned her:

> You will no longer be dependent on me, but upon your husband and your mother-in-law, to whom you owe unbounded obedience and true love. You will no longer take orders from me, but from them. . . . Love your husband with a pure and fervent love, obey him in everything; you will not be submitting to him but to God, for God has given him to you and made him your master. If he is cruel to you, then you will bear it all patiently and oblige him. Don't complain to anyone. People will not come to your assistance, and all you will do is expose his weaknesses, and bring dishonor on him and yourself.[68]

Anna Labzina claimed to have received the same advice from a friend, the prominent Russian Enlightenment figure Mikhail Kheraskov, and other good people. Unless Labzina was using this as a rationalization for her submission to a husband who womanized, gambled, and drank, the advice she recorded must have constituted a powerful cultural code.

During the first half of the year following his wedding, Ivan was permitted to spend most of his time with his young wife either at home in Dmitrov or with his parents at one of their mills near the Volga, a honeymoon of sorts. Life in the grain business, the need to be on the road much of the year in bad weather and good, gave Ivan a keen appreciation of home life. In Dmitrov he enjoyed all the conveniences of the family's large, two-story timber house (featuring an addition of guest apartments recently completed in masonry), a staff of servants, and the respect of his fellow citizens for the leading family of the city. Ivan found it hard to give up these pleasures and go on the road where he often lodged in post stations, on barges, and even in open fields. Some days when on the road he had to work and ride through the night with no rest. It is not hard to know how he felt about this when, after the honeymoon, he had to return to his work. At the end of each year he noted wearily in his diary the distances he had traveled and the exact number of days he had been separated from his wife. And the laments started the very first year of his marriage. At the end of his summary for 1773 he wrote: "In this year I covered 2,219 verstas, riding to various places. I was separated from my wife for 51 days." This was the year of his honeymoon. More typical were the following years when his travels averaged between 5 and 6 thousand verstas, and his absences from home amounted to 195 days in 1774, 193 days in 1775, and 190 days in 1776.[69]

*   *   *

Ivan began to keep regular diary notes only in 1773, the year of his marriage. The entries for his childhood and after until 1773, on which this chapter is built, are sketchy and in part a reflective account that he inserted once he decided to write a daily journal. Most other authors of memoirs and journals from this time began their works by stating their motivation for making such a record, which was almost invariably that the memoir was intended for the edification of their family and progeny. Curiously, Ivan did not offer such a motivation or give any reason at all for why he wished to keep a diary. We may nevertheless be in a position to suggest his reasons as we get better acquainted with Ivan and his life.

As for this early stage of his life, although Ivan was born and grew up in a dynamic, rapidly changing Russia and was a child of relative privilege, the setting and social identity into which he was habituated were not remarkable or unusual for a young male of his station. The district towns throughout central Russia in this period contained people of wealth and prominence similar to his father and grandfather. Ivan's upbringing, rudimentary education, and early apprenticeship on the waterways of central and northern Russia were normal for a provincial grain merchant. The dangerous and distant travel and the taxing physical work, despite the assistance of agents and hired bargemen, did not leave Ivan with a feeling of privilege and leisure. Indeed, he found that the rigors of life on the road held little appeal. The trips to the capital cities and ancient river ports nevertheless introduced him to spectacular sights and re-fined ways of living that unquestionably appealed to him. Moreover, the eman-cipation of the Russian nobility from obligatory state service that was granted in 1762 just before Ivan began his apprenticeship generated a broad movement of nobles to their country estates and district towns, accompanied by a rich flowering of estate architecture, gardens, and provincial social life and culture. The journal that Ivan began at this time constitutes an account of his develop-ing identity as a person who wished to participate in the formation of this new, more cultivated life of his community. It is a reflexive account in that Ivan monitored his own life and the styles of living that he encountered in the capital cities and country estates to which his work took him, and he sought to make these features part of his own life. But strong notions of traditional limits and inherited practices likewise were expressed in his thinking, as we can see from his comments about how fate had determined a particular woman to be his spouse. Ivan was a man whose experience featured elements of two kinds: those we associate with the more fixed and bounded character of a traditional society and those we associate with the modern reflexive project of self-identity.

One element in Ivan's developing identity will be a prominent civic role. This, one could say, reflected merely Ivan's desire to follow in his father's footsteps. Yet Ivan's participation in the civic affairs of his community was different from his father's. Before continuing with Ivan's life in the 1770s, it may therefore be helpful to look at the character and development of politics in his city during his father's time, before Ivan himself became active in civic affairs.

2

Local Politics during Ivan's Youth

POLITICS IN DMITROV

In March of 1767 my father was elected from our city as a deputy to the Commission to compose a project for a new law code, and in June I went to Moscow, where I lived for a period of time.

In January of 1768 the deputies were dismissed and told that they should appear two months later in Petersburg. . . . In the first days of March my parents rode to Petersburg, and I remained at home until March 31st when I rode to the Tvertsa River to the village of Mel'nikovo for the loading of barges.[1]

Local politics and administration placed burdens on merchant families. Russia was a centrally governed state, and each province and district was subject to the power of government-appointed police and administrative officials: governors-general and governors at the provincial level and *voevody* (singular *voevoda*) at the district level. Central fiscal affairs were in the hands of local treasury agents, who collected taxes and other levies and sent them up the line to the capital cities. While these officials could and did intervene in local affairs on occasion, towns were in principle self-governing corporate bodies composed of officially registered citizens, who were classified by their activities and tax obligations as either merchants, artisans, or others usually referred to in Western literature as "posad people" (a translation of the Russian *posadskie liudi*) or later as "lesser townspeople" (*meshchane*).[2] Citizens elected their own leaders, who served on the town magistracy and in several other capacities. The city assembly (*skhod*), with the confirmation of the magistracy, distributed obligations among the citizens in accordance with their tax-eligible status. The magistracy managed the licensing of business activity and sat in judgment over civil legal cases. Although the affairs of other urban dwellers, such as peasants, clergy, and nobles, were beyond the competence of the town offices and belonged to the corporate bodies of those social groups (the peasant communal councils, the spiritual administration, and a variety of offices for noble affairs), when persons from these other groups had disputes with townspeople or needed to use assets or receive permissions concerning town property, they too would be subject to the jurisdiction of the magistracy court. Moreover, leading merchants maintained business and social connections with persons in the other groups and regarded such connections as important to the functioning of their town and their family enterprises.

The structure of urban governance in Russia had acquired new forms and European language labels in the reforms of Peter the Great. Peter introduced an urban statute in 1721 calling for the creation of town magistracies composed of elected burgomasters (*burgomistry*) and councilors (*ratmany*).[3] In large cities the magistracy was headed by a president. The number of burgomasters and councilors in each town depended on the number of registered townspeople (as distinct from other groups such as nobles or peasants who might be living in a city). Though the magistracies were conceived initially as bodies independent of local agents of the central government and subordinate to only the Chief Magistracy in Petersburg, this arrangement did not long survive the death of Peter the Great. In 1727 the Supreme Privy Council, which then ruled the central state, abolished the Chief Magistracy, renamed the town magistracies "city halls" (*ratushi*), and subordinated them to the state administrators in their localities, the voevody. Peter the Great's daughter, Elizabeth, seized the throne in 1741 and reintroduced many of the institutions of her father's time, including the Chief Magistracy and the local town magistracies. They served as administrative and judicial instances for the local merchant and artisanal society. Even so, the authority of the local agents of central power remained decisive whenever they felt the need to intervene.

The Dmitrov town magistracy at the time of Ivan Tolchënov's youth, when his father played a leading role in city governance, was composed of a burgomaster and two councilors. In addition, the city elected a large number of other officers of lesser rank to manage tasks associated with the collection of taxes and recruits, registration of urban dwellers, the billeting of troops and policing of the markets and warehouses. Citizens were also chosen to serve as judges on the "verbal court" (*slovesnyi sud*), which handled small civil disputes relating primarily to commercial affairs. Election and service on the magistracy were the preserve of the members of the merchant guilds, the wealthiest citizens. The rest of the registered urban populace voted on and served in the lesser offices, and their choices were then confirmed by the members of the magistracy.

Soviet historians of the early modern town stressed the class conflict in the cities of the eighteenth century. They detailed a number of incidents of conflict between the wealthy merchants and the ordinary tax-eligible citizens in the cities of Orël, Iaroslavl, and Arkhangel'sk.[4] Conflicts of another kind flared up from time to time between townspeople and the agents of the central government, who not only enforced the tax obligations of the tsarist regime but also demanded a variety of services from the townspeople and even imposed changes in the administrative order, housing requirements, and placement of streets and roads, not to mention the personal payments and perquisites they expected for their efforts.[5] Dmitrov was not free of tensions of both these types. Indeed, in Dmitrov these tensions went back several decades. In 1732, for example, lesser merchants had to flee the city to avoid being arrested and sent off as army recruits to fill the town's quota.[6]

I have already mentioned the election of Ivan's father as the representative of his town to the famous Commission on Laws convened by Catherine II in 1767. Her stated intention was to bring together representatives of the non-servile social groups to create on the basis of modern principles a new law code for the empire. The last general code had been promulgated in 1649, and in the intervening period the reforms of Peter the Great had transformed Russia and the Russian elites such that the old code and the welter of subsequently issued government decrees provided a poor legal guide to the citizens, administrators, and judges of this rapidly modernizing and expanding empire. The empress drew the legal principles for the new code from the writings of European jurists of her time and recorded them in a Grand Instruction. Other working documents for the commission came from the cities and districts whose citizens met beforehand and drew up their own "instructions," which contained statements of the needs of each representative group (nobility, townspeople, free peasants, non-Russian tribes). The towns occupied a prominent place in the Commission on Laws. Of the total 564 deputies, well over one-third (208) represented the towns.

Historians have found the instructions of the town deputies and their speeches at the commission's general assembly to be a rich source of information about the aspirations of the merchants at this time. Some historians have made much of the potential class conflict expressed in the arguments that arose in the assembly between the town deputies and the leading defenders of exclusive privileges of the nobility. In a number of cases, merchant deputies asked that townspeople be given the exclusive right to engage in commercial activities in the cities, that nobles be limited to selling only what they produced on their estates with the resources of their estates, and that peasants not be allowed to trade in the cities unless they enrolled as citizens and shared the taxes and service obligations of the townspeople.[7] Deputies complained that townspeople had to pay the demeaning "soul tax" and were subject to corporal punishment. Some deputies and instructions, speaking for the wealthiest merchants, asked that first-guild merchants be allowed to carry a sword (a right limited to the nobles), that members of the magistracies be given officer ranks, and that merchants be permitted once again to purchase bonded servants. While it is true that these requests seem to have made some spokesmen of the conservative nobility jittery and defensive, Soviet historians were inclined to find class conflict nearly everywhere and may well have exaggerated the tensions between the nobility and the merchants at this time.[8]

In reality, very few town instructions asked that merchants be granted special privileges and rights that would place them on the level of the nobility. Take the request about owning bonded servants. This is sometimes interpreted as an effort on the part of merchants to acquire a privilege that belonged to the nobles. But the truth is that the merchants were attempting to recover a right that had been usurped by the nobility. Not only merchants but many other non-nobles had long enjoyed the right to own bonded servants. Lesser townsmen, even peasants, as well as merchants owned serfs right into the middle of the eighteenth century. In 1746, however, the Governing Senate began to define serf-ownership as an exclusive right of the nobility. It was this innovation that the merchants were reacting against. They were asking that the nobility not be allowed to arrogate to itself alone this traditional privilege.[9] As it happened, merchants continued to own serfs either because they had purchased them before the ban or had worked out an arrangement to hold them in the name of someone legally qualified to purchase serfs. The Tolchënov family, for example, had several bonded servants working in their home and retained these people for decades beyond the passage of laws assigning exclusive serf right to nobles.[10]

The Russian scholar Andrei Demkin argues in recent studies that the merchants at the Commission on Laws usually expressed their desires timidly. Apart from their requests either to ban urban commerce by nobles and peasants or to make them bear urban tax and service obligations if they did so, the merchants mostly wanted improvements in the financial and taxation instruments that concerned their day-to-day activities. One of these was the law on bills of exchange (*veksel'nyi ustav*). While generally satisfied with the law, merchants wanted more protection for creditors. For example, they asked for much clearer and more detailed rules on bankruptcy. They wanted the government to come down hard on those who declared bankruptcy intentionally to avoid payment of debts or those who ruined themselves "through extravagance." Merchants asked that such people receive severe sanctions such as liquidation of all their assets to pay creditors and payment of their remaining debts by day labor.[11] Had this stance been accepted and enforced uniformly, it would have had a bearing on Ivan Tolchënov's fate in the 1790s when his fortunes turned. But bankruptcy legislation remained confusing and often ineffective until the end of the century, after the crisis in Ivan's finances.

Other common concerns involved the billeting of troops and confiscation of horses by the military and central government officials. Merchants complained that the military took over whatever parts of their homes and stables they wanted, knocked out walls to suit their convenience, and beat the merchants if they protested. The merchants could sue the officers for "dishonoring" them, but the effort was expensive and the fines too trivial to deter the abuse. For this reason, merchants asked that the government build barracks in towns for the housing of troops.[12] Likewise associated with merchants' feelings of dignity and place was their objection to the poll (or soul) tax. Some of them had been addressing letters to the Commission on Commerce about this long before the Commission on Laws, complaining that despite the great contributions of merchants to the economy, they continued to be subject to the degrading poll tax, which placed them socially in the same category as the lowliest peasant or urban worker.[13] Merchants saw themselves as people who stood on a much higher level, and they sought to emphasize their separation, a striving that also revealed their great anxiety about slipping back into what they regarded as the contemptible position of peasants and urban workers.

Finally, merchants expressed dissatisfaction with the laws on inheritance. According to V. I. Sergeevich, the merchants operated on the principles of the Byzantine *Ecloga* and wished to continue to do so.[14] The *Ecloga*, which influenced early Russian legal compilations, gave parents broad discretion in changing or withholding property endowments in their wills in response to the behavior of heirs.[15] The civil courts established by Peter I did not, however, recognize these principles, and, consequently, merchants did not have an inheritance system that they felt comfortable with. Preferring the old way of doing things, they now asked that it be brought into the proposed new legal system.

It would be interesting to know what Ivan Tolchënov's father and the other merchants and townspeople of Dmitrov thought of these issues and to compare their opinions to those of the people of other towns and to those of the local nobility. Unfortunately, the statement (*nakaz*) that the Dmitrov townspeople sent to the Commission on Laws was one of the briefest and least revealing of all those submitted. The townspeople merely introduced their chosen deputy, the diarist's father Aleksei Il'ich Tolchënov, and expressed full confidence in his abilities. The drafters then added that "neither when the request [for a statement] was first considered nor later when the statement was being written were any requests for corrections offered, and the [town representatives] declared that they did not have any general needs to present in regard to conditions in the city." The statement concluded with warm thanks to the empress for her concern in convening the Commission on Laws and wished her good health.

Although the Dmitrov statement expressed satisfaction with current conditions, life in the city was not all peace and harmony. Dmitrov suffered the same stresses, the social and personal discord, as other towns. Unfortunately, the diary of Ivan Tolchënov does not tell us much about these conflicts, nothing at all really for the period of the Commission on Laws. The diary only begins in 1769, a year after the plenary sessions of the commission, and is very thin in its first few years. Even when Ivan's jottings become more frequent in the mid 1770s, they do not say much about local politics, as the diary is mainly a record of the author's travels, daily schedule of visits and visitors, family events, and remarkable sights. Other dimensions of town life can nevertheless be found in the archives of local institutions. In the years preceding the Commission on Laws, they reveal a series of conflicts in town governance and even an acrimonious election fight that prompted orders from the central government for a second election.

In 1760, the Dmitrov magistracy voted to dismiss from their offices the burgomaster Pëtr Loshkin and two councilors for offenses to the merchants and to replace them with Ivan Il'ich Tolchënov (the diarist's uncle) as burgomaster and Danil Popov and Pëtr Karavaev as councilors.[16] The bitterness provoked by this battle is reflected in a complaint filed by the defeated Pëtr Loshkin early the next year against Stepan Borisovich Tolchënov, whom he accused of assaulting him at a meeting of the magistracy and yelling out all manner of criminal charges at him. Evidently Loshkin, a member of one of the town's prominent families and a man who had served for sixteen years as burgomaster (at the time city officials served indefinite terms), could not accept being turned out. Four years later, when Ivan Il'ich Tolchënov and Pëtr Karavaev asked to be allowed to step down, a new election was held, and it too provoked angry opposition.[17] Two leading merchants, one of whom was the diarist's maternal grandfather, Fëdor Makarov, complained that they had gone to the assembly and duly elected two new persons, Stepan Karavaev as burgomaster and Pëtr Semënovich Tolchënov as councilor, to serve as replacements for the retiring officials. According to the plaintiffs, after they left the building someone vacated that decision and called for another vote, which resulted in the election of Aleksei Semënovich Tolchënov as burgomaster and Stepan Karavaev as councilor. But this election should be considered invalid, they argued, because Aleksei Semënovich Tolchënov was mixed up in the affair of the discredited Pëtr Loshkin and, besides, his election was confirmed by only one first-rank merchant, who was a close relative at that, and signed by some other non-propertied persons, altogether no more than forty-five persons. The upshot of what appears to have been an attempted coup by people close to the ousted Pëtr Loshkin and backed by lesser tradesmen with resentments against the wealthiest merchants was a subsequent election in August of the same year. In this next election the forces maneuvering against the wealthiest merchants must have mobilized their people effectively, because the balloting again returned Aleksei Semënovich Tolchënov as burgomaster and Stepan Karavaev as councilor.[18]

It is not surprising that tensions sometimes ran high between the top officers of the city administration and the other merchants and tradesmen. The top officials were responsible for seeing that the many tax-collecting, supervision, and maintenance tasks of the town were done, and they could suffer heavy fines and punishments if state demands were not met. But the needs of the lesser townsmen's own families and businesses occasionally prevented them from performing the services they were elected to carry out. The magistracy officers then had to come down hard on the shirkers. For example, when the diarist's father, Aleksei Il'ich Tolchënov, was burgomaster in 1767, he found that the person in charge of selling salt was not on duty during a major holiday, and a large number of people were lined up to purchase salt from the town warehouse. When a search for him proved fruitless, Aleksei Il'ich demanded that this shirker be severely punished as an example to other lower-level officials. The officers of the magistracy complied and ordered that absent salt officer be hauled before them and lashed mercilessly.[19]

The mystery is why these tensions did not surface in the town's statement (*nakaz*) to the Commission on Laws, which instead offered a bland assurance that the townspeople had no needs to present to the commission. A possible explanation is that the leading officials sought to keep these local conflicts and tensions local and to produce a statement so innocuous that everyone could agree to sign it and give the central authorities the impression of harmony in the town. The one thing that stands out in this short document is the large number of townsmen signatories. In addition, it contains an unusually large number of signatories from the clergy, which appear in a prominent position.[20] Could it be that Aleksei, the diarist's father, who had been chosen to represent the town at the commission, and his colleagues sought to assert the unity of the town leadership, lay and clerical together, and to counter the character of the Commission on Laws as a secular forum in which local clergy were not permitted representation?[21] Merchants and clergy in Dmitrov, and elsewhere, were close and cooperated on projects in church construction, furnishing, and renovation, in which the merchants made large contributions and took great personal and civic pride. The city leaders, seeing that the clergy was excluded from the Commission on Laws itself, may have wished to include it in the local discussions. In any case, the city's statement would have had to be uncontroversial if it were going to achieve unity and paper over the fissures between rich and poor, and possibly laity and clergy, that characterized any town of the time.[22]

If the merchants of Dmitrov wanted to allege an untroubled life in the city, the nobles of Dmitrov district took a very different approach. In their statement to the Commission on Laws, the nobles painted a dark picture of conditions in the countryside. There, all was conflict, insecurity, fear, and frustration with the legal system. The nobles filled their statement with requests for changes that would increase their ability to control local conditions. They expressed concern about the lack of law and order in the countryside. Their statement told of trespassing, robbery of crops and other thefts, and personal insults that frequently led to terrifying fights in which thuggish gangs intimidated and beat their peaceful neighbors into submission. Suits filed to protest these assaults, the statement claimed, bogged down in distant courts and proved ruinous to the plaintiffs. Journeys to these far-off courts were costly and robbed the plaintiffs of time and money they needed to run their farms. The nobles who drafted the statement asked that courts be established closer to home. They proposed a set of district courts, four for Dmitrov district, in which judges elected from among the nobility would preside over substantive cases in their resident locale and ride a circuit three times a year to deal with more trivial matters that could be resolved quickly. This detailed and thoughtful proposal included protections against abuse by judges and also the use of the same judges as a protection for nobles against interference by agents of the central government such as the provincial voevoda.

The nobles also had strong words about the need for a reform of the inheritance system that would give every noble complete freedom of testamentary disposition. In this their approach was similar to that requested by the townsmen. They resented having to provide for all sons and wanted the ability to keep the family estates intact and productive by willing them to prudent and industrious sons. They also wanted more flexibility to provide for daughters, signaling a broader trend among the nobility that was shifting provision for daughters from a contract between her parents and her husband-to-be to a deed from her family to her.[23]

The nobles likewise spoke of the importance of educating all children of the nobility—and not just them. Elementary education for peasants was also advised. And, indeed, one outcome of subsequent reforms by Empress Catherine was the founding of local schools, including one in Dmitrov.

The writers added a popular physiocratic injunction of the day that all the arable lands in the district should be under cultivation so as to bring greater prosperity, low grain prices, and a surplus that could be marketed abroad. Finally, they asked for the establishment in all cities of banks for the nobility similar to those that now existed in Moscow and Petersburg. Nobles should have access to easy credit in their own neighborhoods.

In contrast to the merchant statement with its plenitude of signatures from all levels of Dmitrov society, the noble statement contained only fourteen signatures out of the more than three hundred noble landlords registered in the district. It seems clear from the prominence of the Orlovs and Saltykovs among the signatories (six of the fourteen) that this assertive statement was the work of a few families with a well-defined agenda for reform. In view of the participa-

tion of the Orlovs, who were then ascendant at court, the agenda no doubt
represented ideas that already enjoyed the empress's support.

SCANDAL IN THE VOEVODA OFFICE
AND OTHER TENSIONS

*[1772] In March there was established in our city a commission for an inquest
and investigation of tangled affairs in the voevoda office and for a decision on the
continuation of precautions against the plague. The leading official on the commission was State Secretary and Assistant to the Governor of Moscow Nikita
Ivanovich Bestuzhev, who took up residence in our home for about four weeks.*[24]

Another site of tension in the city was the relationship between the townspeople and the central government officials: the voevoda, assistant voevoda,
and secretary. The job of the voevoda was to enforce government regulations,
taxation, billeting, and other burdens on the citizens. The citizens naturally
preferred to arrange their affairs on their own terms. A typical case occurred in
1764 when a large conflagration in the middle of town consumed 19 forges, 141
shops, and 3 residences. A local merchant blamed the smiths for starting the fire
and asked the magistracy to see that the smithies be rebuilt in a place of the
magistracy's choice. The central government, in response to a fire that consumed much of the city of Tver in May of the previous year, was just then
formulating rules that would diminish the losses caused by urban fires. The
crowded and untidy shape of Russian towns, built almost entirely of wood,
provided ample kindling for infernos that periodically destroyed whole communities. The voevoda chancery in Dmitrov frantically demanded an order
from the central authorities that would forbid merchants and smiths from
rebuilding their shops and forges where they had stood before the fire. A year of
wrangling ensued before the town magistracy and the central government
officials were able to agree on a compromise solution, even though in this era
relations between the central officials and the magistracy were not as strained as
they later became. The magistracy ordered that the smithies had to be moved to
a new spot and allowed the merchants to rebuild their shops where they had
been, but (in response to the voevoda's concerns) with a certain distance between each structure.[25]

Tensions between the voevoda office and the townspeople became more
serious in the next decade, in part because of scandals in the voevoda's office
itself, in part because of the reordering of urban life that the central government began to impose on the cities in the mid-1770s.

A new voevoda and his deputy were appointed to Dmitrov in 1770: Pëtr
Alekseevich Zherebtsov and Guards Ensign Aleksandr Savich Malygin. Voevody were usually former army officers, and they came to government service

with a military approach to affairs. The normal give and take of civilian governance was alien to them. Zherebtsov and Malygin were of this cut. Malygin in particular seemed to rub local people wrong. Soon after his arrival we find him filing complaints against local merchants, including one against Ivan Il'ich Tolchënov, a former burgomaster and uncle of the diarist.[26] Malygin had just arrived in March, and in May he charged that Ivan Il'ich Tolchënov had accosted him at the home of a local chancery clerk, called him a drunk, hurled numerous curses at him and threatened to cut him to ribbons. Tolchënov allegedly also sat next to Malygin's wife and treated her rudely. Unfortunately, the file on this case does not explain why one of Dmitrov's prominent citizens would take such a dislike to the assistant voevoda within weeks of his arrival. The case was settled quickly, however. Like many other such personal insult or dishonor suits (*beschest'e*), the parties agreed within a month to settle it "amicably" after the defendant paid a small fine.[27] The cause of friction in this instance was probably the billeting of Malygin's people in a house owned by Ivan Tolchënov and his brothers in the commercial district, a house that would continue to be a bone of contention between Malygin and the Tolchënovs for some time into the future. This type of conflict was quite common in towns and, as mentioned earlier, constituted a major complaint of townspeople at the Commission on Laws. Government officials frequently came to towns and simply occupied, sometimes by force, prime properties, refusing to accept the billets designated for them by the local magistracy.[28]

Further trouble between the voevoda's office and the townspeople surfaced in a scandal late the following year. This concerned the theft of goods from households that had been infected during the outbreak of plague in 1771 and a number of accusations of bribery and malfeasance that were swirling about Voevoda Zherebtsov, the secretary of his chancery Pëtr Grekov, and a local noble serving as a private inspector, Captain Pëtr Khitrovo.[29] As Ivan reported in his year-end summary excerpted at the head of this section, the central government in Moscow sent a commission in March 1772 under the leadership of State Councilor Nikita Ivanovich Bestuzhev to investigate the case. During the four weeks that the commission sat, Bestuzhev resided in the diarist's family home.[30] The investigation ended on April 11 somewhat inconclusively. Bestuzhev relieved Khitrovo of his duties as inspector, but Zherebtsov and Grekov were allowed to remain at their posts because of insufficient evidence to convict them of a crime.[31]

Captain Khitrovo, who had moved to the area just two years earlier, proved to be a remarkably disruptive figure, a petty tyrant, who was continually stirring up trouble. Engaged in the supply of liquor and collection of liquor taxes in Dmitrov, he filed many complaints, on the one hand, about the shortcomings of the voevoda office, while apparently, on the other hand, also trying to bribe the voevoda's secretary Pëtr Grekov. In one incident he was accused of paying off Grekov with an expensive golden tobacco case. Khitrovo responded that he simply wanted to give Grekov a gift. Grekov, for his part, explained that while he was at Khitrovo's home on a dinner invitation, the squire offered him the tobacco case, which he refused to accept, and then on returning home found that the case had been slipped into a pocket of his kaftan when he was not looking. Another time, we find Khitrovo thumbing his nose at the sumptuary laws by visiting the assistant voevoda in an unauthorized coach and six. He was also frequently in conflict with the clergy of his estate church and at war with the episcopate about replacing them, difficulties that continued for nearly two decades.[32]

Although Ivan soon after got to know Khitrovo and regularly visited his Podlipich'e estate for the early July holiday associated with his Icon of the Kazan Madonna estate church, at the time of the Bestuzhev Commission inquiry in 1772, Ivan may not have known Khitrovo well enough to take an interest in the case. Again, we learn nothing from the diary entries about the substance of the accusations against Zherebtsov, Grekov, and Khitrovo, even though Ivan was living in Dmitrov and staying in the same house as State Councilor Bestuzhev. But this was a time when Ivan's diary was still primarily a record of this travels. He mentioned the investigation only in his retrospective notes on 1772 composed about 1790. Though mentioning the investigation in general terms, he seemed most interested in reporting that his family had hosted a high central government official for four weeks. His identification with figures of authority and prominence was a key to his identity; these were the contacts that he most sought to affirm in his diary.

After the investigation by State Councilor Bestuzhev, bad blood between the voevoda office and the Tolchënovs continued. In 1773, another of the diarist's uncles, Mikhaila Il'ich Tolchënov, filed a complaint with the magistracy on behalf of himself and two of his brothers about the continuing occupation of their house by the voevoda and his people, a situation that, according to the complaint, not only caused the family commercial losses but had also led to a severe injury of one of the brothers. The building had been taken over by the voevoda office in February of 1772 and had been under continuing occupation for nearly a year and a half. Since the house was in the merchant section of town, the petition read, it was "very burdensome" for the family to have it appropriated by state officials, and the family had made repeated oral requests to the magistracy about this. The magistracy had offered to give the voevoda other quarters, but the house of the Tolchënov brothers was still being occupied in June of 1773. Because we are currently adding rooms to that house, Mikhaila Tolchënov continued, we need to have free access to it. "But this June 12th when my brother Ivan Il'ich Tolchënov went to inspect the building, a minion of

Voevoda Zherebtsov attacked him without any provocation and beat him severely." The petition then asked on behalf of the three Tolchënov brothers, the diarist's uncles, that the house be freed from billeting. The brothers also announced that they were suspending the new construction on the building because of the danger of entering it and because of the continual abuse, losses, and insults they risked in doing so.[33]

This case was the culmination of a particularly unpleasant and violent winter and spring in Dmitrov. The year 1773 opened with an allegedly unprovoked assault on the diarist's father, Aleksei Tolchënov. In a complaint filed on January 8 he claimed that the previous day when he was at a meeting of merchants of one section of the city, the merchant Fëdor Shestakov "attacked me for some unknown reason and pummeled me on the face and head, injuring and dishonoring me."[34] Soon after, Assistant Voevoda Malygin brought a complaint against another family member, Iakov Stepanovich Tolchënov, a cousin of the diarist's father and uncles. Malygin asserted that on his return to Dmitrov in early February, he had stopped near the grain barns, and "in an abuse of my honor for some unknown reason this merchant Tolchënov asserted that I was worse than an animal and that I procured young women for my sexual pleasure."[35] Although both these cases were settled in the summer without court battles, they reveal the tensions between some of the citizens and between citizens and central government officials.

Then for a time the acrimony appears to have subsided. The reason was undoubtedly the Pugachëv rebellion. This popular uprising, which broke out late in 1773 and came close to the Moscow region in late 1774, quickly drew the elites together in self-defense, as it threatened anyone with property or position.

But as soon as the danger passed, conflicts began to reemerge, and the battle to end billeting of the voevoda's people in the residence owned by the Tolchënov brothers once again flared up. This time the brothers were able to obtain an order from the magistracy that called for the voevoda and his people to vacate the home of Uncle Ivan and his brothers and to move to lodgings that were being made available to him in the home of Semën Borisovich Tolchënov. Evidently the voevoda office continued to resist this move, for the local magistracy then took the matter to the Chief Magistracy in Moscow and obtained a decision in April of 1775 affirming the order of the Dmitrov magistracy to change the lodgings of the voevoda.[36]

That same month, Assistant Voevoda Aleksandr Malygin again appeared as the focus of troubles. The burgomaster Fëdor Loshkin complained to the magistracy that he was assaulted by Malygin in the midst of a fire fighting operation. He and the city policemen had hauled fire fighting equipment from the magistracy building and were in the process of extinguishing a fire that was consuming two neighboring homes when Malygin showed up "excitedly and instead of assisting in the fire fighting as his duties required, attacked me without any cause and called me a rogue and cursed me with all manner of foul words." In short, instead of helping, Malygin allegedly blamed Loshkin for not having the right fire fighting equipment and generally made a nuisance of himself. Luckily the fire did not spread farther, reported Loshkin, but he asked the magistracy to order that Malygin or any other personnel of the voevoda office in the future not interfere in fire fighting operations or hurl insults but render only appropriate assistance.[37] These were particularly serious accusations because of the terrifying specter of fires in urban Russia. Persons responsible for lighting or spreading them were not treated gently.[38]

This altercation between Malygin and Loshkin may have been an aspect of the conflict between Malygin and the diarist's uncles. Fëdor Loshkin was a close associate and business partner of the Tolchënovs and was later married to Uncle Ivan's daughter Matrëna.

Aleksandr Malygin was accused of causing another unpleasant incident a few months later. About three in the morning on a day early in September 1775, he and two of his men ran to the cathedral and demanded at knifepoint that the bells be rung for a general alarm. They also ordered the night police to set up a hue and cry along all the streets. These drastic measures were normally reserved for emergencies such as a fire or other calamity threatening the city. When people reacted in the usual way and converged on the places where the alarms were sounded, they were surprised to discover no fires or other crises. They then went to Malygin's dwelling and found that there, too, nothing alarming was happening.

For his part, when questioned by the authorities, Malygin claimed that men had invaded his residence and beat him and that this was the reason he raised the alarm. His stories turned out to be somewhat inconsistent. A police elder reported that on the night in question, when he asked Malygin why he was ordering an alarm sounded in the streets, Malygin told him that a few men appeared at his apartment and "beat him up" (*pribili*). In a memorandum a few days later, Malygin wrote that this "villainous assault" was perpetrated by a large body of men who "beat him and wished to beat him to death," and it was to avoid the murder of himself and his men that he ordered the alarm sounded.[39] Since it evidently remained unclear who the attackers were and no outsiders could be found at the time in Malygin's residence, it is hard to imagine what he was up to. It is perhaps not surprising that Malygin might feel under threat in a city where he had made a habit of picking fights with members of the leading families and (as later became clear) even with his own superior, but whether he was actually attacked or not, the citizens of Dmitrov did not think his plight that night justified a general alarm.

Another case in the magistracy archives indicates that Malygin had cultivated at least a few friends. This case likewise shows that citizens sometimes sought to settle disputes between themselves with the help of a clergyman and turned to the magistracy court for a resolution only after the informal arbitration efforts of a priest failed. In this case, two members of the Tugarinov clan (both lesser townsmen and not from the wealthy branch of the family) went to their common confessor at the Prophet Elijah Church to ask him to settle a dispute about how much one of them owed the other for a piece of property that they both initially claimed to own. The priest made some progress but ultimately could not win an agreement between the two men, and the matter landed in the magistracy court. One of the testimonies in the case came from Aleksandr Malygin, but when questioned about it the priest said that he did not include it in his own testimony because Malygin could not be regarded as impartial. He had been godfather for one person in the dispute and was friendly with him, and moreover the person in question still owed Malygin money.[40] Malygin's personal bond with the family of this lesser townsman may indicate that he had cast his lot with the less wealthy artisans and traders of the city, and this may explain why he held a grudge against and picked fights with the leading families and finally with his own superiors, whom he may have seen as in a corrupt alliance to dominate the weaker citizens.

After the Pugachëv rebellion, these wealthier people close to the diarist's family seemed to be again firmly in control of the town magistracy. Aleksei Stepanovich Tolchënov had been burgomaster in the early 1770s. He was a cousin of the diarist's father and brother of the Iakov Tolchënov whom Malygin had earlier accused of assaulting him. When Aleksei Stepanovich had to step down in 1773 because of ill health, the townspeople elected as his replacement Fëdor Semënovich Loshkin, who, as already mentioned, was a close friend and business associate of the diarist's family. The lead signature on the document affirming Loshkin's election is that of the diarist's father Aleksei Tolchënov, followed by the signature of his brother and Loshkin's future father-in-law, Ivan Il'ich Tolchënov.[41] Two years later at the regularly scheduled elections, Fëdor Loshkin was again returned as burgomaster in an especially important race.[42] The central government was in the process of enacting a major reform, the Institution of the Administration of the Provinces of the Russian Empire (1775), which promised a significant enlargement and reorganization of local administrative and judicial institutions. This close associate of the diarist's family would be in a key position to name people to subordinate posts in the city administration, including the many tax-collection agents, and to guard the interests of his friends and relatives during the implementation of the reform.[43]

Among the changes initiated that year was a reclassification of city people that increased the tax levies on guild merchants and separated them from the rest of the urban taxpayers, who were now to be grouped together as "the lesser townspeople" (*meshchane*). In noting this change in his yearly summary, Ivan wrote in the names of the leading merchants in order of their declared capital, heading off the list proudly with "my father Aleksei Il'ich." The rest of the list of first and second guild merchants included respectively "Ivan Il'ich Tolchënov and his brothers, Stepan Sergeev Loshkin, Pëtr Sergeev Loshkin, Aleksandr Vasil'ev Loshkin, Ivan Semënov Tolchënov, Pëtr Semënov Tolchënov, Stepan Karavaev, Artemei Tugarinov, Pavel Ivanov Tolchënov, Aleksei Semënov Tolchënov, and Gavrilo Shestakov." Eleven more families filled out the third guild of the town.[44] The names come as no surprise. These are the families whose leading members also appear in the top city offices in these years.

It is interesting to observe the variation in Ivan's presentation of names in the passage quoted above. Usage of surnames and patronymics among merchants was in transition at this time. Before the eighteenth century members of commercial groups were usually identified by first name, although the very wealthiest merchants might bear surnames. Usage of surnames among merchants more widely seems to have been spurred by the introduction of the poll tax early in the eighteenth century, and merchant families increasingly used surnames as the century wore on. Even so, a specialist on Russian genealogy, Aleksandr Aksënov, found that as late as the end of the century about 10 percent of first-guild merchants in Moscow were still not using surnames and being identified only by first name and patronymic.[45]

In the documents I have been using for the second half of the century, forms vary. Officially, first name and the full patronymic (-ovich, -evich) was supposed to be used only by persons occupying the first five places on the government Table of Ranks. It was a mark of aristocratic distinction. Ranks six to eight were to use the partial patronymic (father's name in -ov form followed by *syn* [son]).[46] But outside of official documents, in private writings such as Ivan's journal, nobles were normally listed with surnames and the full -ovich form of patronymic regardless of their rank, whereas merchants appeared sometimes with -ovich, but most often with the partial patronymic. In the names quoted above from Ivan's journal he favored his father and uncle with the full patronymic, dropped the *syn* in the partial form for some others, and in the case of Karavaev, Shestakov, and Tugarinov omitted the patronymic altogether, possibly because no other members of those families had the same first name (Tugarinov was at least as wealthy and distinguished as those listed with patronymics). It seems that the wealthier merchants were gradually adopting the -ovich form typical of the nobility. This might be seen as another sign of the aspiration of this upper echelon of commercial people to be recognized as having dignity and an importance for the state equal to those of the nobility.

The administrative reforms of Catherine the Great took some time to implement and were only gradually introduced over the next several years. Ivan, who was still spending much of his time on the road in the second half of the 1770s, unfortunately reported little about the politics of the town. He merely noted his presence at the general town assembly at the magistracy building in July of 1776 and his father's return to the city from his northern mills in July of the next year to take part in the biennial balloting for the magistracy, which resulted in the election of Ivan Artem'ev Tugarinov as burgomaster and Vasilii Karavaev and Dmitrii Nemkov as councilors.[47] So, familiar names again appear, except for Nemkov, a member of a third-guild merchant family that was to play a growing role in the town leadership in the following years.

DISHONOR SUITS AND THE QUESTION OF CREDIT

November 12th, 1775, the Dmitrov magistracy received the merchants listed below, who declared that this past November 8th they were invited by the Dmitrov merchant Stepan Semeonov Korovaev to his home, where there happened also to be the Dmitrov merchant Pëtr Semënovich Tolchënov, who without any cause in the presence of many people of different ranks and sexes, heaped upon the staff of the magistracy and those merchants and lesser townspeople who had been there two days earlier many swear-words, and he called the mayor and deputy and the magistracy councilors and everyone who was at the town assembly, whether of the first, second, or third guild or lesser townspeople, rogues, scoundrels, thieves, and swindlers, and continued this tirade for no less than three hours. . . . They ask that he be dealt with according to the law. . . .

Last year, 1787, a complaint was filed by the Dmitrov posad person and city elder Efim Vasil'ev Shumilov, who asked that suit be brought against a posad person of this city, Maksim Alekseev Bakakin, who on December 13th in the city of Dmitrov on the market square at the time he was buying bread accused him of being dishonorable. . . . The plaintiff and the accused, after consulting together composed their difference amicably and agreed not to pursue the matter further in the future. —Cases from the Dmitrov magistracy[48]

As we have seen in some of the cases referenced here, questions of honor occupied a prominent place in conflicts between the citizens of Dmitrov and between them and the officials appointed by the central government. The Russian historian Aleksandr Kamenskii has recently discussed this question in his book about everyday life in the north Russian town of Bezhetsk in the first three-quarters of the eighteenth century. There, too, and presumably in much of urban Russia of the time, accusations and counteraccusations of defamation, which were a central feature of life in pre-Petrine Russia, continued to play a role in the eighteenth century. Kamenskii refers to the analysis of the American medievalist Nancy Kollmann in her book on this subject and her contention that because clan and other collective bodies formed the essential context of life in early Russia, people were under enormous pressure to bring suits against anyone who had insulted or defamed them, for an insult to one member of a group that was left unanswered would bring dishonor and a loss of position to the entire collective. People were accordingly quick to respond to an insult by filing a suit. Surviving records indicate that only a small proportion of the suits actually went to trial and reached resolution in that process. Kollmann believes that the important thing was to declare publicly that one was prepared to defend one's honor in court, a stance that would often lead to an out-of-court or "amicable" settlement.[49] Kamenskii, after assessing a number of dishonor suits in Bezhetsk, "cautiously concludes" that the number had been going down in part as a result of the increasing separation in the modern era of the individual from the collective bodies that determined one's identity and standing in earlier times. "However paradoxical it may seem," he writes, "to the degree that we see the development of the emancipation of the individual, the formation of civil society and the rights of man, the idea of honor seems to recede into the background."[50]

While Kamenskii's general point about the declining relevance in the eighteenth century of defamation suits prompted by the need to protect a social collective seems well grounded, it is easy to see that concerns about dishonor of another kind, namely personal dishonor, continued to be important for some social groups in Russia. We have the well-known orgy of dueling and assertive "hussarism" that gripped the elite noblemen of the first half of the nineteenth century. The frequent accusations of dishonor that are reported in the cities of Dmitrov and Bezhetsk (and presumably elsewhere), hurled by merchants at one another or by merchants at officials, would seem again to have the purpose of defending one's personal honor and not that of a collective that would be threatened with humiliation and displacement in a hierarchy of such groups. In this case, honor was most likely linked to trust and to protection of the social capital that allowed one to obtain the credit and funding required to operate a commercial enterprise.

Financial credit was notoriously costly in Russia at this time because of the difficulty and expense of enforcing contracts and recovering payment on promissory notes and other financial instruments.[51] The cost of credit naturally increased in relation to doubts that a lender might have about the capacity of the borrower to repay. Russian merchants often operated on the basis of government contracts, and the archives of the Dmitrov magistracy are full of sworn statements made on behalf of the city's merchants, attesting to their probity and ability to undertake contracts of a certain financial magnitude over a specified period of time. The statements are signed on behalf of one merchant by other merchants, often current or former officials of the magistracy.[52] A merchant had to be in good standing in his community in order to obtain this certification. He could not let stand an accusation of dishonor or lack of probity without incurring some cost to himself in his efforts to negotiate state contracts, loans, and, what is the same thing, deferrals of payment for supplies or labor. The maintenance of one's credit was so important to commercial survival that it required not merely a defense of honor but in some cases even a positive self-presentation designed to convey the impression that one occupied a secure and trustworthy position in the community and had sufficient collateral to back up one's promissory notes and other contractual obligations.

FURTHER SCANDAL AND DEPARTURE OF THE VOEVODA

In February [1778] the assistant voevoda, Aleksandr Malygin, secretly departed for Petersburg and submitted a petition to Her Majesty in which he explained all the misdeeds and malfeasance of Voevoda Zherebtsov and his secretary, Grekov. As a result, the government set up a special investigatory commission in Moscow, and the voevoda and Grekov were dismissed from their posts. —From Ivan's yearly summary notes for 1778.[53]

The weather in 1778 was unusually stormy. February opened with what Ivan described as "an entire night of immense and rare northern lights with frightening columns of fire." Toward the end of April the weather turned harsh. Ivan had just returned to Dmitrov, where a powerful northern wind whipped the city all day. Farther northeast on the Volga River the same wind drove a blizzard across the Nizhnii Novgorod region, where many grain ships were sailing in long reaches. Thirty-six of the boats, including those of Dmitrov merchants, were swamped, some with as many as 4,000 sacks of grain. Ivan reported that although "the heavenly Creator preserved our own shipments from misfortune because they had moved beyond the hardest-hit reaches, four of Uncle Ivan Il'ich's boats went under as did one of the Loshkin family." What grain could be retrieved, mostly expensive wheat, had to be sold on the spot for almost nothing. In September of the same year Dmitrov suffered "a ferocious thunderstorm. Terrifying lightning continued for more than three hours and instilled everyone with horror." A month later snows and rains followed close on one another, flooding the city.[54]

The politics of Dmitrov matched the unsettled weather of the year, as a crisis enveloped the voevoda's office and by extension the regular citizens. The initiator was just the person one might expect, the assistant voevoda, who liked to pick fights and who may have instigated the earlier accusations against his boss that led to the Bestuzhev commission of inquiry in 1772. Now in 1778, as the summary report by Ivan excerpted at the head of this section explains, Aleksandr Malygin sneaked away to Petersburg and informed on his superior Pëtr Zherebtsov and Secretary Pëtr Grekov.[55] The result was the formation of another special investigating commission, this time in Moscow, to sort out the accusations and impose penalties. One of the most startling discoveries, and possibly the one that caused the central authorities the greatest concern, was the alleged receipt by an ordinary citizen of a sealed envelope containing a personal edict from the empress. False edicts, or authentic ones that fell into the wrong hands, often sparked bloody riots when malcontents used them to claim tsarist authorization for action against local officials—a common occurrence in the recent Pugachëv rebellion. Although Malygin's action was primarily an assault of one central government agent on his colleagues, the townspeople of Dmitrov could scarcely remain bystanders, because the work of the voevoda's office necessarily implicated many of them. A number of issues figured in the case, including mismanagement of salt shipments and taxes, the theft of goods from a home that was quarantined during the plague epidemic, and a possible cover-up of the evidence by the subsequent destruction of the home in question. The investigation touched a number of Tolchënovs. Vasilii Tolchënov, a chancery clerk in the voevoda's office, was mentioned in connection with the edict. Uncle Ivan Il'ich had apparently purchased the ill-fated home under quarantine at some point. Other Tolchënovs were involved in salt shipments and sales.[56]

Although the background remains hazy—was the voevoda excessively exploiting his position for personal gain, or were some townspeople conspiring with him to shift their financial and service obligations to others?—the scandal ended the voevodaship of Pëtr Zherebtsov. In the minds of the townspeople, it had even more fateful consequences for the voevoda chancery secretary, Pëtr Grekov. Zherebtsov, who left town soon after the scandal broke, was apparently little lamented. We hear no more about him in the diary. The Tolchënov family, at this time the most prominent in the town, was not close to him personally, as the diary rarely records social contacts with him and those contacts occurred on holidays and official occasions. The secretary Grekov was, by contrast, settled in the town and a social acquaintance, if not a close friend, of the Tolchënov family. They had exchanged personal visits, and Grekov traveled with the family to Moscow on at least one occasion.[57] Not surprisingly, then, they showed concern when, following the scandal and dismissal of Grekov, his health precipitously declined. During the post-Easter rounds of visiting friends and neighbors in early April of 1779, the diarist and his father paid a last call on Grekov, who was already gravely ill. Three weeks later he was dead. In his year-end retrospective listing of acquaintances (*znakomye*) who had passed away in that year, Ivan noted that, according to what people said, Grekov's "death resulted from the unbearable sadness he suffered following the denunciation by Malygin."[58]

The advent of a new voevoda in September of 1778, Second Major Nikolai

Iur'evich Andreanov, did not change the atmosphere for the better. Another military man, Andreanov proved to be a stickler for form and accused the magistracy officers of doing their work poorly and tolerating a large backlog of cases. He also attacked the officials of the salt board for not doing their job and raised questions of malfeasance on their part. Perhaps his inability to work cooperatively with the community was the cause of his short tenure in the district.[59] Matters between the city leaders and the central government agent in the town seemed to improve only after the arrival in 1782 of Anton Letstsano. (This European surname was no doubt Lezzano in Latin letters. The transliteration from the Cyrillic, though accurate, is unfortunately a bit clumsy.) Letstsano served in the new position of police commissioner (*gorodnichii*) that was to replace the office of voevoda. Letstsano was much more accommodating of local interests than were his predecessors. Evidently, too, the diarist Ivan Tolchënov played a positive role. Letstsano's arrival coincided with Ivan's elevation to a leading position on the town magistracy, and he and Letstsano became frequent companions and, in view of the time they habitually spent together, one could even say good friends. This bond seemed to bring civic peace to the town for much of the 1780s. When at the end of the decade town life again suffered serious disruption, the cause was an assault not from within but from the governor-general in Moscow. In this conflict, Police Commissioner Letstsano, though a central government appointee, sided with the townspeople against the demands of his superior in Moscow.

*   *   *

This glimpse into local politics reflects the administrative structure of the city and the social tensions that were evident as it was entering the modern era. Although settlements of traders and artisans (known collectively as "posad people") had formed around fortified points in Russia since earliest times, the first major legislation to devote a chapter to them was the Law Code of 1649. This was a sign of the growing importance of registered city dwellers as a social and political force. Before that time, the law made no distinction between posad people and peasants.[60] The 1649 code sought to end the division of towns into taxed and untaxed sectors (the latter being private domains) and to group citizens in occupational and social estate categories, each enjoying particular privileges and bearing particular obligations to the state. This basic arrangement continued into the eighteenth century augmented on occasion by new state administrative structures such as the Chief Magistracy. Historians generally agree that although the town officials were elected by their peers, they acted more as tax collectors for the state than as representatives of the electorate and were in the unenviable position of having to meet the demands of the central state for revenue or suffer confiscation of their own wealth and even brutal corporal punishment. Not until the second half of the eighteenth century did urban dwellers begin to form an estate consciousness and show an ability to act with common purpose.[61]

This consciousness had been gradually emerging through the century, shaped by the contacts that merchants developed in their trade and by institutions such as the Chief Magistracy and Commission on Commerce that the central government had created specifically to serve the commercial groups. The abolition of internal tariffs at mid-century and the increasing tempo of trade undoubtedly also increased the awareness on the part of merchants of their importance. The Commission on Laws must have played an important role as well because of the high concentration there of townsmen, who came to the assembly from all over the country and could measure their strength as a group. A literature on commerce was beginning to appear and was very much encouraged by the empress and her top officials. The empress also established a Commercial School, which, though unsuccessful at first in attracting merchant sons, nevertheless stood as another symbol of the state's solicitude for commercial people and desire to assist them.

The reforms introduced by Catherine II in the 1770s and 1780s sought to unify the life of the city further by bringing the different social estates into a shared body known as the "common duma," and into administrative and judicial offices which, though defined and staffed by separate social estates, were functionally articulated and mutually reinforcing. This effort to unify the urban dwellers of various estates in a common enterprise proved premature—the nobility was not ready to participate—and governance continued into the middle of the nineteenth century to be exercised by separate institutions defined by social estate. Even so, the reforms were a sign of major change in the character and outlook of the wealthy townspeople. The rights and privileges accorded to the merchant guilds in the Catherinian reforms both responded to and fostered the development of a self-conscious commercial elite aware of its growing importance and with a taste for the finer things of life. Behind this change were larger forces, including the dynamic growth of commerce in eighteenth-century Russia, the formation of a national market, the movement of large numbers of nobles to the countryside and provincial towns after their emancipation from state service in 1762, and, as a consequence, the exposure of ever more townspeople to the Europeanized culture of the court and nobility. This striving on the part of commercial people for a cultivated life appeared first among the wealthiest of the townspeople, the families of the first and second merchant guilds. It is this group and this era of change in Russian provincial life that shaped the consciousness and aspirations of the diarist Ivan Tolchënov.

Another change that was becoming apparent was the diminishing importance of larger family and kin loyalties. Dishonor suits were, as a result, showing a different character. As the individual was becoming disembedded from the extended family and clan matrix that was important to social life and identity in earlier times, dishonor suits were not initiated so much to defend the place of the kin group within a hierarchy of other such groups as to defend the reputation and probity of individuals. Suits were to serve as an assertion of a person's social identity as an honest dealer who could be trusted to pay his debts. Another way of making the same point was to fashion an impressive self-presentation that would convince others that one had the resources necessary to conduct a successful business and to meet one's financial obligations.

The role that Ivan Tolchënov later played in the politics of his city was, in part, a feature of such a commanding self-presentation. But even though he may have used his civic role as a cover for financial troubles, he would also prove to be very helpful to his fellow citizens by improving cooperation between the elites of his town during the 1780s. His ability to make friends with the local nobility, state officials, and his own peers in the offices of municipal government was to bring an era of calm and cooperation to his town quite different from the stormy politics of the 1760s and 1770s reviewed in this chapter.

3

Junior Member of the Family Firm: Merchant Life in Dmitrov

THE YOUNG GRAIN TRADER

[1773, September] 19th In the morning they fully opened the sluices and at 7 o'clock on the same day the barges moved out, and I went with the first caravan and left the trailing one under the supervision of Afanasii Popov. After passing the Solpa rapids we stayed overnight near the village of Gryzhino.

20th We sailed safely into Noshkinskaia wharf and, having obtained pilots, we also stayed overnight there.

21st At dawn we were under way and toward midday sailed safely into Basutinskaia wharf. I ate dinner at the home of the local commissar, Ensign Pëtr Alekseevich Mazovskii, and since there were no pilots available, we also stayed the night there.

22nd In the morning I obtained some pilots and we got under way. We descended the Opoki rapids and stopped for the night.

23rd In the morning we went through the Zhadin rapids and because of the density of barges ahead of us we moved over to the left bank and stayed there all day and overnight, and I walked down the line and had supper at Secretary Ivan Stepanovich Mukhin's.

24th In the morning I descended all the way to Opechenskaia wharf, and getting pilots, we set out at midday for the Borovichi rapids. I sailed on a government barge and, after having reached the city of Borovichi, went farther in a boat to Poterpil'skaia wharf and on the way had the great satisfaction to see that all the barges had come down and were moving safely and soon they all put in on the left side because of the lack of space on the right from the crowding of barges. Having settled up with the pilots and extra workers, I rode back along the line by land at 3 in the morning for the dispatch of the trailing caravan and turned over the forward one to the supervision of Maksim Sychëv.

. . .

30th The fog did not last long and we cast off early and in 2 verstas we got through the Sumy rapids, and after that in 2 more verstas we passed the Flat spit, the village of Kuznetsy, and the rocks named the Bitch with Puppies. Then in 3 verstas we passed the village and shoal of Shliapki [Hats], where the forward barges made a stop and caused one of my barges to strand on a rock. The others, having sailed by that spot, went about 5 verstas filled with spits and shoals and, finding a convenient place, put in, and the stranded barge, having been pulled loose, joined up with them. All the barges continued on their way and on the right side sailed to the village of Morkonitsy and then to the hamlet of Kashira, and beyond it stopped for the night on the left side.[1]

Ivan's marriage in January 1773 signaled the end of his apprenticeship in the family business. While he remained a junior partner in an enterprise dominated by his energetic father, Ivan was now regarded as capable of directing transport and trading operations on his own, including the hazardous passage down the northern waterways from Vyshnii Volochëk. In September 1773, his father for the first time entrusted him fully with one of the family's grain shipments from central Russia. He dispatched Ivan to Vyshnii Volochëk where the family's grain barges were waiting to join the third and final shipping caravan of the year. Ivan's notes from this trip reflect his new level of responsibility and also provide a vivid picture of the difficulties that merchants encountered in moving their goods to market.

The fall caravan was moving through the locks in a series of columns. The first, with 139 barges, started through on September 14. The next day another 236 moved out in two columns, one in the morning and one in the afternoon. Ivan had 13 barges divided between these two. The following day, still more barge columns departed, placing Ivan's barges in the middle of a lengthy, tightly-packed string of vessels. The real test began when the columns slid through the locks leading from Lake Mstino into the Msta River. From here until the river emptied into Lake Ilmen the barges had to pass through eighteen rapids, including the feared Borovichi rapids, plus nine treacherous shoals, not to mention other obstacles such as enormous rocks (each bearing a colorful name) and occasional narrows. Ivan worked out of his barges in the front column but often rode ahead in a government boat, to judge the hazards and hire local river pilots to guide the barges through difficult stretches. He also traveled back upstream to check on his barges in the trailing column.

On September 24 Ivan reached the Opechenskaia wharf just above the Borovichi rapids. He hired a pilot to run his barges through the rapids and rode on ahead in a government boat to the town of Borovichi to await their arrival. Luckily, all of the barges in this column came through unharmed. The trailing column was, however, stalled in heavy traffic above the rapids. Ivan rode back by land and found that a knot of boats was going to delay entry of his seven trailing barges into the rapids until late in the day. What was he to do? Should he send them on their way at last light? Nervously, he decided to dispatch five of them and hold the last two back until morning. The five got through, but one of them so filled with water that it had to be pumped out all night. Even then it proved unseaworthy, and Ivan transferred its contents to his other vessels. The remaining two barges arrived safely the next morning, but probably only because their crews had shifted sixty sacks of flour from them to a third craft known as a lighter (a low-draft boat used in shallow waters). The lighter, however, sank, and this mishap further delayed Ivan while his men reloaded the flour from the disabled lighter onto other barges.

The rest of the way down the Msta, low water and fog made the remaining rapids and shoals exceptionally dangerous. The barge Ivan was riding on again and again stranded on rocks and ran aground in sand bars, each time having to be pulled free by other boats and slowing the column's overall progress. When Ivan's first barges finally reached the town of Bronnitsy, a few kilometers above Lake Ilmen, Ivan rode forward to the estuary and discovered that haulers were having to drag barges through the shallows with great effort, managing to pull no more than ten or twenty barges a day into the lake. Riding back to find his barges in the trailing column, he located them about seven kilometers above Bronnitsy, where a government boat was aground at mid-river. It quickly became clear that his trailing barges could go no farther. He hired stevedores to unload the cargo on the river bank for overwintering. Ivan then went downstream and was able to get some of his barges from the first column down to the estuary, but strong winds off the lake and heavy rains sank nine nearby barges (fortunately, not his own). Ivan faced a dilemma. The weather was unsettled. Winter was closing in. Should he risk going farther or give up and fail to get any of the family's fall shipments to market? A big decision for a young man just turning nineteen years old. On October 14, he shifted some sacks from three barges onto a fourth empty one to make the vessels more seaworthy, evidently expecting to proceed into the lake. However, the next day, his birthday, Ivan trudged a long way through swamps to the ancient city of Novgorod and prayed for guidance at its St. Sofia Cathedral. When he returned to the boats, he decided to call it quits. A wise decision. Later the same day, as he moved back upriver, Ivan ran into strong winds and a blinding snowstorm that trapped him on the water at night and nearly prevented him from reaching the safety of his upstream barges. He had halted his shipments none too soon.

Although the family firm ended the year with barges stranded all along the waterway (Ivan's on the Msta and others on the Tvertsa), this was not unusual. When the ice broke up the next spring and the high water from the melt lifted the boats and sped them to Petersburg, Ivan found that their cargo was in great demand. Brisk sales recouped the losses of the previous year.[2]

THE YEAR 1774 AND THE THREAT OF POPULAR
REBELLION IN THE MOSCOW REGION

*[1774 July] 27th I went with my father for the first time to visit Prince Ivan
Fëdorovich Golitsyn at his Danilovskoe village and had dinner.*

29th I went to visit him again by myself on business.

*31st In the afternoon, Prince Ivan Fëdorovich met with a large group of nobles
at the chancery to consult on taking precautions against the criminal Pugachëv
and then came to our house.*[3]

The year 1774 opened with Russia in its fifth year of war with Ottoman
Turkey. Even as the war was going well for Russia on the battlefield, it was
proving costly and difficult to bring to a close. More disturbing, a popular
rebellion was raging in the southeast of the country. Despite government efforts
to stamp it out, the rebellion shifted from place to place and kept renewing
itself. As the year wore on, the rebels moved north into the Russian heartland
and for a short time came within striking distance of Moscow. The leader of the
rebellion was a Don Cossack by the name of Emel'ian Pugachëv. A fugitive from
justice, Pugachëv escaped to the lands of the Iaik Cossacks north of the Caspian
Sea and played on their resentments at recent government retaliation for their
protests against a loss of inherited privileges and freedoms. The rebellion began
in the autumn of 1773 when Pugachëv led the Iaik Cossacks in an armed assault
on government outposts in the southeastern steppe lands. Passing himself off
as Peter III, the rightful tsar who had been illegally dethroned by Empress
Catherine and her favorites, Pugachëv enjoyed enough success initially that he
was able to rally to his side a large number of disaffected groups, including
religious dissidents such as the Old Believers, non-Russian peoples whose lands
were being colonized by Russians, workers in the Urals metallurgical factories,
and enserfed peasants. In time, he was fielding units of several thousand armed,
if not always well disciplined, followers.

At first the war and the rebellion were confined to the southern and eastern
regions of the country and did not affect the grain trade of the Tolchënov
family. Ivan started out the year 1774 in Moscow with his in-laws, where he
was making preparations for a purchasing trip to Promzino Gorodishche in
Simbirsk province to the southeast. On the trip, he passed through the towns of
Arzamas and Alatyr that just a few months later would fall to the rebels. But for
the time being the area was calm. Although Ivan would likely have picked up
information about the disturbances when he was in Moscow or on his travels to
Promzino Gorodishche, he wrote nothing about them in his diary entries from
this period. The government was keeping a tight lid on information about the
rebellion, and people, including at least one merchant, had been detained for

carrying news of the disturbances into central Russia. If Ivan knew about the rebellion at this time, he prudently did not commit the information to paper.[4]

After his trip to Promzino Gorodishche, Ivan spent much of late January and February in and around the Volga port of Lyskovo downriver from Nizhnii Novgorod, where he was organizing further purchases of grain and renting storage barns to hold it for transshipment. He dispatched agents to purchase grain in more distant ports or to gallop to Moscow to fetch money for the transactions.

It is apparent from a new element in his diary that Ivan had recently acquired a pocket watch, an expensive accessory that had come into use among well-to-do nobles, officials, merchants, and manufacturers both in the capital cities and in the provinces after the middle of the century. Peter the Great had ordered that all government offices should have clocks, and, according to the Russian historian Boris Mironov, most did so.[5] If he is right, the timepieces must initially have come from outside the country. The first Russian manufactories for clocks were established as late as 1769, and then only on the initiative of the government, one workshop in Petersburg and one in Moscow. The Petersburg workshop produced timepieces principally as gifts and awards to persons in recognition of their service to the state. The Moscow facility, which produced for the market, may have been the source of Ivan's watch.[6] Ivan's new timepiece allowed him to record his movements with an imagined to-the-minute precision, which he did first mainly in his travels. For example, on the trip home from his stay later in the year in Petersburg, he wrote "I left [Pavlovsk village] at 3 h. 47 min. in the morning, passed the village of Zakharovo at 6 h. 12 min., Borshchovo at 8 h. 10 min., Tresviatskoe at 10 h. 14 min., and arrived in Rogachëvo at 11 h. 48 min. and ate dinner there."[7] Ivan's fascination with this new mechanical device is apparent, even if it offered only a false precision, since no watch in his era could keep time to the minute.[8] Its significance lies in Ivan's need to show off his watch in his travel notes, and undoubtedly in his life as well. It is also a sign of Ivan's marking of abstract horological time and in this sense his association with systems of temporal and spatial tracking that extended beyond his personal ken and placed him in a matrix of modernity.[9] Yet it is characteristic of Ivan's betweenness—his fascination with the new even while continuing his reliance on convention—that he used the watch for certain matters more than for others in a way that reflected his strong continuing attachment to inherited practices. Here we see him marking his travel times, but later he used precise clock measures most often to record fateful family events and religious services.

To return to the earlier part of the year 1774, after his work downriver on the Volga, Ivan went home in late February. Thereafter, he traveled back and forth between Moscow and the family's northern mills until April 8, when he left for the city of Tver to buy barges, hire bargemen, and load the grain for the spring caravan to Petersburg. On April 30 he and his uncle Mikhaila left by land for Petersburg, where they arrived twelve days later to supervise the sale of the family's grain shipments that had been stranded in the waterway late the previous year. Except for a brief trip home for Easter, he was in the northern capital for much of the spring and summer. Unfortunately, Ivan records almost nothing of his more than two-month stay in Petersburg. Only two occasions seemed to him worth remarking. On Pentecostal Sunday (June 8), he noted his church attendance at the Nevskii monastery (where his mother was buried), dinner with another Dmitrov merchant and friend Semën Korob'in, and a promenade he attended at Ekaterinhof, a palace park southwest of the city on Neva Bay, "where Her Majesty and His Highness [Grand Prince Paul] deigned to appear, and the crowd was very large." The next day he told of walking in the imperial summer gardens. Then nothing for twenty days. Finally, he again took up the pen and reported that "I rode to [the suburban palace of] Peterhof, where I visited court purveyor Pavel Ivanovich Tolchënov,[10] had dinner with him, and spent the day walking in the gardens. From 7 o'clock onward through the entire night I attended a masquerade at the palace and in its gardens, enjoying the magnificent decoration of lights." Here was an event worth recording to the minute. "I left the masquerade at 1:55 and started out for Petersburg at 3 in the morning."[11]

This first opportunity for Ivan to rub shoulders with the rich and well born of the capital city made a big impression on him, and it presaged a closer acquaintance that was soon to develop between Ivan and the noble elite of his own town.

Ivan's few notes about his pleasant social occasions in Petersburg captured none of the troubled mood of the court and higher officials at the time. At court, a major change was in progress; Grigorii Potëmkin replaced Grigorii Orlov as the favorite of the empress. This shift signaled a broader adjustment in policy and personnel, making those currently in charge of affairs justifiably nervous.[12] The war with Turkey, though soon to be concluded, had been dragging on, and Russia's enemies were encouraging the Ottomans to hold out longer in hopes that the social upheaval on the Volga would work to Turkey's advantage. Of most immediate concern, the Russian military could not pin down Pugachëv or extinguish once and for all the flame of rebellion he had ignited. Just a week before the masquerade party at Peterhof, Pugachëv had resurfaced with a large army east of the city of Kazan and taken a series of towns along the Kama River. Three weeks later, on July 16, Ivan Tolchënov, having finished his business in Petersburg, left for home. While he was en route, Pugachëv and his forces moved down the Kama and attacked Kazan, looting and burning the city. They then fanned out across the Volga into the areas of Nizhnii Novgorod and Penza provinces that Ivan had visited for grain purchases earlier in the year. There the rebels rounded up and executed dozens of noble landlords and local officials in a region that lay just 440 kilometers from Moscow.

The news of the rebel advance westward struck fear in the hearts of every property owner in central Russia. The government in Petersburg was near panic. Empress Catherine briefly considered going to Moscow to lead the defense of the city but was dissuaded when advised that her presence in Moscow would most likely increase the panic in the country's heartland. At the same time, Moscow Governor-General Mikhail Volkonskii swung into action. On July 25 he called an extraordinary session of the Moscow Senate departments to announce measures for the defense of the city, placing each of the eight Moscow senators in charge of a particular city section.[13] Orders also went out to the government offices in the district capitals of Moscow province, instructing the local voevody to "report on rebel movements [and] send their treasuries to Moscow if the insurgents approached."[14] The voevody were instructed to begin working with local nobility and townspeople to organize and arm a militia. The towns east of Moscow and closest to the threatened areas sprang into action even before receiving these orders. Others farther away, like Dmitrov, responded quickly once the orders arrived.

This was the situation that greeted Ivan just after his return from Petersburg late on the day of July 25. His diary notes are, as usual, frustratingly short. As excerpted at the start of this section, he recorded that he went with his father to visit Prince Ivan Fëdorovich Golitsyn at his Danilovskoe village for the first time on July 27 and that two days later he rode out on his own to see him again "on business." On July 31 Golitsyn returned the visit after he had come into the city to meet with a large group of nobles to consider measures the community should take in response to the popular rebellion being led by Pugachëv. If these daily notes were all we had, we could infer much of what was going on from the general context and the orders that had come from Moscow. Luckily, we need not speculate, for Ivan gave a fuller description of the events of that time in his retrospective notes when he was transferring his daily jottings into leather-bound volumes many years later.

In these summary notes he referred to two great tragedies of 1774: the upheaval led by the pretender Pugachëv and an accompanying widespread crop failure and famine. With regard to the first, Ivan reported that Pugachëv not only wreaked havoc throughout the lower Volga region but "threatened even the capital city of Moscow and its surrounding towns." Ivan continued: "As a result, on July 27th a Senate order about taking precautionary measures was received in Dmitrov by urgent courier. Following that, on the 31st the district nobility assembled in the town under the chairmanship of General-Major and Cavalier Prince Ivan Fëdorovich Golitsyn. By general agreement they decided to form a militia from their serving people, appropriately armed and based on one person per 100 male serfs." Although Ivan reported these decisions many years later as being by general agreement, the language used in the resolution at the time suggests that some nobles may have raised objections or expressed less than full commitment. The statement of the noble assembly read pointedly that the people to be recruited for the defensive force should be given by their masters "without any reservations." In Dmitrov, as was the case in a few other districts, some people evidently believed that the local leadership was asking more of them than they were capable of giving.[15] However arrived at, this decision about forming a militia was what Golitsyn carried to the Tolchënov home immediately after his meeting with the local nobility (the visit to which Ivan referred in his daily jottings). Ivan's father then called a meeting of his fellow merchants, who promptly "passed a resolution in conformity with that of the nobles."[16]

If Pugachëv had actually moved into Moscow province and the local elites had had to make good on this promise, Dmitrov would have had to organize and equip a force 200 men strong (drawn from the 20,000 privately-owned male serfs of the district). This would have been a risky proposition if the atmosphere of distrust and fear described by police and noble memoirists of the time was accurate. The people responding to the government appeal were the noble serfowners and the first-rank merchants, some of whom also owned bonded servants. These propertied elites did not involve others in their plans because they did not feel sure of the loyalty of those further down the social ladder. They understood that Pugachëv and his legions were not just dangerous in themselves but that they might also ignite uprisings among bonded people in areas beyond the battle front. The famous diarist and landowner Andrei Bolotov commented, referring to this time, that "we were all positive that all the lower orders and the rabble, and especially all the slaves and our servants, if not openly, then secretly in their hearts were committed to this miscreant [Pugachëv], and were already rebelling in their hearts and ready at the least inflammatory spark to make fire and flame."[17] Fortunately for the elites, the loyalty of the serf defensive force was not put to a test. Ivan reported, "on August 6th the Senate sent an order to suspend the mobilization because by the mercy of God the malefactor Pugachëv and his confederates had been thoroughly defeated by regular army forces in the region and took off running into the steppe."[18]

The spirit of cooperation between the local elites that marked these two weeks of panic carried over for a time into personal relations. An event of great importance to the Tolchënov family happened in the week following the end of the rebel threat. On August 11, Ivan's wife Anna gave birth to their first child, a son, who according to Russian custom was given the name Pëtr because that saint's name day fell close to the day of christening.[19] A week after the birth,

Ivan and his father rode to Moscow to announce the event to Anna's parents and to bring them to Dmitrov for the baptism, which took place on August 22 at the Dormition Cathedral. No Russian christening was complete without a two-day celebration and, if possible, prominent guests. Ivan could report with satisfaction that "the celebration was attended by plenty of people, including Prince Ivan Fëdorovich Golitsyn and Andrei Ivanovich Molchanov," another prominent local noble. To add to the importance of the event, Ivan was able to recruit a third remarkable guest. Learning that Archbishop Antonii had arrived in town from his diocesan seat in Pereslavl the first night of the celebration, Ivan rushed to the monastery the next day and invited him to dinner the following day. On that day, Ivan wrote, "His Grace said mass at the cathedral, where I was in attendance, and then he dined at our house together with Prince Ivan Fëdorovich and other local nobles."[20] A few days later the archbishop said mass at a church close to the Tolchënovs' house and then visited briefly in their home before they all went together to Prince Golitsyn's estate for dinner.

Although the Tolchënovs seemed to have been close to the clerical elites of the region, their social contact with Prince Golitsyn at this time may have been a temporary response to the threat of rebellion. It might, too, have had something to do with the special position of Prince Golitsyn. Though a leading member of the local nobility, Golitsyn was in disfavor with Catherine's court, isolated from sources of information, and under police surveillance. He came from an ancient aristocratic family, was educated in Europe, and had risen rapidly in government service. At the time of Catherine's coup d'etat in 1762, Golitsyn was an adjutant on the staff of Emperor Peter III and remained loyal to the fallen ruler, refusing to take an oath to Catherine.[21] He retired to live in internal exile in the Moscow region, where a number of discontented officers and courtiers had taken refuge and spent their time complaining to one another about how affairs were being conducted in Petersburg. In Golitsyn's case, the fact that Pugachëv employed the guise of the returned Peter III must have made his position particularly uncomfortable. He undoubtedly craved news of the changes then occurring at the Petersburg court and of the government response to the Pugachëv rebellion. Possibly, Ivan's two invitations to the Golitsyn estate immediately following his return from Petersburg were prompted by the prince's desire to learn more in this time of crisis about events in the capital, where Ivan had just spent four months. The quickness with which Ivan's father mobilized the leading merchants in support of the nobles' decision to form a militia must have further solidified the relationship.

Once the rebel threat receded, however, the social contacts between the Tolchënovs and Golitsyn seem to have faded. The appointment of General Pëtr Panin as leader of the forces in pursuit of the fleeing Pugachëv may have satisfied the local nobles that their interests would be protected, obviating the need to cooperate closely with other social groups. Panin was another internal exile and champion of the disgruntled Moscow nobility. After Pugachëv's capture, life settled back into its normal pattern. Ivan did not record any more social visits from Prince Golitsyn until three years later, in mid-1777, when Golitsyn showed up at the Tolchënov house for a dinner in honor of the new archbishop of Pereslavl, Feofilakt. But this was more an official than a private occasion. A year earlier, when Ivan was preparing to celebrate the birth of his daughter Evdokiia and had ridden out to Golitsyn's estate personally to ask the prince to attend the christening dinner, Golitsyn turned down the invitation.[22]

Ivan's aspiration to share in the social life of the local nobility was clear. But this goal still eluded him. Socializing with Prince Golitsyn and others of high rank was possible only on exceptional occasions when either the elites as a whole were under threat, as in the Pugachëv upheaval, or when the visit of a prominent clerical or government official prompted a general gathering of the top people of the city and the surrounding landed estates. Also important in this connection was no doubt the attitude of Ivan's father. His low-key performance in the Commission on Laws and his unceasing work in the family grain business suggest that to the extent he sought out relationships with the nobility, he did so primarily for business purposes. He may even have disapproved of the kind of social climbing that appealed to Ivan. Only after the death of his father did Ivan's contacts with the local nobility, including Golitsyn, come to occupy a central place in his life.

In summing up the year 1774, Ivan spoke not just of one tragedy but of two. The first was the Pugachëv rebellion. The second was the widespread crop failure and famine that struck the central and lower Volga provinces in the insurrection's wake. Ivan understood the famine as a result primarily of the disturbances in the region. It was at this time, by the way, that Ivan's father tried to take advantage of the sharp rise in prices in the south by dispatching Ivan and the family agent Afanasii Popov to the northern waterway to buy up at low prices the grain stranded in barges along the route to Petersburg. Years later, when Ivan was composing his retrospective notes, he reported the effects of this crisis on the people sympathetically, noting that "around Astrakhan and Saratov the price of rye flour reached [such high] levels that in many places people resorted for nourishment to grasses, crushed goosefoot, and acorns, and they were bringing these things to market for sale. There was even insufficient straw for livestock. About all one can say in conclusion," Ivan continued, "is that in four provinces (Orenburg, Astrakhan, Kazan, and Nizhnii Novgorod) a very great number of people perished as a result of these two calamities."[23]

Although Ivan could scarcely have avoided mentioning these terrible events in his later retrospective notes, he characteristically did not dwell on the negative and even hastened to mention positive achievements of the year both for the country and his family. He noted that God did not merely "pour down his wrath on Russia but also favored her" with a victory over the Turks. "The Lord, having punished [Russia] within her borders, sent down in external affairs a glorification of her armed might and, having crowned her with victories, delighted her with an advantageous peace, concluded . . . with the Ottoman Porte." He then added information about improvements to his family's properties that occurred in 1774, including the building of a masonry storehouse at their home in Dmitrov and refurbishing of the wooden rooms in the main house. These notes, written when Ivan's fortunes were already in decline, reveal not only pride in his country and family but also his ability to balance the positive and the negative when assessing his past, an indication of his capacity to restore balance in his own life.

The culmination of the year 1774 took place just after its close in Moscow, when Pugachëv and several of his confederates were executed on January 10, 1775. Ivan had been in Moscow a few days before the execution but had left on a grain buying trip to Orël on January 6. Much more important to him, it is clear, was to be in Moscow in time for the entry of the imperial family later the same month. He finished his work in Orël on the seventeenth and rode back to Dmitrov.

On the 21st at noon I left with my wife for Moscow, where my father was then staying.

23rd I had to ride back home once again to get some necessities.

25th in the morning I returned to Moscow, and in the afternoon on Tverskaia St. we viewed the solemn entry into this capital of Her Imperial Majesty and Their Highnesses [Grand Prince Paul and his wife].[24]

Compared to the many other trips he took between his home and Moscow, Ivan's turnaround time on this trip back to Dmitrov was unusually fast. He was obviously in a hurry to make it back in time for the entry of the imperial family. The opportunity to participate in the pageantry and pomp of power and to be in the presence of the sacred figures of the dynasty was of great significance to Ivan throughout his life and an indication of the quality of his patriotism.

IVAN'S "GRADUATION":
COOPERATION AND CONFLICT WITH THE STATE

[St. Petersburg, 1775] June 1st In the evening I strolled in the garden of the imperial palace.

2nd At dawn the barges arrived safely.

8th I was summoned along with the other merchants to the Main Police Headquarters, where they endeavored to persuade us to sell our rye flour for no more than 3.50 rubles a sack. But all the traders gave their final price as 3.80.

16th Along with the other merchants I was called on the same matter to the Winter Palace, where, in the absence of the court, Military Governor General-Fieldmarshal Prince Aleksandr Golitsyn was residing, and he too tried to persuade us to reduce the price on rye flour; however, everyone refused because of the lack of any profit.

25th I visited Kiril Filipovich Popov.

29th I attended mass at the Nevskii [Monastery] and in the evening went for a stroll in the garden of the imperial palace.[25]

The excerpt from the diary that opens this section relates to the second of two events that touched Ivan the following year, 1775. The first was a labor dispute on the northern waterway that threatened to cripple the transport of grain to Petersburg.

As usual, the year began for Ivan south and east of Moscow on trips to buy grain at major depots such as Orël and Promzino Gorodishche. When spring arrived and the ice on the northern waterway broke up, he rode north to join the first barge caravan, which was lining up at the Vyshnii Volochëk locks for the journey to Petersburg. This time, however, he found the caravan at a standstill in front of the locks because of a labor dispute. Migrant workers, who arrived each spring from all over central Russia to work the barge traffic, were demanding higher wages than the merchants were willing to pay. Nothing was moving. This situation prompted the energetic young governor-general of the province, Jakob Sievers, to take action. He deployed a couple of stratagems to defeat the workers. He first ordered the merchants not to pay workers any more than a certain set wage, well below what the workers were asking. Then he told the merchants in the front column to hire only workers from the surrounding Vyshnii Volochëk district and to hire them only for the first portion of the trip. This united front of government and merchants, plus the threat to exclude the migrant laborers altogether, quickly broke the resistance of the workers, and they agreed to sign on for the wage set by the governor-general. Ivan was very impressed with Sievers's fast and effective action and called him "a staunch defender of merchants in the water-borne trade to Petersburg."[26]

When the grain shipments reached Petersburg three weeks later, Ivan saw a less accommodating face of government. As the diary excerpt at the head of this section reveals, a few days after the barges arrived, he and the other grain merchants were summoned to the central police headquarters of the city and asked to sell their rye flour at a price no higher than 3 rubles 50 kopeks a sack. The police in Russian cities were responsible not just for criminal matters but for urban security more generally, including the maintenance of grain reserves. Since Petersburg was an extraordinarily expensive city, the police were under pressure to keep bread prices down. Rye bread was the dietary staple of the working people of the city, and in the wake of the recent popular disturbances, the government sought to hold down rye prices and remove a likely source of discontent. The merchants, however, stood their ground and refused to sell their flour at anything less than 3.80 per sack. A week later, Ivan and the other merchants received a second summons, this time to a more splendid and intimidating venue: the Winter Palace. Although the court was away at the time, the merchants were greeted by the highest-ranking military officer in the country, General-Fieldmarshal Aleksandr Golitsyn, commander-in-chief of the Petersburg garrison. He, too, did his best to persuade the merchants to reduce the price on rye flour. And he, too, failed. Ivan reported that the merchants again refused to budge, pointing out that the price requested by the government would deprive them of their profit.[27]

This trip to Petersburg illustrates a number of circumstances about merchant life and about the relationship of the tsarist government to merchants. First, merchants enjoyed a cozy relationship with government officials, especially when authority was under challenge. As was true elsewhere in Europe, the government and commercial elites were more often in league than in conflict. The government understood that the wealth of the nation depended on the health of its commerce and protected merchants against the demands of workers for higher pay. Moreover, as Ivan's story about the summons to the Winter Palace demonstrates, Russian merchants were not the cringing servants of government power that they have often been portrayed. They were prepared to defend their private interests. By the same token, the monarchy, however absolutist it claimed to be, was not so foolish as to assault the laws of supply and demand. The relationship between government and the commercial classes was one of negotiation and accommodation.

We could well designate this as Ivan's graduation day, when at age twenty he stood together with his fellow merchants in the Winter Palace and rejected the entreaties of the leading tsarist military official.

THE POWER OF A MIRACLE-WORKING ICON

[1777, May] 4th At 6 in the evening I left with Andrei Fëdorovich [to join the grain barges at Volochëk]. We stayed overnight in Rogachëvo.

5th Having arrived at Klin, I released our own horses to return home, and we traveled the rest of the way on postal mounts. We stayed overnight in Gorodnia. My ailing health kept getting worse, and I was suffering from an extraordinarily severe headache.

6th At 10 in the morning we passed through Tver and in the evening arrived at Torzhok, where with difficulty I made my way on foot to the lodgings of Uncle Iakov Stepanovich. At night we rode farther.

7th At 11 in the morning we arrived in Volochëk and stopped at the apartment

of Andrei Zaitsov. Toward evening my illness got so bad that I was no longer able
even to walk.

8th The barges entered Volochëk, and I decided because of the illness to
return home.

9th At 10 o'clock in the morning I left and toward evening arrived in Torzhok,
where I spent the night, and during the night I became so weak that I could not
ride any farther. For this reason, at 10 in the morning I told Uncle Iakov Stepa-
novich about my condition, and out of his love for me he had me ride over to his
apartment and to rest there. But I felt my life was in danger and therefore decided
to confess my sins and ask repentance and did so in sound mind to the confessor of
the local parish church of St. Clement, the archpriest Timofei Ivanovich Zborov-
skii, who tried to boost my sagging spirits with wise exhortations. But I had
lost all hope and as a result was seized by overwhelming feelings of gloom and
despondency.

11th After mass I had the honor of receiving the sacrament of communion
at the apartment, and though conscious, I suffered somewhat from confused
thoughts, and later the very same day a violent fever overtook me. They sent
news of my illness home to my father urgently by post horses.[28]

The year was 1777. It was May and time to follow the spring barge traffic
north out of the Vyshnii Volochëk locks to Petersburg. Ivan, who was now age
twenty-two and experienced in this work, was taking with him his young uncle,
Andrei Fëdorovich Makarov, the son born to Ivan's grandfather from his second marriage late in life. Andrei was twelve years old at this time and living as a
ward of the Tolchënovs in their home. He was just beginning his apprenticeship
in the grain trade. But this trip was not going to work out as planned.

The spring weather had not been auspicious. The thaw came late and in a
series of warm days followed by refreezing of the rivers. When Ivan had been
working in April to get barges into position on the Tvertsa River to move
through the locks northward, he had encountered continual difficulties. The
water was high. Off-and-on flooding over ice-bound rivers presented great
dangers for the crossings that he and his workers had to make. When the waters
flowed, they did so slowly because of the jams caused by the ice break-ups and
refreezing. After the exhausting work of loading and moving the barges forward in these conditions, Ivan returned home to Dmitrov for a few days before leaving again early in May for Vyshnii Volochëk and the canal traffic to
Petersburg.

Even before leaving home this second time, he began to feel ill. Two days
before his departure, he wrote in the diary that "I sensed a change in my health
yesterday evening, that is I felt shivery and drained, and in the night I had a
fever." Even so, after packing up and completing other preparations the follow-

ing two days, he and Andrei left to join the canal traffic. As described in the quotation starting this section, they traveled to the continental divide at Vyshnii Volochëk fast, first on the family's own horses and then on rented postal mounts. Even though Ivan kept feeling worse, he pushed on to their destination. Only after arriving so exhausted and sick that he could not walk did he decide that he could not continue and had to return home. He had reached Volochëk on May 7, the family barges entered the locks on the eighth, and on the ninth Ivan started home.

On the return trip, he got only as far as Torzhok. Too weak to continue, he contacted a nearby relative whom he had visited just days before on the trip north, "Uncle" Iakov (his cousin once removed), and told him of his condition. Iakov invited him to stay at his place to rest. Ivan was sinking fast and fearful enough for his life that he summoned a priest to say confession. Although the priest did what he could to encourage Ivan to think more positively, Ivan continued to despair. The next day, May 11, he arranged to have communion administered where he was living, but it did not have the curative effect that Russians often hoped it would. Indeed, he was seized by a "violent fever" the very same day that left him delirious and out of touch with his surroundings.

In the meantime, word of Ivan's illness had been sent to Dmitrov, prompting his father to set out immediately to be by his side. Ivan wrote that the arrival of his father on the fourteenth lifted his spirits a bit and calmed his fears, even though he was still delirious with fever. It was not until four days later, on the eighteenth, he continues, that "for the first time I came to, but I was still so weak that I could scarcely move. I nevertheless began to have some hope of recovery and to believe that the all-generous Creator had seen fit to prolong my life, and in the next days I felt somewhat improved." In fighting off the illness, Ivan noted that he made no use of medicines and "relied solely on God's mercy and on the purest of prayers to his Holy Mother and the saints to snatch me from the jaws of death."

A week after he had emerged from his delirium, his father and he decided it was time to start for home. Before leaving, they agreed to stop on the way at the church in the village of Vedernitsy, about twenty kilometers west of Dmitrov, the shrine of a miracle-working icon much revered throughout the Moscow region. At the same time, two relatives and a family friend were converging on Vedernitsy to meet them and to pray for his renewed health. "We rode into Vedernitsy and there, to my surprise, we were greeted by my father-in-law Aleksei Ivanovich, Uncle Ivan Il'ich, and Andrei Korobov, and we all spent the night there." The next morning the clergy brought Ivan the miracle-working icon and anointed him with holy water. Afterward the group continued to Dmitrov and attended mass, even though Ivan could barely manage because of

Nikolo-Pesnoshskii Monastery near the town of Rogachëvo.

his continued shaking and shivering. The sick and weary traveler was happy to be home at last. "By the grace of God I was able to see my home and the people of our household, which I had never expected to see again."[29]

The icon at Vedernitsy represented Christ at the sheep basin curing a sick man. Housed in a wooden church at the time of this visit by Ivan in 1777, the icon had been attracting so many pilgrims and their monetary offerings that three years later the parishioners replaced the decaying wooden structure with a masonry building covered with intricate baroque designs.[30] After Ivan's near-death experience, the shrine at Vedernitsy became a regular site of pilgrimage for the Tolchënov family, as it was for a large number of people from Moscow province, including many of the leading nobles and high government officials. Trips to Vedernitsy usually included a stop at the nearby Nikolo-Pesnoshskii Monastery, which contained graves of noble families from the region. Ivan's diary contains references to dozens of people who passed through Dmitrov on their way to Vedernitsy, often finding lodging at one or another of the large merchant homes of the city or merely stopping to have dinner with a prominent local family. Pilgrims from Moscow, such as the governor-general or the Tolchënovs' own Muscovite in-laws, would visit Vedernitsy and the Nikolo-Pesnoshskii Monastery as one point on a triangular excursion that went from Moscow to the Trinity–St. Sergei Monastery, then westward through Dmitrov to Vedernitsy before returning to the capital. The first such trip by Ivan's family following his life-threatening illness took place in October of the same year.

21st At 2 o'clock in the afternoon I rode together with my wife and Petrusha [their first son] to Vedernitsy, where we arrived at 5 o'clock and stayed overnight.

22nd We attended the vigil and then prayed, and for mass we rode to Pesnoshskii Monastery. However, we found that mass was not being said and so, after praying there, we left for home and arrived safely at 4 o'clock in the afternoon.[31]

Ivan's recovery took a long time. He complained of having no strength and of suffering from severe constipation. Not until two weeks after his return did he even venture into the garden of his home. More than a month passed before he went again to mass at the local parish church. Ivan was the sole surviving child in his family, and his parents no doubt insisted that he be fully recovered before resuming his usual activities. Ivan remained house-bound for nearly the entire summer. He first began to venture out in August, taking short trips to local monasteries, strolls in the woods, or joining in at the harvesting of apples. From mid-August onward he visited Moscow and the family's mills near the Volga, but for the rest of the year he made no long trips to supervise barge traffic or purchase grain. In November he was again sick, first briefly with diarrhea and vomiting and then more seriously with a large boil and fever that put him in bed.

It is interesting to observe that in neither of these severe illnesses did Ivan seek out the help of a doctor or surgeon and, significantly, in the first instance even reported explicitly that he took no medicines. Reliance was placed entirely on religious practices and long periods of rest and recuperation. Ivan's diary entries from this period show that he very much thought of God as acting directly in the world and that Divine intervention, facilitated by the "purest of prayers to his Holy Mother and the saints," was what had spared his life. When his three-year-old son Pëtr had become dangerously ill in July of the same year and was expected to die, Ivan likewise did not seek medical help. But Ivan's failure to seek medical assistance probably did not stem from a rejection of modern practices so much as from a lack of familiarity and access.[32] He had acquired a timepiece and later showed an interest in telescopes and other scientific instruments as he matured and came into contact with them. When a few years later medical doctors began to be stationed in district capitals, Ivan got acquainted and even became friends with some of them. After these experiences he began to consult physicians and later, too, specialists in Moscow about illnesses in his family. Yet these medical specialists did not displace Ivan's belief in curative religious practices, and in some later illnesses Ivan became angry and frustrated with the unsuccessful interventions of doctors and placed greater hopes in religious objects and practices.

IVAN'S NEW INTERESTS

[St. Petersburg, 1778, September] 4th. In the morning I was at the Senate and at 2 at the department about the case of Mr. Deriushkin [a member of a regional court], and from there to the Academy [of Sciences] bookstore, to the market, and in the evening I visited with Pavel Tolchënov.

5th In the morning I was at the Senate again and the market.

6th I was at the Commodity Exchange and from there went to see three very unusual things, namely: 1. a model of the bridge over the Neva River made by the Russian engineer Kulibin, 2. the nearly completed monument of Emperor Peter the Great, 3. a model of St. Isaac's Church and other marble things there. Then to the market.

7th In the afternoon I was at the market.

8th I heard mass at the Nevskii [Monastery] conducted by Bishop Gavriil, and in the afternoon strolled in the Summer Gardens of the court.

9th Mass at Nevskii àgain, and in the afternoon I went to the Lutheran church out of curiosity, and then to the market.[33]

In the 1770s Ivan spent much of his time away from home, working in the family's grain trade. This took him to Moscow and farther south and east on grain purchasing trips in the winter. Middle to late summer usually found him in Petersburg, where he supervised the unloading and sale of the grain and flour that his family had shipped to the northern capital. Here during the mid- to late 1770s when Ivan was in his early twenties, he came into contact with the diversions of the educated urban elites and began to develop a taste for them.

We have already seen Ivan during his 1774 trip to Petersburg, his first without parental supervision. He recorded at that time his promenades in palace gardens and attendance at a masquerade in the grounds of the summer palace at Peterhof. The next year, when he stayed in Petersburg from late May to mid-August, he began to cultivate an interest in more serious matters. This, it will be recalled, was Ivan's "graduation day" trip when he had to stand shoulder-to-shoulder with other merchants and resist the government's high-pressure efforts to force down the price of grain in the capital. Once Ivan overcame this challenge, he set out to learn more about the city's cultural attractions.

His first stop was at the Academy of Arts, an institution founded in 1757 to teach painting, sculpture, and architecture to Russian students. The government of Empress Elizabeth had hired foreign instructors to show Russians how to produce objects of culture with which to adorn their surroundings and give them a look of Western high society. On display at the Academy of Arts were some of the works produced there, and the institution accordingly functioned as an incipient national gallery. Ivan wrote simply that he had gone to view the "curious things" on display there. Possibly, this type of artistic expression was not to his taste, for the academy did not become a regular stop on his trips to Petersburg. Soon after this outing, Ivan visited another important cultural institution, the Kunstkamera. This was in essence Russia's museum of science and ethnography. Founded by Peter the Great in 1714, the Kunstkamera initially housed curiosities and anatomical grotesqueries that Peter had collected during his trips to western Europe. Other ethnographic and archeological materials were soon added, and in 1727 the museum acquired its own beautiful baroque building on the Vasilevskii Island embankment of the Grand Neva River. By the time of Ivan's visit, the Kunstkamera was part of a suite of buildings belonging to the Imperial Academy of Sciences. The famous scientist, poet, and historian of the eighteenth century, Mikhail Lomonosov (who died ten years before Ivan's visit), had worked in the Kunstkamera and taken astronomical observations from its tower. Unfortunately, Ivan failed to record his impressions of the Kunstkamera collections. As in most of his daily entries, he merely noted his presence at the institution.

One aspect of Russian life that Ivan seemed to enjoy greatly and liked to describe in detail was public celebrations. Just one day after visiting the Kunstkamera and failing to comment on its collections, he attended celebrations of the Russian peace treaty with the Ottoman Porte and reported on them at length. "I heard mass at the Kazan Cathedral, which the Bishop of Smolensk conducted, and where the military governor of Petersburg and all high personages were present. Then from the church all the way to the Winter Palace two ranks of guards and field regiments lined both sides of the street, and during the singing of the wishes for a long life [*mnogoletie*] they fired three volleys. Cannon fire from the fortresses and church bells could be heard all day long. In the evening," Ivan went on, "until after midnight people continued to celebrate along the main streets, which just like the two fortresses were richly illuminated, and the throngs of people were large."[34]

The following year, 1776, Ivan was in the northern capital from late September through November. His sojourn began with a very special event, the wedding of the heir to the throne, Grand Prince Paul, to Maria Fëdorovna. This was Paul's second marriage. His first wife had died in childbirth the previous year. Ivan had the good fortune of observing the ceremony close up, thanks to a personal connection of one of his business acquaintances, a man by the name of Kheruvimov. "In the morning I walked to the palace and found an opportunity through the confessor of the nephew of Kheruvimov to pass through the court church to the altar and from there to enjoy a good view of the marriage ceremony and hear the prayers of thanksgiving and the sermon preached by the bishop of Moscow, Platon. Then I witnessed the guard regiments' congratulatory greetings at the palace."[35] Two days later he was back at the palace to see the popular entertainments associated with the marriage festivities, including provision to the public of two bulls and wine flowing from fountains.

Although Ivan, like most other Russians, loved to view the imperial family and its associated pageantry whenever an opportunity arose, his personal development can be measured better by other activities. On this trip, he again visited the Academy of Sciences bookstore and for the first time began to record instances of attendance at theaters. This latter interest apparently originated with Ivan himself. The diary contains no evidence that his parents attended the theater. Early in October he noted that after a trip to the market, "I went to see Kheruvimov, and in the evening together with him we went to the palace, where we first saw a French comedy and ballet and then went to a masquerade and stayed until midnight." Two days later we find him at the "free theater in the home of Count Iagushinskii." It was not sophisticated entertainment. On that evening the theater featured a performance by the English tight-rope walker Sanders, "the leaping in the air" of Pallis, and a pantomime.[36] The next month he was back at the Iagushinskii Theater for another performance by Sanders. Soon after, he joined up with Kheruvimov again to visit the court theater and see another French comedy.[37]

Trips to Petersburg regularly thereafter included stops at the Academy bookstore and visits to the theater. These tastes were becoming built in as a part of Ivan's new identity as a cultured man of the world. He had acquired a love of reading, as he told us, when he spent the summer of 1768 with a private teacher in Petersburg. Interest in the theater came a few years later and continued to be not only a part of his own life and identity but was also transferred to his children, one of whom became a prominent actor. He also shared this interest with his wife, Anna, who began to accompany him to theatrical performances closer to home. In January 1779 he traveled to Moscow with her and their son to visit relatives and conduct business. Ivan first went to the theater there by himself. Then a few days later, after dinner with his in-laws, the entire family attended the theater to see the comic opera "Good Soldiers" followed by a ballet.[38] Another trip to Moscow with his wife and son in May found him again at the theater with his in-laws, although it is not entirely certain that Anna accompanied him on this theater outing. Ivan wrote that "we dined with the Kaftannikovs [the family of Anna's sister and brother-in-law] and in the evening I was with them at the theater." By July, they were back home in Dmitrov and enjoying theater in the provinces. It is clear that this was something they had now begun to do together. Ivan reported that on the eighth, after going to mass at the nearby Podlipich'e estate church of Squire Pëtr Khitrovo (a trip the family made every year in connection with the early July festival of that church), they had dinner there and spent the day, including attendance at the estate theater, where they saw two plays: "Friend of the Unfortunate" and "Rebirth."[39]

Ivan's interest in theater was not unusual. The popularity of theatrical performances was growing rapidly in just this period, and merchants and trades-
people made up a large part of the audiences. The people who accompanied
Ivan to the theater were people like himself, a fellow merchant in Petersburg
and his merchant brother-in-law in Moscow. The plays that Ivan and his wife
attended at this time were popular melodramas by Mikhail Kheraskov, a moralistic writer and Freemason who served as director of Moscow University from
1763 through much of the rest of the century and cultivated the talents of a
number of young Russian writers.[40]

Another of Ivan's new interests was gardens. This pursuit was evidently
again a matter of his personal initiative. The first reference in the diary to his
interest in gardens appears in September of 1775 when he traveled with his wife
to Moscow for five days. It was apparently a visit to family members because,
apart from noting their attendance at mass in the Kremlin's Dormition Cathedral, Ivan recorded only that "I rode out to the German settlement to the
garden of Mr. Demidov." This was the expansive twenty-acre estate and gardens
of Nikita Akinfievich Demidov, scion of the family of industrialists who owned
much of the Urals metal industry. The estate was laid out on terraces that
descended toward the Iauza River, a stream that flowed through the northeast
side of the city. The property contained by some accounts seven, by others as
many as ten orangeries, the largest of which measured 68 by 9.6 meters. Separate structures were devoted to vegetables, peaches, grapes, plums, pineapples,
and cherries. Three greenhouses also served the estate. A count made in 1774, a
year before Ivan's first visit, recorded 9,000 plants, among them yews, laurels,
cedars, palms, and box trees, geraniums, roses, 15 types of aloes, 8 types of ficus,
5 species of pineapple, citrus fruits, peaches, apricots, watermelons, grapes, and
a wide variety of flowers.[41] What a feast for the eyes, nose, and palate! Although
this trip took Ivan to the urban estate of the Nikita Demidov, an even more
impressive botanical garden was owned by his older brother Prokofii, a well-
known eccentric, philanthropist, and pioneering botanist. Prokofii Demidov
had sold off his metallurgical holdings and lived in splendor in Moscow, where
he endowed a number of charitable projects proposed by the empress, including the imperial foundling home and a commercial school. He was an avid
apiarist and even wrote a tract on the care of bees. Gardens were, however, his
consuming interest.[42] He maintained a number of them in different Russian
cities. His best-known garden was at his "Neskuchnyi" estate on the banks of
the Moscow River. Although Ivan's first trip to a Demidov garden was to
Nikita's in the Basmannaia section of Moscow, both Demidov gardens, and
several others developed by nobles and merchants in Moscow, would play a role
in Ivan's plans for creating gardens of his own in Dmitrov. These plans may

indeed have already been developed. Ivan wrote about visiting nearby villages to do grafting of apple trees in the spring of 1776, and then mentioned an orchard at his family's home in Dmitrov the following summer. After the first hard frosts in August of 1777, we find him in Moscow purchasing fruit trees from a priest in Vorontsov Field.[43]

Trips to Petersburg now also provided an opportunity to see other inspiring gardens and the kind of exotic plants that could grow only in an orangery. During his stay in the northern capital in 1778 to conduct grain sales, Ivan joined a fellow Dmitrov merchant, Semën Korob'in, on a trip to the imperial summer residence at Tsarskoe Selo south of the capital. They hoped to see "all the magnificent things there so worthy of comment," as Ivan phrased it. Korob'in knew the court herald, who let them into the palace. "We examined all the rooms in the palace," Ivan wrote, "the court church, the gardens, grotto, hermitage, and other small pleasure houses and conversation nooks, as well as the orangery." It was on the orangery, however, that he dwelled, remarking that "We saw a flowering aloe tree, which through the skillful work of gardeners had flourished for 37 years from its beginnings."[44]

This experience left a strong impression. Ivan was eager to enjoy the expansive gardens of the capital cities and the exotic plants that were a mark of distinction for their owners and a joy to cultivate and observe in themselves. Whether or not he was taken by the "poetry of the gardens," as the Russian scholar Dmitrii Likhachëv called it—that is, the consciously symbolic and emblematic qualities of gardens—is hard to say. It is difficult to believe that any persons living in Ivan's time could remain unaware (as most people are today) of the didactic character of gardens, even if they may not have been familiar with the classical allusions through which the symbols and structures spoke.[45] Even so, Ivan did not write about this aspect of gardens, concentrating instead on the variety of plants and their fascinating presentation. And sooner than he expected, or could have hoped, he was going to have an opportunity to indulge his taste for the exotic and impressive.

UNEXPECTED DEATH IN THE FAMILY

[1779, August] 13th In the morning was a hard freeze that damaged all the cucumbers. At 3 in the afternoon father left for Pereslavl-Zaleskii to visit the bishop during the days of the Dormition.

15th I attended mass at the cathedral, had dinner at the archpriest's, and from his place I went to call on the chancery worker Sergievskii. At dusk my father-in-law Aleksei Ivanovich and brother-in-law Kaftannikov arrived from the Trinity Monastery.

16th I attended the vigil and mass at Presentation Church, then we fished in the river above the Lower Mill, and in the afternoon we rode to the Meadow Mill to take a stroll.

17th I was at home and our Moscow guests arrived in anticipation of the return of my father. In the evening Uncle Dmitrii Il'ich visited with me. This evening I felt a great melancholy.[46]

The Tolchënov family was having an exceptionally good year in 1779. Life in their town had settled down. The social upheaval led by the pretender Pugachëv of the mid-decade was far behind them, and the repercussions of the scandal in the voevoda office the previous year had begun to recede. Ivan's life-threatening illness of 1777 was also behind him, and he was fully active again in his family, business, social, and cultural life. His father, too, had survived a serious health crisis in 1778 and was vigorously pursuing his commercial work. Indeed, the volume of the family's grain trade had reached an all-time high in 1778, and in the current year, 1779, Ivan's father was reaping huge profits, amounts in excess of the declared capital assets of most other merchant families in the city.[47] The family seemed to be developing a positive relationship with the new voevoda, Major Nikolai Iur'evich Andreanov, and their social contacts with the noble families of the town and surrounding district had become more frequent.

Then tragedy struck. As recorded in the diary entry that starts this section, Ivan's father had left on August 13 for the diocesan center at Pereslavl-Zaleskii to visit with the bishop during the feast of the Dormition (a fixed holy day that occurs on August 15). Ivan and the rest of the family, including Ivan's in-laws who were visiting from Moscow, were waiting for his father's return in the next days. Ivan describes in his diary what happened on August 18:

At 2 in the morning there was an unexpected and alarming knock at our gate that I took for the arrival of father from Pereslavl, but what did it turn out to be? Instead, Uncle Dmitrii Il'ich was standing there and announced the death of my dear father, unbearable and unexpected news that a messenger had just brought urgently from Trinity Monastery. Oh, time of affliction! Oh, moment of grief! Most precious father of mine, Aleksei Il'ich, left home completely healthy . . . on his own horses, going to Pereslavl, taking with him [our] agents Sava Balabolin and Nikifor Sokolov. At Trinity Monastery, he caught up with Prince Ivan Fëdorovich Golitsyn and rode with him the rest of the way to Pereslavl, and they spent Dormition Day there happily in the company of the bishop. But on the following day, the 16th, at night the first misfortune befell him, when thieves stole from his lodgings all three horses that he had with him. He regretted this loss but not terribly. 16th he dined and stayed overnight with the bishop, and then in the morning on rented horses he headed for home still in good health.

Ivan's father had taken one worker with him on the journey home and left his two agents to search out the stolen horses. After riding just 15 kilometers, Aleksei Il'ich suddenly "felt weary and drained, soon after bloody vomiting started, and he became listless." Aleksei told his worker that "he sensed he was not going to make it home." Although they continued on, they traveled barely three more kilometers when Aleksei ordered his driver to stop so that he could get out.

[A]t the same time a stroke hit him in the right ear so hard that he could not stand it and they laid him on the ground. Meanwhile, a driver galloped to Trinity Monastery to get the monastery priest for a [last] confession. Until he arrived two hours later, father lay in the same place, in such anguish that he was beating his arms and legs on the ground. He had lost the power of speech, and only when people called loudly would he for a brief time move his eyes. When the priest arrived, not being able to conduct confession or do anything else with him, they placed him in the carriage so they could at least get him to the monastery, but having just reached the monastery and begun to ascend the hill to Klement'evo, there he surrendered his soul to his Creator. Such is the fate of human life![48]

Ivan called this "the saddest day of my entire life." The memory of this time clearly left a very deep imprint. "Memory" is the right word, because it is doubtful that the passages in the diary about his father's death were written at the time of its occurrence. Ivan interrupted his usual lapidary notes at this point in the journal to write a detailed description of the events connected with his father's death and of the funeral that followed. The style and elucidation have much more in common with his later interpolations in the form of yearly summaries, which he began composing in the 1790s when he transferred his daily jottings to leather-bound volumes. The passages about his father's death are from a more mature period of his life when his writing rose to a literary level and was influenced by the sentimentalist literature of the time. A persuasive sign of this reworking can be seen in the final sentence of the passage quoted at the start of this section, which was the last entry before Ivan reported on his father's death: "This evening I felt a great melancholy." This recording of a deep sadness *before* he had heard of his father's death is unquestionably a later insertion and probably the beginning of the long interpolation about the death and funeral. In this regard, note also that Ivan repeated the phrase "This evening" in two consecutive sentences. This was not something he did in his regular daily notes and is another sign that the passage is a later insertion.

We are indebted to Ivan for a detailed description of a merchant funeral in a provincial town. He wrote that the body arrived at dawn just two hours after the family had first learned of his father's death. As soon as the body was laid out amid the sobbing of the family, the parish priest began to chant the *panikhida,* the service commemorating the dead, which in the Orthodox Church is sung before the burial and then on the third, ninth, twentieth, and fortieth days after death (the days corresponding to the steps of the soul ascending to heaven).[49] The abbot of the Boris and Gleb Monastery and the entire local clergy, according to Ivan, went into action to prepare the funeral. People from throughout the city began to arrive. "[O]ur house was filled every minute with a large throng of people saying their farewells because the deceased was so well loved." That evening Ivan went to the monastery to pick out a spot for the burial, which took place on the third day, August 20. The weather on the day of the funeral was clear and hot.

In the morning the body was laid in the coffin in the appropriate way. The coffin was upholstered in scarlet velveteen with silver braid. The clothing was as it should be: a light-blue robe suit, in his hands lay a Persian scarf, and on his feet were white silk stockings and yellow shoes. Right up to the time of burial the body did not change and with each passing hour became more vibrant. Only the place where the paralysis struck had become dark. The hearse cloth was covered in gold brocade, from which afterwards chasubles and albs were sewn at the monastery. At the 11th hour, upon the gathering of the entire clergy, the body was lifted and carried ceremoniously to the monastery, and after the mass was performed there, the prayers for the dead were said and the body was lowered into the grave, which was laid out in brick in the church opposite the iconostasis on the southern side. Presiding at the burial was Iakov, abbot of the Boris and Gleb Monastery, along with the archpriest, and up to 20 priests and 10 deacons, plus a very large number of people were in attendance.[50]

Following the mass, the entire clergy, the Tolchënov relatives, and "a considerable number of admirers of the deceased" returned to Ivan's home for a dinner.

At this time, Ivan was just twenty-four years old and the sole surviving child of his parents. He was heir to the family business, wealth, and the personal and social responsibilities of his much admired father.

*   *   *

These years of the mid- and late 1770s were defining for Ivan. As he entered his twenties he was fully engaged in the work of a young grain trader for which his father had prepared him, and he operated comfortably in the conditions to which he had been habituated. Acting under the general supervision of his father, he traveled in the winter to the south and east to make grain purchases, and in the summer he conducted a caravan of the family's barges north to Petersburg and oversaw the sales of flour and grain they contained. He worked with the pilots, bargemen, and stevedores who moved goods down the water-

ways, and he stood together with his fellow grain merchants to resist government pressure to lower prices.

At the same time, Ivan was acquiring aspirations that went beyond the
requirements of his commercial activity. He was not content to remain at his
barges at the Smolnyi grain wharves in Petersburg or at the family's sales office
in the market. At first occasionally and then more frequently, he explored the
attractions of the city and indulged in the new consumerism of the age. He
began to show off in his diary entries his wearing of a pocket watch, his outings
to parks and palaces, his visits to cultural institutions, attendance at a masquerade in Peterhof, and his opportunity to observe at close range the wedding of
Grand Prince Paul. To gain entrée to these places and events he at first exploited
his personal connections with merchants resident in Petersburg. Later, on his
own initiative, he sampled the growing intellectual and cultural life of the
capital available to a person of his station. He purchased books at the Academy
of Sciences bookstore, visited gardens and greenhouses, the theater. Ivan was
curious enough about his surroundings that he even looked in at the Lutheran
church to compare it to Russian Orthodox places of worship. His field of
habituated activity had brought him into proximity with the fields of elite
culture and social life, which themselves had been expanding rapidly in this
period of noble freedom, growing wealth, and the encouragement of an Enlightenment monarch. It was at just this time, the middle 1770s, that Ivan
turned his diary keeping into a daily practice rather than an occasional travel
log and began reflexively to write himself into an interesting new life of cultivated tastes. It may indeed have been one and the same urge that pushed him
into daily diary keeping *and* propelled him along a line of social expansion. It
was at this time, too, that we see in his invitations to Prince Ivan Golitsyn an
aspiration to associate with the nobles of his district, people who were educated
for things considered more lofty than commercial affairs and who, along with
wealthy and knowledgeable merchants, were likely to share Ivan's new interests
in a gracious and stylish life.

In the diary entries of this period we can see something of Ivan's thinking,
his allegiances, the quality of his patriotism, and his worldview. He thrilled at
sightings of the imperial family and the opportunity to be in close proximity to
its power and pageantry. He found the public celebration of Russia's victory
over the Turks more worthy of detailed description than his visits to cultural
institutions or the theater. He was clearly under the spell of autocratic authority
and, as Richard Wortman has analyzed in regard to the nobles, derived gratifi-
cation and affirmation from being in the presence of the imperial family and
government dignitaries. His manner of expression also makes clear that he
viewed God as an active force in the world. Not for Ivan was the God of
Enlightenment deists, a creator who set the world in motion and then allowed it

to operate on natural principles. In referring to the Pugachëv Rebellion Ivan wrote that God had unleashed his wrath on Russia (but also tempered this anger by allowing Russia to defeat the Turks). He also gave God credit for "seeing fit to prolong [his] life" when he fell critically ill on the road to Petersburg in 1777. Although Ivan continued to grow and develop new interests and attitudes, he did not abandon the idea that God was present and aware of individual human acts and could be angered or mollified by individual behavior.

The unexpected death of his father was a disorienting shock that thrust Ivan suddenly from his habituated station as a junior member of a family firm managed by his energetic father into the leadership of both the firm and the family. This is a fateful moment for the development of identity. While it did not change Ivan's social identity—he continued to occupy the position of a first-guild merchant that he had enjoyed as a member of his father's household—it greatly altered his opportunity to refashion a personal identity. Emotionally, such fateful breaks in the continuity of one's life have a powerful impact, and, as we can see in Ivan's language, the death of his father affected him deeply. He had to mourn not just the loss of his father and the security that his father's enterprise and status conferred; he also had to mourn the loss of his own protected position within the family and business arrangements his father had created. But a loss of habituated place and attendant identity, however traumatic initially, also carries with it the opportunity, even necessity, to remake oneself and one's surroundings in ways that may produce a new and more satisfying personal identity.

4

Young Paterfamilias

HEAD OF THE FAMILY FIRM

[1779, November] 24th I attended the vigil at Presentation Church and heard mass at the cathedral. The abbot and Uncle Ivan and his family dined at my house, and after 3 o'clock I left for Moscow; we stopped overnight at Sukharevo.

25th I arrived with my father-in-law at his home before 10 o'clock in the morning. Then I went to the post office and the city center.

26th In the morning I received money on bills of exchange from Popov's agent and Uvarov, and just after noon dispatched [my agent] Prokofii Tiut'kin to Lyskovo for the purchase of grain. Then I rode to the orangeries of Mr. Demidov and in the evening made some purchases in town.

27th I heard mass at the Dormition Cathedral, dined at my brother-in-law Kaftannikov's home and in the evening went to the theater. . . .

[In Moscow again in December] on the 8th I heard mass at the Monastery of Our Savior by the Icon Shops, dined at Kaftannikov's and then went to see the races and after that was at the Znamenskii Theater.

9th I was in the city and was dispatching agents to the southeast for the purchase of grain, and in the evening I accompanied them as far as Rogozhkoe.

10th In the morning I was at the Boloto [market] and in the city. I ate dinner at the home of my brother-in-law Kaftannikov, and then visited my cousin Pëtr Andreev Tolchënov, and in the evening was in Sushchëvo to see my father's mother-in-law.

11th in the morning I rode out to Mr. Demidov's orangeries and received from his gardener a plan for the construction of my own greenhouse, later called an orangery, and from there I proceeded to the post office and the city.[1]

The death of his father plunged Ivan into a flurry of activity. Responsibility for arranging the rituals of prayer and remembrance for his father, for the operation of the family's grain trade and other businesses, and for the family members themselves, including his stepmother, the widow left by his father's untimely death (and visits to her mother, as the diary excerpt above reveals)—all these matters now fell on Ivan's shoulders. The days following the burial of his father were marked by further requiem masses and prayers. These included a mass and office for the dead at the monastery twenty days later, at the halfway point to the very important remembrance that Russians conducted forty days after a death. Ivan also organized a series of additional ceremonies just before the forty days elapsed; he took advantage of a visit by Archbishop Feofilakt to town and convinced the prelate to say a special mass for his father. It turned out to be a big day for the family. "24th [September] I went with the entire family to the monastery for the mass that was said by the bishop together with six priests. And this was followed by the office for the dead, performed with most of the clergy of the city. Afterwards dining at my house were, first of all, the archbishop, then Prince Ivan Fëdorovich Golitsyn, Mr. Boltin, Messrs. Obreskov, Maslov and his family, the treasury officer Mr. Nazimov and his family, assistant voevoda Mr. Gorokhov, Squire Khitrovo together with the two Princes Volkonskii, the abbot and the entire suite of the archbishop, and they stayed until 5 pm." Every one of the laypeople mentioned by Ivan was a noble, either a local official or someone with estates in the vicinity. We know from other entries that Ivan's own family members and in-laws were present as well, but in the entry quoted here, a memento of the exceptional guests, he did not include them. To finish the day, Ivan reported, "at dusk I rode over to the monastery to show my appreciation to the archbishop." The wording of this entry leaves little doubt that the trip included the delivery of a gift or contribution.[2]

While concern for the soul of Ivan's father demanded time and energy, the living family also needed tending to. Ivan's wife, Anna Alekseevna, was in the last stages of pregnancy when his father died. Because her two most recent births had ended in the deaths of the infants in their first two weeks, Ivan must have been worried about the outcome of this impending birth. On September 20 Anna delivered a son, Aleksei, at the same time that Ivan was running to and fro arranging the mass by the archbishop. (The name Aleksei chosen for this child, incidentally, conformed neatly both to the custom of naming children after saints whose feast days occurred close to the date of birth and to the wish to honor the memory of Ivan's father.)[3] In the midst of dealing with the archbishop and the town elite, Ivan was organizing a baptism and accompanying dinner and summoning in-laws from Moscow to participate in the christening. To add to his cares, the following month Ivan's first-born son, Pëtr, fell ill with smallpox. Pëtr was just five years old, still vulnerable to the scourges that carried off many Russian children, including all of Ivan's siblings. Pëtr lay sick for two weeks, but then, to his parents' relief, gradually recovered.

The time Ivan could spend worrying about Pëtr and the newborn Aleksei was limited, because the family business also demanded his attention. Within a few days of his father's burial, he was on the road to the family's northern mills to load and dispatch barges of flour to Petersburg through the treacherous northern waterways. On his return trip he stopped off just north of the city at the Peresvetovo estate of the aristocrat Sergei Mikhailovich Golitsyn, whose mill the family rented, and was delighted to report that he was received there "affectionately." Soon he was on his way to Moscow to make purchases. By the first of October he was again riding north to the mills near the Volga, this time to send off another consignment of barges together with those of his Uncle Ivan. But, as he had come to know well, late season shipments frequently ran into trouble. This time the barges floated scarcely a kilometer before stranding in shallow water. Uncle Ivan rode in and they spent a day trying to drag the barges through the shoals, to little effect—then they gave up. The diarist made another trip to the mills a couple of weeks later in the company of his father-in-law, who seems to have joined Uncle Ivan in the role of senior counselor during the time the young Ivan was taking over responsibility for the family enterprises. It was late October. Ice was forming, and the barge season was over. After "conducting a survey of affairs" at the mills, they even ran into difficulty getting home. The crush of moving ice made their return trip across the Volga exhausting and perilous.[4]

The efforts for his business and family were inevitable attributes of Ivan's new role as head of the family and its enterprises. What most accurately prefigured his future, however, were the choices he made for himself, some of which we can see in the passages from the diary that begin this chapter. In the midst of Ivan's runs between home, the north mills, and Moscow, he was establishing the pattern of his new life. At home, when not tending to remembrances for his father and consulting with his family business partners, he was stocking and rearranging his fish ponds. In Moscow, he visited with relatives and made purchases for the family business and charitable projects. He obtained cash and furnished it to agents for grain purchases downriver. But he also allocated a portion of his time to the races, to theater-going, and visits to the orangeries of prominent families. Of these avocations, gardens seemed to be what interested him most. He was in contact with some of the best gardeners in Moscow, and before the end of the year he had ordered and obtained a plan for his own orangery in Dmitrov.

Yet his life turned out to include much more than the conduct of business and the pursuit of his personal interests. His business interests led him into politics and positions of responsibility in his town's governance, and these positions, in turn, brought him into social contact with the local nobility, central state officials, and the high clergy.

THE RHYTHMS OF DAILY LIFE

On the night of September 30th [1778] Dmitrov experienced ferocious thun-
derstorms and horrifying lightning strikes that continued for more than three
hours. Everyone was terrified. On October 1st and 2nd a huge snow fell just like
those of winter so that in some places the snow drifts made the roads almost im-
passible. Then from the 5th a warm-up set in and the rivers filled from the run-off
of melting snow. Snow and rain continued to fall again until by the 16th the melt
water was like the spring floods and smashed apart the floating bridge. The
Shkurin home on Carriage Road was standing in more than two feet of water.[5]

Ivan Tolchënov's life was lived within a context of community that followed
a familiar and reassuring rhythm of time and ritual. Ivan's temporal orientation
operated at several levels. The first was the rhythm of the seasons, the freezing
and thawing of the river and land routes so critical to long-distance trade in
agricultural commodities. Ivan continually tracked the weather and seasonal
changes, noting their effects on the movement and pricing of products. At the
close of each year's diary entries, he summarized the weather for that year,
tracing the principal shifts in the patterns of heat and cold, precipitation and
drought, as well as specific memorable events. Among the last were cases of
lightning bolts that killed people or set homes afire, early or late frosts and
heavy snowfalls, floods, and "terrifying northern lights"[6] (literary touches suggesting, again, that he was influenced by the sentimentalist writings of the age).[7]
Weather changes were not only important markers of time but also matters of
personal safety, especially for a person who traveled frequently by river and
road. As already noted, the unexpected formation or early break-up of ice on
rivers often made Ivan's crossings treacherous or impossible.

A second order of time-keeping was religious. Marking the movement of
time through each year was the sequence of holy days, fasts, masses of remembrance, blessings of the waters, plus folk holidays such as Maslenitsa (Shrovetide) associated with religious observances. Ivan was steadfast in his religious
practice, and one purpose of his diary may have been to monitor and record his
fidelity in attending to his religious duties, much like the English Puritans, who
were the first diary keepers. Ivan noted each religious service he attended,
whether it be mass, matins, vespers, or a vigil. He also recorded the name of the
church or monastery at which he attended the service and, on special occasions,
the priests or prelates who presided.

The year began with the Epiphany and the procession to the rivers for the
blessing of the waters. Ivan often observed this holiday in Moscow with the
relatives of his wife, Anna Alekseevna. This was a time of the year when Ivan had
to be in Moscow to orchestrate the dispatch of agents on grain purchasing trips

and to furnish them with money from Moscow government offices. The next big holiday was Maslenitsa, the pre-Lenten celebration marked by sleigh rides, visiting, hosting, and general merriment. Ivan and his family must have enjoyed these festivities immensely, as he always noted them prominently. We know, too, from other memoirs, about the centrality of this holiday to merchant socializing, display of wealth, and marking of the pecking order.[8] Lent followed and led to the annual pre-Easter confession and communion, which Ivan usually recorded laconically in the diary. On a few occasions, however, he announced this obligation in an especially unctuous rendering, as he did in 1782 in the following entry. "On March 25 I attended a vigil at the Presentation Church and afterward made my confession to the Most High, and later at Mass, though unworthy and in hopes of mercy from our Redeemer, had the honor of taking the all-pure, divine, life-giving, and awe-inspiring sacrament of communion; and of our family members Anna Alekseevna, Andrei Fëdorovich, and our son Petrushka also took communion."[9] Perhaps this year these rituals took on special importance because Ivan had recently become burgomaster, and it was the first time he was performing them as a public figure and appearing with his young family in a distinguished position. The private celebrations of Easter were most often shared with the family of Uncle Ivan. The spring holy days wound down through the following week with the diarist's daily attendance at mass.

Other important occasions that marked the movement through the year included the August 1 blessing of the waters and summer pilgrimages to important religious sites such as the Trinity–St. Sergei Monastery and, equally important, to the nearby shrine at Vedernitsy, with its famous miracle-working icon that the family believed to have played a role in saving Ivan's life. A central ritual for the family and the local religious community took place each August 17 when they attended a special mass in memory of the death of Ivan's father and the clergy shared a meal at the Tolchënov home.

Secular events likewise gave shape to the flow of time. The weekly markets on Mondays and Thursdays supplied not merely goods but also a regular rhythm for the community.[10] Once a year, in September, the town hosted a large fair that attracted peddlers and buyers from a wide circle of surrounding towns and hamlets. The city council and other periodic meetings of the citizens for the discussion of affairs and election of officers were important occasions. These meetings did not, however, occur on a fixed schedule, as the new statutes of 1775 and 1782 on local governance brought change in the number, character, and functioning of urban institutions. Each year the meetings and elections fell at slightly different times, and yet they represented important stages of urban life.

A third order of time-keeping was the daily rhythm of morning, afternoon, and evening. Ivan often tracked his days in this way. "In the morning, I was at the market. In the evening, I visited Uncle Ivan." "In the morning, I went to the Meadow Mill; after dinner I rode over to see off the district treasurer, Stogov, who was leaving for Ruza."[11] Sometimes, he marked time in more precise ways that indicated the presence of a clock. He noted the hour or even the minute some activity began or ended, indicating that he must have been carrying his pocket watch. As mentioned earlier, the entries he produced in this way bore only a fictive precision, since Ivan had no readily available standard by which to set his watch and, in any event, no pocket watch in his day could accurately render time to the minute.

This intrusion of a device of the age of rationalism with its precise divisions of the day into hours and minutes, while implying Ivan's association with disembedded conceptual systems of tracking time, seems in his case at least as much a personal status marker. In the diary as a whole, the precision of the clock is accorded less often to business functions than to traditional observances such as important family events (births and deaths), and religious practices, especially pilgrimages. For example, his son Vladimir died "at the start of the 6th hour in the afternoon." His daughter Ekaterina was born at 5:20 pm and died a year later at 7:28 am. Another daughter, Varvara, was born at 11:45 in the evening.[12] Easter services were noted with similar precision. "Easter mass began at 7:35" is a typical entry for this important holiday.[13] The family's trips to the shrine at Vedernitsy were recorded with similar attention to the clock.[14]

In 1768, when Ivan was fourteen years old, his parents took him on a trip to Rostov and Iaroslavl to pray at the icon of the Tolsk Blessed Virgin. Twenty years later, when his own eldest son, Pëtr, was fourteen years old, Ivan made the same trip, recording it with the kind of precision that to his way of thinking pilgrimages, and perhaps only pilgrimages, warranted.

[1788, August] 28th We left Ozeretskoe at 4:20 in the morning, arrived at Sergiev Posad at 7:38, and went to the monastery, where we visited the vestry and saw all the treasures kept there. Then we heard mass and prayed at the Holy Trinity Church. We had dinner at the home of my wife's cousin, the tax-farmer Aleksei Petrov, and continued on our way at 1:45 in the afternoon.[15]

The entire trip, running for nearly two weeks, was recorded with this same to-the-minute accuracy. Ivan operated within the modern, rationalistic field of precision time-keeping, but he deployed this knowledge in the service of traditional family and religious obligation. If there was an element of efficiency or modernity in these efforts to sequester time, it was not the kind we are familiar with. Perhaps it was again punctiliousness similar to that of English Puritans, who built a daily record of fidelity to religious duty. Or, more likely, it was a device that afforded Ivan a sense of control over a life that was offering him new experiences and the prospect of new and preferred identities. Yet it could as readily be understood as akin to the behavior of present-day parents who take a video-camera or pair of binoculars along on a vacation trip in order to preserve or sharpen their observations (while displaying a status symbol), devices less often used at home, where other status markers are in evidence.

The display of the signs and symbols of a cultivated life, in fact, occupied much of Ivan's time and attention after he became head of his household and family business firm.

PERSONAL PROJECTS FOR A CULTIVATED LIFE

[1780, May] 14th Before 6 in the morning I departed for Moscow; I ate dinner in Sholokhovo and arrived at the home of my father-in-law at 8 in the evening.

15th I heard mass at the Archangel Cathedral, where Bishop Platon conducted it and gave the sermon. Afterward I visited my brother-in-law Kaftannikov; in the evening I strolled in the garden at Znamenskii meadow at the home of Dmitrii Ivanovich.

16th In the morning I went to make purchases of trees for our newly built orangery and was at the orangeries of Count Stroganov, the lady-in-waiting Golovinskaia, and the gardener Miller. Later I was in the city and at the home of Kaftannikov.

17th I attended mass at the Dormition Cathedral. In the evening I visited Kaftannikov.

18th I spent the morning at the orangeries of the gardener Beliaev. Later I was in the city, and in the evening I visited Ivan Egorov Osorgin.[16]

Even as the death of Ivan's father brought new responsibilities to the young heir, it likewise permitted him to indulge the tastes he had been developing in his formative years. What most interested Ivan was the creation, if only on a small scale, of the kind of life he had seen and admired among the wealthy merchants and nobles of the capital cities of Petersburg and Moscow. The external expression of this cultivated life included a masonry townhouse, orangeries, fish ponds, and elegant carriages. Ivan set out to get these trappings of the good life.

His family may already have owned some local ponds, for Ivan had mentioned fishing as a productive activity earlier, and he had been fishing actively in the months before his father's death. Even so, this activity now commanded greater attention. In early November 1780, he supervised the drawing out of the fish, presumably for winter preservation or sale, in both his domestic pond and in the ponds connected to the Lower Mill that his family rented on the north side of the city.[17] Soon after the weather broke the next spring he was out with his workers fishing and restocking the ponds. The availability of fresh fish close to his home is mentioned in the diary more often from this point on. For example, we glimpse his work in seeding the supply chain periodically in reports such as the following one in November 1780, when he noted that "I released into the ponds at the Lower Mill the fish that we had brought in barrels from the Migoloshkaia Mill."[18] The need to transport fish in barrels rather than catch it locally may have arisen from what people regarded as pollution in the nearby Dubna River, which had turned red and rusty from the runoff of swamps and manufacturing.[19] In May of the next year Ivan and his workers caught the fish from these ponds at the Lower Mill and transferred them to his domestic pond.[20] This activity bore the marks of a privatization of what had earlier been a tsarist concession. In the late seventeenth century the city of Dmitrov had maintained ponds for supplying live fish to the tsarist court in Moscow. Fish were transported from the Volga and its northern tributaries, the Mologa and Sheksna, in specially built river boats "cut through" with holding tanks. A "tsarist fish office" in Dmitrov kept accounts and delivered the fish to the Moscow court.[21] This activity evidently died out when the court moved to St. Petersburg early in the eighteenth century. Six decades later, when the emancipation of the nobility from lifetime service in 1762 spurred rapid development of civic and country estate life, the elites began appropriating these formerly regal luxuries for themselves. Priscilla Roosevelt described the decorative and no doubt also practical series of ponds on the Apraksin estate near Dmitrov.[22] The remains of similar elaborate ponds can still be found on the estate of Prince Ivan Golitsyn, where the diarist was a frequent visitor, and at other homes in the countryside surrounding Dmitrov. A merchant could not own a country estate, but Ivan, whose family rented mills and adjoining ponds near the Volga and close to home in Dmitrov for its grain business, was in a perfect position to exploit this water resource for the delivery of fresh fish to the family table. The family also owned a sufficiently large urban property to have final holding ponds close to its home.

Gardens, and especially the exotic plants that were cultivated in orangeries, fascinated Ivan. Ever since the mid-1770s when he began visiting the Demidov and other gardens and orangeries in Moscow, Ivan's interest in horticulture had been intensifying. Recall his excitement during his trip to Petersburg and Tsarskoe Selo in September 1778 when he viewed an aloe plant "that through the skilled work of the gardeners had flourished there for 37 years."[23] He did not, however, have the leisure in those days to build on this enthusiasm. And his father might not have shared this interest and may even have thought of greenhouses as frivolous. Although the family had gardens next to its home in Dmitrov earlier, no mention is made in the diary of plans for a greenhouse until after the death of Ivan's father. Then, within weeks, Ivan was throwing himself into a quest for an orangery and very soon had acquired an architectural design for one of his own.

Ivan's youth had been accompanied by the blossoming of Moscow as a center of wealthy noble and merchant domestic elegance and delight in gardens and greenhouses. Before their emancipation from lifetime service, Russian nobles had little time to improve their home life. Empress Catherine recalled her visits to Moscow when she was grand duchess in the 1740s and 1750s and complained about having to stay in the drafty, rundown homes of leading nobles of the city.[24] Matters rapidly improved in the 1760s and 1770s, however, as nobles flocked to the city and built new townhouses or refurbished existing ones, outfitting many of them with gardens and greenhouses. Well-to-do merchants imitated this fashion, and soon gardens and exotic tropical trees and flowers, raised under glass, became all the rage.[25]

The most splendid example was the urban estate of Prokofii Demidov, the eccentric scion of an artisan family that had made a fortune in metallurgical manufacturing and risen into the nobility. Beginning in 1756 Demidov built gardens adjoining his palace on the high right bank of the Moscow River, near the Donskoi Monastery. His estate looked northwestward across the river to a meadow and the New Virgin Convent below. The gardens were described by the famous naturalist Peter Simon Pallas, who stayed at Demidov's home for nearly a month in the late 1770s and produced a detailed catalog of the structure and of the flora and fauna of the estate. The site, Pallas explained, did not come ready-made. It had to be dug out of a steep ravine, and Demidov employed 700 men for two years at the job of carving the ravine into the shape of an amphitheater intersected by a series of five terraces, each about 100 meters across. All the terraces but one held orangeries, several of which were forty meters in length. The lower sections boasted the largest orangeries, which housed palm and tropical fruit trees. The very lowest section near the river featured a large pond surrounded by trees and containing rare birds and waterfowl from many parts of the world.

Pallas told of Demidov's love of botanical gardens and the large sums and personal attention that he lavished on his project. Demidov carefully preserved and cultivated seeds of rare plants, "placing them in saucers with clay and covering them with moist cloths," then moving them to progressively larger containers. Through such careful manipulation he was able to grow trees and plants well beyond their natural average sizes. Pallas commented that "this garden not only surpasses anything of the sort in all of Russia but may be compared to many celebrated botanical gardens in other countries by virtue of the rarity and number of plants that it contains."[26] Ivan Tolchënov frequently recorded trips to the Demidov gardens and orangeries in his diary, but he rarely indicated which one he had visited. On a couple of occasions he made clear that he was at the estate of Nikita Demidov, the twenty-acre spread in the Basman-naia section of the city described in the previous chapter. But he undoubtedly

was also drawn to the celebrated gardens of Prokofii Demidov. Within four
months of the death of his father, Ivan had obtained a plan for his own orangery from a gardener of the Demidov estates (see the diary excerpt for
December 11, 1779, on the first page of this chapter).[27]

Ivan began to implement this plan as early as April of the year after his
father's death. Following a trip to Moscow that month during which he made
his usual visit to the Demidov gardens, he mentioned his own greenhouse in his
daily notes. We get a fuller description in his later summary of the year 1780. "In
this year, because of my interest in gardens, I began to put them gradually in
order. To this end, I hired a gardener, the freeman Pëtr Pankrat'ev, and in the
spring, in the corner opposite the pond on the northern side [of our property],
an orangery of 8 sazhens[28] was constructed with a belvedere over the center of
the hall." To this structure was added in the fall a small greenhouse "for keeping
early cucumbers." That same fall Ivan began to fill the orangery with plants. He
made the rounds of his favorite orangeries in Moscow and purchased "wild
orange, lemon, laurel, peach and other fruit trees up to 70 in number. I likewise
bought flowering bulbs and actual flowers and seeds in sufficient number to get
a good start."[29] Interestingly, in late September he also visited the home of
another prominent merchant family in Dmitrov, the Tugarinovs, for the re-
moval of orangery pear plantings that had been grafted in the spring.[30] This
diary entry makes clear that the fascination with orangeries and exotic plants
was not a personal quirk of Ivan's but a trend that was spreading rapidly from
Moscow to the provincial elites more broadly. Indeed, a young official passing
through the Urals city of Ekaterinburg at about this same time made a point of
visiting a factory owner there in order to see his "superb orangeries" that were
filled with pineapples.[31] It was the Moscow region, however, that saw the greatest burst of activity in these years. Referring to the 1770s and 1780s, Pallas
reported in his book of travels that in Moscow

> Horticulture has within these few years been brought to such perfection, that
> all kinds of vegetables and fruits are in superabundance; being the only pro-
> ductions of the country which are sold cheap and which probably will become
> cheaper every year. The largest shoots of asparagus are reared here in the midst
> of winter in hot-beds, and in such plenty that they are transported to St.
> Petersburg. Early fruit is neither scarce nor dear in Mosco: it is not inferior in
> flavour to that produced in England. In summer the most delicious species of
> cherries, apricots, peaches, pears and apples, nay even ananas, are commonly
> sold at a reasonable price.—All these improvements, made since the year 1770,
> are chiefly the effects of indefatigable exertion. The numerous private or-
> chards, kitchen-gardens, and hot-houses lately established by the nobility and
> gentry, have contributed much to the great abundance of vegetables.[32]

Ivan was caught up in this enthusiasm and eager to share in this productive
and enjoyable pastime and status symbol. To advise him on the development

of his new gardens, he invited to Dmitrov his favorite Moscow gardener, a man named Beliaev, who owned gardens in the north Moscow settlement of Sushchëvo.[33]

Another sign of Ivan's new opportunities and growing association with the local nobility was his participation in the fall hunts of the elite. The first year after the death of his father this seemed to involve merely an invitation to dinner on the day of the hunt. Ivan wrote on September 25, 1780: "In the morning I rode out to the Peresvetovo estate of Prince Sergei Mikhailovich Golitsyn, who was there to run with the hounds together with his brother Court Chamberlain Prince Aleksandr Mikhailovich. I was invited to dinner, to which Prince Ivan Fëdorovich [Golitsyn] also came." By the following year Ivan had managed to get an invitation to join in the hunt itself, this time at Prince Ivan Golitsyn's estate. "I had dinner at the Danilovskoe estate of Prince Ivan Fëdorovich and then rode with him until dusk, following the hounds in the hunt."[34]

As these social expressions of Ivan's new status increased, so too did the material signs. Among these would count the orangeries Ivan was having constructed and filled with exotic plants, plus new carriages, an apartment in Moscow, expansion and improvement of the family's home, and then in the years 1785 and 1786 the construction of an altogether new and stunning masonry home in the style of noble townhouses, the first masonry private residence ever built in the city of Dmitrov.

PHILANTHROPY: CONTINUING HIS FATHER'S WORK

In this year [1783] I resolved to construct at my own expense a chapel in the Prophet Elijah masonry church on the right side of the nave. The chapel was named for three miracle-working saints of Moscow and all Russia: Pëtr, Aleksei, and Iona. The work got started in July with the iconostasis and was finished with the painting of the icons and the fashioning of the appropriate ecclesiastical utensils.[35]

The diary passage above is from Ivan's retrospective notes when he was later transcribing his daily entries into leather-bound volumes and was building a record of the life of affluence that he could see coming to end. It describes succinctly one of his early charitable initiatives. It may have taken on more importance in his thinking when he recalled it years later than it did at the time it happened. In 1783 when he was supervising the construction of the chapel and paying for it, this activity was one of many in a very busy life. His business was prospering, he was serving as a city official, and he was building his elegant life. Although he recorded in the diary events associated with the chapel construction, they nearly get lost amid several other activities. For example in July

1783, when the work was beginning on the chapel, Ivan made a trip to Moscow and reported that "in the morning I rode to the timber stalls and purchased boards for the iconostasis of the Prophet Elijah chapel. Then I was at the orangeries of the merchant Makarov, and in the evening at the theater. [The next day] in the morning I visited Beliaev [the gardener] and again went to Makarov's. I had dinner at my brother-in-law Vandashnikov's and then remained in the city until the evening."[36] Picking up materials for the chapel was squeezed in among visits to orangeries and the theater, activities that occupied the bulk of his attention. Ivan was in and out of Dmitrov on business and family visits for the rest of the summer and fall. On a couple of occasions he noted having looked in on the work on the iconostasis at the chapel.[37] But he wrote nothing more about the progress of the work or his financial contribution. Only when the chapel was completed did he include more detail, this time on the events associated with its consecration. This occurred in mid November 1783 just after Ivan had returned from a trip to the family's grain mills on the Volga.

18th I arrived home safely at 10 in the morning. After dinner I rode to the Prophet Elijah Church to see to the preparations of the chapel for consecration, and from there I rode to see the abbot.

19th I attended the vigil in preparation for the consecration of the church and then attended the actual consecration, which was conducted by the abbot, Pavel, and the clergy in the name of the three miracle-working saints of Moscow and all Russia: Pëtr, Aleksei, and Iona. Then the abbot, the clergy, and Uncle Ivan Il'ich and his household had dinner at my house.[38]

This was just one in a number of philanthropic contributions that Ivan made, in keeping with the role and responsibilities of a wealthy townsman.

Ivan's father and grandfather had made similar contributions. They were among the wealthiest citizens of Dmitrov, and the townspeople and the religious leaders depended on their generosity to provide the facilities and financial support necessary for the ritual performances that bound the community together. Distributions to the poor on the occasion of the death or remembrance of a prominent citizen were one expression of community solidarity.[39] The beneficiaries would offer prayers for the deceased in return for the alms that provided a brief holiday from want. These charitable acts, noted earlier in connection with the death of Ivan's father, were common throughout Russia. More lasting contributions came in the form of material gifts of the kind represented by the chapel in the Prophet Elijah Church. A decade earlier Ivan's grandfather, Fëdor Makarov, had built an entire church in the west end of the city, the Church of the Presentation of the Virgin at the Temple, founded in 1764. Makarov's wife and Ivan's grandmother, Marfa Matveevna, died at the time the church was being constructed and was buried in its nave. This church soon after became the parish church of the Tolchënov family. Ivan's father and he himself continued to contribute to its expansion, and later Ivan built his new masonry townhouse just down the street. From Ivan's retrospective notes we learn of the active participation of his father in the church construction just before his death in 1779. "In this year, through the efforts of my father, improvements were made to the Presentation Church. In place of wood, the cupola was covered with sheets of tinned iron purchased at the Demidov factory, and the central roof, though initially done out of proportion, if only slightly, was then redone twice and covered with sheets of tinned iron. And the altar and entryway were covered with sheets of dark iron and later coated to produce a sheen." After the death of Ivan's father, we find Ivan's widowed stepmother making contributions of her own to the church by sewing chasubles, surplices, and ecclesiastical stoles.[40]

Although the church was not solely the responsibility of the Makarov-Tolchënov family alliance—another merchant of the town, Mikhaila Osetrov, provided a crystal chandelier for the chapel—Ivan continued his family's contributions. Soon after his father's death Ivan was spending large sums of money to outfit the church further. In February of 1780 he traveled to Moscow to complete a number of business tasks, and on the same trip "rode out to the bell factory to purchase medium bells for the belfry of the Presentation Church."[41] Just two months later, to celebrate Easter, he boasted of having bought and arranged for installation in the Presentation Church a chandelier made of copper, which consisted of seven tiers of lights and weighed nearly 600 pounds. Unfortunately, Ivan could not be on hand in April of 1780 for the hanging of this impressive ornament. His daily entries indicate that on the day in question he was accompanying his young step-uncle part way on a journey to Vyshnii Volochëk to work with the grain barges. We learn about the large chandelier not from his diary entries but from his later year-end summaries.[42]

Other charitable projects that Ivan took part in during the 1780s, besides his contribution of the new chapel in the Prophet Elijah Church in 1783, included his purchase of tiles in 1782 for the ovens in the new Magistracy building. The building had burnt to the ground the previous year when rotting chimney tubes caught fire, and Ivan, a new member of the magistracy court, had taken responsibility for this aspect of the building's reconstruction.[43] In 1786 he recorded the laying of the foundation of a bell tower for the Presentation Church, a project for which he had engaged the architect and to which he made large financial contributions in 1786 and 1787.[44] In all these charitable endeavors Ivan was adhering closely to the traditions and expectations of his social group. Merchants throughout Russia were the primary benefactors of local churches and monasteries, which they built and furnished with chapels, porches, bell

Exterior of the Church of the Presentation of the Virgin at the Temple (Presentation Church), built by Ivan Tolchënov's family.

towers, icon walls, large bells, fresco paintings, expensive jewel-encrusted icon covers, and more. They also left substantial sums of money in their wills for the upkeep of churches, the clergy, and contributions to the poor.[45] Merchants characteristically regarded wealth, however gained, as a gift from God and considered it the duty of the recipients to contribute to the community, the church, and the poor "in God's name" if they were to have hope of winning forgiveness after death. Natal'ia Kozlova has pointed out that in some merchant wills the authors even refer to specific injunctions in Holy Writ about the opportunity of clemency for persons whose wealth, even if acquired dishonestly, was properly used for the good of the community.[46]

Later in the decade Ivan would be deeply involved in another major church-building project, one much bigger than he or his community had undertaken before: restoration of the magnificent Dormition Cathedral inside the old walled city.

Seven-tiered copper chandelier that Ivan Tolchënov purchased for
the Presentation Church.

MANAGER OF FAMILY RITUAL AND CONTRACTS

[1781, October] 29th Because of the agreeable intention of my stepmother to get married to the Moscow merchant Ivan Petrov Bykov, I sent word home this morning that [my wife] Anna Alekseevna and our children should come [to Moscow], and I set out to find an apartment where we could hold the wedding dinner, which I rented in the parish of the Georgian Virgin, which is in Vorontsov Field.

Russian society was highly patriarchal in its values and structures. As a man and the sole surviving child of his father, Ivan inherited responsibility not only for the family business but also for all members of the household that his father had left behind, which included Ivan's own immediate family, his father's widow, his young step-uncle and ward Andrei Fëdorovich Makarov, and the family's bonded servants. For the people in his charge Ivan now had to play the leading role in the most important social and ritual functions of their lives. He arranged and sponsored their baptisms, funerals, and weddings.

Some of the additional duties incumbent on a prominent citizen and household head also fell to him. For example, in the year after his father's death, Ivan, despite his youth, was asked to serve as godfather to the son of the archpriest of the city's cathedral, a task that seemed to please and even flatter Ivan. "This morning I served as godfather to Mikhail, the son of the archpriest, attended mass in the cathedral, dined and spent the rest of the day with the archpriest."[47] In short, very soon after his father's death Ivan was being called on to perform the respected social role that his father had long played in the community. In Russia, age was not as important in defining a person's role as was one's place in a social hierarchy. Indeed, the terms "young" and "old" had as much to say about place and function as they did about biological age.[48] Ivan could be, and actually was, a church elder and senior (*starshii* or "old" in Russian) clan member despite his youth.

Funerals and baptisms were highly ritualized and therefore relatively uncomplicated activities, however painful or engaging they may have been personally. Soon enough, Ivan was faced with more challenging family responsibilities. In October of the following year, 1781, he was involved in the arrangements for two marriages in quick succession. The first, the marriage of the daughter of a Tolchënov household serf, Sergei Osipov, to a young man of the town, was the more straightforward of the two and probably did not cost Ivan more than the future services of the woman and a nominal dowry or merely the woman's trousseau. The contract was settled on October 7 at Ivan's home, and the accompanying supper included Uncle Ivan Il'ich and his family, a cousin and frequent visitor Pëtr Alekseev Tolchënov and his family, and Fëdor Loshkin, a leading merchant, city official, and husband of Uncle Ivan's daughter, and his family. This set of people constituted a close inner circle, beyond Ivan's immediate household, who often participated in private family occasions. The wedding was celebrated two weeks later, and Ivan hosted a supper for relatives.[49]

The second marriage, which is referred to in the diary entry that opens this section, was more complicated, for it involved the remarriage of Ivan's stepmother. Remember that Ivan's mother died of consumption while living in Petersburg at the time her husband was serving on the Commission on Laws in 1768. Within fourteen months of her death, Ivan's father remarried, this time to a woman from the Moscow merchant family the Kholshchevnikovs. This woman, Mavra Petrovna, widowed by the death of Ivan's father in 1779, had now found a suitor and summoned Ivan to Moscow to manage the arrangements. Unlike the briefly described arrangements for the marriage of his servant woman, the negotiations leading up to his stepmother's wedding were lengthy, as were the celebrations that accompanied the wedding. The entire process occupied the better part of a month and offers a glimpse into a side of merchant life seldom illuminated before.

Ivan received the summons from his stepmother three days after the wedding of his servant in October 1781 and hastily departed for Moscow. He arrived on October 27 and the next day was "in consultations about the man who had made the proposal of marriage" to Mavra Petrovna. The suitor was Ivan Petrov Bykov, a Moscow merchant. By the following day it must have been clear that the negotiations were going to succeed, as Ivan sent word to his wife in Dmitrov that she should come to Moscow and bring their son Pëtr. In the meantime, Ivan busied himself in finding an apartment to rent for the wedding dinner, while also taking the opportunity to attend the theater and a wedding dinner of a friend. Autumn was the favorite season for weddings in Russia. On November 2, Ivan got together for a meeting with the groom Bykov and his friends that lasted until midnight. Here no doubt were worked out the arrangements for a dowry. First thing the next day, Ivan went to the Office of Deeds (*Krepostnaia kontora*), which handled property transfers, including the transfer and sale of serfs, and then again that evening Ivan met with the groom and the groom's brother until midnight. Property and financial arrangements must have been completed at this stage. The next few days were consumed in visits with in-laws and friends, and only once again with the groom and his brother. On the seventh Ivan's step-grandmother, Fedos'ia Mikhailovna Makarova, and his Uncle Ivan Il'ich arrived from Dmitrov. The next evening the two parties to the marriage met at Ivan's apartment to sign the official contract, and they and their guests stayed on and celebrated until midnight. On the eleventh Ivan went to the home of the groom for further "negotiations," lasting four hours. Unfortunately Ivan did not write about what the negotiations involved, although, to judge by the actions that immediately followed, they may have concerned the final timing of the dowry transfer. The next morning Ivan was at the Office of Deeds and then recorded that "at dusk I released the dowry and at 9 pm the wedding took place in the Church of the Resurrection of Christ in the Goncharsk region" southeast of Kitaigorod.

Now the festivities began in earnest. The wedding was followed by a large dinner and party at the home of the groom lasting deep into the night. Ivan and his wife did not get home until 1 am. The second day the newlyweds had dinner at the Tolchënovs' apartment, and in the evening everyone reconvened at the groom's house for supper and a ball that again went until midnight. Ivan got a break on the third day, which the newlyweds may have reserved for the groom's family, although Ivan stayed up until past midnight on a visit to a member of the Chief Magistracy, a government office of great importance for merchants. The fourth day found his family again in the role of host. They gave the final dinner of the wedding cycle, the *otvodnyi stol* or the meal hosted by the bride's family and associated with the movement of the married couple to their new lodgings.[50] This, too, was a big affair that included the new relatives and Ivan's friends and lasted until midnight. After this exhausting round of celebrations the Tolchënovs rested up for a couple of days in Moscow. Ivan used the time to pay one more visit to his favorite gardener, Beliaev. Then on the eighteenth the entire family rode back to Dmitrov. Ivan had spent twenty-three days in Moscow on this important family mission.[51]

Ivan recorded his participation in other marriages in the following years. A second daughter of his servant, Sergei Osipov, was betrothed in the Tolchënov home to a local townsman in October of 1784. Ivan noted the engagement ceremony in his diary. The wedding that followed the prescribed two-week interval does not appear in Ivan's diary entry, although he did mention it in his later summaries of events of the year.[52] Again, in 1786 two of Ivan's "people," Aleksei Ivanov and Mar'ia Larionova, were married. In this case, Ivan made no mention of a preceding betrothal agreement or any fuss over the wedding itself. The two household serfs being married evidently had no property worthy of a marriage contract. His guests that evening were the same close inner circle of Uncle Ivan Il'ich and Fëdor Loshkin and their families.[53]

Ivan will sponsor further marriages of members of his immediate family, marriages that reveal social changes occurring in the merchant estate and also something more of Ivan's aspirations. But these marriages belong to the period of time covered in a later chapter.

IVAN JOINS THE MAGISTRACY

[August, 1781] 24th At 7 in the morning I rode to the magistracy for the voting for local offices, which began after 10 am and continued until 2 in the afternoon. After dinner Uncle Ivan Il'ich visited me as did the wife of the district treasurer.

25th I spent the day at the magistracy for [more] voting. In the evening cousin Pëtr Alekseev visited me.

. . .

[December, 1781] 2nd In the morning I was summoned to the magistracy, where my election to burgomaster was announced and the edict about my entry into office was read; along with me were elected as magistracy councilors my cousin Ivan Ivanov Tolchënov and Mikhail Semënov Nemkov. We then repaired to the cathedral and there swore the usual oath, and, returning to the magistracy, we entered into our offices; in the evening I was visited by the voevoda and his family and the wife of the assessor, Mrs. Maslova, and her children. This evening [my step-uncle and ward] Andrei Fëdorovich returned from Petersburg.

3rd Before the dinner hour I was serving at the magistracy. At my house for dinner were the new and former officers of the magistracy; then the gardener Beliaev arrived from Moscow. In the evening we all visited Stepan Tiut'kin.

4th In the morning I was at the magistracy.[54]

For a prosperous small-city merchant, public service was difficult to avoid. Philanthropic activities were expected, and we have already seen some examples of Ivan's charitable work. Another area was service in the administrative offices of local self-government. On the one hand, merchants were expected to fill such positions, and they also had good reason to do so, for they needed to keep an eye on their business and family property interests that could be affected by the administrative process. Moreover, some positions could be filled only by merchants of a certain rank, and the number of eligible officeholders in a small city was limited. On the other hand, public service was risky. It robbed merchants of time and resources they needed to invest in their businesses if they were to prosper in a highly competitive market. We have seen in an earlier chapter that merchants sometimes had to step down from public office before their term ended in order to restore their financial position. The strain that municipal public service placed on merchant finances occasionally led to bankruptcy.[55]

Ivan, like his father, who had served on the Dmitrov magistracy and also represented the city at the Commission on Laws of 1767–1768, was certain to feel pressure to play a civic role and was unlikely to be able to escape participation in the political life of his town. But he could no doubt have delayed such an assignment for a time and worked with his relatives and business partners to ensure that someone they trusted would serve and keep an eye on their interests. Even so, Ivan decided to accept a position in public service within two years of his father's death. Considering that he was only twenty-seven years old, his decision to run for burgomaster may well have been a choice and not a response to an appeal pressed insistently on him by relatives and partners.

The 1770s and 1780s were a time of rapid political and administrative change in Russia. In the wake of the ferocious popular rebellion led by the Cossack pretender Emel'ian Pugachëv, Empress Catherine hurriedly completed her Law on Local Governance. Promulgated in 1775, this law sought to create a well-articulated judicial and administrative organization in the district towns to supplement and partially replace the undifferentiated executive, police, and judicial authority of the centrally appointed administrator (known as the *voevoda*). The voevoda system was an arrangement inherited from Muscovite Russia that had proved inadequate to the demands of the rapidly developing imperial Russian economy and society. The complaints of the delegates to the Commission on Laws about the deficiencies of the legal process, the under-administration and insecurity of the rural districts, the deterioration of natural resources such as forests, were underscored by the ravages of the Pugachëv Rebellion, which revealed the perilous lack of police and administrative offices through large stretches of the Volga basin and Ural Mountains. In essence, the standing army created by Peter I had been serving as the administrative and policing arm of the state in the provinces, where the army was billeted during peacetime. The officers acted as officials for the purposes of tax collection and military conscription. Soldiers did the footwork. If this arrangement functioned well enough to supply basic needs in peacetime, it was unworkable in time of war. War drew most of the domestic administration out of the towns at the very time it was most needed to furnish conscripts and revenue. All that remained of the domestic administration was a few widely scattered police officials. It was this vacuum of power that allowed Pugachëv and his followers to lay waste the Volga-Urals region and execute a large number of nobles while the army was away fighting in the Turkish War and pacifying Polish militias that resisted the partitioning of their republic. It was also the reason that the empress commanded local nobles and merchants to organize and finance their own local militias in a matter of days when the Pugachëv Rebellion threatened the central provinces.

Within a year of the end of the Pugachëv Rebellion Catherine announced her plan for reorganizing the local courts and administration into a multi-tiered system of district and provincial institutions staffed by elected representatives of the nobility. At the district level on which Dmitrov stood, these included a district court, a lower land court, and a noble guardianship, plus a surveyor, a medical doctor, and a few other technical specialists, offices and agents that were gradually introduced over the next several years. Since the personnel had to come principally from the members of the nobility who had retired to the provinces, the reform constituted a return of the emancipated nobility to state service. But few nobles protested this move to put them back in harness. After the sobering spectacle of death and destruction by the rebels, the instinct for self-preservation was sufficiently powerful to convince nobles of the need for a more stable and reliable domestic administration.

The structure of urban government was also changing, but less noticeably. The town elites continued to dominate decision making. They themselves were subject to intervention and sometimes angry recriminations from state authorities when the imperial government was pushing a specific policy or change that the town leaders did not agree with. But for the most part urban elites were left to their own devices in deciding local matters, such as whom to accept into the urban community and whom to elect to local office. The town magistracies settled conflicts between members of the urban commune, enforced contracts, and allocated taxes and other burdens among the townspeople. As time went on, the names of some offices changed and the number of offices expanded, but the same families of the local merchant elite continued to occupy the key positions.

One of the top city officials during Ivan's youth was Fëdor Loshkin. Married to Ivan's cousin, Matrëna Ivanovna (the daughter of Uncle Ivan Il'ich), Loshkin was an in-law, close family friend, and sometime business partner of the Tolchënovs. He had served as burgomaster on the magistracy. He was a frequent visitor at Ivan's home in the years following the death of Ivan's father, often appearing there with one or more of Ivan's uncles, men of the same age as Loshkin. These men must have discussed with Ivan many times his new role as head of the family and the family businesses and the need for him in these capacities to play a role in the politics of the urban community—if not right away, then in the future.

In the first year after his father's death Ivan did not get involved with local politics or even pursue many contacts with the district nobility, something that he later obviously enjoyed. He made occasional visits to the estates of the Golitsyn family northeast of the city, including the Danilovskoe estate of Prince Ivan Fëdorovich Golitsyn, which later became a site of frequent visits by him, and the Peresvetovo estate of Prince Sergei Mikhailovich Golitsyn, from whom the Tolchënovs rented a mill and purchased grain. It will be recalled that he was invited to Peresvetovo for a dinner in connection with a hunt as early as September of 1780, and the next year he joined the hunt itself at Danilovskoe. But these outings were unusual for this period. The noble family with which Ivan and his wife socialized most frequently at this time was the Obreskovs, the family of a retired guards captain who lived on the heights of Shpilëvo just south of the city. Ivan's father and mother seem to have been close to the Obreskovs, and Ivan was probably just continuing an established connection. This friendship, which did not seem to have a political dimension, was reinforced in mutual hospitality that continued long after the retired captain died suddenly in 1781. The Tolchënovs visited with the Obreskov widow and her growing children for many years thereafter (a connection that would eventually have some important business payoffs for Ivan). Typical of the kind of outing this young merchant and the Obreskovs enjoyed was a day trip in early October 1780 to the highly praised porcelain factory north of the city owned by Franz Gardner. A few days later, Ivan and his wife took her Moscow relatives to visit the same factory, after which they threw a dinner for them, the Obreskovs, and another local noble, Squire Pëtr Khitrovo. Perhaps Ivan wished to show off for his in-laws his acquaintances among the local nobility. But for now this type of socializing was limited to a few people and occasions. Ivan's political participation was even less remarkable, consisting of obligatory attendance at a couple of meetings of the city's general assembly (*obshchestvennyi sovet*). In 1780 Ivan concentrated on organizing his personal life, adapting to his new role as head of the family and its businesses, and cultivating his interest in gardens.

The following year brought a change. Early in February the magistracy delegated Ivan to accompany the mayor of Dmitrov to Moscow to present the town's good wishes to the new governor-general of Moscow province, Nikolai Arkharov. Although Ivan did not yet occupy an official position, he must have enjoyed the trust of his fellow merchants and exhibited the type of personality that they knew would make a good impression for the town. This assignment led to a return visit from the new governor-general when he toured the northern districts of Moscow province a few months later and dropped in on Ivan. Ivan's unusually detailed diary entries about the visit reveal how flattered he was by the attention:

[June] 9th I remained at home in anticipation of the arrival, announced in advance, of Governor-General Nikolai Petrovich Arkharov, who at 9 pm actually drove directly to my house. In his suite were Colonel and Member of the Economic Collegium Ivan Semënovich Litvinov, Provincial Treasurer Andrei Ivanovich Zverev, the architect Mr. Osipov, and others.

10th In the morning the governor inspected the city and government offices, and I was invited to join him for dinner. Afterwards the governor left for the porcelain factory—to which I also rode at his pleasure. I returned at dusk.

11th After dinner, the governor departed for the Trinity Monastery.[56]

On some of Ivan's subsequent trips to Moscow, he made what were evidently return courtesy calls on the governor-general.

   It is hard to know whether Ivan sought this assignment to represent his town before the governor-general or whether it came to him unbidden, but it obviously left a strong impression. He enjoyed associating with the powerful and well born and, to judge by his diary entries, drew a significant portion of his identity from such associations. Although this particular experience as a representative to the governor-general may not have been determining, from this point onward Ivan began to play an active role in politics and government. As can be seen in the diary excerpt at the start of this section, later the same month, August 1781, he recorded his presence at the balloting for local administrative offices, at which time he must have won election as first burgomaster, for toward the end of the year, when he returned from a trip to his Volga mills and a harrowing on-foot river crossing over thin ice, he was summoned to the magistracy to be inducted into this office. At the same time, two councilors were installed, one of whom, Ivan noted, was his cousin Ivan Ivanovich Tolchënov. The second was Mikhail Nemkov, a member of another prominent merchant family. They then took the oath of office at the cathedral and got down to work. The same evening Ivan hosted the voevoda and his family and Mrs. Maslova, wife of the district treasurer, and her children.[57] Even before his entry into office, Ivan was beginning to cultivate some of the political elite. For example, in late September he had hosted a dinner for the voevoda and Prince Nikolai Petrovich Obolenskii, brother of a newly elected judge of the district court.[58] Obolenskii with time became one of Ivan's closest acquaintances, and they and their families exchanged many visits.[59] Ivan's role in the administration of his town invited him into a wider social circle that included the central government officials and the officers of the new estate-elective courts in his district.

   Ivan's new position in the town and district elite and the responsibilities of his office became clear in the first year of his service, 1782, which proved to be quite eventful. His trips to Moscow now included calls on officials of the Chief Magistracy, which supervised the affairs of the town magistracies of the entire central region of the country. He was also personally closer than before to officials, clerics, and nobles at every level, and even served as godfather for the son of a district collegiate assessor, a member of the nobility. We see him consulting with such people ahead of important meetings of the town general assembly and city council. On June 3, after attending a religious procession to pray for the end of a drought, Ivan hosted a gathering of the town's two magistracy councilors and his Uncle Mikhaila and the mayor, Ivan Tugarinov, a meeting that may have been in anticipation of a visit later that month by a planning commission that was to redesign the city streets and arrange for a replatting of the entire town, a major and threatening disruption of the city's life. Ivan understood the importance of this visit for the future of the city and spent a lot of time with the members of the planning group and especially with its leader, Lieutenant-Colonel Shchelin, despite other important work he had to attend to, such as the consecration of a new magistracy building constructed to replace one that had burned to the ground the previous year. Ivan's diary entries record his attention to Shchelin and effort to guide the planning work during the five days the commission resided in Dmitrov.

[June] 20th In the morning I was with Lieutenant-Colonel Shchelin . . . and then at the magistracy. And in the afternoon Mr. Shchelin was at my house.

21st Mr. Shchelin and his officers dined at my house and stayed until evening.

22nd In the morning I was at the magistracy and after dinner I visited Mr. Shchelin, took him for a walk around the city and for a visit to Fëdor Loshkin.

23rd I heard mass at the cathedral, and after that there was a consecration of the free-standing building constructed for the magistracy, and it was the first time I had been in it. In the afternoon I visited Mr. Shchelin and went fishing with him in the river close to the floating bridge, and then we visited Mayor Tugarinov.

24th I heard mass at the Annunciation Church and then was with Mr. Shchelin, and in the evening he came to my house to visit with Uncle Mikhaila Il'ich and Fëdor Loshkin.

25th In the morning I was with Mr. Shchelin, who at 9 am departed from the city.[60]

Unfortunately, Ivan failed to tell us what his friends and associates discussed with the lieutenant-colonel. The redesign of the city, as we shall see, was a project of enormous consequence for the townspeople. Were Ivan and the others using this opportunity to urge Shchelin to minimize the disruption of their community? In Ivan's own case, we can be sure that he conferred about the location of a new house for his family. Plans for this home were already in gestation, and Ivan later recorded that he sited it in accordance with the street pattern developed from Shchelin's survey.

Two months later, in August 1782, Ivan had the heady task of entertaining the powerful military governor of Moscow and former president of the state War Collegium, Count Zakhar Chernyshëv. He first heard about the projected visit on August 14 when his wife Anna was desperately ill. Even so, he had to get to work on preparations. The importance of this visit can be judged by the speed and anxiety with which Ivan, amid other worries, rushed to fulfill his responsibilities. For example, the news of Chernyshëv's impending arrival in Dmitrov reached Ivan just after he had returned from the yearly requiem mass in remembrance of his father. He learned that Chernyshëv was to arrive that evening, August 17, and was coming from the Trinity Monastery. Ivan had to quickly gather the top merchants of the town and transport them to a village on the southeast approaches to the city in hopes of meeting Chernyshëv and his entourage en route from the monastery. However, no doubt much to Ivan's relief, it turned out that Chernyshëv had diverted to the Danilovskoe estate of

Prince Ivan Golitsyn northeast of the city to stay overnight, and Ivan could spend the evening making final preparations for the visit. Luckily, his wife Anna had just started to show some improvement, reducing another source of concern.

At dawn, Ivan, together with the voevoda and the town magistracy councilors, headed off to Danilovskoe to greet the count, whom they met at 7 am. Ivan recorded in the diary that "we all immediately rode back to town and were received by the assembled merchants at 8 am at the entry to Birch Street. The count continued directly to the cathedral and from there to the chancery and the storeroom. As he exited the storeroom, he announced his intention to visit me, and we proceeded on foot to my house while discussing commerce and other matters. Arriving at my house were Chamberlain Prince Mikhail Vasil'evich Dolgorukii, Actual State Councilor Pëtr Nikitich Kozhin, and General Adjutant Ivan Petrovich Turgenev. The count was kind enough to stay for a half hour, having tea, and the others also vodka, and then got in a carriage and rode to the magistracy and from there to have a look at the new chambers for the government offices." During this entire time, Ivan was also housing in-laws from Moscow, including two of Anna's sisters, who must have been helping in her care. After the departure of Chernyshëv and, two days later, his Moscow relatives, Ivan rode out to Prince Golitsyn's estate "to thank him for the recommendation."[61] Ivan understood that Chernyshëv's attentions to him were prompted by Golitsyn's endorsement, something that no doubt drew Ivan closer to Golitsyn as time went on.

Life for Ivan was becoming busy and interesting. A week after the Chernyshëv visit he went with his eight-year-old son Pëtr on a five-day trip to check on his north mills and the barges being readied for the late summer caravan of grain to Petersburg. Ivan then took his wife and two sons to Moscow for recreation and visits with in-laws. Ivan visited the orangeries of his gardener friend Beliaev and of Squire Khitrovo twice, and made single visits to those of Demidov and the merchant Makarov. They also attended what Ivan still called the Znamenskii Theater (although after a fire in 1780 that had destroyed it, the structure was rebuilt as the Petrovskii Theater and was also known as the Medoks Theater).[62] Ivan twice called on the governor-general, checked in with a secretary of the Chief Magistracy, visited a Moscow merchant, and, before leaving the big city, purchased flower bulbs for his gardens back home—a full schedule for a five-day stay.

At home more responsibilities awaited him. As mentioned in chapter 2, it was at this time that the new centrally appointed police commissioner (*gorodnichii*) was assigned to Dmitrov and its surrounding district. This was the key representative of the imperial government in the localities, a powerful figure and a replacement in many respects for the voevoda, a position that was being phased out in connection with the introduction of the local government re-

forms announced by Empress Catherine in 1775. The appointee, Anton Letstsano, arrived on September 16, 1782, and Ivan immediately went to him for an
"official visit," which Letstsano returned the very next morning. A few days later
Ivan rode out to the estate of Prince Ivan Golitsyn for mass and dinner, at which
time he no doubt sought his agreement to attend a dinner that Ivan planned to
host two days later in connection with the annual fair and to introduce the new
police commissioner to the town elite. Ivan's entry for the day of the dinner
proudly recorded that "today dining at my home were Prince Ivan Fëdorovich
Golitsyn, the police commissioner, the voevoda and other government officials,
and the top merchants, and they stayed until 4 in the afternoon, and then we
strolled through the lanes of booths at the fair. Afterward, I visited with the
voevoda and then with the district treasurers Nazimov and Lopatkin." These
activities were merely a prelude to ceremonies and celebrations the next month
for the official introduction of the local government reforms in Dmitrov. In the
meantime, Ivan and his extended family went on their annual pilgrimage to the
village church of Vedernitsy and its miracle-working icon along the road to
Rogachëvo west of town.

    The next month, October 1782, the new offices of local government pro-
jected in Empress Catherine's decree of 1775 were introduced into Moscow
province, starting early in the month in the city of Moscow "with great fanfare,"
as Ivan wrote in his later annual summary, and then proceeding to the district
centers. Ivan was in town for the entire month, busy at his usual civic and social
tasks. He put in his hours at the magistracy and the town market, attended a
christening dinner for the child of his cousin, one of the town councilors, and
served as godfather for the child of another merchant, all the while keeping up a
steady round of visiting and hosting with the new police commissioner, the
district treasurer, and his uncles. Then on October 20 Naval Captain First Class
Vasilii Nikitich Kurmanaleev arrived in Dmitrov to conduct the ceremonies
prescribed for the election and opening of the new government offices. Ivan
reported that this important naval official lodged at his home during his stay,
and the diary entries described the scene.

*On the morning of the 21st the police commissioner and the new judges from
the nobility visited with Kurmanaleev and then heard mass at the cathedral. In
the chambers of the magistracy balloting took place among the merchant and
lesser townsmen estates for the mayor, the magistracy, and other local offices, at
which I was again elected first burgomaster. I had dinner with the district judge
Prince Ivan Petrovich Obolenskii and then returned to the balloting through the
evening.*[63]

The elections for local offices in Dmitrov usually took a great deal of time,
lasting deep into the evening and sometimes into the wee hours of the morning.
A lot of offices had to be filled, including those charged with maintaining the

salt and other common provisions of the town, and maneuverings to obtain or escape these duties could sometimes be quite intense. In this case, possibly because of the unusual attention of the central authorities, the balloting extended only through the evening. The next day, the local offices were opened "with a prescribed ceremony that was new to our city," Ivan wrote. The officials and Ivan then rode out to the Danilovskoe estate to have dinner as guests of Prince Ivan Golitsyn. The following day, it was Ivan Tolchënov's turn to play host to the elite, and he wrote that dining at his house were "Prince Ivan Fëdorovich Golitsyn, Mr. Kurmanaleev, Prince Obolenskii, the police commissioner, and all the district judges and most prominent merchants." Although this dinner brought the festivities connected with the opening of the government offices to a close, a new relationship between the merchants and nobles of the district had begun to develop, and the attention merchants were receiving from state officials and the nobility seemed to foster in the leading commercial people a consciousness of themselves as a social group whose importance was recognized and who could take pride in their contributions to the economy and society.

In Russia, where the private and public spheres were not conceptually delineated and distinct, political interactions were also social interactions, and an increase in the number of government offices necessarily expanded social contacts. The introduction of new administrative and judicial instances created a social bond across the town and district elite that continued to grow. Two pillars of this relationship were obviously Prince Ivan Golitsyn, the marshal of the local nobility, and Ivan Tolchënov, the first burgomaster and most visible merchant. Their respective roles brought them into a close and frequent social relationship.

We can see the change the very next month, November 1782. It started with Ivan going out to the estate of Prince Ivan Golitsyn for dinner and staying on until dusk.[64] Back home in Dmitrov Ivan almost daily hosted or visited with either the police commissioner or district treasurer. Other occasions included the officials of the new courts. On the ninth of November, he noted that "in the evening I hosted Prince Obolenskii and his children and nearly all of the judges of the district." Then on the twenty-first he took advantage of the feast of the Presentation of the Virgin (probably because of its association with the church his family had endowed) to invite an impressive list of guests for dinner. "Dining at my home and staying until the evening were Prince Obolenskii, all the nobles of the town, and the most prominent merchants, altogether more than 30 persons." This crowd was large enough that it challenged the Tolchënov household's supply of china, for Ivan recorded in his diary the next day that "I spent a short time at the magistracy in the morning and then rode out to [the porcelain factory at] Verbilki for the purchase of china plates and dishes."

As for Prince Golitsyn, although he had moved to Moscow for the winter,

Ivan continued to drop in on him when he traveled to the city on business. When Golitsyn returned to his Danilovskoe estate the next summer, Ivan's visits for Sunday mass and dinner become a frequent affair. In the next two summers he visited there at least once a month. By 1785, the frequency had increased. Ivan was out to the Danilovskoe estate for dinner with Golitsyn once in March, twice in May, twice in July, once in August, once in September, twice in October, and once in November.

WIFE AND CHILDREN

[April, 1784] 18th At 7 in the morning my wife and both children [Pëtr and Aleksei] left for Moscow. We ate dinner in Sholokhovo, and at 7 in the evening we arrived at the apartment I had rented at the Nikitskii Gate from a priest at the Ascension Church, Father Antipa.

19th In the morning I visited Prince Ivan Fëdorovich Golitsyn. After dinner I was in the city and other places. In the evening Vandashnikov and Kaftannikov [in-laws of Ivan's wife] visited us.

20th In the morning we took our son Pëtr Ivanovich to the school [pansion] run by the teacher Horn. Afterwards I visited the governor and Prince Obolenskii and after dinner I was in the city and with [the architect] Agafonov.

21st [Sunday] At the beginning I was at the home of Prince Ivan Fëdorovich. Then at the Dormition Cathedral to hear Mass and prayers. After dinner I visited the orangeries of Beliaev and then went to the theater.

22nd I spent the morning in the city. Had dinner at Vandashnikov's and then rode to the Demidov orangeries.

23rd In the morning I went with my wife to Dr. Ferzeksh, and then until 2 o'clock stayed in the city, and in the evening at the apartment.

24th At 6 in the morning my wife and Lëniushka left for home, and Petrusha remained in Moscow for his studies and was living with my father-in-law Aleksei Ivanovich.[65]

An ideal paterfamilias was also a devoted husband, at least in the merchant estate, if we can judge from the small amount of evidence for this era. The kind of open marriages and permissive sexuality that characterized the court nobility was not apparent in merchant families. For his part, Ivan eagerly took on the role of devoted husband. It is worth recalling the laments of his younger years about his long absences from home. This was when his father was still alive and dispatched him from one end of Russia to the other for work in the family grain trade. He marked these days on the road as "days separated from my wife." Although his marriage to Anna had been arranged, Ivan clung to her and looked after her as strongly as if he had chosen her himself.

When, after the death of his father, Ivan was free to dispose of his time as he liked, he stayed closer to home and to Anna. He still had to travel frequently, but his trips defined a much smaller area. From Dmitrov he would journey north to the family's mills near the Volga and south to Moscow, travels requiring no more than a day or two on the road. In both cases, the trips were for recreation and socializing as well as for business. Throughout the 1780s Anna was often his companion on these trips. Although quick trips to the north mills to check on the grain processing and barge loading did not include her, each summer the entire family took an extended vacation at the mills. Much of this vacation time Ivan and Anna spent socializing with extended family members who also had mills in the area and with neighboring landowners and others who were also escaping to the countryside for relaxation. Anna likewise accompanied Ivan on many of his trips to Moscow, where she visited with her relatives and joined Ivan on trips to the theater and to parties.

While they could enjoy these activities together, Anna may have found them to be only brief distractions in what was an otherwise difficult time in her life, filled with personal losses and sorrow. Soon after the burial of her father-in-law in 1779, she gave birth to her fourth child, Aleksei, amid the disruption caused by this sudden death and the reorganization of the household under the authority of her husband. This meant that she, too, had to take on much enlarged responsibilities as the mistress of the house. At the same time, her own mother, who lived in Moscow, began to suffer "severe fevers," a scourge that afflicted her for a half year and led to her death in late April of 1780. Ivan, Anna, and their son Pëtr had traveled to Moscow in the first days of that April to visit Anna's ailing mother (though Ivan did not fail to visit Demidov's orangeries at the same time). The news of the mother's death reached the Tolchënovs on Easter Saturday, just ten days after their return to Dmitrov. As soon as Easter Mass finished the next day, Ivan and Anna rode again for ten hours without stops to her family in Moscow so that they could attend the funeral the next day.[66] A month later Anna returned to Moscow on her own for observance of the forty days following the death of her mother, while Ivan stayed in Dmitrov to participate in the religious procession from the Dormition Cathedral to Prophet Elijah Church to pray for good weather during the summer growing and transport season.

Early the next year, 1781, Anna gave birth to a daughter and lost her to death after two and a half months. At the start of 1782, Anna again gave birth, this time to a son, Vasilii, and lost him as well after two weeks. This sort of loss was taken in stride by Russian families of this era, but it must have been painful for a mother. In the middle of the same year, 1782, the Tolchënov household was shaken by a senseless murder next door, when two brothers got into a fight and one killed the other. Not long after in August Anna got sick with an infection that nearly caused her death. "It started with a pain in her tooth," Ivan recorded, "and then led to shooting pains in the right ear and cheek, with a fever." For several days the infection intensified, and the family feared for her life. But after a week of torment, Ivan could report with relief that "by the grace of God my wife's illness began to subside."[67]

Worse came for Anna the following year. Early in March 1783 her sister Mar'ia Kaftannikova died in Moscow from what Ivan described as consumption and fevers following a premature birth. Ivan was in Moscow at the time on business and was lodging at the Kaftannikovs'. The end was nearing when he had to depart for home, "leaving [Mar'ia] with a severe illness and no hope of recovery." The news of her death reached him shortly thereafter at the inn where he was staying on the way home.[68] Anna and he did not go to Moscow for the funeral, perhaps because she was expecting another baby herself. This child, a daughter, Aleksandra, was born in April and survived for only thirty-eight days. Three days after the burial of Aleksandra, and perhaps to get their minds off this loss, Ivan and Anna traveled to Moscow, visited relatives, strolled in Count Sheremetev's beautiful suburban estate of Kuskovo, and went to see some of the city's orangeries.[69]

Despite this reprieve, the year still held further emotional shocks for Anna. In the fall, tragedy again struck her natal family. In late September, while Ivan was at the north mills supervising the loading of the fall grain barges, he recorded that "I received the urgent news of the unexpected death in Moscow of my sister-in-law Vera, and because of this I hastened my departure for home. I left at 11 am and, without stopping except to stay overnight in Prigary, . . . I reached home at 11 [the next] morning." Anna's sister Vera was barely twenty-three years old and unmarried when she died without warning.[70] Ivan must have understood that the death of this young sister after so many other recent losses was going to throw Anna into despair. He dropped everything and rushed home to be at her side. And Ivan continued to be solicitous of Anna's health in subsequent months. Although committed to be at the magistracy daily, on December 12 he recorded that "because of the illness of my wife, I did not leave home today. Aunt Marina Semënovna came to visit."[71] Aunt Marina, not a frequent visitor, was evidently summoned especially to provide care and companionship to Anna.

This difficult year for Anna seems to have brought the couple closer. From this time forward through the 1780s the diary records Anna more often than before in company with Ivan in their socializing in the city of Dmitrov and adjoining country estates and on trips to Moscow and to various vacation spots and shrines in the surrounding area. Ivan's desire to keep Anna close may have stemmed from the experience of losing his own mother at an early age after her many personal losses.

If devotion to the well-being of one's wife was a responsibility of the paterfamilias, another was the education of his children. Ivan took special care of the education of his first son, Pëtr. In these early years, he still had the means to provide the best, and he arranged for Pëtr to attend an expensive private school (*pansion*) in Moscow. It will be recalled that Ivan himself received the more traditional home schooling of a merchant son. Judging from his own retelling, he learned reading and writing without a regular teacher and mostly on his own. His father stepped in to guide him through the rules of arithmetic. After that, his education consisted of practical experience in the family grain trade both locally and on the road, except for a break of a few months in Petersburg in 1768 when his father placed him with a monk from the local seminary for advanced training in geography. This type of training, home schooling followed by an apprenticeship in the family business, was the norm for merchants in this period.[72]

Efforts to get the sons of Russian merchants a formal education in commercial skills had begun as early as Peter the Great's reign. The government launched a program in 1723 on the model of Peter I's own example of studying European techniques in Europe. The plan was to send at least fifteen sons of merchants abroad for study. A number of candidates were summoned to Petersburg for consideration, but the plan faltered when officials discovered that none of the boys knew enough German or arithmetic to benefit from study abroad, and the candidates were sent home.[73] Later, books on commerce began to appear but languished without adequate sales. For example, a series of lectures on trade by Jacques Savary, published in French as early as 1675, came out in a Russian edition in 1747 in a press run of 1,200 copies on the initiative of a government office, the Commerce Collegium. Despite encouragement to merchants to purchase the book, four years later only 112 copies had been sold. When the government, chastened by this experience, next sponsored a similar publication, it limited the press run to 400 copies.[74] About twenty other books on commerce appeared in the second half of the eighteenth century in Russia, but they too did not enjoy strong sales. It is likewise worth remembering that the commercial school established by Catherine II in Moscow in the 1770s failed to attract many students from the merchant estate.[75]

Merchant fathers seem to have fallen into one of two groups. The largest number no doubt reasoned that a liberal education was more likely to alienate their sons from the commercial life than to make them happy and successful at it. These fathers considered a practical introduction to business the proper training for their boys. Indeed, as late as 1846 an advice book by a merchant appeared in which he prided himself on this approach and recommended it. "I have a foundation in practice and not in theory. Commerce demands exclusively a resolute and more practical understanding of its ideas than a theoretical one."[76] In contrast, merchants who aspired to a life more cultivated than was typical for this group and who wished to associate with the educated nobility, whether or not they themselves had hopes of rising into the nobility, sought for their children the new liberal education with its emphasis on a broad knowledge of history, geography, foreign languages, and comportment. And this was the ideal increasingly promoted by the government and educational authorities in Catherine II's reign for nobles and merchants alike. The first thorough development of this model came from Empress Catherine's adviser on education, Ivan Betskoi, the author of a number of educational manuals and plans, including most prominently a tract titled "The Education of Youth of Both Sexes."[77] The commercial school mentioned earlier was also designed by Betskoi (and constructed with financing from the philanthropist Prokofii Demidov, the same person who owned the elaborate orangeries described earlier). It is curious that, despite Demidov's love of botany, he did not agree with Betskoi about the advantages of a broad curriculum of liberal arts and sciences for merchants and argued for a purely professional program of studies at the commercial school. In a classic dialogue between the humanist and the technician, Betskoi rejected Demidov's view and contended that his own approach would contribute to the spread of enlightenment in the country and prepare students for other walks of life should they shift their career goals from commerce.[78] As it happened, the dispute had little impact on merchant education. Most Moscow-area merchants of the time who wanted something beyond home schooling for their children avoided the commercial school, possibly because of its close physical association with the Moscow Foundling Home, and opted instead for European-type schools that emphasized languages and culture.[79] It was this broad liberal education that Ivan sought for his son Pëtr.

After checking with his friends in Moscow, Ivan decided on a school run by a Prussian immigrant, Johann Christian Horn. Pëtr had been schooled at home and gained some practical experience by accompanying his father on business trips. His entry into formal education at the Horn Pansion at the age of nine was a big event for the family. As the diary entries quoted at the start of this section reveal, Ivan, Anna, and their younger son Aleksei went along to Moscow in April 1784 to see Pëtr off. The family took residence in an apartment by the Nikitskii Gate on the west side of Moscow that Ivan had begun to rent from a priest of the Ascension Church and that would become the family's base in the old capital. The trip was also an occasion for the usual round of visits to Anna's family and other in-laws, and for official stops to see the governor of Moscow province and the marshal of the Dmitrov nobility, Prince Ivan Golitsyn, as well as for Ivan's trips to orangeries, consultations with an architect about plans for a new home, and attendance at the theater. In addition, he and Anna stopped in to see a medical doctor, Dr. Ferzeksh, possibly to consult on medicines for Anna.[80] But the main purpose of the trip was to install Pëtr in school.

We know something about this school because the very next year after Pëtr began his studies there Empress Catherine ordered a review of the private schools that had recently sprung up in Moscow. In response to her directive, the governor-general of Moscow, Count Iakov Brius, formed a commission composed of two members of the Office of Social Welfare, two scholarly clerics appointed by the Orthodox Church, and two professors from Moscow University. Their assignment was to learn whether instruction in the schools was being done by qualified teachers and whether "superstitious" ideas were being purveyed. In regard to the school Pëtr Tolchënov was attending, the commission reported that Johann Horn had obtained the proper certification from the university to operate a pansion and that its student body consisted of sixteen boys and seven girls. Interestingly, the entire contingent of girls was of non-Russian Orthodox faiths (*inovernye*), presumably of Protestant or Catholic background. The commission report noted that "the children were making good progress in French and German, especially the girls. . . . In geography, history, and Latin and Russian languages, and likewise in the catechism of each student's confession they responded to questions well, except for the Russians, of which there were only six, and they did not know their catechism."[81]

The last observation is interesting but not surprising. As mentioned in chapter 1, teaching of the catechism was not common in Russia before the mid-nineteenth century, as we know from the frequent urgings of the Holy Synod that it should become more so. Ivan himself evidently did not receive training in the rules of his faith, as he commented on other aspects of his education but said nothing about catechism. In the journal as a whole, while he unfailingly recorded his attendance at church and visits to and from clergy of every rank, he did not make any remarks about doctrine or the rules of his faith. On rare occasions he mentioned the topic of a sermon (and then only those delivered by a bishop or metropolitan) but included nothing of substance about the sermon. Given this background, it is little wonder that the Russian students at Horn's school scored poorly on religious education.

To return to the report on Moscow private schools, while the commissioners did not find any evidence of "superstition, corruption, or temptation" at the Horn school, they observed disapprovingly that the boys and girls were being taught together in the same room and recommended that they be given instruction separately. They also noted that "the Russian language teacher was not qualified or competent to teach children" and should be replaced.[82] Indeed, the certification for teaching that Horn received from Moscow University in August of 1780 cleared him for the teaching of German and French and a number of non-language subjects, but not for teaching Russian.[83]

Pëtr continued his studies at this and another private school for several years and was no doubt one of Russia's best educated merchants by the time he finished. This investment in him may have helped the family when it fell on difficult times. Pëtr remained in the merchant estate even after his father had fallen to the rank of lesser town dweller.

*   *   *

After adjusting to the sudden and unexpected death of his father, Ivan got thoroughly and enthusiastically into his new life as head of his wealthy and prominent family. He seemed to enjoy his responsibilities for arranging the personal affairs of members of his household and participating in the rituals of marriage, birth, and death of his extended family and friends. The amount of time and effort that went into these matters was remarkable and indicates the centrality of these practices to the maintenance of community and a sense of control these Russians sought to exercise over their lives. Ivan also continued the philanthropic work of his father and grandfather, contributions that were expected of wealthy merchants and that they themselves understood as a payment for the blessings that God had bestowed on them. He likewise took on important civic responsibilities by becoming a member of the city magistracy. And much sooner than Ivan could have imagined he was free to indulge the tastes he had been acquiring for a life of elegance. As he threw himself into projects to beautify his life, he also inscribed his new circumstances in his diary, carefully noting the people and places he visited and the guests who came to him, which included an increasingly elite mix of officials, landed nobles, and clerics, in addition to his fellow merchants.

This life of a prominent citizen in the bosom of his family was enormously satisfying. But it kept Ivan from attending closely to his business interests and to the profitable grain trade on which his local position ultimately rested. His aspiration to a different kind of life from his father's disciplined commercial activity, supplemented by civic leadership, was turned around in Ivan's case. Civic leadership and the entrée it was giving him to the social elite of his district exerted such a strong pull on him that he had little time left for the close supervision of his business enterprises.

5

Leading Citizen

In this year [1785] I began the construction of a masonry home. First, in April the entire family moved from the wooden residence that my father built in 1774 on the street to the old, tall wooden residence in the yard, and the former home was taken apart and transported to Birch Street on the land that had been purchased from Sergei Voropanov for the construction of the [new] home. On the same spot we constructed the two-story masonry building with a mezzanine on the side facing the yard. The ditches were dug starting on the 23rd and the foundation laid on the 27th of May. The masonry construction was finished on September 15, and then during the autumn they did the beams and rafters and the lathing, and covered the top with iron roofing sheets. And all the rooms were fitted out with wooden floors and ceilings.[1]

Ivan's position as a government and business leader propelled him toward an ever more expansive personal life. The major physical expression of his status and aspirations was a large new home constructed of brick and finished on the outside in stucco in the style of the finest noble townhouses. Although his father had bought land on the west side of town as early as 1776, probably as an eventual site for a home for Ivan and his growing family, plans for the specific design of a new house began to take shape only after the father's death and Ivan's rise to prominence in his city.[2] It was in October of 1783 that Ivan initiated a relationship with the Moscow architect Mikhailo Iakovlev Agafonov, whom he invited to dine at his home in Dmitrov. Ivan may have become acquainted with Agafonov at the estate of Prince Ivan Golitsyn; the architect had designed buildings for the prince's estate at Danilovskoe.[3] From January through July of the following year Ivan met with Agafonov at least once a month, alternating the visits between Moscow and Dmitrov, as plans for the

Exterior of Ivan Tolchënov's masonry house in Dmitrov.

new home gradually developed. At the same time, Ivan began to make trips out to the brickyard at the Danilovskoe estate, evidently to arrange for the production of materials for the home.[4]

The consultations with Agafonov often included Ivan's wife Anna and sometimes other family members as well. Ivan must have considered the house a collaborative affair that concerned other members of the family just as much as him. And the consultations usually involved socializing, as business and social life in Russia habitually merged. Agafonov's visits to Dmitrov included dinner with the Tolchënovs. In Moscow, Ivan and Anna would sometimes dine at the Agafonovs', or on occasion Ivan would host a dinner in the capital, as he did in early June of 1784, when he invited Anna's sister along with Agafonov and his wife. This was just after the entire family had returned from a pilgrimage to the Savin Monastery west of Moscow and the New Jerusalem church complex built by the reforming patriarch of the seventeenth century, Nikon, where they had seen impressive structures whose features Ivan may have wished to discuss with Agafonov; for in addition to working on the Tolchënov townhouse, Agafonov was designing the bell tower for the Presentation Church mentioned in the previous chapter as another of Ivan's contributions to this shrine that his father and grandfather had built.

By the time the weather broke the next year, 1785, everything was in place to start the new home for the Tolchënovs. In late May workers dug the foundation and laid the cornerstone. Around the same time, Ivan was again making frequent trips to the brickyard, evidence that he was closely involved in mobilizing resources and supervising the project. In his year-end summary for 1785,

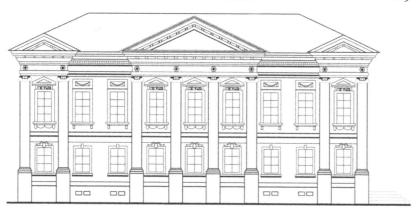

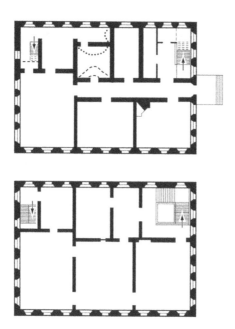

Exterior elevation and floor plan of the Tolchënov house.

quoted at the start of this section, Ivan described the family's preparations and the progress of the work on the new home. They had moved out of the wooden house that his father had built along the street in 1774 and taken up residence in an older, taller home that stood in the back yard. The home built in 1774 was then dismantled and moved to Birch Street, where he placed it on the land purchased for the new home. It was on that property, bordered by Birch Street and Klin Road, that the two-story masonry home was erected.[5] As Ivan noted,

Interior of a room in the wing of the Tolchënov house.

most of the basic construction work was completed by the end of the year. The
finishing of the inside then took up much of the following year.

In the meantime Ivan continued his routines of serving at the magistracy,
entertaining local officials, and taking short trips to Moscow to conduct business, dispatch agents and money for grain purchases, and visit with friends,
relatives, and officials. Now that he had an apartment in the old capital, Ivan
often took the family along so that they could visit with their son Pëtr. The trips
invariably included as well stops at Moscow orangeries and evenings at the
theater. Ivan's trips to the north mills to supervise the work there continued,
too, but were less frequent and shorter in duration than the Moscow visits.

The time was also punctuated by the occasional introduction of new offices
and visits to Dmitrov by state dignitaries. The spring and summer were especially busy, starting in May 1785 with the sitting of the district court, where
Prince Ivan Golitsyn presided as the chairman of the district nobility. He then
joined Ivan Tolchënov, the police commissioner, and a number of judges at
Ivan's for dinner. The next day Golitsyn returned the favor by inviting Ivan for
dinner at Danilovskoe. This was the year Empress Catherine promulgated her
new charters of the nobility and of the towns, defining the rights of the privileged estates. In the case of the towns this meant the institution of new offices,
and Ivan spent four days in mid-June preparing and then participating in the
election of persons for these positions. A few days later the town was favored by

Front entry staircase of the Tolchënov house.

a visit from Count Fëdor Andreevich Osterman, the former governor of Moscow province, who was taking his family on a pilgrimage to the shrine at Vedernitsy. On a previous such trip in 1777 Osterman had stayed in the Tolchënov home, but as the Tolchënovs were now temporarily in an old wooden house in their yard, the governor's family was lodged in the rooms of another merchant, Prokofii Tiut'kin, then an agent for the Tolchënov firm. Neverthe-less Ivan played the central role in receiving the governor, as he reported in the diary:

I was at home in the morning, and all the town officials rode over to my place to await the count's return from Vedernitsy. On his arrival . . . to Tiut'kin's, I and the others met him. After dinner the count and everyone else went for a stroll in my garden and orangeries, and then at 5 in the evening he left for Moscow.[6]

Less than two weeks later, when Ivan was in Moscow with his wife and children having dinner with his in-laws and the architect Agafonov, he received an urgent message about the impending visit of Pëtr Vasil'evich Lopukhin, the civil governor of Moscow province. (Catherine's administrative reforms had divided the former Moscow governorship into two offices: a civil governor and a military governor or commandant.) Dropping everything, Ivan left at four in the morning "traveled alone, without baggage and making no stops and arrived at eleven the same morning." Unfortunately for Ivan, although he dressed for the occasion and waited patiently all day with his friend Prince Obolenskii, the governor did not appear until the next day, when Ivan and other officials met him at the west end of town by the Presentation Church. The next day Ivan accompanied the governor on an inspection tour at which, to Ivan's relief, he found the files of the magistracy in proper order and thanked Ivan for the good work. Lopukhin, who like Osterman was on the pilgrimage circuit from Moscow to Vedernitsy to the Trinity Monastery, left the next morning for the Trinity Monastery accompanied by Ivan to the outskirts of Dmitrov, as was customary.[7]

August brought another important guest to Dmitrov, Iakov Aleksandrovich Brius, the military governor of Moscow and the most powerful official in the old capital. The visit lasted three days and included a thorough tour and inspec-tion. Brius arrived on the twenty-sixth and was lodged in the home of Ivan's friend, Fëdor Loshkin. Ivan worked at the magistracy until five in the evening, getting ready for the tour with Count Brius. He reported that "the magistracy officials and I then followed along with the Count, who strolled around the town on foot, starting at Tugarinov's cloth factory and then proceeding to Samoilov's leather factory. From there we continued along the embankment to the Koniushennaia sloboda section of town and went to our house to see the garden and orangeries. The count, having praised everything and expressed his appreciation, walked back to his lodgings and at the floating bridge released me and the others to our homes." The next day was devoted to showing Brius's provincial councilor around the town offices while he inspected the handling of business there. The day after that, Brius himself appeared at the offices for an inspection and then, if we are to believe Ivan's report, expressed his thanks to

Ivan and the other officials for their good administration of affairs. A final visit by Ivan to Brius at six in the morning the next day to wish him farewell and accompany him to the edge of town ended what must have been a stressful, if ultimately successful, review—and even gave Ivan another opportunity to show off his horticultural achievements. He was probably sorry that his new home was not yet available for housing and entertaining such a distinguished visitor.

The rest of the year was free of important visitors, except for Bishop Feofilakt, whom Ivan had a chance to entertain when he passed through town in September. Ivan could enjoy watching the workers complete the masonry construction on his new home in September and then observe in the autumn the building of the rafters and placement of the metal roof. Ivan was also able to relax on a grouse-hunting trip in October to villages near Klin owned by his friend Viktor Nazimov, the Kashin district treasurer (the Tolchënov family rented mills in the Kashin area on the Volga). A few days later he celebrated the birth of a daughter, Varvara. Finally, an event of importance for the town occurred in December when it was able to open Dmitrov's first public school, one fruit of Catherine II's reforms. The school was launched with fanfare and an inaugural speech by the teacher, a priest from the city's Annunciation Church, in the midst of the year-end town elections when plenty of people were present. The only shortcoming was the lack of a schoolhouse. Ivan noted that classes would have to be held in a room of the magistracy building until a school could be built.[8]

In the winter of 1785–1786, Ivan took more trips and spent more time than usual in Moscow: five days in December, nearly two weeks in January, a week in February, two weeks in March, and a week in April. The trips included work on the grain business, purchases of stone and ovens (probably for the heating of his new home), visits with in-laws and with his aristocratic acquaintances from Dmitrov who spent each winter in the capital, including Prince Ivan Golitsyn and Prince Nikolai Obolenskii, plus calls on government officials. He and his wife Anna also took in theater performances in January before the theater closed for Lent. It seemed that they were becoming more integrated into the Moscow social scene, as they attended the wedding of the daughter and son of two Moscow merchant families in February. But perhaps this was to be expected. Anna was herself a Muscovite by birth and upbringing, and Ivan's building projects had brought him into increasing contact with Moscow suppliers.

Something else happened that was not characteristic of Ivan's experiences in Moscow up to this time. He made regular stops at the Financial Board for Moscow province, the office responsible for collecting taxes, customs, and other duties, including the sale of government liquor franchises. Ivan's diary entries about this from January through early March are not very revealing, recording merely that he went to the Financial Board on a particular day. More interesting was the entry of March 18, in which he noted that he had hosted in his apartment "Secretary Strashnov and staff members of the Financial Board." When we learn that early the next month Ivan was back in Moscow and recorded that this time he went to "the Financial Board for the auction of the Dmitrov liquor franchise,"[9] it suggests that Ivan's visits to the Financial Board were in preparation for the auction and that he had invited the officials to his place to press his case for receiving a liquor franchise.

For entrepreneurs with energy and good connections, a liquor franchise produced a substantial income. Some of the wealthiest merchants in imperial Russia had begun their climb to the top as liquor franchisees. This system, known as tax farming, was instituted in 1755 and then made obligatory for all provinces in the empire except Siberia in 1765–1767. Franchisees paid in advance for the right to sell vodka for a particular time in a particular jurisdiction and then retain whatever revenue they earned in the course of their lease. Successful franchisees would usually take their earnings and invest them in other more secure and lasting commercial enterprises.

But why would Ivan now be trying to get into this business? He had after all inherited a successful commercial enterprise and was the beneficiary of his father and grandfather's efforts that made them the wealthiest merchants in Dmitrov. The answer can be found in Ivan's later retrospective notes. Although the daily entries in the diary for this period give no hints other than this unusual and failed bid to win a liquor franchise, we can see in the year-end summary for 1785 that Ivan was beginning to experience what we would today call cash-flow problems. In the summary notes for 1785 Ivan tallied up his grain purchases and sales and noted that he was able to bring in a profit of 9,000 rubles. However, "the construction of our new masonry house, various domestic and other losses to debtors reduced my capital by 11,000." He also complained that receipts from Petersburg were slow in arriving as a result of the muddle his agent, Stepan Tiut'kin, had made of his affairs there, and, he added, he had not been aware in 1785 of how serious this problem was becoming. The upshot was that in order to make purchases for his business in 1786, he had to borrow 6,000 rubles. Borrowing on this scale at the high interest rates typically charged at this time was a recipe for catastrophe. No wonder then that Ivan was casting about for another source of income such as a liquor franchise. It did not, however, occur to him at this point to take a more direct hand in running his business, especially the important Petersburg end of it, which was the principal site of revenue collection.

A modern financial adviser might propose a cutback on personal expenses, but to a Russian in Ivan's position, this was not an option. Besides, he was now in the midst of major building projects, and his expenses could only mount. In addition to the house still under construction, he was re-doing and expanding outbuildings. "We removed the roof from the former malt house and added height to the brick walls. The barn was dismantled, and the malt house was made into a building that served as a stable, carriage house, two storerooms and a vestibule with storage closets that led into living space. Over this was a drying room for dresses, and the whole structure was covered with a wooden roof. A new wooden building was also constructed, consisting of a covered hut, two cattle sheds, and an open barn, all of which were likewise covered with a wooden plank roof. In the garden on the side by the yard a gate was erected along with a latticed fence."[10] Finally, apparently to provide fuel for the new home, orangeries, and other buildings, Ivan purchased a nearby grove, where he and his wife enjoyed strolling on a holiday.[11]

The centerpiece was the home itself. Its design followed the usual pattern of luxurious noble townhouses of the day. From the main entry on the eastern side a large hand-carved wooden staircase rose with two turns up to the second floor and a suite of three large, high-ceilinged rooms with enfilade doors along the south wall. In other words, the rooms were linked by a series of interior doors that provided a vista through nearly the entire length of the house when the doors were open. Ivan lovingly described the final phases of the work on the home in his summary notes for the year 1786.

This year the floors were installed in the house on all levels, the doors made, the frames and panels, and likewise wooden staircases on the inside. On the outside the porches done in masonry were built. [The builders] laid down the ovens and a metal worker finished them. Likewise the ceilings in all the rooms were plastered, as were the walls in some of them, an iron balustrade with frontons was mounted on the roof and frames placed on all the windows. In the lower story all the work done by the joiners was painted. With the ovens installed, we began to heat the building, and on October 15 for the first time we had guests in the lower rooms.

These first guests came for supper and included Colonel Gal'berg of the Shlis-sel'burg regiment and his family. The regiment had been billeted in Dmitrov for the past month and a half, and Ivan had regularly invited the colonel and quartermaster in for visits. A few officers of the regiment, the state-appointed police commissioner, and the locally elected police chief completed the guest list. What figured as the grand opening of the magnificent new home came four days later in the main room on the second story; it turned out to be an all-day affair. Ivan noted proudly in his diary passage for that day that "dining with us was Prince Ivan Fëdorovich [Golitsyn], the colonel [Gal'berg] and his family, Major Supov and several officers, the police commissioner, Squire Pëtr Khitrovo and other local judges and relatives. The evening was spent listening to music played by the regimental band, and the prince stayed on until after 7 o'clock. The colonel and several guests remained for supper and departed after midnight."[12]

This inaugural celebration of the house actually preceded the family's move. This took place two weeks later, when, as Ivan expressed it in his later notes, "with the help of the Creator we fully moved over to live on the lower floor and during the winter did not experience any harm from dampness or furnace fumes." In this first masonry house in Dmitrov, Ivan obviously harbored some concerns about ventilation. Even so, Ivan and his family must have found it exhilarating to occupy such a splendid building, surrounded by the gardens, greenhouses, stables, and ponds that Ivan had invested in and developed over the past few years. The house and grounds were the envy of the entire community, an urban estate that rivaled the country homes of many nobles of the day.[13]

All this cost money. In Ivan's report on the weather for the year 1786, he noted that conditions in the north central part of the country caused crop failures and a very hard winter for many peasants, who were reduced to eating chaff and even hay. But the harvests in the south and in Penza province were abundant, keeping down the price of grain generally and enabling grain merchants to do well. Ivan could write that his trade turned a "very handsome profit," as he had earned a total of 13,000 rubles, or 34 kopecks on the ruble— quite a nice return. The difficulty in 1786 was again on the expense side. "The outlays were not small," he wrote in his financial report. "Finishing work on the masonry house cost 4,860, another 2,960 was expended on the construction of a masonry bell tower for the Presentation Church, upkeep of the family and home, interest payments and other expenses coming to more than my profits reduced my working capital by about 1,500 rubles." At the end of the year he figured his available capital, including the portion that would eventually go to his young uncle and ward, Andrei Makarov, amounted to 40,000 rubles. This was not enough to carry the business through the next year, and Ivan had to resort to further borrowing, this time 16,000 rubles worth. Here again he blamed some of the difficulty on the slow collections of payments in Petersburg and mistakes by his business agent there, Stepan Tiut'kin, but he eventually also had to acknowledge his own failings.

Looking back some years later, Ivan could see that his change of fortune could be traced to the year 1785 when, despite continuing good returns from the grain trade, the receipts from sales in Petersburg, which constituted the bulk of his income, were delayed. As a consequence he was forced to borrow to finance his purchases and labor for the following year's trade. The combination of the ruinous interest rates in Russia's credit-poor and mistrustful commercial world and Ivan's extravagance made it difficult for him to recover. Perhaps he could have saved himself if he had acted decisively, but at the time he was apt to focus on good news and to hope for a fortunate turn. The year 1787, for example, gave him some reason for optimism. His business did exceptionally well, earning an income of 14,600 rubles, while expenses for interest on his loans and for his household and living, additional work on his new home, schooling for his son Pëtr, and further contributions to the construction of a bell tower at the Presentation Church came to only 10,500 rubles. This net gain of over 4,000 rubles allowed him to pay off a portion of his debt and reduce his overall obligations to 13,000 rubles. It was still a large sum—nearly his entire income in a very good year—and interest rates continued high, but the profits gave Ivan hope that he was beginning to work his way back to solvency.

The danger was that so long as he needed to borrow to keep his business going, he dare not make any changes in his way of living. It was his place of prominence in his community and his manifestation of wealth that provided the collateral for Ivan to continue borrowing. His social capital was very much also his working financial capital. Skimping was not wise. An obvious reduction in his scale of expenditures would raise questions about his creditworthiness. In any case, this option would not have appealed to Ivan, as his identity was tightly bound to his position as a wealthy trader and leading citizen who could entertain the elite of local society and even important Moscow officials and clerics. Ivan's new house was a marvelous site for such entertaining as well as evidence of his business success and eventually collateral for loans. Work on the interior continued through 1787, and Ivan described the new touches in his later summary.

In this year all the woodwork was painted in the upper floor and the mezzanine, and the carving, niche, and doors in the entryways were primed . . . , plus frescoes were painted on the walls of the great room and some other rooms, and those that were not done with frescoes were covered with wallpaper, a silk blend in the bedrooms and niche and paper on the others. Mirrors were placed in the upper chambers and drapes hung on the windows, and other appropriate finishing touches were made. Outside, a gate was raised and a masonry fence built along the street, and running off from it around the large yard were wooden fences. In the cattle yard they made a gate and the entire roof was painted. The cost of all this work was 2,000 rubles.[14]

While the family was settling into this impressive urban estate, life continued through the first half of the year almost routinely. Ivan's second term as burgomaster had ended. He was no longer serving daily at the magistracy and could make frequent trips to the northern mills and even more often to Moscow and the family's apartment there. In Dmitrov, he socialized with the police commissioner, the district police captain, and his new friend from the local nobility Afanasii Iushkov. Iushkov had recently been elected a district judge, and just as

in the case of Prince Obolenskii a few years earlier, the election of a local noble
to the district court gave Ivan the opportunity and the desire to meet with the
person and to cultivate a friendship. Ivan was also a frequent visitor to the
noble widow Anna Obreskova and her children, who seemed almost an extension of his own family. His association with the Golitsyns, especially Prince Ivan
Fëdorovich, likewise continued.

LOVE OF THE PAGEANTRY OF POWER

*[1787, June] 27th A day of celebration in the capital. The occasion was the entry
into the city of Her Imperial Majesty after her safe return from the southern provinces. After 7 o'clock in the morning the entire family went to the Kremlin where
for this occasion we had rented ahead of time an elevated space at the porch of
the Dormition Cathedral. The most august monarch, coming from the village
of Kolomenskoe, and the grand princes Aleksandr Pavlovich and Konstantin
Pavlovich, who had recently joined her there from Petersburg, arrived at the
cathedral after 11 o'clock and amid great splendor heard mass conducted by
Bishop Platon. After mass they departed for the home of the Moscow Commandant on Tverskaia Street. After dinner I stayed in our apartment.*

*28th This morning we again took the entire family to the same rented space
in the Kremlin, and the empress and their highnesses came to hear mass at the
cathedral and from there went to the Palace of Facets. In the evening I was back
in the Kremlin where a ball was being held in the Palace of Facets with the august
personages in attendance. Later I attended the vigil at the Dormition Cathedral.*

*29th In the morning I visited Vandashnikov, and later we again rode to our
rented space in the Kremlin, and after the arrival of the monarch and the grand
princes mass was said. Bishop Platon of Moscow, who had conducted it, was afterward declared by her majesty worthy to be promoted to metropolitan. Having
dined at our apartment, after 4 o'clock in the afternoon we set out for home, taking Petrusha with us. We spent the night at Sholokhovo.*[15]

This passage from the diary captures Ivan and his family during a trip to
Moscow for three consecutive days of viewing the imperial family on the occasion of Empress Catherine's return from her highly publicized tour of the newly
opened provinces of southern Russia in the company of Joseph II of Austria.
This was the trip famous for the "Potëmkin villages" that Catherine's former
lover and builder of southern Russia had supposedly hastily erected along the
route to impress her and her guest. Ivan had evidently spent a substantial sum
of money to rent space on a viewing platform in a very privileged location right
by the steps into the Kremlin Dormition Cathedral so that he, his wife Anna,
and their two boys, Pëtr and Aleksei, could see everything at close range. They
must also have spent money to outfit themselves for this extraordinary chance

to participate in the pageantry and pomp of power when Catherine was at the height of her popularity. Ivan was fascinated with ceremonials of power and the opportunity to be in proximity to the imperial family. He even returned alone to the Kremlin during the evening of the second day where a ball was being held and later attended a vigil. His account leaves unclear whether he also attended the ball. Perhaps his viewing platform rental included an invitation to the ball.[16]

What is remarkable about this occasion is that its attraction for Ivan was such that it overrode a heartrending family event that occurred unexpectedly and almost simultaneously. Tragedy had again struck Anna's Moscow family soon after she and Ivan arrived in the capital. Ivan had just begun to indulge his favorite pastime of visiting orangeries of nobles and merchants when he received news of the grave illness of Anna's sister Elizaveta. Although Ivan gave no information about the illness—was it the childbed fever that Anna's sister Mar'ia had died of a few years before or something else—it ran a rapid course, and Elizaveta died just two days later. The family arranged an impressive funeral that was conducted by a bishop and the heads of two monasteries. Here is the diary account of those days:

[June] 23rd In the morning I went to Demidov's orangery. From there, I rode over to Vandashnikov's and had dinner there. Extreme unction was administered to my sister-in-law. In the evening I attended a vigil at the Ascension Church.

24th I heard mass at the same Ascension Church. Toward 1 o'clock in the afternoon Vandashnikov let us know that Elizaveta Alekseevna was drawing her last breaths, and my wife and I immediately rode over there but found that she had already expired at 1 o'clock. And we stayed there until after 6 o'clock. . . .

26th After 6 o'clock in the morning we rode to Vandashnikov's for the funeral, which was conducted by Bishop Anfim, the Greek metropolitan, assisted by the abbot of St. John Chrysostom [Monastery], the father superior of the Intercession Monastery, and the parish clergy. First the body was borne into the St. Nicholas parish church, where mass was said, followed by prayers for the dead, and then the body was interred in the Intercession Monastery. I had dinner at Vandashnikov's and returned to our apartment after 5 o'clock.

The family scarcely had time to grieve, for the very next day, June 27, the empress was scheduled to make her entry, and early in the morning they hurried to the Kremlin to be in attendance. Perhaps it was a distraction that Anna in particular needed after having lost a third sister within a short time. Although she did not attend the evening events that Ivan reported in his diary, she did evidently witness the daytime ceremonies at which the tsarist family appeared.

Another important family event of the year 1787 was a change in Pëtr's school. In March Ivan was in Moscow to arrange this. It is not clear whether

Pëtr had outgrown the school run by Johann Horn or whether Ivan wished to make a change for other reasons. But he visited a man whom he variously named Bardenkov and Bordenov, the owner of another "pansion," and was evidently satisfied with what he found there, for the next month he returned to Moscow and moved Pëtr from the Horn school to the new pansion. This school would be Pëtr's last. In two years, when he reached age fifteen, Ivan would dispatch him to the grain wharves of the central Volga to make purchases for the family business, just as Ivan himself had done at about the same age.

Ivan continued this year to host occasional visits from powerful Moscow officials. Count Fëdor Andreevich Osterman, senator and former governor of Moscow province, stopped in again to visit when he and his family were on the way to the shrine at Vedernitsy. This time he dined with Ivan and inspected the new local school. In July, Moscow Civil Governor Pëtr Lopukhin came to town with his family, also on another Vedernitsy pilgrimage, and he took over Ivan's home for a few hours to use as an office, ate dinner with Ivan and the police commissioner, and then inspected the local government offices. Finished with his work, the governor invited Ivan and Anna to accompany his family to Squire Pëtr Khitrovo's nearby estate at Podlipich'e before the Lopukhins left on the next leg of their trip, the Trinity Monastery. In early September another visit took place when the new Moscow Commandant or Military Governor Pëtr Dmitrievich Eropkin descended on the town for two days of inspections. These predictable, if unscheduled, visits by powerful persons did not greatly disrupt the affairs of the city and even provided opportunities for municipal leaders to show hospitality and develop useful acquaintances. More difficult and threatening interventions from Moscow, however, loomed on the horizon.

If Ivan's social position and personal identity were secure for now, personal losses and concerns for the health of his family could appear unexpectedly, as was the case with the sudden death of Anna's sister. To take another example, in May 1787 Ivan's young step-uncle and ward Andrei Fëdorovich Makarov was stricken with scarlet fever. Ivan learned of this just as he returned from a pleasant vacation in Moscow with Anna and their sons Aleksei and Pëtr. He had visited orangeries and the Golovin court gardens, and the family had gone with friends on Pentacostal Sunday to stroll in the beautiful suburban estates of Ostan'kovo (later Ostankino) and Petrovskoe. On returning to Dmitrov, they found Andrei aflame with a fever that lasted five days. Oddly, we do not learn about this in Ivan's daily entries but in the later summary for the year. Perhaps it was enough for him to record the visit of Count Osterman that was taking place at the time Andrei was ill. But possibly, too, the scarlet fever took on greater significance when Ivan's own children fell ill a few months later with a similar infection that had a worse outcome, and, consequently, in retrospect Ivan thought it worth recording Andrei's illness in the year-end summary notes.

In those same notes he wrote in great detail about the weather for the year and commented on a remarkable and frightening phenomenon in the early fall. "The end of September and beginning of October saw a period of more than two weeks of the loveliest warm, dry weather. Not a single drop of rain fell, and the atmosphere remained clear. But at night we often had terrifying northern lights, and especially on October 3rd fiery columns raced across the sky the entire night and objects were illuminated and appeared as if a continuous conflagration were occurring very nearby." In view of what happened to his children just a few days later, this alarming spectacle in the night sky may have taken on added meaning.

EMOTIONAL ATTACHMENT TO CHILDREN

[1787, October] 14th I spent the entire day at home. In the evening Uncle Mikhaila Il'ich visited.

15th I heard mass at the cathedral, and the rest of the time I spent at home feeling miserable over the illness of my children Lëniushka [Aleksei] and Katen'ka [Ekaterina].

16th I did not go anywhere.

17th I attended the vigil and mass at Presentation Church, and in the evening Uncle Mikhaila Il'ich visited.

18th I spent the entire day at home.

19th I attended the vigil and early mass at Presentation Church. In the evening the district police captain, the public prosecutor, and the [collegiate assessor] Gruzdev visited me.

20th I did not go anywhere.

21st The same

22nd I attended the vigil and mass at Presentation Church and in the evening visited at the homes of the police commissioner and of [Squire] Iushkov.

23rd I spent the entire day at home.

24th I attended the vigil and mass at Presentation Church. My wife and I dined and spent the evening at the estates of Iushkov.

25th I did not go anywhere. In the evening my cousin Pëtr Alekseev visited.

26th I heard mass at Presentation Church and spent the day at home.

27th I spent the day at home and in the evening visited my cousin Pëtr Alekseev.

28th I spent the day at home again and in the evening visited Iushkov.

29th I was at home in the morning, and after dinner my wife and I rode out to Lar'kovo to visit the district police captain and spent the evening with him.

30th I did not go anywhere.

31st I attended the vigil and mass at Presentation Church. In the evening Iushkov, the police commissioner, and Gruzdev visited me.

November 1st I did not go anywhere.

2nd I spent the day at home and the evening at the home of the police commissioner.

3rd I spent the entire day at home. We lost hope of my daughter Katen'ka's survival.

4th At 7:28 in the morning she passed away to my deepest regret for she had been a joy. After dinner I rode to the monastery to ask the abbot's permission to bury her there. Uncles Ivan Il'ich and Mikhaila Il'ich and their families spent the evening at my home.

5th In the morning we took the body of our deceased daughter to the monastery, and after mass the funeral service was read by the abbot together with the brothers and the clergy of the Presentation Church, and then she was interred. All the clergy who participated in the funeral dined at our house together with Uncle Ivan Il'ich and Fëdor Loshkin and their families. Also, the Moshinskii women[17] spent the evening with my wife.

It was unusual for Ivan to spend a series of days at home unless he were himself very ill. Yet in the three weeks excerpted from his diary above he rarely left home, and he did so mainly to go to church. He made a few evening visits to friends and relatives, but except for two trips he and Anna made to nearby noble estates for dinners and visits lasting into the evening, they stayed close to home. At the beginning and end of the excerpt we see the reason, their worry and fears for their two sick children, one of whom did not survive.

In the past many children died in infancy and early childhood. This was true everywhere. Among Russians the toll was unusually high. Reliable statistics on infant mortality in Russia were not available until the second half of the nineteenth century, and they show that as late as the 1890s Russians were losing nearly half of their children by age five. Outcomes were unlikely to have been much better in earlier times. Although we lack accurate counts of childhood death for the eighteenth and early nineteenth centuries, the evidence of individual families indicates heavy losses. An extreme case is the highly decorated general Pëtr Panin, who fathered fourteen children and saw only one live to maturity (this surviving son became Russian foreign minister under Emperor Paul). But other elite families also lost a high proportion of their children. As noted earlier, every one of Ivan Tolchënov's own siblings died in childhood. Of his parents' nine children Ivan was the sole survivor. In the next generation Ivan and his wife Anna produced sixteen children in the years from 1774 to 1794, nine boys and seven girls. Of these just four, all boys, survived for more than a year. This toll was not unusual. Other accounts from this period tell a similar story. Look, for example, at the memoirs of N. A. Naidenov. His grandfather, a successful merchant in the late eighteenth century, fathered at least eleven children and saw only three survive early childhood.[18] Another merchant of this time, Ivan Rychkov, lost eleven of his twelve children (more about this family later in this chapter). Or consider the recently published diary of the noblewoman Varvara Tatishcheva. She had eleven pregnancies between 1804 and 1819 and suffered two miscarriages and three stillbirths. Of the six live births, only three survived past early childhood.[19] Elizaveta Ian'kova, another noblewoman, whose childbearing years extended from 1794 to 1807, gave birth to seven children and brought only three to maturity.[20]

Historians have for some years been debating the depth and timing of the emotional attachment of people to their children in earlier times. Some believe that the toll of childhood death was so high that people shielded themselves emotionally by not forming an attachment with newborns until they had survived for a certain period of time. Others question this view.[21] The evidence of Ivan Tolchënov's diary may be helpful in defining the emotional boundaries within which people operated in this early modern period of teeming death of small children.

It would also be useful to know if the degree of attachment varied for the mother and the father. Ivan Tolchënov's diary, unfortunately, does not speak about the feelings of his wife Anna, and so we cannot compare her emotional responses. In this regard, Ivan wrote more about his mother. He linked her early death to the grief she experienced over the loss of nearly all of her children, noting that from the time of the death of the ninth child, "who to my parents' great sorrow expired unbaptized on the day of its birth, my mother began to feel the illness that turned into tuberculosis and cut short her days."[22] Toward the end of this discussion, I will cite some accounts by women to test their responses. In these cases, as in Ivan's sometimes lengthier remarks, the evidence consists less in direct emotional statements than in what people found worth recording about the birth, death, or survival and growth of their children.

Incidentally, the infant mortality rates in the Tolchënov family of 75 to nearly 90 percent, plus other evidence in the diary such as the short birth intervals, suggest that these merchant women were not breastfeeding their children, a sign probably of their aspiration to set themselves apart from the laboring classes.[23]

As for Ivan's reports on the deaths of his own children, his remarks reveal a pattern. If a child died within two months of birth, he merely noted the time of death and invoked a common expression: either "she passed into eternal bliss" or, on a couple of occasions, the variant "by the power of God she passed away." One or two perfunctory sentences followed about arrangements for the funeral and burial. Some examples:

August 1st [1776] At noon I left [Moscow] for home. I spent the night in Ignatovo. Today my daughter Evdokiia passed away after having lived for 15 days.

2nd I arrived home safely in the morning and we buried our daughter in the Boris and Gleb Monastery. The abbot and brothers dined with us.

. . .

[September] 17th [1777] At 2 o'clock in the morning our son Sergei passed away into eternal bliss, having lived on the earth 12 days and 18 hours. I heard mass at Presentation Church.

18th We buried our deceased son in the Boris and Gleb Monastery. The abbot and brothers dined with us.

. . .

[January] 11th [1782] I spent the day at home, and in the evening our Moscow guests [relatives who had come for the christening of Vasilii] and I visited Uncle Ivan Il'ich.

12th Before dinner I was at the magistracy. After dinner our Moscow guests departed for home, and I accompanied them to the far side of Khomilovets. In the evening Fëdor Loshkin visited me. Today our son Vasilii got terribly sick and suffered sharp pains.

13th I spent my designated hours at the magistracy and the rest of the time at home. At the start of the seventh hour after noon our son Vasilii passed away into eternal bliss.

14th In the morning I was at the magistracy and at the abbot's. After dinner I rode to the Meadow Mill.

15th We buried our deceased son Vasilii in the monastery on the left side of my father by his feet. The abbot and brothers, the clergy of the Presentation Church and Uncle Dmitrii and his household dined with us.

Ivan wrote nothing about these children or others who died young (with one exception) in the year-end summaries inserted into the diary a few years later. In these summaries he commented on the weather through the course of the year, crops and the harvest in various places, the grain trade, and unusual happenings, after which he placed a brief section on the deaths during that year of national figures, local people, and relatives. However, the death of even an immediate family member did not rate inclusion in the summary if he or she was under a few months of age.

Three of Ivan's twelve children who died in infancy survived beyond two months, and about them the diary had a bit more to say. The first was Mariia, who was born in 1781 and lived for two and a half months. Two weeks prior to her death Ivan mentioned that she had fallen ill. He did not give this kind of early alert for the children who died within a month of birth. The next we hear of Mariia is the entry on her death. "At 3 this afternoon my daughter Mariia by the will of God consigned her infant soul into His holy hands." He then noted that she was laid to rest beside his recently deceased father in the local monastery. Another daughter, Varvara, lived for five months before dying in March 1786. In this case, instead of the usual formula about passing on to eternal bliss, Ivan wrote about her illness, noting that "she passed away at 6 in the morning, having suffered for more than month with a stomach ailment, vomiting, and diarrhea. I spent the entire day at home." The next day the funeral and burial took place at the monastery, and she too was laid to rest at the feet of Ivan's father. Although Varvara had been sick for over a month, Ivan had not noted the onset of her illness, as he had for Mariia and for older children. He had been back and forth to Moscow on business that month; he arrived home from one trip at 10 pm on the very eve of Varvara's death and wrote that she "was beyond hope of living." It is difficult to believe that Ivan had formed much of an emotional bond with either Mariia or Varvara in view of his brief comments, but he had enjoyed enough of a history with them that he could get beyond the pat phrases he used for the other children and write something, however brief, about their illnesses. He also found a place for them in the monastery church next to his father, whereas later children who lived only a short time were interred in the local parish cemetery. Ivan wrote nothing about Mariia or Varvara in his year-end summaries.

Altogether different was Ivan's reaction to the death of a child who survived for nearly a year. This was Ekaterina (Katen'ka), born on November 12, 1786 (less than eight months after the death of Varvara in this world of near-continuous pregnancy for fertile women). The diary leaves no doubt that Ivan had fallen deeply in love with this child. The daily entries on her illness and death, excerpted above, are brief yet telling. Twenty days before her death, he mentioned the onset of illness: "I went to mass at the cathedral, and the rest of the day I spent at home feeling miserable over the illness of my children Lëniushka and Katen'ka." During the following two and a half weeks we find Ivan uncharacteristically home nearly the entire time. After a week his son Aleksei suffered a brief but severe crisis and began to recover. Katen'ka, too, rallied but then went into decline. On November 3 Ivan writes that "we lost hope of my daughter Katen'ka's survival," and the next day: "At 7:28 this morning she passed away to my deepest regret, for she had been a great joy."

Katen'ka was different from the other deceased children in receiving not just mention but extended comment in Ivan's year-end summary. In this section, Ivan abandoned the diary form and adopted a narrative style as he looked back on the year's events. Touched by the death of the child of one year, this man of affairs who had no formal education penned some expressive passages. He spoke of how the illness first attacked his eight-year-old son Aleksei and then a day later the nearly one-year-old Ekaterina. The illness, which presented as a fever and rash accompanied by a severe sore throat, may have begun as scarlet fever or other streptococcal infection and moved rapidly to pneumonia in the boy. He felt such weakness and pressure in his chest that by the third day he asked his father to allow him to say confession and receive the last rites. Ivan explained:

During the night of October 12th our son Lëniushka suddenly got sick with a fever and was extremely weak. At first we considered it due to an eruption of the pox and therefore did not treat it with anything. Then the fever intensified to an extreme level with delirium, and his throat was terribly sore, his nose ran and mouth drooled. On the evening of the 13th, to add to our sorrow . . . our daughter Katin'ka, who was completely healthy when she was put to bed, began to moan in her sleep and woke up with a fever and started crying uncontrollably, and we noticed that she would not let anyone touch her sides, and my wife and I spent the night in great distress and almost without sleep. On the morning of the 14th we brought in Dr. Kazotti, and after examining the children, he began to treat them. He placed pepper plasters on our son's spots and told us to swathe his throat with oil but advised delaying further treatment as he suspected that the illness was smallpox. In the evening we bathed our daughter Katerina, and she was somewhat calmer during the night, except that on her back a red rash appeared.

Ivan continued with a detailed explanation of the treatments for the children. After Aleksei received the sacraments and further medical treatment of laxatives and powders to control his temperature, he began to feel some relief. Though Katen'ka was still quite ill, she too saw some improvement as her rash started to dry up. By the end of a week, Ivan reported, the children were both much improved, "for which my wife and I were inexpressibly happy."[24]

But while Lëniushka had fully recovered a few days later, Katen'ka, though back to her usual play and learning to walk when held by the hand, continued to show disturbing symptoms. She refused solid food, the rash came and went, a fever lingered. Then on October 27 she took a turn for the worse. "On the 31st she was so weak that she could not sit up using her arms for support, and her chest was so congested that she lost her voice and could only with great difficulty swallow water or milk. Now my wife and I succumbed to all the sadness that only a parental heart can know when being deprived of such a lovely child." In the next days, Katen'ka weakened further, exhibiting a larger and darker rash and increasingly severe symptoms of the pneumonia that finally claimed her life on the morning of November 4. Ivan described those days.

*On November 1st we took her to mass and administered extreme unction, and
then having slept a bit, she was so altered that we couldn't even hope for her to
live out the day. The rash spread and darkened. On the 2nd she lay in the same
condition, and on the 3rd she couldn't even raise herself on her arms. While we
lived in hope of the intervention and help of the Creator, we came to a decision
out of human feeling to take whatever measures we could [to save her], and we
summoned the doctor. He came at 11 in the morning, examined her, and said that
the pulse was not yet dangerous, that she suffered from fever and that we might
still be able to try something. So, after midday we gave her whale oil to break up
the congestion and soothe the fever, but it didn't help at all, and she got steadily
weaker and closer to the end of life. In the night of the 4th she became terribly
melancholy, and in the 7th hour of the morning they suddenly called me to her
side, and I saw her for the last time as she released her soul into the hands of God
at 7 hours and 28 minutes.*

This account, though included in the summary report added years later, must
have been based on notes that Ivan took soon after the events it describes and
then preserved with his diary notes. Even though memories associated with
powerful emotions are better retained, it is hard to believe that Ivan could have
recalled so many specifics years later.

And it continues. Ivan described in loving detail the white calico, gold
ribbon, and silk stockings and slippers in which she was buried as well as many
other details of the funeral, including the role played by Katen'ka's favorite
horses in pulling the coach bearing her coffin. Then he added: "So, by the
power of God and in punishment for my sins I was deprived of this extraordinarily lovable child. Right from her birth she was completely healthy and
well-behaved, and as she grew she was always sprightly and happy, and her
games and play were in advance of her years, just as her intelligence was well
ahead of her age, for she understood everything right away and even went
beyond what you would expect. For example, seeing that a door in a room was
not closed or that . . . jars of kvas were not covered, she noticed all that herself
and was not content until the things had been put right. She loved horses and
cows, and her favorite thing to do was to visit our sorrel horses and to feed them
oats, pet them, and kiss them. She loved fruits very much, and she developed
quite a taste for them when she was but a half year old, and when she was only
eight months old she was already picking cherries from the tree. Her face
resembled mine exactly and she was so very sweet, and she had two teeth, one of
which at her death remained not quite fully grown out. She had not yet begun
to walk on her own but could make a circle around the chairs without support
—and to me she was exceptionally affectionate."[25]

While this sentimentalist narrative summary makes a contrast with the terse diary entries, in both accounts sympathy and engagement—love—are expressed of a quality not seen in reports of children who had died younger. Can we know if the age-defined boundaries of emotional expression that Ivan allowed himself were typical of people of his time and place?

Indeed, confirming evidence about what feelings could appropriately be expressed in regard to the death of children can be found in other sources from this time. One is the memoirs of Pëtr Ivanovich Rychkov. Rychkov was the son of a merchant who had worked the trade to Arkhangel'sk in the early eighteenth century. His father, Ivan Rychkov, obtained enough education for Pëtr that he was able to enter government service and rise into the nobility through the Table of Ranks. Like Ivan Tolchënov, Pëtr Rychkov was the only surviving child of a large progeny (twelve siblings in his case). He himself had fifteen children by two wives and lost ten of them to early death. His reports on their deaths follow the pattern of Tolchënov's. For a child who died very early, he wrote simply that "she passed away, having lived three months," and offered no expression of sorrow. But a son who died at age two was described in detail as very intelligent and clever and passed away "to the great grief of me and his mother." He also detailed the burial of this son. The loss of a nine-year-old daughter brought expressions of "indescribable sadness" and explanations that she already spoke German.[26]

We see the same pattern in the memoirs of another noble, the artillery major Mikhail Vasil'evich Danilov, whose account was penned in 1771. For a death of a very young child, he wrote simply that "on our arrival in Riga our daughter died, after having lived for two months." In contrast, the deaths of older children elicited an emotional response. The year 1761 brought him and his wife particularly bad news. "My son Dmitrii, who was then one year and six months of age, got sick with diarrhea while we were traveling and to my great sorrow died, causing us indescribable sadness and tears. We had not yet finished mourning the death of my son when our grief was deepened further. My younger stepson Aleksei in the fifth year of his life died from smallpox, which was so severe that even old people in their 60s were falling ill."[27] Again, the threshold for the expression of grief was somewhere well above two months.

What about the response of mothers? Can we see a difference in how they reacted to the death of children? Unfortunately, the available sources do not give much to go on. Of the women mentioned earlier in this section, Varvara Tatishcheva kept a journal that was even more lapidary than the one Ivan Tolchënov wrote. She gave birth in 1804 to a daughter, Agrafena, who lived for nearly two years. Tatishcheva wrote simply that "At 1 o'clock in the morning of the 23rd of February my daughter Agrafena passed away." Six years later she lost a son, Nikolai, a few days after his first birthday. She wrote: "He died in 1810 on August 30, a Wednesday, in the afternoon. He was sick for only ten days." This entry seems to have been made some time after the death and grieving period and may lack emotion for that reason. However, a child born in 1815, who lived just four months, elicited a similarly flat report. "May 2nd at four o'clock in the afternoon son Fëdor was born at Peleshko. Iurii Vasilevich and our eldest daughter Varvara were his godparents. He died in the same year on August 30th at twelve o'clock in the afternoon. He was sick with a severe cough."[28] In two cases of stillbirth and miscarriage, her focus was on her own illness, excessive bleeding, and loneliness.

The memoirs of Elizaveta Ian'kova were a record made by her grandson and composed long after the facts they describe. Accordingly, though presented in her voice, they come to us at some remove. Temporally, the composition falls in a much later time when the conventions of expressing (or feeling?) attachments to small children may have changed, though it is true that Ian'kova would have remained in some measure under the influence of the conventions of her youth. She lost four children of seven. The death of her son Pëtr at age one was explained in some detail interspersed with perhaps exculpatory comments about her own delicate state of late pregnancy and residence in a drafty home in winter.

> Grandfather proposed that we should move to his house where it was warmer, and I was myself in such a condition that I had to take care of my health, and the main thing: Petrushka was coughing and wheezing all the time, and I was very fearful for him. My sisters wrote that I should not get upset on his account and should just give him Harlem drops as needed. I was privileged to give birth to Anna and to recover after that, but my boy was not fated to live; he died on February 12, 1797. The funeral mass was at the parish church, and we interred him at the Virgin Convent.[29]

The death of Ian'kova's seven-year-old elder daughter Sof'ia (she later had another daughter Sof'ia) hardly rated a mention in the memoirs. More space went to a three-year-old Elizaveta, but here she recalled the kindness of a neighbor more than the death of her child:

> While [my husband] was away, on January 24th my youngest daughter Lizan'ka died, and at this time our very caring neighbor Ekaterina Dmitrievna Burtseva was a great help. I was not well myself and all the children had gotten sick, and she took my daughter two verstas to a village cemetery and had her interred there. Such deep sympathy will never be forgotten. Many years have passed, and I still recall how Ekaterina Dmitrievna cared for me.[30]

In noting the death of her third child, Sof'ia the younger, at age fourteen of wasting disease, she told of three instances of clairvoyance that the girl experienced toward the end. In her story Ian'kova emphasized not the death but, on the one hand, her discussion with a doctor who explained the phenomenon of clairvoyance and, on the other, her relation to the French governess whose charge the dead girl had been. Interestingly, to the extent that Tatishcheva and Ian'kova expressed concern in connection with the death of children it was as much about their own health and their relations with the adults in their lives as it was about the children themselves. The men reported on the events of illness and death and in some cases on the grief they and their wives felt, but they did not focus on their ties to others, except for the usual arrangements for burial and other ceremonial functions. Recall, too, that when the Tolchënovs' Katen'ka died, Anna spent the evening with other women (see the diary entry for November 5 at the head of this section). If this small sample is any guide, women were more attuned than men to the intimate social support system provided by their female relatives, neighbors, and even employees, and they expressed their concerns for their physical and emotional health in this context. It is worth remembering that women's worries about their social support system and physical health (Tatishcheva's bleeding, Ian'kova's delicate condition) were very much to the point, because not only infant but also maternal mortality was significant in this period. A mother had good reason to worry about her own health and about the fate of her children should she not survive. These were fears that other women could understand, and they were therefore available to sympathize and help when needed; men were frequently absent on business or service responsibilities.

The diary of Ivan Tolchënov and the other sources referenced here allow us to obtain some measure of the emotional life of his community by fixing the range of permitted comment on a fateful event such as the death of a son or daughter. Judging from the material presented here, Russians were not expected to form an emotional attachment to their infants before they had survived for at least two months. After that, attachments could develop gradually through the first year and be expressed in an increasingly powerful emotional register.

MAYOR OF THE TOWN

[1788] December 3rd [Moscow] I did not leave the apartment. At 10 o'clock in the morning I dispatched Dmitrii Zherebin to Lyskovo for the purchase of grain. In the evening [collegiate assessor] Gruzdev and [architect] Agafonov visited me.

4th In the morning I visited Karachinskii, and at 2 o'clock in the afternoon I departed for home. I stayed overnight in Sholokhovo.

5th I arrived safely to my house before 9 o'clock in the morning, and the rest of the time I spent at home.

6th I attended the vigil at Presentation Church. After 11 o'clock I rode out to Danilovskoe and had dinner there with the prince and stayed through the evening and had supper.

7th I did not go anywhere. In the evening the district police captain, Kvashnin, and his wife visited me.

8th I was at home during the day and in the evening visited the police commissioner.

9th I did not go anywhere.

10th I attended the vigil and mass at Presentation Church. In the evening Miss Moshinskaia visited us. At 7 o'clock someone came from the magistracy, where voting was then in progress to elect town officials for the next three years, to inform me that the society had elected me mayor. Accordingly, that very hour I departed for the assembly and assumed the office, and I was present for the continuation of the voting until midnight.

11th In the morning I was at the magistracy and with the police commissioner, and in the evening I was again at the voting until past 10 o'clock.

12th In the morning I visited the police commissioner. Then at the cathedral for prayers and from there to Iushkov's. In the evening I hosted at home all the members of the local nobility and their families.

13th In the morning I was at the magistracy and the rest of the time at home. In the evening Uncle Dmitrii Il'ich visited me.

14th During the day I was at home and in the evening I visited Iushkov.

15th In the morning I was at the magistracy, and after 2 o'clock in the afternoon I departed for Moscow. I stayed overnight in Sholokhovo.

16th Before 9 o'clock in the morning I arrived at the apartment. After dinner I was in the city.

17th Before 9 o'clock in the morning I visited Governor Lopukhin to present a report on the newly elected officers of the magistracy. I heard mass at Ascension Church. The rest of the time I was at the apartment.[31]

The passages above refer to Ivan's election to the post of mayor of his hometown at the end of the year 1788. The background to this move included a number of important family events and a deepening acquaintance by Ivan with members of the district nobility.

Two months after Katen'ka's death, new life came to the Tolchënov family. Early in 1788, Anna gave birth to a son, Pavel, one of the four of her sixteen children who survived childhood. The godparents were the elder son Pëtr and Ivan's cousin, Matrëna Ivanovna Loshkina, the daughter of Uncle Ivan and wife of Fëdor Loshkin. It is probable that the survival of Pavel endowed this particular choice of godparents with special significance, for they would be called on to play the same role for the next few children born to Anna and Ivan. And the children kept coming. They arrived on the same, almost yearly, schedule until 1794, even though Anna suffered some scary seizures and fainting spells after the birth of Pavel and would endure a series of health crises in the next four years.

The year 1788 also marked the twentieth anniversary of the untimely death of Ivan's mother, which occurred on May 6 in Petersburg when she was accompanying her husband for the second session of the Commission on Laws in 1768. Ivan was then in Novgorod traveling with the family's grain barges and had to rush to Petersburg to be with his father. This anniversary called for a special charitable act in remembrance of her. In keeping with merchant practices, Ivan hosted a large dinner for the poor of the city, feeding by his count about 175 people.[32]

Ivan's diary was a record of the people he knew and spent his time with, and even on the day of this open dinner for the poor people of Dmitrov, we can see that Ivan was able to fit in a visit to his new noble friend Afanasii Iushkov between early mass and prayers for the dead and the big midday dinner. Ivan more and more often was in the company of the local officials and landowning nobility. His frequent visits with Prince Ivan Golitsyn continued, as did his even more frequent, at times daily, visits to the widow Anna Obreskova and her children, the friends who were so close as to be virtually members of the Tolchënov family. Others with whom he spent a great deal of time when he was in the city included the police commissioner appointed by the central government, Anton Letstsano, and the district police captain elected by the local nobility, Ivan Kvashnin. In the case of Kvashnin, Ivan and Anna often visited him and his family at their nearby Lar'kovo manor. Others from the local nobility who appeared at the Tolchënov house regularly and whom Ivan and Anna visited at their rural estates were Afanasii Iushkov (and his brother Nikolai) at the village of Seliuvkino, Prince Ivan Obolenskii at his Botovo estate known for its superb gardens, and Pëtr Khitrovo, who hosted theater performances at his Podlipich'e manor. Two others whose country homes they visited were Lieutenant Nikolai L'vovich Vakhromeev, and I. I. Vel'iaminov-Zernov, although these two more often appeared at the Tolchënovs' home in the city.

Summer trips by the Tolchënovs to the north mills when Ivan checked on the loading of his grain barges provided other occasions for socializing. Ivan mixed work and pleasure on these trips. The noble landowning family that the Tolchënovs most often visited for dinner while sojourning there for the past eleven years was the Rakovskiis. In return, Ivan opened his home in Dmitrov to the Rakovskiis and put them up for the night when they were traveling south to Moscow. This summer of 1788 the Rakovskiis had a guest, Lady Kiova, about whom we learn little more than her name and that she had a home of her own in the area, to which Ivan and Anna later paid a visit. Prince Sergei Mikhailovich Golitsyn also had an estate here, on which sat the Miglosh mill that Ivan rented, and Ivan visited this other Prince Golitsyn on business and for dinner. He and the family also attended mass at Sergei Golitsyn's estate church.

Another family outing in 1788, probably a rite of passage for Pëtr, was a pilgrimage in late August to Rostov and Iaroslavl. Pëtr turned age fourteen on August 22, the same age Ivan had reached when his father took him on a similar pilgrimage to these ancient cities to visit the churches, monasteries, and business centers, marking Ivan's entry into the family business as an independent worker who no longer needed to be accompanied by a senior agent of the firm. The pilgrimage this time included Anna and her father, plus Andrei Fëdorovich Makarov (Ivan's step-uncle and ward who was now twenty-three years old and coming into his inheritance), and the Tolchënovs' next eldest son, Aleksei. The journey went by way of the Trinity Monastery in Sergiev Posad, where the travelers stopped to hear mass and visit the vestry to see "all the precious stone treasures collected there." Continuing on, Ivan recorded the trip with his watch in hand and with greater detail than his usual entries.

[August] 29th We left [the village of Tiribrovo] at 3:54 in the morning. Arriving at Pereslavl, we heard the bells announcing mass and therefore rode to the former Gortskii Monastery and attended mass there, and then we stopped at an inn in town at 10:20. Having finished dinner, we strolled through the city to the fishermen's quarter and there inspected the fishing equipment and smoke sheds before taking a boat ride on the Turbzha River all the way to the lake. However, because of the high waves we did not go very far [into the lake]. From Pereslavl we departed before 4 o'clock and rode to Nikitskii Monastery, where we heard vespers and prayed to Saint Nikita Stylites [Stolpnin].[33] Then we continued, stopping in the village of Krivoi Pogost for the night.

30th We left at 5:10 in the morning. We ate dinner in the village of Diubly and, continuing on, arrived in Rostov at the village of the Iakovlevskii Monastery at 4 o'clock in the afternoon, and we strolled around the city and through the trading lanes.

31st We heard early mass at the Iakovlevskii Monastery. Afterward we prayed to Saints Dmitrii and Iakov, the miracle workers. Then we attended late mass at the cathedral and prayed to the saints buried there. Later we decided to continue on to Iaroslavl at 2:12 in the afternoon on rented horses. We spent the night in the village of Shopsha.

September

1st Continuing on our way, we left at 4 in the morning and arrived in Iaroslavl at half past 7 and stopped at the Danilov inn. At the parish church we heard mass for the feast of Saint Simeon Stylites, which was conducted by Archbishop Arsenii. Afterward, having finished dinner, we walked through the lanes of shops and on the best streets of the city until the ringing of the vesper bells. At this time we prayed to the pious Princes Vasilii and Konstantin, who are buried here. Then we went to the Monastery of Our Savior [Spaskii] and there prayed to the pious Prince Fëdor and his children David and Konstantin. We spent the night in Iaroslavl.

This was the climax of the trip. The next day they returned by the most direct route, stopping only to spend the night and to pray to St. Sergei at the Trinity Monastery. Pëtr soon after went with his grandfather back to Moscow for his final year of schooling.

By now Ivan was so familiar with the nobles of the Dmitrov district that much of his autumn was taken up with visits to their villages. And Ivan's entries on these trips sometimes indicate his comfortable association with the local elite. Take, for example, his entry for September 15, where he wrote that "at about 9 in the morning my wife and I went with Iushkov and other local nobles to Squire Vakhromeev at the village of Alekseevo. We passed Pesnoshskii Monastery on the way and arrived at 2 in the afternoon. We had dinner with Vakhromeev, visited through the evening, and stayed overnight." Twice in October Ivan and Anna spent the day at the Podlipich'e estate of Pëtr Khitrovo, and scattered through this period were their continuing and regular visits for dinner with Prince Ivan Golitsyn at his Danilovskoe estate. For example, on October 22 Ivan and Anna went to Podlipich'e for dinner and the evening. Two days later they were at Afanasii Iushkov's for dinner and supper. Four days after that, Anna and Ivan dined at Golitsyn's estate, and two days later again they had dinner with Khitrovo at Podlipich'e. The following night Ivan was in Lar'kovo village at the home of the district police captain Ivan Kvashnin. The next day he and Anna had dinner and supper at the home of another local noble, Squire Moshinskii.

At the same time, Ivan was doing his own share of hosting the local elite. The socializing seems to have grown in frequency in this period and may have something to do with the forthcoming elections for city offices. According to Catherine II's new law on the cities, top urban officials were to be chosen by a vote of the entire local society and not just the commercial estate. Ivan's diary records on October 19 that he hosted dinner that day for "Prince Ivan Fëdorovich Golitsyn and his family, and all the city officials, Khitrovo and his wife, and our relatives. They stayed all day and through the evening."[34] About a month later, he organized another big gathering with a slightly different clientele. The occasion was the feast day of the Presentation of the Virgin associated with his parish church. "I heard mass at Presentation Church. I hosted dinner for the abbot, Iushkov, the police commissioner, Shokurov [an assessor of the district court], and other judges and relatives, more than 20 persons, and they stayed past 10 o'clock."[35] In short, Ivan was entertaining his acquaintances from the local nobility, plus officials appointed by the central government and those elected locally, who were also nobles, and having them socialize with his relatives from the merchant estate in what seems to have been an effort to foster a socially diverse urban elite.

The next ten days Ivan, Anna, and their son Aleksei were in Moscow on a business and family trip. When Ivan returned, he checked in separately with his

Portrait of the merchant and mayor of Iaroslavl, Ivan Kuchumov, painted by
Dmitrii Kornev in 1784, demonstrating the style of dress and general appearance
Ivan Tolchënov might have shared. Kuchumov occupied the same civic position
as Tolchënov at the same time. No portrait of Ivan Tolchënov exists. Iaroslavl
Historical-Architectural Museum, Iaroslavl.

influential friends in the community: Prince Ivan Golitsyn, and the police commissioner and the district police captain. On December 10 the elections for city offices for the next three years were in progress. As can be seen in the diary excerpt at the start of this section, Ivan and Anna were home that evening hosting a friend of Anna's from the local nobility, Miss Moshinskaia, when at about 7 o'clock he was informed, probably not unexpectedly, that he had been elected mayor and was supposed to appear immediately at the magistracy to observe the further voting.

Why would Ivan have sought out this position at a time when it might seem that he could better have concentrated on his business and halted his slide into debt? The answer is no doubt that his elevation to this position would ensure his inclusion in a new social category created by Empress Catherine in her 1785 Charter to the Towns, the rank of "distinguished citizen" (*imenityi grazhdanin*), which provided highly desirable exemptions and privileges, including things that merchants had long sought for their estate as a whole: exemption from corporal punishment and the right to live in the style of a noble. Although this distinction could be acquired by amassing and declaring for taxation purposes a very large capital, that option must have appeared increasingly remote to Ivan, even if he were able to stem his business losses. Public service was another means to the same end, and Ivan's experience and connections positioned him well to seize this opportunity. Once acquired, this new distinction was difficult to lose. Despite Ivan's later troubles and social descent, he continued to be referred to as distinguished citizen until the end of his life, an honor that accorded him a measure of personal protection and respect and no doubt also opened doors that might otherwise have been closed to him.

RESTORATION OF THE DORMITION
CATHEDRAL IN DMITROV

[1791, September] 26th At 10 in the morning at the invitation of [Squire] Iushkov I rode to Seliuvkino, where that morning the Right Reverend Bishop Serapion had arrived on his way from Moscow to Dmitrov for the consecration of the cathedral, and other guests of Iushkov had gathered there, and in their company I had dinner and spent the day and evening and ate supper before heading back home after midnight. In the meantime, that evening Matvei Orlov and his wife had arrived at my house from Moscow.

27th In the morning I visited the Right Reverend, who was staying at the monastery and had designated the next day for the consecration of the cathedral. For this reason, I also asked him to come to my home for dinner, and I spent the rest of the day making preparations. In the evening I attended the vigil at the cathedral, which was conducted by the Right Reverend himself.

28th I was at the consecration in the cathedral of the restored upper Church of Our Immaculate Lady and her glorious Dormition, which was conducted by the Right Reverend Serapion and the clergy, and Serapion delivered a sermon. Dining at my house with him were Prince Ivan Fëdorovich Golitsyn, Chairman [of the district nobility] Mishkov, [Squire] Golovin and his family, [Mrs.] Obreskova and her children, [Squire] Iushkov, [Squire] Vakhromeev, and other guests and relatives, in all 25 persons, and some stayed for the evening. Vakhromeev and Orlov and his wife stayed overnight.

29th I spent the morning at home with our guests, who stayed for dinner. Orlov then left for Moscow, and I stayed and visited with Vakhromeev and then had supper at Shpilëvo with Obreskova.

30th This morning from 10 to 11 o'clock I visited the bishop and the rest of the time I was at home.

October 1st I attended the vigil and mass at Presentation Church. The mass was said by the bishop, who afterward came to visit me. The rest of the time I spent at home.

Ivan's new position as mayor of Dmitrov shifted the focus of his public service. As a burgomaster serving in the magistracy he had to spend many of his mornings at the office hearing, reading, and deciding legal matters. The magistracy was in large part a court and was becoming almost wholly so as a result of the recent administrative reforms. And the jurisdiction of the magistracy was limited to the affairs of persons registered in the urban social estates of merchant and "lesser town dweller." The office of mayor in the new administrative order was intended to represent the city as a whole, including members of the nobility and other non-commercial people who resided there. In most cities this arrangement did not work out as well as its designers had hoped, mainly because the nobility was not yet willing to participate. But in the beginning the people of Dmitrov seemed able to pull together, in part probably because all the residents of the town had to deal with two difficult and costly challenges. The cooperation may also have owed something to Ivan's ability to develop and maintain friendly relations with his neighbors from all levels of society.

The two challenges that confronted the city more or less simultaneously during Ivan's term as mayor from December 1788 through 1791 were the restoration of the Dormition Cathedral in Dmitrov and the reorganization of the street plan of the city. Let's focus first on the cathedral renovation and then take up the second challenge in the next section.

The cathedral was a splendid architectural achievement of the early sixteenth century, an era not lacking in impressive new structures in central Russia. Dmitrov had benefited at that time from the growing commercial traffic between Moscow and the White Sea, which permitted the townspeople to finance a magnificent masonry cathedral in the heart of the walled city. Later years were, however, not so good to the city. Trade to the north declined in the seventeenth century, and when Peter I, early in the next century, built a new capital at the mouth of the Neva River, the main route from Moscow to Petersburg bypassed Dmitrov. The town lacked the resources to do major maintenance on the cathedral, and the building gradually deteriorated. The central structural elements rested on oak piles driven into sandy soil that allowed rot to creep in. Shifting and settling of the building's supporting columns produced cracks and crumbling of the walls, and this in turn let in moisture that caused further damage to the structure and its objects of devotion. By the 1730s the cathedral clergy was pressing the Governing Senate to provide funds for repairs. The best they could extract were small sums sufficient to pay only for patching up surface damage. This work and a renewed effort at repair in the 1760s proved wholly inadequate.

By the late 1770s the condition of the cathedral bordered on the catastrophic. Settling had increased, and huge cracks appeared in all of the five drums that supported the cupolas. At this point the voevoda, Pëtr Zherebtsov, and the treasurer for the Economic Collegium, Viktor Nazimov, two centrally appointed government officials, stepped in and asked for an urgent architectural survey and cost estimate for repairs. This initiative, which must have been a response to pressure from the local clergy and citizens, marked the start of a protracted fight to obtain funding. Among the problems faced by the city was the refusal of the Holy Synod even to recognize the cathedral as a building for which it bore responsibility. It turned out that because the church had not been associated in early times with a particular type of patrimonial property, it had not been included on the list of state churches. The Governing Senate helped to clear up this mistake and then requested funding from the empress for repairs, which initially she authorized. Everything seemed fine. But then war broke out with Ottoman Turkey in 1787, and the government froze all expenditures for church repairs. After many years of effort the project appeared doomed.

Luckily for the people of Dmitrov, a number of positive circumstances came together just at this time and enabled them to save the Dormition Cathedral. First, the city was enjoying a brief economic renaissance. Its merchant families of recent generations, the fathers and grandfathers of Ivan and his peers, had seized the opportunity to make money by supplying commodities, especially grain, to the burgeoning market created by the rapid growth of Petersburg. They did especially well by getting in early and developing the markets and know-how that allowed them to play a leading role. Although this dominance did not last more than a few decades, the city for a while prospered as never before, and its merchant families contributed a portion of their wealth to spruce up the town.[36] Before mid-century not a single parish church in Dmitrov had been built in masonry. Then from the 1750s to the 1810s every wooden church in the city was redone in masonry—and new masonry churches were added, such as the Presentation Church on the west side of town that the Makarovs and Tolchënovs had heavily endowed.

Second, the city was also fortunate to have on its side at this time an extraordinarily active and effective bishop. The position was somewhat unusual. The man who occupied it, Serapion, had been appointed in May of 1788 to assist Metropolitan Platon. Serapion served as Platon's vicar, and to give him an impressive presence, changes were made in the boundaries of the archdiocese of Pereslavl-Zaleskii, so that Serapion, though he resided elsewhere, could be styled the bishop of Dmitrov. As it happened he took this assignment to heart, and in September of that year he visited the city and got acquainted with the top people, including Ivan Tolchënov. Ivan wrote in his diary that after mass in the cathedral, "I went to see [Bishop Serapion] at the monastery and was invited along with other city officials to dine with him there." Two days later Serapion rode over to inspect the Presentation Church just down the street from Ivan's new home. Ivan met him there, and the bishop accepted an invitation to visit Ivan in his home.[37] Undoubtedly, at these meetings much was said about the deterioration of the cathedral and the urgency of taking action. Serapion immediately took an interest in the matter. Very soon he was pressing the nobles and merchants of Dmitrov to cooperate in amassing the funds needed to do the renovation now that they could no longer count on a substantial government contribution.

It was about this time that Ivan was elected mayor, and he was soon deeply involved in the project. Within a month of his election Ivan was in Moscow to meet with Serapion. Most of the rest of the same day he was with Prince Ivan Golitsyn, whose help would be important in winning the support of the local nobility. The next day Ivan visited a Moscow architect. The project was gaining momentum. In March of 1789 Ivan was back in Moscow and met twice with Serapion, and in May Serapion arranged for two architects from Moscow to do an updated survey of the cathedral. The first to arrive was Captain Pëtr Shishkin, who, Ivan recorded in his diary, on May 14 "came to inspect and make drawings of the cathedral, and he accepted an invitation to stay at my house." During the next days Ivan spent a lot of time with Shishkin and the archpriest of the cathedral while they checked the building and subsoil in the area. On the nineteenth the second architect arrived, Collegiate Assessor and Major Semën Korin. "I hosted them for dinner," Ivan wrote. "Then we walked to the cathedral. They drew their conclusions about the repairs, and both left for Moscow at 6 in the afternoon."[38]

Ivan's leadership was the third positive element in getting the job done. He even seems to have influenced the choice of the architect to supervise the project. Just a few days after the survey by Shishkin and Korin, Ivan was hosting Mikhailo Agafonov, the architect who had built his home and who also worked for Prince Ivan Golitsyn, designing buildings at Danilovskoe. Presumably following the advice of Ivan and possibly also Golitsyn, Serapion soon gave Agafonov the assignment of drawing up a budget and supervising the project. In a memorandum from July of this year the bishop underlined the central role that Ivan had assumed in the overall effort. "The mayor, Mr. Ivan Alekseich [sic] Tolchënov," wrote the bishop, "has assured us that the merchants of Dmitrov will take upon themselves the restoration of the cathedral."[39] Ivan then went to work, in cooperation with the archpriest, to collect the needed funds. He had the fall and winter to do the job, since Agafonov set the starting date for the next spring, having seen that the building materials were not yet purchased and delivered to the city. Ivan asked the bishop for a book with the cord and seal of the Church Administration for use in soliciting contributions.

In a short time and against great odds, Ivan succeeded in collecting 3,000 rubles from the "zealous citizens" of the town, as the church authorities put it in a report from this time. Ivan had informed the church leaders that the city was facing a costly reorganization of its streets and private properties, making it difficult to ask for large contributions. The Church Administration understood and was able to add another 1,808 rubles to the 3,000 that Ivan had gathered, bringing the funds available for the renovation to 4,808.

Although Ivan did not complain about the difficulties and indeed seemed energized by the project, it was unquestionably a stressful time for him. It was just then, late summer 1789, when he was soliciting funds for the cathedral that the governor-general descended on the town, making angry demands about its reorganization. Within days of this unpleasant visit, Ivan's wife Anna suffered a labor so prolonged and exhausting that the family feared for her life. She said confession and prepared for the worst. But, luckily, she was able finally to deliver the baby. Ivan wrote: "I spent the day in sorrow but it ended in joy," as just before midnight Anna gave birth to a son. The boy was given the name of Iakov and was one of the four children of Anna and Ivan who survived into adulthood. This crisis gives us another brief glimpse of the network of support for a woman of Anna's standing. Ivan reported that as she was regaining her health, she was visited by "Lady Khitrovo and the wife of the district doctor, and others."[40]

Late winter and spring 1790 were occupied with ordering and transporting materials for the cathedral work to Dmitrov. Ivan went back and forth to Moscow many times, checking in with Serapion and Agafonov. He also met very often with a man named Matvei Orlov, who apparently was instrumental in organizing the materials for the project. (The diary excerpts at the head of this section show that Orlov and his wife later appeared in Dmitrov for the

consecration of the restored church.) Back in Dmitrov, Ivan frequently inspected the materials that were arriving. The work got underway in earnest as
summer approached, and Ivan was at the cathedral nearly every day right
through the month of September whenever he was in town. In early August
Bishop Serapion came to Dmitrov for a few days to look over the work. Ivan
visited with him often and accompanied him on inspection tours of the work in
progress at the cathedral. To top it off, the bishop accepted an invitation to join
Ivan for dinner, and Ivan recorded with delight that the bishop stayed on until 5
o'clock. The guests included the abbot of the Boris and Gleb Monastery and the
archpriest of the cathedral as well as the top government officials (the police
commissioner and district police captain), the district doctor, the government
legal aide, and a number of locally elected nobles and aristocrats, starting with
Prince Obolenskii, and finally Uncle Ivan Il'ich and others. Ivan made a separate trip out to Danilovskoe on the day preceding the dinner to personally
invite Prince Ivan Golitsyn, but Golitsyn was under the weather and declined
the offer.

As the repairs got underway a surprising discovery was made about the use
of the building. The authorities learned that the holder of the local liquor tax
franchise was using the basement of the cathedral to store large supplies of
vodka for distribution to his drink shops. The initial reaction of the Church
Administration was that the cathedral was an inappropriate place to house such
a business and that the vodka could stay there only until the supply on hand was
sold and only if it did not interfere with the renovation. But it soon came to
light that the rental payments by the liquor franchisee were the sole regular
source of income for the clergy's use in maintaining the everyday operation of
the cathedral churches, and the clergy was loath to give it up. Accordingly, after
a series of memoranda on the matter, the Church Administration agreed that
the contract with the liquor franchisee should continue indefinitely.[41] This use
of church property to earn income was apparently quite common, if one ac-
cepts the judgment of the Russian Freemason Maksim Nevzorov. He criticized
the clergy at this time for being little more than petty tradesmen. "All of the
Archbishopric and monastery buildings in Moscow, which form lairs of inns,
eating-houses, coaching inns and shows, which serve only for luxury, stand in
proof of this."[42] It seems that after the secularization of church property in the
1760s, the finances needed to conduct the Lord's work required concessions to
his adversary.

Most of the renovation was completed the following year 1791, and Ivan was
bending every effort to see that the building would be consecrated before the
end of the year. His term as mayor came to a close in December of that year, and
he desperately wanted the project completed while he could still garner the
satisfaction and credit for having accomplished it. Despite his own sinking

finances, when the funds originally allocated to the cathedral renovation ran out in the summer of 1791, Ivan stepped in and made a very large no-interest loan of 433 rubles, or nearly 10 percent of the entire cost of the renovation, to ensure the work's swift completion. The only thing that did not get finished was the frescoes for the walls of the upper or main church. Serapion raised the question of painting the walls in May and even dispatched to Dmitrov an "iconographer of Greek paintings" to consult on whether to prepare the walls for frescoes or to postpone the job. At this point, Ivan explained in a personal letter to the bishop that although the local contributors very much wished to have the walls painted, "the citizens were suffering greatly this year from both very poor commercial returns and the need to reconstruct their homes." This second point referred to the radical redesign that was being forced on the city. It was agreed therefore to postpone the frescoes and whitewash the walls.[43]

This decision and Ivan's loan cleared the way to finish the work. Ivan inspected the cathedral almost daily through the summer and went to Moscow in mid-August to report to the bishop on the progress. It was probably at this time that Serapion agreed on a date for the consecration, which was set for the last days of September.

In the portion of the diary excerpted at the start of this section, Ivan noted the consecration and related events, including the impressive dinner party that he hosted. The diary entries make clear that he derived enormous satisfaction from his central role in achieving the long-sought restoration. And, indeed, this achievement, won against great odds, filled the local clergy and its supporters with such enthusiasm that they asked to push ahead immediately with the construction of a great bell tower for the cathedral. They had salvaged 80,000 bricks from the walls dismantled in the renovation in hopes of using them for the bell tower. Unfortunately, the same financial difficulties that delayed the frescoes frustrated the hopes to move ahead on the bell tower. This project became a task for later city administrations, which were finally able to generate the funding and finish the job in the second half of the decade.

By that time, Ivan was no longer living in Dmitrov. But his work from 1789 through 1791 on the cathedral had left its mark. He had created an impressive legacy in his final philanthropic effort, and his work received recognition not just in the attention he garnered at the time of the consecration but also in a more enduring form. A stone plaque crafted by a skilled Moscow stonemason and placed in the wall of the cathedral thanked him for his efforts in assembling the funds for the project.[44] A more personal and very satisfying recognition came a year after the consecration when Ivan and his family visited the Trinity Monastery, the seat of the Moscow Metropolitan. Ivan recorded the day in his diary. On September 12, "after early mass at the refectory I received a blessing from their Right Reverends Platon and Serapion, for the latter happened to be at the monastery to visit the metropolitan, and both had heard mass in the refectory, and I was invited by the Right Reverend Platon to his cell for tea and was there for about an hour."[45] As it happened, this diary record of Ivan's personal audience with the best-known and most influential cleric of his day proved more enduring than the stone plaque in the cathedral wall, only a portion of which remains today. If Ivan's purpose in transcribing and pre-serving his diary notes in leather-bound volumes was to leave a record of his important position, he succeeded far more effectively than he might have imagined.

THE "DESTRUCTIVE" REORDERING OF THE CITY

[1790, August] 17th In the morning news was received about the arrival today of the governor-general, Aleksandr Aleksandrovich Prozorovskii. I therefore spent the entire day at the magistracy and on the outskirts of town by the Moscow Road for a meeting of the society, and at 7 o'clock in the evening his excellency arrived and was quartered in my house.

18th [Sunday] The governor-general heard mass at Presentation Church, where I was too. Then I followed him together with all the city officials as we rode in droshkies around the outskirts and in the central areas of the city until after 1 o'clock in the afternoon. I had dinner by invitation with the governor-general. The rest of the time I spent at home.

19th At 11 o'clock in the morning I followed the governor-general to the govern-ment offices, which he examined and then just after noon rode out of town with his suite to the prince at Danilovskoe, and from there continued to Sergiev Posad. The rest of the time I spent at home.

The administrative reforms of 1775 reshaped the provinces and districts of Russia into territories with more or less equivalent numbers of people, 300,000 to 400,000 for provinces and 20,000 to 30,000 for districts. The reform also called for the re-formation of towns along a rational grid of broad streets and squares. The focus of this policy was the old cities of central Russia with their narrow winding streets, promiscuous mixing of private homes, artisan shops and smithies, warehouses and other buildings. The policy was largely a re-sponse to the damage frequently visited on cities by fire, which turned whole sections into ashes. In 1763 fire caused the near total destruction of the ancient Volga city of Tver. Prevention of the plague, which had returned to central Russia in 1771, and which was thought to be caused by crowding, pollution and resultant miasmas, was another consideration.[46] The government also wanted to make it easier for military units and other traffic to move through cities with dispatch. The preferred model of the era was the baroque city of neat rectilinear forms, ordering the urban landscape in ways that gave a sense of greater control than did the historically formed and cluttered street scene of old Russian towns. (Dmitrov was one of the latter, a town that had grown outward from the ancient fortress walls, following old paths.) The policy may therefore also be seen as another example of the rationalist disembedding of Ivan and his contemporaries from their traditional spatial moorings and their displacement into a modern system of abstract ordering, making them part of an extending and homogenizing project of urban design. Another feature of the design was separate city blocks for each social estate, a sign of the governing elite's growing anxiety about the transgression of social boundaries and its desire to fix persons in well-defined and unalterable ascriptive roles.

The process of remaking the city got started in Dmitrov in June of 1782, perhaps spurred on by a recent fire that had almost totally consumed Rogachëvo, a nearby town that served as Dmitrov's port to the Volga. The conflagration at Rogachëvo that May had destroyed two churches and nearly all the other buildings, leaving only four homes standing. In June the Moscow governor-general, Count Zakhar Chernyshëv, sent a team under the leadership of Lieutenant-Colonel Shchelin to survey and draw up a plan for reorganizing the city of Dmitrov along a rectilinear plan with broad streets. It is worth recalling the importance that Ivan attached to this visit and to the work the team was to perform.[47] During the six days Colonel Shchelin was in town Ivan hosted a dinner for him and his officers, met with him once or twice each day, introduced him to prominent citizens, and even took him fishing. And no wonder. Not only did the Tolchënovs and Makarovs own a number of properties that could be affected by a redesign of the city, but Ivan was already making plans for his masonry home and needed to ensure that the new town plan would not pose difficulties for its siting.

The plan drawn up on the basis of Shchelin's work in the following year received confirmation by the empress and was delivered to the police commissioner in Dmitrov, Anton Letstsano, in March of 1784.[48] At the same time, Ivan explained in a report inserted into the diary some years later, the commissioner was instructed "not to allow anyone to repair any buildings and when someone wanted to rebuild a house, it should be sited in conformity to the plan." And, Ivan continued, "my masonry home was in that very same year laid out on the lines designated in the plan." Ivan went on to say that in the next several years nothing much was accomplished on the redesign of the city. The project seemed to interest Count Chernyshëv, but he died suddenly just six months after the plan reached Police Commissioner Letstsano. Chernyshëv's successors, Count Iakov Brius and Pëtr Eropkin, showed no interest in the project. They both made visits to Dmitrov during their terms of office and did not so much as mention the new city plan. Likewise, the civil governor of Moscow province, Pëtr Lopukhin, who visited Dmitrov on numerous occasions, invariably consented to the requests of citizens to be allowed to repair their homes and buildings in place.[49] Given the lack of pressure from the Moscow authorities and what Ivan described as Police Commissioner Letstsano's "naturally charitable inclinations, [Letstsano] permitted everyone to make repairs to current buildings. Only if someone found it impossible to repair an existing building was a replacement erected on a new site in accordance with the plan." As a consequence, by 1790 only about twenty houses had been built as required.

Then, just as Ivan was in the midst of his second year as mayor and working hard to complete the renovation of the Dormition Cathedral, the city received an unexpected shock. The new Moscow governor-general, Prince Aleksandr Aleksandrovich Prozorovskii, decided that reorganization of the cities had to be a priority.

Prozorovskii occupies a prominent place in Russian intellectual history, where he is notorious for having investigated and persecuted the writer, publisher, moralist, and philanthropist Nikolai Novikov. Novikov was also a leading Freemason, and unfortunately for him, Empress Catherine had become very suspicious of the Freemasons and instructed Prozorovskii to look into their activities. Russian Masonic lodges had links to Grand Prince Paul and to lodges in other northern countries hostile to Russia, and some scholars believe that Catherine feared the Masons were hatching a plot to overthrow her and place her son Paul on the throne to further the foreign policy interests of Prussia and Sweden. A recent study argues, in contrast, that internal political pressures were more important. Catherine had found her earlier tolerance for the heterodox ideas of the Freemasons were bringing increasing complaints from the Holy Synod, which regarded the Freemasons' moral writings a challenge to the authority of the Russian Orthodox Church. The country faced two foreign wars, and Catherine needed the support of the Church. Prozorovskii took on the task of investigating Novikov and his associates with vigor and presented Catherine evidence that, while scarcely incriminating, intensified her concerns and led to Novikov's imprisonment.[50] It is worth observing that another of Ivan Tolchënov's prominent acquaintances at this time, Metropolitan Platon, was also asked to evaluate Novikov's ideas, and Platon defended him against accusations of subversion. Nevertheless, Novikov was incarcerated.

Empress Catherine by all accounts was not fond of Prozorovskii. He had a sharp tongue and garrulous manner that offended her. But advisers convinced her that Governor-General Eropkin was not tough enough to deal with the difficult issue of subversion, and she agreed to appoint the energetic, if peevish, Prozorovskii.[51] Ivan and his fellow citizens were soon to get acquainted with this forceful and arrogant viceroy.

Prozorovskii was appointed to his post early in 1790 and made his first visit to Dmitrov in mid-August of that year. The daily entries in Ivan's diary give

little idea of the drama of this visit and what it portended. The passages referring to this first trip are excerpted at the head of this section. As usual, Ivan
reported the surface events only. Prozorovskii came, attended church, met the
city officials, toured the town, had dinner, looked over things at the government offices, and left. All very matter of fact. We know, however, that it could
not have been a pleasant experience. A memorandum drafted for Prozorovskii
on the day of his visit indicates that he had been carefully reviewing the work
of the government offices in Dmitrov beforehand and was not pleased. He
sent a pointed order to the district legal official, accusing him of neglecting
his responsibilities. This was followed by an order listing specific mistakes in
the work of the district courts, the police, and the city magistracy, emphasizing
the lack of proper documentation and the vagueness of reports on cases and
verdicts.[52]

When Ivan was composing his short essay on this history some years later in
his summary notes, he again reported Prozorovskii's descent on the town in
restrained tones, but he admitted in this second report that the visit was not very
encouraging. "Prozorovskii . . . had a distinct inclination toward the regular
construction of settlements, and so from his very arrival the sight of streets and
houses scattered about randomly and little progress having been made on the
redesign made him unhappy. He made this clear to the police commissioner as
well as to the entire citizenry, and he told the former that he had better strive
vigorously to get the reconstruction done and to open up all the new streets."[53]
At the same time, Prozorovskii declared that some aspects of the current plan
for reorganizing the city needed to be improved, and he arranged for the
Moscow province surveyor Kliucharëv to come to Dmitrov in October to draw
up a new plan. The new design followed the previous one but also included
some significant alterations. Then, with scarcely any delay, another surveyor
appeared in town in January of 1791 and planted signs and posts delineating all
the new streets and city blocks. In May an order arrived demanding the immediate opening of the new streets and squares and the razing of fifty homes that
were blocking the route of the new main western artery, Klin Road. This sudden
command to destroy a large number of homes sent their owners reeling. They
rushed to Moscow with pleas to delay the action, but Prozorovskii was unbend-
ing. Their next recourse was to beg Police Commissioner Letstsano's permission
to put off the catastrophe, at the very least until they could harvest the products
of their gardens in the late summer. The ever-accommodating Letstsano, who
had been serving in Dmitrov for nine years and was a frequent visitor and close
friend of many families, acceded to these requests. By Ivan's account, Letstsano
began to enforce the order to raze homes only in September and even then did
not push the matter.

Unfortunately for Letstsano and everyone concerned, Governor-General

Prozorovskii decided to take a detour on his way north to Petersburg in early October and stopped off in Dmitrov to check on the reorganization of the city. Ivan's diary entries on this visit again relate merely the surface events that at six o'clock in the evening on October 3 the governor-general arrived and was quartered in Ivan's home. The next day he inspected the road project and at ten in the morning continued on to Klin. But in Ivan's later short essay we get a much different picture.

Seeing that nothing had been done to implement his personal commands, the governor-general expressed enormous dissatisfaction and heaped reproaches on Police Commissioner Letstsano, who owing to this incident decided to move else-where. Prozorovskii ordered Vice Governor Nikolai Efimovich Miasoedov to come here from Moscow to investigate the situation and to take charge of the work. That very same October he did so and checked all the lines that had been laid out by the surveyors, and several houses that lay close to mine on the new road were torn down, except for some huts, which were left until spring.[54]

All this was done with lightning speed. Ivan recorded that on October 19, just two weeks after Prozorovskii's surprise visit, "the main Klin Road was opened and the floating bridge relocated to this new thoroughfare, and on the 20th traffic began to travel on it."[55]

This process, which Ivan later called "the destructive reordering of the city," continued through the next year and beyond. The opening of the new Klin Road within two weeks of Prozorovskii's angry demands was more a gesture of submission than an achievement of the project. Indeed, the following year the bridge and traffic returned to their former route while the new Klin Road was closed for the paving of one side. At the same time the destruction of homes continued as the government surveyor supervised the re-setting of streets along a rectilinear grid. Ivan checked in with Prozorovskii in Moscow in early June, evidently with a request from the city council to be permitted to allocate properties along the new roads and streets. When Governor Lopukhin stopped in Dmitrov in late June to examine the progress of the project, he would have seen that dozens of homes had been dismantled in and along the principal streets and almost none had been rebuilt. Only by late in the year had some families moved building materials to new locations and begun to lay out the dimensions of new homes. Where all these people spent the winter is not recorded, but presumably they crowded in with relatives who lived in still undisturbed parts of the city.

Reconstruction began in earnest only in the next year, 1793. "In this year," Ivan reported in his later summary, "at the start of spring the floating bridge was moved to the new location by the thoroughfare, and people began to travel on it toward the middle of summer when the other half had been paved.

Though a great hardship on the townspeople, the road was a convenience for travelers. Quite a few homes were rebuilt this year along all the streets, especially on the north side of Klin Road and west side of Birch Street, where nearly all the homes were rebuilt." Ivan's new masonry house stood on the north side of Klin Road and was not directly affected by the new arrangements, but he must have been glad to see that his neighborhood was reforming quickly on the new grid. Parts of the other, eastern side of town proved unable to recover their residential character and were merely used as kitchen gardens until the middle of the nineteenth century.[56]

In early July of 1793 Prozorovskii made another trip to Dmitrov, this time with his wife, and stayed for nearly a week. Ivan was in Moscow during most of this time. He recorded in his diary for July 11 that "I arrived home safely. Governor-General Prince Aleksandr Aleksandrovich Prozorovskii and his wife had been living in my house since the 6th, having come to our town from the Trinity Monastery." And then the next day, the 12th, "At 10 in the morning the governor-general left for Moscow satisfied with everything. . . ." Ivan later added in his year-end summary that "Prozorovskii had examined everything in detail and was satisfied with the success of the reorganization and did not order that coercion be used to get more buildings dismantled in the expectation that the residents would themselves now find it necessary to rebuild."[57]

Even so, the disruption to the city continued for many years thereafter. Just sorting out how much property was lost to various parties and what they should receive in compensatory land for rebuilding was a major headache, as was the issue of where a home should be located, in view of the new plan's designation of specific sections of the city for particular social groups: nobles, merchants, and others. The Dmitrov archives are filled with volume upon volume of cases on these matters for many years into the future, as people naturally sought to preserve as much of their previous homesteads as they could while receiving adjoining land in compensation for what was lost. Their claims inevitably conflicted with one another and with the rules about the socially designated residential sections. A very high proportion of the business conducted by the city magistracy in subsequent years was devoted to these cases. And, as mentioned earlier, some sections of the city did not get repopulated until a half century later.

This story illustrates two characteristics of Russian imperial administration and the articulation of absolutist power. The first is that the theoretically absolute power of the Russian sovereign had to be expressed through her agents at the local level. In other words, she had to delegate with little supervision or opportunity for feedback an enormous amount of her authority to her viceroys, the governors-general. Accordingly, their preferences had much to do with what would get accomplished. In the case of the reorganization of towns on a modern grid, the first governor-general, Zakhar Chernyshëv, seemed to have an interest in this matter and got the ball rolling, but his successors evidently cared little about it—until Prozorovskii took over twenty years later and demanded action. And the action he demanded only happened when he or one of his immediate subordinates physically appeared in Dmitrov and personally supervised the work.

Second, the primary local representative of imperial power, the police commissioner (or before him the voevoda) was likely to fall into one of two patterns of behavior. He could adopt an adversarial stance and remain an outsider to the town social networks. In this guise he could be a strict reporter of local affairs to the crown, turning in people when they bent or circumvented the laws, and could force on the community the policy decisions of the center regardless of local conditions. This approach had the disadvantage of disrupting the established power structures, which were the principal means of getting things done. The former assistant voevoda, Malygin, and the voevoda Andreanov appear to have maintained this outsider stance and been in conflict with the leading local families during much of their time in the city. These families in turn seemed to do what they could to make trouble for the officials.

Or a police commissioner could adopt a cooperative attitude and seek to work closely with the local power brokers. The likelihood in this case was that, like Anton Letstsano, he would be absorbed into the local society and be more responsive to its concerns than to the orders he received from the capital. For Letstsano this stance worked well so long as the central authorities were not trying to change the accepted arrangements in his district. When Prince Prozorovskii arrived with a strong agenda for change, Letstsano's efforts to soften the blow on his local clients got him and them into trouble and ended up costing Letstsano his job. The longer an imperial official's stay in a particular locale the greater the risk he would merge with the community he was supposed to supervise and become less useful as a tool of oversight and change. By the same token, such an official would be helpful in keeping routine matters on track and not upsetting local structures.

Finally, observe the contrast between the responses of the citizens of Dmitrov to these two projects. On the one hand, we see in the cathedral renovation civic action of a high order. The archpriest and cathedral clergy cooperated closely with the mayor and the leading citizens to mobilize government and private support for the project. The bishop assisted in absolutely crucial ways by tapping central government contributions of personnel and money through the Church Administration. He would not have done so had the citizens of Dmitrov not approached the effort with great enthusiasm and major contributions of their own. Despite commercial setbacks and the simultaneous need to rebuild large sections of their city, the civic leaders in Dmitrov pulled together to assemble the architectural talent, skilled workers, and financial means to complete the project in a short time and to do so with no prodding from anyone. On the other hand, the forcible imposition of a new ordering of the city's streets, squares, and residential sections by the stern and inflexible governor-general met with a different response. Here, too, one senses a civic solidarity in resistance, as people bombarded the authorities with appeals for delay and the leading families used their influence with the police commissioner to buy time. But in this case, the citizens did not command the institutional capacity or authority to act effectively on their own behalf and were compelled to submit to the demands of the central government. They did enjoy sufficient autonomy and the institutional means to sort out between themselves the property rearrangements, the claims and counterclaims, of their fellow citizens, and the city's elected representatives spent the next several years at this work. These events help to define the boundaries within which merchants could form their social identity. The autonomy they were able to exercise would be important to Ivan both in shaping his personal identity and also in cushioning the blow to him when he had to depart from his former social estate.

*   *   *

This period marked the high point of Ivan's civic and social life. He had reached the pinnacle of urban governance in the role of mayor, and in that capacity he was working with high clerics and government officials of national importance. He was also included in the social life of the leading nobles of his district. He was a leader among his peers as well and demonstrated an ability to win their support for the cathedral renovation and, until the intervention of Prozorov-skii, to help them modify and delay the "destructive" project to reorganize their city. In short, he had refashioned his self-identity from that of a domestic grain trader of limited education to a person who associated with the powerful and the well-born, and in the process he had embellished his personality with the attributes of a man interested in reading, the arts, and modern methods of sequestering nature.

Another feature of this change that becomes evident in this period is Ivan's entry into the world of medicine. Earlier, when he had become gravely ill while traveling north to supervise the grain barges, he had not asked for a doctor or used any kind of medicine. The advent of district doctors after the local government reforms of the 1770s had put him into contact with a new field of scientific practice. After he settled down in Dmitrov following his father's death, Ivan regularly hosted district doctors in his home and even became close friends with some of them. Their knowledge and Ivan's own aspiration to modernity must have convinced him of the utility of medical intervention. The first mention of Ivan going to a doctor was in April 1784, when he was in Moscow and he and Anna made a visit to a Dr. Ferzeksh. Now again in 1787, when their two children were critically ill, they called on the help of the local physician, Dr. Kazotti. Ivan's trust in medical doctors did not, however, become absolute, and in a later health crisis he resorted again to inherited practices, revealing his characteristic betweenness.

The question for Ivan now was whether having achieved recognition as a civic leader who rose to the position of "distinguished citizen," he would be able to maintain this social identity and personal standing in the face of the increasing financial difficulties caused by his expansive living. The next phase of his life will be consumed with an effort to preserve his material and social accomplishments, or, in short, his new identity as a merchant who could enjoy the same respect and style of life as the nobles of his acquaintance.

6

Eminent Trickster

TWO TRIPS TO PETERSBURG

[1789, October] 22nd [Pëtr and I] arrived in Tosna after 4 in the morning and were delayed there until after 9 o'clock for repairs to our vehicle and replacement of the axle. Continuing on, at 1 o'clock in the afternoon we stopped for dinner in Slovianka and left at 2. By the grace of God we arrived in Petersburg before 6 o'clock and stopped near Nevskii [Monastery] at the apartment of Stepan Tiut'kin.

23rd In the morning I was on our barges. Afterward I heard late mass at the Nevskii Monastery and then inspected the interior of the new cathedral church. After dinner I was at the market and we took a ride around the nicest streets.

24th I spent the morning on the barges and after dinner was at the market.

25th Before dinner I was in the apartment and afterward at the commodity exchange, and from there I rode over to look at the chapel of the St. Isaac Church. In the evening I visited Pavel Tolchënov.

26th In the morning I went to see Rezvyi, whom I did not however find. After dinner I was at Korob'in's and in the evening visited Iamshchikov.

27th I attended early mass at the Nevskii in the Lazarus Church. Then I visited the abbot, Nikander, who had earlier been the father superior at the Boris and Gleb Monastery in Dmitrov, and the rest of the time I was at the apartment.

28th I heard mass at the Kazan Cathedral. For the occasion of the celebration of the recovery of Grand Duchess Aleksandra Pavlovna from smallpox, the mass and prayers were conducted by Innokentii, archbishop of Pskov. From the cathedral out of curiosity I rode over to the Catholic church and observed their service. In the evening Petrusha and I were at the Malyi Theater, where they did the comedy "Twins" and a ballet.

29th In the morning I was at Rezvyi's and then went to the protocol official of *the [imperial] court administration. Later I visited Messrs. Letstsano. The rest of the time I spent at the apartment.*

30th Having left the apartment after 11 in the morning, I was at the court administration, then at the Academy bookstore. I ate dinner at the Novgorod Inn. Then until 5 o'clock I visited Aleksei Rudakov, and from there I was at the theater, where they were doing the opera "Diana's Tree."

31st I spent the day at the apartment and the evening at Ivan Petelin's.

November 1st Before dinner I was at the apartment, and afterward at the bazaar and at Tokarev's. In the evening Korob'in and his wife visited me.

2nd In the morning I visited Pavel Tolchënov and Rezvyi, and was at the apartment from dinner time and Tokarev visited me in the evening.

3rd I heard mass at the Nevskii and spent the rest of the time at the apartment.

4th Petrusha and I attended mass at the Great Court Church, where the empress, the heir, and the grand duchess were present. We ate dinner and stayed until 6 o'clock at Petelin's, and from there visited Pëtr Rudakov.

5th I was at the apartment until noon. I ate dinner and spent the evening with a group at Pavel Tolchënov's.

6th I heard mass at the Nevskii, which was conducted by Metropolitan Gavriil and the confessor of the empress on the occasion of the interment of the lady-in-waiting Polianskaia. I dined and spent the day and evening and had supper at Pavel Tolchënov's on his name day.

7th Before dinner I was at the apartment, and afterward at the market and at Korob'in's. In the evening I visited Petelin.

8th I heard mass at the Nevskii, and in the evening visited Karpov.

9th In the morning I visited Nikolai Andreevich Molchanov, and then Pavel Tolchënov. From there I went to the market and then went with Petrusha to see the Kunst Kamera. I had dinner and spent the day and evening and had supper at Karpov's.

The diary passage starting this section covers the first weeks of Ivan's month-long trip to Petersburg in the fall of 1789 with his son Pëtr. In his later year-end summaries for this period, Ivan lamented that the key to his financial difficulties, apart from his expansive living, was the slow collection of receipts in Petersburg, the end point of his grain commerce, and the shambles that his agent in the northern capital, Stepan Tiut'kin, had been making of his affairs there. Yet Ivan had not been to Petersburg since he took over the business in 1779 on the death of his father. Although he had started borrowing large sums to finance his trade as early as 1785, he did not sense a crisis coming and expected a favorable turn. His hopes were not entirely misplaced. The years 1787 and 1788 had yielded solid profits. We saw that Ivan had netted sufficient returns in 1787 to pay off some of the principal on his loans. Profits the following year were even greater, reaching a total of nearly 12,000 rubles. But this income was more than offset by expenditures, in large part because this was the year Ivan had to turn over to his young step-uncle Andrei Fëdorovich Makarov the capital that the Tolchënovs had been managing for him until his majority. Indeed, Ivan may have delayed this transfer—Andrei was already twenty-three years of age—until he had a year of exceptional profits, for the inheritance amounted to the very substantial sum of 11,000 rubles. Ivan's other expenses included 1,000 rubles for work on the new house, a 500-ruble contribution to the new bell tower and frescoes at the parish church, 800 rubles for his son Pëtr's education, 1,300 for interest on loans, 470 for remodeling of his orangeries, plus 6,000 on household expenses and gambling losses—altogether more than 10,000 rubles. Since his profits, great as they were, barely covered payment of Andrei Makarov's inheritance, Ivan's debts increased. Looking back on this predicament, he sighed that "hence in the midst of very favorable commercial conditions my capital not only did not grow but declined by 10,000 rubles, and I could not reduce my borrowing, even though my trade, as a result of the reduced sums and slow receipts from Petersburg, was decreasing in volume compared to my peers. Because they were more prudent than I, though we started with about the same capital, they were able to increase theirs substantially in these and the following years while I lost everything."[1]

At the time, however, Ivan must have thought that the situation was salvageable. He had enjoyed two profitable years in a row and had paid off the inheritance obligation to Andrei Makarov. More attention to business might still stave off disaster. It was no doubt with these hopes in mind that he finally bestirred himself to travel to Petersburg and look into affairs there, first with his eldest son Pëtr in 1789 and then two years later with his son Aleksei. The trips seem also to have been intended to introduce his sons to the life of the northern capital and the business arrangements of the family firm there. For example, we can see in the excerpt at the start of this section that Ivan took Pëtr to the theater and to the scientific exhibits at the Kunstkamera museum. Ivan himself stopped in to see the Catholic church "out of curiosity," just as he had visited a Lutheran church on an earlier trip. Ivan's interest in the wider world was evident in these visits prompted by "curiosity" during his stays in Petersburg.

The trip with Pëtr began on October 17 with a five-day ride north on post horses that included a stop in Novgorod to visit St. Sofia Cathedral, where "they had the honor of kissing the relics of all the saints." The stay in Petersburg itself was marked by a mix of business, cultural enrichment, and sightings of the imperial family. Although Ivan found time for a couple of evenings at the theater and stops at the Academy bookstore and the Kunstkamera, the diary shows that he concentrated on business, spending much of his time at the

market and with government officials, including a contractor for the imperial
court named Karpov, from whom Ivan was apparently trying to recover a bad
debt. Judging from this and later sections of the diary, Karpov seems to have put
Ivan off with promises of later payment.

Whatever adjustments Ivan made in his business during this trip to Petersburg were either done too late in the year to help or were overwhelmed by
market conditions, for he turned a profit for the year of only 7 to 16 kopeks per
ruble. This poor return and his declining volume of trade netted him a mere
3,350 rubles, or less than one-third of what he had earned the previous year. His
expenses were also down but ran well ahead of his income.[2]

In the following year Ivan was still able to make grain purchases at Lyskovo
and Orёl, though fewer than before because of his shrinking capital. He processed the grain at his mills and had it safely transported to Petersburg. But the
returns were again disappointing, in part because of continuing unfavorable
market conditions. After detailing the purchases and sales in his year-end account for 1790, he summarized the melancholy result.

*Thus, by the power of God, trade this year was unprofitable owing to the high
cost of grain and the increasing number of people competing to purchase it. Total
losses were 2,135 rubles. Moreover, because of the mess my agent in Petersburg,
Stepan Tiut'kin, had made of my affairs, a significant portion fell into debt,
and the slow turnover in receipts and trade meant that nearly all of it had to
be done on borrowed funds at high interest. Add to this my household expenses
and other outlays, and it turns out that the actual reduction of my capital this
year amounted to 9,860 rubles, and a substantial portion over and above that was
tied up in questionable debts. So, this great loss perceptibly disordered my circumstances, and the decrease in my capital year after year reduced my trade. What is
more, not having money at the proper time, I usually had to make purchases at
higher prices than other traders and also pay added expenses for transport.[3]*

Ivan made the second trip to Petersburg in the early spring, 1791, this time
with his eleven-year-old son Aleksei in tow. More of this visit than the last was
devoted to sightseeing and personal interests. On the very first day, after visiting
his sales booth at the port, he went to the Winter Palace and rode through the
nicest sections of the city. Subsequent days found Ivan at the commodity exchange, at two orangeries kept by foreign gardeners, at the Academy of Sciences
bookstore, at an auction of paintings at the Academy of Arts, at the English
Store, and several times at the central bazaar. It may have been at the English
Store that he purchased a telescope, because on the same day he had visited that
store he later walked to the bell tower on Nevskii Prospect to try out the device.
As for the theater, on this trip he could not indulge this interest, as it was Lent

and the theaters were closed. But another kind of theater, the pageantry of the imperial court, was available, and Ivan did not fail to visit the court church for Sunday mass.

What was the purpose of this second trip to the northern capital? It is doubtful that Ivan would still have entertained thoughts of improving his business in Petersburg. To judge from the diary entries for this stay, which was much shorter than the 1789 trip, the principal object was to use whatever influence he may have had with the governor-general of the capital, Count Iakov Aleksandrovich Brius, to recover funds from a government contract. Brius, it will be recalled, had earlier been governor-general of Moscow and had become acquainted with Ivan when he was on an inspection visit to Dmitrov in 1785. Soon after Ivan reached Petersburg he went to the governor-general's office and arranged a meeting, which took place two days later. He wrote that at the meeting he submitted a petition in regard to the court contractor Karpov, presumably to force Karpov to pay for grain deliveries. Ivan also took his case to the civil governor P. N. Konovitsyn. In the end, however, these efforts yielded little, as Ivan was still pursuing Karpov's widow many years later to recover his losses.

When he totaled up his earnings for the year 1791, Ivan pointed to the high costs of barges, supplies, and labor that again prevented him from operating in volume. His profit margin had fallen to a mere 3½ kopeks per ruble, yielding an income for the year of 610 rubles. In fact, as Ivan lamented, "the entire year's trade was useless, and considering that it was done on borrowed money it was very costly, which was gradually dragging me down into a mess and complete ruin, for the reduction of capital this year exceeded 10,000 rubles, including household upkeep and various losses." Some of the losses had stemmed from the long-run unprofitability of the Miglosh mill that his family had been renting for the past fifteen years from Prince Sergei Mikhailovich Golitsyn. Ivan nevertheless seemed to regret relinquishing control of this mill and with it the personal connection that it had brought him to Prince Sergei Golitsyn. Yet, finally, his financial troubles convinced him to let the lease expire.

PËTR MARRIES

[1794, January] 11th I spent the morning at home, and at 2 o'clock in the afternoon my wife and all our children and I left for Moscow, staying overnight in Sholokhovo.

12th We arrived in Moscow after 8 in the morning, and I did not go anywhere all day.

13th In the morning I was at the Boloto [market]. Later at the Dormition Cathedral I attended mass and prayers, and in the evening I visited and had supper with [Mrs.] Obreskova.

14th Before dinner I was at various places, and spent the evening again at the home of Obreskova.

15th I spent the morning at the unloading of iron at the Stone Bridge, and the rest of the time at home [i.e., his Moscow apartment].

16th I spent the entire day at the transfer of the iron.

17th In the morning I was in various places, and then at the transfer of the iron.

18th In the morning I visited Grezenkov and was in the city, in the evening I visited Obreskova.

19th In the morning I visited Sveshnikov and Vandashnikov, and after dinner we rode to the home of the merchant Andrei Vasil'evich Goroshkov to look over his daughter as a prospective bride for our son Pëtr.

20th During the day I was in various places and in the evening at the home of Obreskova.

21st We gave our agreement to our son Pëtr to marry the daughter of Mr. Goroshkov and designated the day after tomorrow as the time for the formal agreement and contract. At noon I was in the city, and in the evening I visited Iushkov.

22nd In the morning I went to see Sveshnikov, Vandashnikov, and Uncle Mikhaila Il'ich to ask them to attend the contract signing the next day, and I spent the after dinner hours at home.

23rd In the morning I visited the Glushkovs and then was in the city. At dusk those I had summoned for the contract signing arrived at our home, and after 6 o'clock we left for the home of Mr. Goroshkov, where, having called upon God's help, we concluded the agreement for Pëtr Ivanovich to marry Anna Andreevna Goroshkova, and we celebrated and feasted until past 3 o'clock in the morning.

24th Before dinner I visited Obreskova and then was at the Stone Bridge for the transfer of the iron, and in the evening I again visited Obreskova.

25th In the morning I visited Grezenkov and was at the Financial Board, and in the evening I visited my new relative Goroshkov.

26th At dawn I visited for necessities Vice Governor Shekshin, and then went to Chobotov's. Later before 3 in the afternoon I was at the Financial Board to get money. In the evening I visited Obreskova, and later Chobotov and his wife visited me.

27th Before dinner I was in the city, and in the evening I visited and had supper with Obreskova.

28th I spent the whole day at the apartment, and in the evening my new relative Goroshkov and his wife, and Afromeev, my cousin Aleksandr Petrovich, and Andrei Fëdorovich visited me.

29th I heard mass with my wife and younger children at the Church of Basil the Blessed in the Intercession Cathedral. From there we rode over to see the wax museum. I spent the evening in the apartment.

30th In the morning I visited Chobotov, Golovin, and Grezenkov, and in the evening was at home.

31st In the morning I visited Glebovskii and was in the city, and in the evening I visited and had supper with Obreskova.

February 1st In the morning I visited Chobotov, and at 10 o'clock I rode over to the house that was rented [for the wedding] from Princess Urusova by the Church of the Savior on the Sands, which is in the Arbat. In the evening I was in the city.

2nd In the morning I went to the private inspector Chipchagov, and then went to see Matveevskii and was in other places. I heard mass at the Church of St. Nicholas the Miracle Worker in Plotniki. In the evening I visited Semënov and later visited and had dinner with Obreskova.

3rd In the morning I visited Iushkov and Prince Ivan Fëdorovich and was in other homes, and after dinner was in the city.

4th From morning until evening I rode around to various homes to invite guests to the wedding. In the evening we received the dowry, at which time we hosted a supper for a number of relatives.

5th Today was the wedding of our son Pëtr Ivanovich, which through the mercy of God was carried off successfully. The ceremony took place at 9 o'clock in the evening at the Church of the Ascension of Our Lord by the Nikitskii Gate and was conducted by Father Antipa Matveevich. The dinner had 37 place settings and featured music and a choir, and the entire ceremony lasted until past midnight.

6th I did not go anywhere during the day, and the usual wedding observances continued. A ball took place in the evening and more than 50 guests attended, and then we had a supper with 48 place settings, and the guests stayed until after 2 o'clock in the morning.

7th I was at the Financial Board and in the city, and in the evening we hosted up to 20 persons at our place and ate supper and visited until after midnight.

The young men of the Tolchënov family were beginning to marry and set up on their own. The diary excerpt above tells of Pëtr's wedding, but the first of the young men to marry was Ivan's step-uncle and ward, Andrei Fëdorovich Makarov. Andrei, who was eleven years Ivan's junior, had been living with the Tolchënovs since the death of his father in 1771, when Andrei was just six years old. When in 1788 he reached the age of twenty-three the family decided that it was time for him to get married, and they entered the Moscow marriage market. Moscow had become the preferred place for the Tolchënovs to seek brides ever since Ivan's father had married a Moscow merchant woman after the death of his first wife—and then found a Moscow bride for Ivan.

As traced in the diary, the process of picking a bride for Andrei Fëdorovich, which occurred early in 1789, reveals something we have not yet seen in Ivan's record of such events: a review and appraisal of a number of candidates before a choice was made. This may have happened quite commonly, but it is rare to get the kind of glimpse of it that Ivan penned in this instance. Because Ivan and Anna were acting as Andrei's guardians, they played a central role. On January 10 they traveled to Moscow with their older children. After making visits to Bishop Serapion and to some of the important nobles of Dmitrov who wintered in Moscow, including Prince Ivan Golitsyn, Prince Ivan Obolenskii, and others, Ivan and Anna began the rounds.

14th I heard mass at Ascension Church. After dinner we went to examine the daughter of the merchant Pëtr Zabelin as a prospective bride for Andrei Fëdorovich. In the evening my wife and I visited and had supper with Blagovo.[4]

15th I stayed at the apartment before dinner, and afterward went to examine as a prospective bride the daughter of the merchant Ivan Kvasnikov.

16th In the morning we got ourselves over to the house rented for the wedding from [the two] Mrs. Bezsonovs on Nikitskaia St., and after dinner we went to examine one more prospective bride, the daughter of the merchant Timofei Shemiakin who lives in Kazënnaia Street.[5]

The decision was made in the next few days in favor of the Shemiakin daughter, and on January 20 Ivan recorded in his diary that "in the evening, having agreed, we rode over again to see Shemiakin and, calling on God's help, negotiated a contract for the marriage of Andrei Fëdorovich with his daughter Fëdora Timofeevna, and we visited until midnight."

The wedding took place early the next month in Moscow. The only hitch was that they lost the house they expected to use when the Bezsonov women returned unexpectedly from their village and wanted to occupy their lodgings. Ivan quickly found another house in the nearby Kislovka section of the city and then invited his important friends to the wedding, which took place at the Church of the Ascension by the Nikitskii Gate. A supper for twenty-nine persons followed. The next day even more guests showed up for a ball and supper with thirty-seven place settings, and Ivan recorded proudly that "among the distinguished guests were Prince Ivan Fëdorovich Golitsyn and family, Ivan Andreevich Molchanov, the Squires Iushkov, Lavrov, Blagovo and others." The third day they hosted another twenty persons for supper. It was a proper three-day wedding with all the trimmings and the quality of guests, demonstrating that Ivan and his family moved among some of the best people of the Moscow region.

Later the same year, 1789, Ivan participated in the arrangements for the marriage of his cousin and close friend Aleksandr Petrovich Tolchënov. Aleksandr's father, Pëtr Il'ich, had been born three years later than his brother Aleksei (Ivan's father) and had died much sooner. He was only thirty-two years of age at his death. Perhaps because of this early death, the family did not enjoy the level of prosperity that would ensure Aleksandr an early marriage. Aleksandr had to work many years to achieve a financial position to marry favorably and was twenty-eight years old when he finally sought a bride in the Moscow marriage market. Ivan, who acted as a kind of older brother to the long fatherless Aleksandr and who invariably referred to him simply as "my brother" in the Russian way, was called upon to serve as a witness and adviser for the final contractual arrangements that occurred in late September.[6]

In the days before, Ivan had been very busy at his duties as mayor in Dmitrov. The civil governor of Moscow province, Pëtr Lopukhin, had been on a hunting trip at his estate and stopped off in Dmitrov on his way there and back and required Ivan's attention. This was the time, it will be recalled, when the city was busy with the huge project of renovating the cathedral. Also under way at this time was the annual fair hosted by Dmitrov, and Ivan had to check on the stamping of foreign wares and other matters. As soon as these tasks were completed, he got into his carriage and rushed to Moscow to assist Aleksandr. Arriving in the middle of the following day, he had little time to relax and get ready before, as he recorded, "I left at 6 o'clock in the evening with my brother Aleksandr Petrovich for the contractual settlement, which concluded the agreement for the marriage to the daughter of the Moscow merchant Mikhail Vasil'evich Papkov, who resides in the Basmannaia section, and I stayed there until after midnight." After having played this role in the negotiations and contract for the marriage, Ivan was evidently unable to attend the wedding. Most likely, the wedding took place the next month at the time that Ivan and his son Pëtr were traveling to Petersburg to check on the problems there with the receipts from the family's grain trade. Ivan and Anna had attended other weddings of Moscow merchants who were merely acquaintances, and Ivan would not have missed the wedding of a close relative and friend like Aleksandr if he were in the vicinity.

Of these two marriages, that of Andrei Fëdorovich had far greater consequences for Ivan and his immediate family. Before Andrei could even consider marriage, Ivan had to transfer to him the inheritance known as the "Makarov capital" that the Tolchënovs had been holding for him. After he was married, Andrei, his new bride, and his mother continued to live in the Tolchënov home for a year until Ivan could get the family's former Birch Street residence spruced up for their occupancy. In February 1790 Andrei and his family moved there, under exactly what financial conditions is unclear. Possibly, Ivan wanted to keep that second home as a rental property or eventually to gift it to Andrei, but three years later when he was in desperate need of cash to invest in new income sources and was also thinking ahead about the need to divest himself of assets that could be seized by his creditors, he sold the home to Andrei for 1,000 rubles.

The marriage of Ivan's son Pëtr in 1794 was still more consequential for the family. In the face of mounting financial troubles, Ivan had to get Pëtr married while he could still find a favorable match and stage the wedding in style. As it happened, Pëtr's new in-laws were also going to prove very helpful in Ivan's maneuvers to salvage something from the wreckage of his family finances.

It is not clear how exactly a fiancée was found for Pëtr. But this time Ivan and Anna did not sample a string of prospective brides (see the long diary excerpt at the start of this section). There was just one young woman in the picture, Anna Andreevna Goroshkova, the daughter of a well-to-do first-guild cloth merchant.[7] Could Pëtr himself have had a say in the matter? He had, after all, been living for several years in Moscow at the home of his maternal grandfather while going to school, and he was working in and out of Moscow in the family grain business for a few years after that. He may well have found Anna Goroshkova on his own or with the help of his mother's Moscow family or even of his paternal grandmother, Ivan's stepmother, another Moscow merchant woman. In any event, by the time Ivan and Anna arrived to conduct the negotiations with the Goroshkov family the choice must have been settled. The language Ivan used in the diary entry for January 21, excerpted at the start of this section ("We gave our agreement to our son Pëtr to marry the daughter of Mr. Goroshkov"), likewise suggests that he and Anna were merely affirming their son's preference. Of course, they still had to examine the young woman, give their official consent, and agree to the dowry and other arrangements. The principal financial matters had undoubtedly been worked out ahead of time by a matchmaker or family members in Moscow, as Ivan did not negotiate over a series of days, as he had in other marriage contracts, but had his witnesses in tow for the final contract and "handshake" on his first visit to the Goroshkovs after having seen the bride-to-be and approved the choice. As was usual, those who acted as witnesses or surety for the contract represented different branches of the family. In this case, they included Uncle Mikhaila Il'ich, and two close in-laws, Aleksandr Vandashnikov, the widowed brother-in-law of Anna, and Tikhon Sveshnikov, the second husband of Ivan's cousin Praskov'ia Petrovna (the sister of Aleksandr Petrovich whose marriage was just mentioned above).

From that point onward Ivan referred to the father of the bride Andrei Goroshkov by the term *svat,* which can be translated into English only as "my relative" or in its earliest instances as "my new relative." The Russian language has a more elaborate nomenclature for family relations than does English, an indication of the great importance Russians have customarily placed on extended family relations. The term *svat* that Ivan now used for Andrei Goroshkov designates the father of one's daughter-in-law or son-in-law and signals the establishment of an almost brother-like connection between the two men. When Ivan married Anna back in 1773, it is worth recalling, a strong bond formed between her father and Ivan's father. Anna's father appeared often in Dmitrov and worked in partnership with the Tolchënovs on some business matters, and the home of Anna's family in Moscow became the first stopping point for the Tolchënovs when they came to the capital. After the sudden death of Ivan's father, Anna's father seemed to serve for a time, along with Ivan's senior uncle, as a mentor while Ivan was getting his bearings as head of the family firm. In other words, Anna's father played the role of another uncle or surrogate father. Now Pëtr's father-in-law would soon have to substitute in some ways for Ivan and also play the role of a second father in order to save family assets when Ivan's luck in escaping his creditors would run out.

Although Ivan did not specify the guests at Pëtr's wedding, the affair must have been impressive. The ceremony took place in the same church in which Andrei Fëdorovich Makarov was married, and the scale of the celebrations afterward was noticeably larger than what had been done for Makarov. This time Ivan hosted a dinner with instrumental music and a choir instead of just the supper organized for Makarov, and the number of guests at the supper the next day for Pëtr and his bride was larger by a third. Since Ivan was still hobnobbing with the same class of people, the guest list must have again included Prince Golitsyn and other distinguished acquaintances of the Tolchënovs from the Dmitrov nobility, in addition to the relatives and Moscow merchant families with whom the Tolchënovs and the bride's family were associated. Finally, catering and hosting the dinners and dances in the home of Princess Urusova in the Arbat had to be enormously expensive, and it was. To mount this impressive event Ivan had paid 3,000 rubles, which was more than he earned in that year and about one-third of what the family firm had made in its very best years of the mid 1780s.

The marriage of young Pëtr and Anna Goroshkova produced a child in the very first year. On December 13, 1794, a son Vladimir was born to them in Dmitrov. Ivan was away in Tver completing the negotiations for the lease of a mill at the time of the birth but arrived home three days later, on December 17, in time for the baptism, where he served as godfather and Pëtr's mother-in-law as the godmother. Much to everyone's delight, Vladimir proved to be a hardy child, survived the dangerous early childhood years, and lived to carry the family name into the next generation.

SEARCH FOR NEW SOURCES OF INCOME

[In Moscow 1793, February]

18th In the morning I rode to the Kuznets section to the apartment of my cousin Ivan Ivanov for the dispatch of Bespalov to the southeast, and in the evening I visited and had supper with Vakhromeev.

19th Before dinner I was at an inspection of Protasov's playing card factory. After dinner I was in the city and in the evening visited Vakhromeev. Then until midnight I visited and had supper with [Mrs.] Obreskova.

20th In the morning I rode over to Mrs. Protasova's to negotiate for the factory, and then left for home after 9 o'clock. I had dinner in Sholokhovo and arrived at home safely at 9 in the evening.

21st I did not go anywhere.

22nd Likewise

23rd In the morning I visited Uncle Ivan Il'ich, and at 3 in the afternoon I left for Moscow. I stayed overnight in Sholokhovo.

24th I arrived at the apartment at 9 in the morning and spent the rest of the time there.

25th In the morning I was at the Protasov factory and in other places. In the evening [Fëdor Sergeevich] Luzhin and Vakhromeev visited me.

26th In the morning I went to see the trustees of the estate of Mr. Protasov, Pëtr Stepanovich Protasov and Mr. Glebovskii, with whom I bargained for the card factory. I ate dinner at the home of Vakhromeev, and after that I went to begin the leasing of the factory, and in the evening I again visited Vakhromeev.

27th In the morning I visited Iuskhov. I attended mass at the Resurrection Church in Bronnaia. I had dinner and lingered until dusk at the home of Prince Ivan Fëdorovich Golitsyn, and in the evening was at a masquerade.

28th In the morning I was at various places. I had dinner and spent the evening until midnight at the home of Iushkov.

March 1st In the morning I was at the factory and at the home of Glebovskii, and the rest of the time at the apartment, where at the request of Chobotov he received guests, one of whom was me.

2nd I attended the leasing of the factory, and in the evening took possession of it.

3rd Before 10 o'clock in the morning I left for home. I had dinner in Sholokhovo, and at 10 in the evening arrived home safely.

The grain trade could no longer provide a living for Ivan and his family. Not only was competition increasing but Ivan slid further and further into debt, and he did not have the working capital needed to earn more than a modest profit. After judging the results of his trade in 1791 as "worthless," he limited his grain purchases in the next year to the Moscow area, and in the diary he recorded his frequent presence in January and February at the Moscow grain markets in the Novoslobodskaia section of the city.[8] As he was unable to exploit the price differentials for grain purchased close to its production point, however, much of the grain he processed in this year had to be sold at cost or even at a slight loss, and the overall profits amounted to only 1,525 rubles. The following year, 1793, he decided to return to the usual method of purchases in the grain-producing regions south and east of the capital, and he sent his son Pëtr to three wharves downriver to buy grain. From the diary entry for February 18 in the excerpts at the start of this section, we can see that he was also cooperating with a cousin, Ivan Ivanov Tolchënov, to send another buyer to the south. This was Moscow merchant Koz'ma Sergeev Bespalov, who was also a relative, the husband of Uncle Mikhaila's daughter Mar'ia.[9] The grain business was very much a family affair. Much of the grain purchased in this year was sold in the central region of the country, either at Rybnyi or at Tver, as the prices were no better in Petersburg and Ivan could save on transport costs. The rest was sent to Petersburg and fetched a better return overall than the year before. Profits amounted to 3,600 rubles. But this was barely enough to cover household expenses, and the interest payments on Ivan's loans exhausted his remaining capital. At the end of the year 1793 Ivan even felt compelled to give up his lease on the Shirin mill near the Volga, a mill that the family had rented for thirty-four years since his grandfather, Fëdor Makarov, first leased it in 1761. This decision was an emotional one for Ivan, for the mill was not just a productive asset; it had also given Ivan and the family a position in the community close to the mill, a place where they could vacation and enjoy social contacts with other merchants and even with the nobles at local estates. But another merchant was willing to rent the mill at a price higher than Ivan considered the dilapidated facility to be worth. As a result, having relinquished the Miglosh mill earlier and now the Shirin mill, Ivan had to give up the opportunity to make money as a miller, and also to part with the social status that had accompanied the mill.[10]

Ivan now had to apply himself to finding new sources of income, and quickly. It will be remembered that he had begun to explore such an option as early as the winter of 1786 when he had made frequent visits to the Financial Board in Moscow to prepare for the auction of the liquor franchise for the Dmitrov area. However, when the auction took place in April of that year, Ivan did not purchase the franchise, perhaps because of the high costs. Four years later liquor franchises were again up for sale, and Ivan, probably with a greater sense of urgency this time, repeated his appearances at the Financial Board. Once again the goal eluded him. He reported in his diary on September 24, 1790, that "I spent almost the entire day at the Financial Board for the auction of the liquor franchises. However, because of the high mark-ups I did not take any anywhere."

By 1793 the situation was becoming dire. Ivan had to acquire new sources of income if he was to survive, and he had to do so while he still had enough credit to borrow. If the condition of his finances became known, he would not be able to raise cash to invest in productive pursuits. His first effort was the one tracked in the diary excerpt at the start of this section: the lease of a factory for making playing cards. This was a smart move. Card playing was a popular pastime in

Russia at this time, one indulged in by virtually the entire society from the imperial court down to the humblest townspeople. With some luck and good management such a factory should have provided a reliable return. In acquiring the factory from the widow of its former owner, Brigadier Protasov, Ivan evidently got help from the wealthy Moscow merchants Ivan Grezenkov and Pëtr Orlov. They appear in later court documents among his major creditors. His noble acquaintances from the Dmitrov district may also have been helpful, especially the Iushkov brothers, Afanasii and Nikolai. Ivan was spending much time with them, and they remained his friends for many years. Another person who appears episodically but especially often just around the time of the card factory purchase was Fëdor Sergeevich Luzhin. He owned the estate of Grigorovo, west of Dmitrov, which his neighbor Elizaveta Ian'kova described as "small but lovely, a delightful little house with a mezzanine and a wooden church." She also reported that Luzhin fell victim to a devastating unrequited love and remained a bachelor all his life.[11] Luzhin took an interest in Ivan about this time and may have been another of those Ivan tapped for a loan, having convinced him that it was a good investment. Luzhin even invited Ivan and Anna to be overnight guests at his estate.

Playing cards were an important source of revenue for the Imperial Moscow Foundling Home, a large facility in the center of the city that managed not only a high volume of abandoned children but also a lying-in hospital and a school for midwives.[12] The revenue came through a stamp tax; each packet of cards was to receive a stamp, initially through a government office and later directly from the foundling home itself. By the 1790s sixteen factories were operating in Moscow and producing large numbers of playing cards, as many as two million packets according to one estimate. But the income to the foundling home was nowhere near what it should have been even with a much smaller number of cards because of the counterfeiting of stamps and a high instance of noncompliance with the stamping requirement. Although the authorities struggled with this problem, even threats of vigorous prosecution from Governor-General Prozorovskii could not bring it under control, and in time the government permitted the foundling home to sell this source of revenue as a monopoly franchise so that it could generate a reliable stream of income.[13] This change came toward the end of the decade with serious consequences for Ivan's business. For the time being, the stamp tax system continued.

After having acquired the card factory, Ivan turned its management over to his wife Anna's brother, Ivan Osorgin. The family for a time also relocated its Moscow lodgings to an apartment at the factory. This was, however, only a temporary arrangement, as Ivan had to find a new home for the factory within a year. The following February he was able to rent space for the operation, including an apartment for his family, on Nikitskaia Street, one of the main roads extending west from the Kremlin. This location became the Tolchënovs' principal residence in Moscow for several years. The new business was up and running soon, and profits in the first abbreviated year of Ivan's ownership, 1793, amounted to 788 rubles. The following year the return more than doubled to 1700 rubles. But after that something happened. Just when Ivan was desperately in need of additional income, Ivan Osorgin apparently made a mess of the card factory work. Merchants liked to keep business operations within the family, but that made them dependent on the talents and knowledge of a limited number of people. If we are to believe Ivan, Anna's brother Ivan Osorgin turned out to be the wrong choice for manager of the card factory. The factory evidently yielded no income in 1795, and the next year things got worse. In this year when Ivan's creditors were finally catching up with him, he learned that his brother-in-law had somehow squandered or been swindled out of the entire capital of the card factory on a trip to the Volga to purchase materials. "Neither the money nor the materials showed up," Ivan wrote, "and the factory fell into debt." That destroyed his trust in Osorgin, and he regretfully replaced him with his own son Pëtr for a time and then in the fall turned management of the factory over to his second son Aleksei.[14]

To return to the year 1793, after acquiring the card factory, Ivan spent much of the rest of the year in his usual relaxed style of life, socializing with family, officials, and his friends among the local nobility. He finally got into motion only at the very end of December when he went again to the Financial Board in Moscow to bid on a contract to transport government iron supplies from the Volga port of Dubna, north of Dmitrov, into Moscow. He won the contract, supervised the work during the first months of 1794 and made 1,054 rubles. Evidence of his work on this contract can be seen in the diary excerpts for January 15–17, 1794, at the start of the section in this chapter titled "Pëtr Marries." In 1793 Ivan had also recovered a small portion of the inheritance he had transferred to his step-uncle, Andrei Fëdorovich, when he sold the family's former timber home on Birch Street to Andrei and his new family for 1,000 rubles.

Despite the dwindling of his grain trade and the decision to give up the Shirin mill, Ivan could not relinquish the idea of having a mill of his own. A mill was primarily a commercial asset, but it also seems to have given Ivan a feeling of a small country estate to retreat to, a place of relaxation in a natural landscape akin to that his noble friends enjoyed on their country estates and another sign that a merchant could live like a noble without having to be a noble. Possibly smitten by the fashion for the pastoral that was seizing the imagination of the Russian elites at this time, Ivan was loath to surrender this summer escape to which he had become accustomed since childhood.[15] Accordingly, just as the lease on the Shirin mill was running out, Ivan took trips in

July and August of 1794 to the Financial Board in the city of Tver to bid on another mill in the upper Volga basin in Tver province. The first trip doubled as a family outing and introduction to Tver for his six-year-old son Pavel.

[1794, July] 15th At 5 o'clock in the morning my wife, my son Pavel, and I left for Tver using our own horses. We had dinner in Doroshevo. Then we passed through Klin before 6 o'clock in the evening and stayed overnight in the village of Seliuvino.

16th Continuing on, we crossed the Shosha at 8 o'clock in the morning. We had dinner in Slobodka and stayed overnight in Pribytovo.

17th At 7 in the morning, having arrived safely in Tver, I was at the Financial Board, and then later we strolled around the city and attended vespers and prayed at the cathedral.

18th We continued our stay in Tver, and I spent most of my time at the Financial Board on the matter of leasing the Skniatino mill.

19th In the morning we rode to the Zhëltikov Monastery and heard mass there and afterward prayed to St. Arsenii. Returning to Tver, I was at the Financial Board. At 5 in the afternoon we left for home and stayed overnight in the village of Gorodishche.

The mill on which Ivan was bidding was in the village of Skniatino on the Nerl River where it enters the Volga, just south of the town of Kaliazin. A final trip to Tver in December sealed the deal, and on January 1, 1795, Ivan took possession of the facility. His objective was to rebuild a rather inefficient mill with an undershot wheel into a more productive mechanism with an overshot wheel, which delivers more power. At the same time he wanted to add to the existing five millstones four new ones for grinding wheat flour.[16] And, indeed, he accomplished all this in the spring of 1795, using loans that he was able to scrounge from a well-to-do peasant in the village of Kimry near the mill and from a merchant in the town of Rybnyi, lenders who lived far enough from Dmitrov to have no inkling of Ivan's mounting financial difficulties.[17]

Ivan now also became more active as a fisherman and created a fishery on his property. One reason may have been the death in 1794 of the Dmitrov fishmonger Stepan Makarov. Ivan reported that he was "the sole person in the entire city who gained his living by fishing and supplied the city with fish, and he went by the nickname 'crayfish.'"[18] Just before his death Makarov, a neighbor of Ivan's along the banks of the Iakhroma River, had ceded some property to Ivan there, which no doubt contributed to this enterprise. Ivan boasted in his summary for this year and the next about the huge catches of fish that he and his cousin Aleksandr were pulling in and seeding in his pond, including over 100 bream, huge pike, chub and many others. Another source of support was occasional sales of plants. For example, in June of 1794, Ivan recorded that

"Count Andrei Ivanovich Tolstoi and his family visited me for the purchase of trees from my orangery."[19]

But the grain trade that had been the family's principal source of income and its route to wealth and influence over four generations was finally grinding to a halt. Ivan did not even report earnings for 1794, writing simply that the grain trade was "of no importance." The following year he stopped dealing in grain altogether. With a twinge of nostalgia, Ivan recorded in his summary for 1794 the death of the merchant Afanasii Grigor'ev Popov. "He had served as my deceased father's favorite agent for many years, and I was detailed to him as a youngster to learn about commercial affairs." Ironically, Ivan's grain business and his mentor in that trade died the very same year.

More discouragingly, Ivan described the overall condition of his family business firm as "similar to a ship that had lost its mast and was being tossed about in the sea at the whim of the winds." And he went on to describe his own state of mind at the time with remarkable frankness, writing that "a kind of nonchalance took control of my reason, as I struggled against melancholy and despair. I was ashamed to reveal my dire situation not only to friends but even to my own family, and I spent much of my time with chimerical thoughts and gambling, which hastened my ruin, and I attempted to console myself and push away unpleasant thoughts by using my remaining assets on other diversions." This assessment fits well what we see in the diary of his efforts the following year. While Ivan still seemed to have some credit and now and again would cast about for additional opportunities to earn income, these efforts for some reason did not pan out. In February he went to the Tatarskaia sloboda section of Moscow, south across the Moscow River, to inspect a gold wire–drawing factory, but nothing more came of that. In late September, during a trip to Moscow, he went to the bank for an auction to transport copper money from the port of Dubna down to Moscow. But he failed to obtain the job. Were these opportunities too expensive? Was he too dispirited to make the effort to secure the needed capital for them? It is unclear. But even if he had been able to acquire these businesses, they could not have produced the huge profits he had once earned in the grain trade and therefore could not have saved him from financial collapse. What energy he mustered in 1795 he devoted to shielding his remaining assets. In the meantime he kept up an impressive front so that he could continue to borrow.

MAINTAINING APPEARANCES

1796 January 1st I heard mass at the cathedral. In the evening I visited and had dinner with Obreskova.

2nd In the morning I stayed home, and at 2 o'clock in the afternoon my wife, younger children, and I departed for Moscow. We stayed overnight in Sholokhovo.

3rd We arrived at the apartment at 10 o'clock in the morning. In the evening I visited Iushkov.

4th In the morning I was at various places, and in the evening I visited L'vov and then Obreskova, where I had supper.

5th In the morning I visited my relative Goroshkov and the gardener Engel'meier, and then Vlasov. I attended vespers at the Epiphany Monastery and had dinner and spent the evening at the home of Iushkov.

6th I heard mass at the Exaltation of the Cross Monastery. I had dinner and lingered until dusk at the home of my relative Goroshkov, and in the evening I visited Zamiatin.

7th In the morning I visited Grezenkov. I had dinner and spent the day and evening at the home of Prince Ivan Fëdorovich Golitsyn.

8th In the morning I was at various places. My wife and I had dinner and stayed until dusk at the home of L'vov and in the evening visited Glushkov.

9th In the morning I visited Obreskova and Bakhmetev. I had dinner at Zamiatin's and spent the evening at the English Club.

10th In the daytime I was at various places and in the city, and in the evening I was at the hall of the Noble Assembly to hear choirs sing on the occasion of placing there a chest image, or bust, of the empress.

11th My wife, children, and I attended mass at the Dormition Cathedral. After dinner I was in the city and in the evening visited Iushkov, and then Obreskova, where I had supper.

12th In the morning I visited the Right Reverend Serapion. Later I visited L'vov, and after dinner Obreskova. I spent the evening at the English Club.

13th I attended mass at the Dormition Cathedral. I had dinner at the home of Zamiatin, and my wife and I spent the evening at a masquerade in the halls of the Noble Assembly.

14th I spent the day in the apartment and in the evening visited Iushkov and later my relative Goroshkov, where I had supper.

15th In the morning I was at various places and in the evening visited and had supper with L'vov.

16th In the morning I visited Golovin, and after dinner I was at the club and then visited and had supper with L'vov.

17th In the morning I visited Iushkov, Golikov, and Grezenkov. The rest of the time I was at home and was visited in the evening by Vel'iaminov and his brother and my relative Goroshkov and his family.

18th I had dinner and spent the evening at the home of Iushkov.

19th In the morning I visited my relative [Goroshkov], then was in the city, and I had dinner and spent the evening at the home of Obreskova.

20th In the morning I visited Prince Andrei Mikhailovich Obolenskii. I had dinner and lingered until dusk at the home of Obreskova and in the evening visited and had supper with my relative Goroshkov.

21st In the morning I visited Golovin and L'vov and had dinner and spent the evening at the home of Iushkov.

22nd Before dinner I was at the apartment, and afterward in the city and at the home of L'vov.

23rd In the morning I visited Iushkov. I had dinner and spent the day and the evening at the club.

24th In the morning I visited Golovin. Later I was at the office of the Provincial Administration and then visited Grezenkov, and in the evening I visited and had supper with Zamiatin.

25th In the morning I visited Iushkov and Obreskova, and in the evening my wife and I visited and had supper with Gruzdev.

26th Before dinner I was in the apartment and afterward in the city. In the evening I visited and had supper with Obreskova.

27th In the morning I visited Iushkov. I heard mass at Piatnitskaia Church and later the last parts of the mass at the Church of Nicholas the Miracle-Worker in Zaiatskoe. Afterward I went with my relative [Goroshkov] to the merchant Sergei Sveshnikov for a loan of money, and I had dinner and spent the day and evening and had supper with my relative.

28th In the morning I visited Vlasov and in the evening visited and had supper with Obreskova.

These passages from the diary for the month of January 1796 indicate that despite the steady decline of Ivan's financial position, he continued even at this late date his expansive style of life and his friendships with members of the nobility and wealthy merchants. This was intentional. In his yearly summary for 1792, Ivan recalled that even then he had consciously decided to act as if everything were fine. This was not in spite of but because of his increasingly desperate situation. After remarking on the poor returns from his trade and his continuing outlays for household expenses, interest on loans, and "unfortunate, though not large, gambling losses," he added that "the disorder of my finances had increased to the point that I scarcely could muster the strength any longer to fight against it. To conceal my unfavorable circumstances and not completely lose credit, I did not change my way of living and continued to hope for a fortunate turn of events."[20]

Indeed, Ivan did not just continue his former way of life. He seemed to live even more expansively in the next few years in hopes that his display of prosperity would enable him to obtain further loans and delay the day of reckoning. For example, in the diary excerpt above for early 1796 we see Ivan spending time dining and socializing at the Moscow English Club. He first visited this exclusive social club for nobles and wealthy merchants five years earlier, soon after he had stepped down from his position as mayor of Dmitrov and enjoyed the title

of "distinguished citizen." Doors were open to him at that time. Less than a
week after he had turned the reins of government over to the new mayor, Ivan
Tugarinov, in December 1791 he was invited to the beautiful Ol'govo estate of
Stepan Stepanovich Apraksin, where he had dinner and enjoyed a performance
at the estate's impressive stand-alone theater that boasted its own actors and
musicians. This must have been quite a treat for Ivan, who was not a regular
guest there. The estate house, which stood in the midst of an English park with
several ponds, had recently been expanded by the Italian architect Francesco
Camporezi into a magnificent, sprawling semi-circular mansion.[21] Two days
later Ivan and Anna went to the Botovo estate of Prince Obolenskii for dinner.
Then two days after that Ivan was invited to spend two days and nights at the
estate of his friend Nikolai L'vovich Vakhromeev, a Dmitrov district noble
landlord of lieutenant rank. On arriving in Moscow a few days later, Ivan first
visited his increasingly close and trusted friend from the Dmitrov district nobility, Afanasii Iushkov. That evening he visited the Moscow English Club,
possibly with an introduction from Iushkov or even from Governor Pëtr Lopukhin, who had been in the leadership of the club in Petersburg since 1780 and
who knew Ivan well in his role as mayor of Dmitrov. A month later Ivan was
back in Moscow and officially enrolled as a member of the English Club.[22]

The history of the Moscow English Club is better known for the nineteenth
century, when it was manifestly the most difficult of the several social clubs to
gain entry to and when its membership embraced the political, cultural, and
social elite of the nation. The club, which was founded in 1772, was closed by
order of Emperor Paul in 1798 and only reopened four years later, after his
death. Most historical accounts start with its reopening in 1802.[23] But surviving
archival documents make clear that the club in the eighteenth century was also
a luxurious and exclusive domain of the elite. Just before Ivan became a member, the club had moved from its former location in the foreign suburb section
of the city into the spacious home of Prince Iurii Dolgorukov on Tverskaia
Street (where the Moscow mayor's office is now located). The club provided
reading rooms furnished with an array of journals and newspapers, as well as
billiards and other rooms. Supper was served each evening and dinner on
Wednesdays and Saturdays. The membership was limited to three hundred and
was not cheap: 25 rubles to start with and 15 at the beginning of each year.
Presumably, Ivan kept up his dues payments despite his financial straits; members who failed to pay on time were to be excluded and their place offered to
another.[24]

It was in this same year, 1792, that Ivan became a regular visitor at the home
of another elite noble house in the Dmitrov region. This was the estate of
Countess Elizaveta Fëdorovna Orlova (nee Rtishcheva), the widow of Ivan
Orlov, the eldest of the brothers who organized the coup d'etat that brought

The Intercession Church on the Andreevskoe estate of
Princess Elizaveta Fëdorovna Orlova.

Catherine II to the throne of Russia. According to the countess's neighbor
Elizaveta Ian'kovo, Orlova was a good-hearted and not especially bright woman
who kept at her Andreevskoe estate just southwest of Dmitrov an overlarge
household of servants typical of the time. She even had a sharp-witted fool
named Matrëshka who would spout such wisdom to her as: "You think you are
a big lady because you are able to sit there with arms folded, receiving guests. . . .
But the truth is that you work for us, and we are your masters. Well, what good
would you be without us? We are the masters: you collect quitrent from the
peasants and give it to us and barely get to keep dick-all for yourself."[25]

Ivan's acquaintance with Countess Orlova began on June 1, 1792, and was
facilitated by his friend Nikolai Vakhromeev. Vakhromeev had come to town
two days earlier for Sunday dinner at the Tolchënovs', and Ivan gathered a few
other friends, including the Obreskova daughters, the district police captain
and his wife, the district doctor, and the local liquor franchisee to spend the day.
Vakhromeev stayed overnight, and the second day, Ivan wrote, "I went with
Vakhromeev to the village of Andreevskoe to visit Countess Elizaveta Fëdorovna Orlova, had dinner at her house, spent the day, and ate supper." He must
have made a good impression because he was invited back with his wife Anna
just two weeks later to spend the entire evening and stay for supper. The visits
continued off and on for several more years. In 1792, Ivan was back at Andreevskoe either alone or with Anna on July 8, August 8, October 22, and

November 15. Two days before the last visit, Ivan and Anna had hosted in their home an evening and supper for the countess and her mother, her brother Nikolai Rtishchev (who later became governor-general of Georgia), her cousin Ivan Likharev, and Anna Obreskova and her daughters, and other guests. During the next two years contacts with the countess were more episodic, and then they picked up and became more frequent than ever in 1795.

These were the years Ivan was spending a lot of time in Moscow trying to find new ways to make a living, and in 1794 and 1795 some of his visits to the Countess Orlova took place at her Moscow residence. But Ivan was still in this period indulging his taste for the estate life of his noble friends and behaving as if everything in his own life was in good order. He was simultaneously maintaining a necessary front to keep up his credit and acting in the role he had created for himself as an important merchant and public official who associated with nobles and lived in their style. His regular visits to the estate of Prince Ivan Golitsyn for dinner continued. Twice in the summer of 1792 he spent a few days at the estate of Nikolai Vakhromeev, where he joined the hunt. On one of these occasions his wife Anna and son Aleksei went along. He and Anna were back for a three-day vacation there in December and then again the following month for two days. These estate holidays continued several more times through 1793 and 1794 either at Vakhromeev's village, at the Seliuvkino estate of Afanasii Iushkov, or at the Grigorovo estate of Fëdor Luzhin. In 1794 and 1795 he added to these stops a couple of overnight stays at the estate of Countess Orlova's brother, Nikolai Rtishchev.

As Ivan's fortunes sank further and he saw the end approaching in late 1794 and through the next year, his contacts with Countess Orlova became more regular and frequent. He visited or entertained her at least once or twice every month. In April he went to her Andreevskoe estate "to take care of some gardening needs." His attentions increased toward the end of the year. On December 2 he was at Andreevskoe for dinner and stayed through the evening and until past midnight. The next week he hosted an evening and supper for the countess, plus Anna Obreskova and her children, Nikolai Rtishchev, and other guests. On the thirteenth he and his wife Anna were at Andreevskoe for a visit and supper. Ivan was down with a severe cold the next week, but soon after recovering on the twenty-sixth he had dinner at Orlova's and spent the rest of the day, staying for supper. But his friendship with Elizaveta Orlova was soon to end. The ground was shifting under Ivan, and when his actual circumstances became known, most of his noble acquaintances would not want to associate with him further.

By early 1795 Ivan's situation was becoming better known and therefore precarious. He wrote in his diary on February 20, 1795, that a delegation from the Dmitrov magistracy that included the police commissioner and a few other citizens visited him to do an assessment of his house. Documents in the archives of the magistracy make clear that the assessment was ordered by the Moscow Financial Board to determine the home's value as collateral.[26] The intensification of his cultivation of the countess at this juncture suggests that Ivan may have been using his connections to persons of national prominence like Orlova and her family, the Rtishchevs, to wheedle loans from other nobles. Two days after the assessment on the house was done, for example, Ivan and Anna went for dinner and the rest of the day to the Dedenovo estate of Vasilii Vasilievich Golovin, son of the famous and long-lived Petrine servitor of the same name. Three days after that, while on the way to Moscow, Ivan stopped off at Dedenovo "to receive the money from Mr. Golovin." The documents on the assessment of Ivan's house indicate that some of his creditors, perhaps even Vasilii Golovin, had raised questions about his ability to repay. More ominously, just six weeks later the Dmitrov magistracy received a subpoena from the Moscow Court of Arbitration demanding that the Dmitrov officers locate Ivan and send him to the Moscow court.[27] Time was running out.

Another person who appears frequently in the excerpts of the diary presented in this chapter requires some comment. This is Anna Fëdorovna Obreskova (nee Ermolova). She was the widow of a retired imperial guards captain, Vasilii Ivanovich Obreskov, and lived at her family's Shpilëvo estate in the hills immediately south of Dmitrov. Her association with the Tolchënovs went back to the 1770s. She and her husband socialized with the Tolchënov family when Ivan's father was still alive. Her husband, Vasilii Ivanovich, died just three years after Ivan's father, and Ivan and Anna continued to socialize with his widow and her children. In fact, as time went on, Anna Obreskova and her children became almost as much a family to Ivan as his own wife and children. The families did things together, as can be seen in this diary excerpt from August 1792:

10th I spent the day at home and in the evening visited and had supper with Obreskova.

11th At 9 o'clock in the morning my wife and I rode to the china factory in Verbilki in the company of the Obreskovs, and we had dinner there, took a stroll, and returned home at 9 in the evening.

12th I spent the day at home and the evening at Obreskova's.

13th At 8 o'clock in the morning my wife and I together with the Obreskov daughters went on foot to [the shrine at] Vedernitsy. We had dinner in Sin'kovo and arrived at Vedernitsy at 3 in the afternoon and prayed there and stayed overnight.

The increasing frequency of their meetings can be dated to about the same time that Ivan struck up his friendship with Countess Orlova. Starting in late 1791 and continuing for the next several years, Ivan was in contact with Anna

Obreskova once or twice a week when they both happened to be in the same city, either Dmitrov or Moscow. Some weeks he was at her home almost every evening and spent entire days there. Look, for example, at a diary excerpt from the first eight days of November, 1793:

1st I spent the day at home and the evening at Obreskova's.

2nd I did not go anywhere. In the evening the police commissioner visited me.

3rd I spent the day at home and the evening at Obreskova's.

4th In the morning I was at the magistracy and the rest of the time at home.

5th I spent the day at home and in the evening visited the police commissioner and then Obreskova.

6th I heard mass at Presentation Church and spent the day at home. In the evening I visited Obreskova.

7th In the morning I visited the police commissioner and the district police captain. I ate dinner and spent the day and the evening at Obreskova's.

8th Vakhromeev had dinner at my house and spent the day, and in the evening I visited Obreskova.

On some occasions, Ivan would check in at Obreskova's more than once in a day on his way to and from other places.[28]

It would be interesting to know more about the nature of this relationship. Modern readers might jump to the conclusion that Ivan was having an affair. At times he seemed to be spending more time at Obreskova's home than his own. Or was he cultivating Obreskova to get loans from her or to reach others through her whom he might solicit for loans? Ivan's lapidary entries give no reason to suspect any of this, and she is not listed among his creditors. Wherever we find a reference to Obreskova beyond the most surface remark about visiting her or having her and her family over for dinner (and such remarks are rare), they indicate merely that she was a family friend. This is explicit in Ivan's note on her unexpected death at the end of the century. He entered in his list of the deceased during the year 1800 that "on September 26th at 7 o'clock in the evening our friend [*priiatel'nitsa*] Anna Fëdorovna Obreskova died unbetimes in Shpilëvo from a pain in the chest and was buried on the 29th in Boris and Gleb Monastery in Dmitrov." Ivan did not use the term "our" unless he is referring specifically to his wife Anna and himself as a couple. Most likely, Ivan had found the Obreskova home a refuge from the mounting pressures he was feeling and Anna Obreskova herself a sympathetic listener and kindly counsel. It was altogether characteristic of this society of arranged marriages and large households that a person's emotional needs were met by a variety of relatives and friends and were not concentrated solely on the spousal relationship.[29]

Indeed, Ivan's wife Anna may well have been upset and angry about his mismanagement of the family's finances and unable to listen sympathetically to his concerns. Moreover, Anna was again enduring a series of personal crises. She was afflicted in the first years of the 1790s by one stillbirth and three more deaths of infant children, plus a number of illnesses. She nearly died after delivering the stillborn baby in 1790. Three years later she started vomiting and suffered excruciating pains in her side for days and was thought to be dying. Extreme unction was administered. Two months after this she suffered a severe siege of chest pains. Perhaps Anna was unable in these circumstances to sympathize with Ivan and may even have blamed his profligacy and inattention to business for the crises she was experiencing. Someone close to her and Ivan but outside the family, like Anna Obreskova, could better play the role of a concerned and sympathetic female friend. Obreskova, at any rate, was in a different category from most of Ivan's other acquaintances from the local nobility. We have seen that a number of women from the Dmitrov elites knew Anna Tolchënova, visited with her and tended her when she was ill or in child birth. Anna Obreskova, in contrast, was the one woman who seemed to be a confidante of Ivan more than of his wife.

As we will learn, this longstanding and deep attachment to Anna Obreskova and her family proved helpful to Ivan years later when he was living in Moscow, and Anna Obreskova's son Nikolai became the civil governor of Moscow province.

BANKRUPTCY AND ARREST, 1795–1797

[1796] November 1st The same [i.e., Stayed home]

2nd The same. After dinner Andrei Fëdorovich visited me.

3rd I did not go anywhere

4th The same.

5th The same. In the evening I was visited by my cousin Aleksandr Petrovich and Andrei Fëdorovich and their families.

6th I spent the entire day at home.

7th The same.

8th I spent the day at home and the evening at my cousin Aleksandr Petrovich's.

9th I did not go anywhere.

10th The same.

11th The same. In the evening my cousin Aleksandr Petrovich and Andrei Fëdorovich visited me.

12th In the morning I received by post from Moscow a letter from my son Pëtr Ivanov in which I was informed of the sudden death of our most gracious monarch Empress Catherine II. Having shed the suitable tears, I spent the entire day at home. In the evening my cousin Aleksandr Petrovich and Andrei Fëdorovich visited me.

13th I again spent the entire day at home.

14th The same. This morning, in accordance with an edict sent by special courier, the taking of an oath to His Imperial Majesty Emperor Paul Petrovich occurred in the cathedral.

15th I did not go anywhere. In the morning Andrei Fëdorovich visited me. In the evening I took the oath at home in the presence of a clergyman.

16th I spent the day at home. In the evening I was visited by Police Commissioner Sal'kov, my cousin Aleksandr Petrovich, and Andrei Fëdorovich and their families.

The passage above captures Ivan at the end of 1796, approximately one year after his financial woes became widely known, his credit collapsed, and the bill collectors were besetting him. Afraid to be seen in public, he had been hiding out in a variety of locations. At this point he was back at home and claiming to be too ill to appear at the magistracy or anywhere else, and he remained holed up in his house, receiving only his closest family members and friends. As this passage from the diary reveals, he refused even to make the obligatory trip to the cathedral for the community recital of the oath to the new monarch and instead arranged to take the oath at home like an invalid and with a member of the local clergy serving as witness.

Ivan had reached this point, which was not yet the lowest, after a long and steady decline in his financial fortunes, episodes of which we have already traced in his diary. The diary entries themselves, at least up to 1795, do not reveal an awareness of just how desperate Ivan's situation was becoming. For a long time he continued to hold out hope for a fortunate turn of events, a big business success or a gambling coup, that would halt the downward spiral and get his finances moving in a positive direction. In the meantime, he continued his high living to give his friends and creditors the confidence that his circumstances were unchanged and possibly even improving. Yet the diary entries also reveal an increasing number of days when Ivan was doing nothing useful or productive. Occasionally, he would bestir himself to get to his mill to supervise grinds or go to Moscow to pursue some potential new source of income, but these efforts were few and far between.

A lot of his time seemed to be spent cultivating people who could lend him money or extend current loans. The diary does not make this explicit. It merely records Ivan's many personal contacts. The specific details of his indebtedness have to be sorted out from the record in the Dmitrov archives. But Ivan did sketch an informative picture of the beginnings of his troubles and subsequent process of financial decline in the year-end summaries that he attached to the clean copy of the diary. In these summaries we see him transformed from a diarist into a biographer of his earlier diary-keeping self. What is most curious

and revealing, he was transcribing his daily entries for the years 1786 onward
into leather-bound volumes and appending yearly summaries at the very time,
1796, when he was hiding out at home, much of the time apparently overcome
with sadness.[30] Yet he was doing something psychologically useful and doing it
in two ways. First, he was taking what were probably perishable daily jottings—
unfortunately, there is no record of the form in which he kept the original diary
notes—and transcribing them into beautiful parchment volumes that would
preserve indefinitely a record of his life as a wealthy trader, public official, and
philanthropist who had associated with the rich, the well-born, and the powerful. Second, he was engaging in the kind of self-analysis that is reminiscent of
the earlier European diary writers, the Puritans and pietists, an exercise in
assessing and acknowledging one's guilt and responsibilities. This type of self-
monitoring and reflexive assessment of where one has been and where one is
headed is a key to effective management of a present crisis and the ability to plot
a future course. This practice may well have helped Ivan come to terms with his
situation and to carry on.

Examining these yearly summaries, we find the first hint of trouble in the
one for 1785, a year in which his grain business was still going well and yielded
profits of 9,000 rubles. But as Ivan admitted, his expenses that year exceeded his
profits. He nevertheless wanted to believe that his difficulties were caused not so
much by his reckless spending as by the slow receipt of money from Petersburg.
Without sufficient working capital to launch his purchases for the next year,
Ivan explained, "I had to start borrowing up to 6,000 rubles with interest,
which in time led not only to the termination of my grain trade but also to my
complete ruin."[31] He blamed the slow receipts on his agent in Petersburg but
claimed that he did not understand the problem until much later. Ivan mentioned the same problem in the summary for the following year. Trade again
had been good, and he still had a working capital fund of about 40,000 rubles if
he counted the inheritance due to his young step-uncle Andrei Fëdorovich
Makarov. Yet high expenses and the continuing delay of receipts from Petersburg forced him to borrow 16,000 more rubles to finance his commerce the
next year. In his reflections appended to the diary notes for 1786 (but composed
in the 1790s), he first acknowledged his own failure to have seen the situation
for what it was. He wrote:

*In general, although all three years in a row, i.e. 1784, 1785, and 1786, my com-
mercial dealings were very favorable, I was unable to make any substantive
increase in my capital. To be perfectly honest, I cannot attribute this to anything
other than my poor management, for I did not give a thought to saving money
and did not restrain myself from unnecessary expenditures, thinking that "of
my abundance there could be no end," as the psalmist writes. Therefore I spent*

money, denying myself nothing that I desired. I paid little attention to my com-
mercial affairs and everywhere handled them through agents and perhaps
improperly. Not only was I lazy, but I also undertook the building of a house
beyond my means and pursued other unnecessary projects and acquaintances
merely for the enjoyment of them; and it should be said that I could not [find
time] to go to Petersburg but instead allowed Tiut'kin to make a mess of my
affairs there, and I scarcely ever went to my mills [to check on] the grinding of
grain and when I did so I did not stay long, and the grinding took place with poor
supervision and was not done as it should have been, the result being that a lot
more flour was lost than was the case in the past. In a word, these prosperous
years were wasted due to my inattention, and later I did not have such an
opportunity.[32]

As noted earlier, although Ivan continued to earn good profits through the year
1788 and even paid off some loans, the grip of high interest rates and the need to
turn over the 11,000 ruble inheritance to Andrei Fëdorovich continued to erode
his working capital until he could no longer finance grain purchases and his
trade came to an end.

In looking back, Ivan could see that it was about 1792 that he realized the end
was in sight and that he chose to keep up appearances as long as possible so as
not to lose credit. From then on, as he wrote in his notes reflecting on the year
1794 cited earlier, he was fighting off depression and entertaining delusions that
things might turn out well in the end. Right through 1795 he believed that his
desperate circumstances were not well known, and indeed, at that late date, he
was still able to borrow sufficient capital to lease the Skniatino mill and to
refurbish it. But that was his last gasp. In his hometown, people were becoming
aware of his plight. The mask was falling away, and he decided to go into action
to save what he could of his remaining assets.

In February of 1795, as we have seen, a delegation from the Dmitrov magistracy did an assessment of his house as collateral for loans. Even so, Ivan had
no intention of allowing the home be confiscated to pay off his debts. As he
reported later, "I was compelled to make some tortuous moves to keep my
house from the creditors. I resold it to my relative Goroshkov and in November
gave him a title to it in his name." Goroshkov was the father-in-law of Ivan and
Anna's son Pëtr. In return for the nominal sum of 500 rubles Ivan handed him a
deed not just for the masonry townhouse (as he mentioned here) but also for
the associated gardens, orangeries, and exotic fruit trees, plus a wooden house,
three shops on Bread Lane, and an empty lot—in short, the bulk of his material
assets.[33] We learn later that Goroshkov very soon mortgaged these to his wife to
remove them yet one more step from the grasp of Ivan's bill collectors. This was
a preventive move, for as yet Ivan's situation was not widely known, and his

creditors were not pressing him. But this was about to change. Just six weeks later the summons for him came from the Moscow Court of Arbitration.[34]

By early 1796, the bill collectors were deluging the Moscow provincial magistracy with demands for payment, and that body in turn ordered the Dmitrov city magistracy to open the case against Ivan Tolchënov, which it did on February 25. But Ivan still had some time and, like the gambler he was, a few tricks up his sleeve. We have seen his ability to put on a show of wealth and to socialize with wealthy and prominent people. This impressive self-presentation enabled him to delay the day of reckoning for several years and bought him additional time to conserve his assets. He kept up this front to the very last minute. The diary excerpt at the head of the section on "maintaining appearances" shows him visiting the English Club and then attending a masquerade with his wife at the Moscow Noble Assembly in January 1796, just a month before the court opened the case against him.[35]

If Ivan's impressive self-presentation served him, so too did the clumsiness of the Russian legal system. Commercial affairs in early modern Russia, as elsewhere, depended on contracts and credit. Merchants and entrepreneurs regularly borrowed and transferred money through promissory notes and bills of exchange. Because commercial operations often spanned large areas, merchants might have loans and pre-paid contracts recorded in a number of places. Moreover, before the early decades of the nineteenth century, forms for business transactions were not standardized and therefore did not enjoy full validity in the eyes of the law.[36] When defaults occurred on outstanding debts, communications between the various offices in which loans and contracts had been recorded proved to be time-consuming. Difficulties arose in confirming the reliability of contracts and the transfer of debts to third parties for collection. Officials likewise had trouble locating and bringing debtors to court.

Aggrieved creditors had to be persistent—and they were. A large portion of the cases in the archives of local magistracies concern claims of creditors for overdue payment on promissory notes. Failure to pay led to seizure of the debtor's property, and if the debtor did not have sufficient property to settle a debt, the resolution often came down to an agreement on the part of the borrower to indenture himself to the creditor or to a third party at the rate of twenty-four rubles per year until the debt was paid off.

Despite the sluggishness of the process, the tenacity of creditors and local authorities was impressive, as it had to be if the system was going to work at all. A notorious case involved a leather merchant from Nizhnii Novgorod who was robbed while returning from a sale of his goods in another city in 1780. He decided his only hope of recouping the loss and supporting his wife, three children, and parents was to get to Petersburg and find a job. There he hired on as a seaman for a run to France with a shipload of masts. At a stop en route, he was dragooned into the service of another country. One thing led to another, and this sorry landlubber from central Russia ended up seeing a lot of the world, including the islands of the Caribbean, North Africa, Turkey, Greece, Romania, and Poland. When he arrived home six years later after many adventures, he was promptly arrested by his local magistracy for failure to pay his second-guild merchant dues during the intervening years and, when this obligation was forgiven, held for debts owed to others to the tune of 230 rubles. When he not surprisingly proved unable to pay, he was condemned to serve for ten years as an indentured laborer at a nearby salt works until his debt was fully discharged. Luckily, this reluctant adventurer won the notice and sympathy of the local bishop and governor, and through their assistance in finding patrons in Petersburg he was able to obtain the funds needed to retire his debt and rejoin his family.[37]

Most of the cases in the archives of the Dmitrov magistracy ended less happily but more or less satisfactorily. The usual debt case did not involve a large sum of money, and the debt could be worked off in a year or two. The creditor got paid, and the debtor could continue his life at home while working off the debt and even spend time on his own business affairs in hopes of reestablishing his creditworthiness. Evidence for the city of Moscow indicates that, just as in Dmitrov, bankruptcy among merchants was not uncommon, something we might well expect in view of the risks of commerce and lack of insurance in Russia in this period. The scope of the problem can be judged by a glance at the number of auctions of merchant property that appear in the principal periodical source of information for Moscow, the publication *Moskovskie vedomosti*. During the years 1775–1778 it carried more than thirty descriptions of the property of bankrupt merchants and merchant wives. One of these was the former president of the Moscow magistracy, D. I. Serebrennikov, a man who was on his second bankruptcy. He first suffered the loss his of property in 1769 for a debt of 8,160 rubles but managed eventually to get back on his feet. However, in 1778 when he went into bankruptcy again, he was not able to recover.[38] Serebrennikov's public service may well have played a role in his commercial misfortunes, as it did for other merchants whose civic duties prevented them from giving needed attention to their businesses.

Ivan's case, not surprisingly in view of his ability to delay its discovery, involved large sums and exceptional complexity. The Dmitrov magistracy had to devote several months to sorting out its details. In the meantime, Ivan began to cash in or transfer his remaining assets. We saw that in November of the previous year he had arranged a formal but deceptive sale of his home and other principal assets to Andrei Goroshkov, who then mortgaged them to his wife. Three months later, in early February 1796, Ivan formally ceded his parental authority over his son Pëtr and transferred him to the household of the same

Goroshkov, Pëtr's father-in-law.[39] This ensured that the assets of Pëtr, now a businessman in his own right, could not be seized in payment of Ivan's debts. In March Ivan parted with another asset when he sold his serf Aleksei Volkov, along with Volkov's wife and two children, to the renowned military commander and diplomat Count Aleksei Grigorievich Orlov-Chesmenskii. At about the same time he sold off his expensive orangery trees and remaining movable property to other people. The trees went principally to his friend and creditor, the nobleman Afanasii Iushkov. Then in May Ivan offered his masonry home and gardens for purchase to the man who succeeded him as mayor of Dmitrov, Ivan Tugarinov, the owner of a very profitable cloth factory in the city. Tugarinov appeared on May 10 with his eldest son to examine the house and returned the very next morning to complete a contract to purchase the house for 15,000 rubles. In view of the complication that the Goroshkov family held the official deed, Tugarinov agreed not to take possession until the following year, and Ivan, as he later wrote, was able to continue "to reside there as full owner."[40]

Once Ivan's creditors learned about his ruin and the sale of his principal asset, they pursued him aggressively. He felt the heat. When he went to Moscow later the same month that he had sold his house to Tugarinov, May 1796, he rode directly to the apartment of his in-law Andrei Goroshkov and stayed there, writing in his diary that "because of payment demands being submitted I could not possibly go to my own apartment." While in Moscow he helped his son Pëtr find a home to purchase near the New Virgin Convent on the west side of the city, a purchase no doubt financed by the money earned on the recent property sales and calculated to shelter these assets by turning them over to Pëtr now that he was under the protection of Goroshkov. This done, Ivan returned to Dmitrov, stopping for only a day, and then left with his son Pavel for the Skniatino mill in Tver province near the Volga, where they hid out for two months. Anna and Iakov soon after joined them at the mill. Ivan's creditors did not know where he was. For them he had simply vanished. We can see from the diary, however, that Ivan was not idle. He was conducting grinds at the refurbished mill and earning a bit on that. He also appeared a few times in the local Kaliazin court, possibly trying to recover a bad debt owed to him there.

Around this same time Ivan transferred to his wife receipts from some of the assets he had liquidated. The available documentation does not reveal the precise mechanism or amount, but it is likely that he returned to her the amount he had received as a dowry. The amount was sufficient for her to establish herself and her three other children as a third-guild merchant household separate from Ivan and thereby retain for herself and her children the privileges and exemptions of that status, including freedom from military recruitment, corporal punishment, and payment of the poll tax.[41] Having placed

Pëtr and his wife and child under the protection of the Goroshkov household in Moscow and his own wife Anna and their remaining children in a legally separate Dmitrov household, Ivan had done what he could to remove all the members of his immediate family from liability for his debts.

At the end of July Ivan sneaked back home and hid in his house in Dmitrov, for a long time pretending simply not to be there. He confined himself to the house and received only the closest family members and friends. The people he saw on a regular basis, outside his immediate family, included his step-uncle Andrei Fëdorovich Makarov and his cousin Aleksandr Petrovich Tolchënov and their families. Occasionally the district doctor, Dr. Kepeng, or Ivan Tugarinov dropped by, or even more rarely the archpriest or an Obreskova daughter. That was all. Even his uncles by blood, formerly frequent visitors, failed to appear, except in three scattered instances. Perhaps Ivan was not eager to see them because they were among his major creditors. When it came to the attention of local officials in late summer that Ivan was actually in the city hiding out at home and they summoned him to appear in court, he claimed that he was too sick with fevers to be able to leave the house and appear at court. Luckily for Ivan, his friend Dr. Kepeng was kind enough to testify to this phony illness.[42] Ivan even neglected to sponsor the annual August 17 mass and dinner in memory of his father, an unprecedented, if understandable, omission. (A few days later his wife, Anna, took an arduous pilgrimage on foot to the Trinity Monastery, perhaps to perform the remembrance along the road on which Ivan's father had died and to call on spiritual strength in the family crisis.) As mentioned at the head of this section, Ivan even managed to avoid leaving the house in November following the death of Empress Catherine II when an edict ordered citizens to appear at the cathedral to take the oath to the new ruler. Ivan admitted to his deceptions and vanishing acts in his later notes, but he excused himself on grounds that he needed to avoid detection "until I could find some means of turning things around."

Turning things around was going to be quite a task. The records piling up at the magistracy court revealed truly breathtaking debts: 1,000 rubles to the Moscow merchant Tikhon Sveshnikov, the husband of Ivan's first cousin, Praskov'ia Petrovna; 2,000 to the Dmitrov district noble Vasilii Golovin; 5,000 to Brigadier Appolon Gal'berg (who had become acquainted with Ivan when he quartered troops in Dmitrov); 5,100 rubles to Ivan's brother-in-law Aleksandr Vandashnikov; 5,100 to the Moscow merchant Ivan Grezenkov; 5,390 to the Moscow merchant Stepan Kulikov; 8,400 to the Petersburg merchant Aleksei Ivanov; 14,558 to his uncles Ivan, Dmitrii, and Mikhaila; nearly 30,000 to the Moscow merchant Pëtr Orlov. There were several others, including 4,000 to his nobleman friend Afanasii Iushkov and nearly 8,000 owed to Andrei Goroshkov.[43]

When the Dmitrov magistracy summoned Ivan in September and he feigned illness, he nevertheless had to offer some response. Accordingly, he sent his son Aleksei (the eldest son in his household since Pëtr had been reassigned to the Goroshkov family) to explain the state of his finances and his inability to pay what altogether amounted to a whopping debt of 90,928 rubles. His tactic was to ask that his creditors be patient, allow him time to reestablish his finances and eventually repay his debts. Reporting on the statement from Ivan delivered by his son, the magistracy explained to its superior court in Moscow that

> because of his losses in commerce and further substantial losses to his capital caused by his former agent in Petersburg, the Dmitrov merchant Stepan Tiut'kin, he is not now in a position to pay his debts and has no cash or property of any kind and owns only unrecovered funds for goods he distributed to various persons on credit or on account, amounting to 11,000 rubles, and for this reason requests most humbly that his creditors would take into consideration his unfortunate situation and be lenient toward him in regard to payment of his debts and permit him an extension of three years and allow him in that time to be at liberty so that he might more reliably seek the means of collecting the money owed to him and in this way be able to pay his debts.[44]

As the magistracy gathered information on the case through the winter of 1796–1797, it found that some creditors were willing to accept this offer, others were not. Among those willing to wait three years were several of the larger creditors: Goroshkov, Ivanov, Kulikov, and Orlov. Another creditor, Vandashnikov, allowed a one-year extension.

The rest were less charitable. Vasilii Golovin argued that Ivan was a liar of the worst sort who time and again had assured him that he would pay up. Tikhon Sveshnikov likewise demanded prompt payment as did the heirs of Ivan Grezenkov. These people and a number of others contended that Ivan did not deserve postponements since he had knowingly deceived and cheated his creditors. What most angered them was Ivan's success in shielding his assets from confiscation. They resented being taken in and found it infuriating that he had continued to maintain appearances and reassure his creditors that he would repay them, all the while divesting himself of every last asset that might be seized in the event of default. They also pointed out that Ivan had not suffered the type of misfortunes that the law recognized as grounds for leniency and postponement of debts, and they demanded, despite sale of his house, that the property be seized and sold to pay them back what was owed.

From the point of view of each individual creditor, this approach may have made sense. But to the magistracy officers viewing the larger picture, the normal way of dealing with debtors simply could not work. Ivan had piled up debts far beyond anything that the magistracy was used to dealing with, and in his affidavits he even listed debts incurred elsewhere and not yet known to the local magistracy, perhaps to make the impossibility of recovery still more obvious and to convince the magistracy of the futility of invalidating the sale of his home, not to mention indenturing him for the usual twenty-four rubles a year. At that rate, his creditors could expect to get repaid in about 4,000 years!

Ivan continued his life as if the solution he proposed would eventually be accepted by the authorities. The family made preparations to move to Moscow but continued to live in the elegant Dmitrov townhouse through the winter. At the end of February 1797, the new owner and his family moved in or, as Ivan put it in the diary, apparently unable to let go of the idea of owning the home, "on this day Tugarinov moved into my house to live by mutual agreement, and we moved down to the lower floor until our departure." In the meantime, Ivan had been running back and forth to the Skniatino mill to take care of one final piece of business. He had to negotiate a transfer of his lease on the mill to a merchant from the nearby city of Kashin, and "with God's help" he managed to do this and get out from under an obligation to pay quitrent and run the mill for two more years. Then on March 16, 1797, at 2 in the afternoon, Anna and the children and servants along with their personal property departed to their new life in Moscow. Ivan followed the next day.

Moving to Moscow did not end Ivan's troubles. Since his case had not yet been resolved, the creditors who were demanding payment continued to pursue him and finally convinced the government to act. On May 7 Ivan received a subpoena to appear before a bailiff and, when he did so, was detained at the request of the heirs of Ivan Grezenkov and dispatched to the offices of the provincial administration and held there for two days and nights. He was then ordered to appear without delay before the Dmitrov magistracy. He left the next morning and arrived the same evening, staying in Dmitrov with his cousin Aleksandr Petrovich. The next day he was in court, where the officers, who were his former neighbors and colleagues, sorted through his complicated case. The work continued for several more days, and Ivan was then allowed to go to Moscow. He returned to Dmitrov in the first two weeks of June for completion of the case and obtained the resolution that he had hoped for.

Contributing to Ivan's ability to evade his colossal debt was undoubtedly the inadequacy of bankruptcy laws in Russia. The Decree on Bankruptcy of 1740, the most recent law on this issue, was a long-winded exhortation against undue risk that drew a clear distinction between inadvertent bankruptcy and intentional, deceitful bankruptcy of the kind Ivan had engineered. While it was not as harsh as the seventeenth-century French law that recommended the death penalty for financial deception, it did provide penalties up to and including many years of hard labor.[45] Despite the law, "the clumsiness of the judicial system," as Arcadius Kahan called it, afforded little protection to private lenders.[46] Ultimately, assuming the central government or ruler did not get involved, the decisions rested with the local magistracies, and they were inclined to arrange matters in the best interests of the community's commercial elites. As always, personal relations counted. Tolchënov had been a good citizen of the town, carrying out a number of large and small charitable projects, bearing a heavy burden of public service, and defending the town against intrusions on the part of the central authorities. He and his family had enjoyed a close association with members of the magistracy who settled the judgments on him, and indeed, at least one of those magistrates was a Tolchënov. Another was a Loshkin.

But the well-known "familyness" of Russian politics—the kinship and patron/client relations—cannot provide a complete explanation. These relationships were embedded in a larger social context, constituted by the merchant and posad community, whose interests had to be protected and balanced. For example, Ivan's own uncles protested the sale of his properties in Dmitrov to a non-family member. They cited Russian property law that allowed kin to claim precedence in the purchase of alienated property and demanded the right to purchase the elegant townhouse that had been sold to another merchant.[47] The magistracy rejected this claim, however, and did so deceitfully. It referenced a 1775 law (article 290) of the Decree on the Governance of the Provinces, saying that when the sale of the property was filed in Dmitrov, the uncles should have registered an objection and, not having done so at that time, they could not now claim the property.[48] The magistracy officers neglected to mention that the very same article 290 allowed for a two-year delay in protesting such sales, and the uncles' claim arrived within that deadline.[49]

The magistracy's decision on the three-year extension of debts that Ivan requested also rested on a loose interpretation of precedent. The creditors who were demanding immediate payment rightly pointed out that Ivan did not qualify for leniency because he had not suffered the kind of misfortunes provided for in the law and, still worse, had lied and manipulated his finances in order to transfer his principal assets to members of his immediate family through third parties. The members of the magistracy obviously knew exactly what Ivan had been doing and did not offer a rebuttal to the claim of these angry creditors. Instead, they used as a precedent a case from 1784 concerning a merchant in faraway Olonets in which creditors with lesser claims in a bankruptcy case were expected to concede decisions to those with superior claims. Accordingly, in the view of the Dmitrov magistracy, because the creditors willing to grant Ivan an extension were owed more than those opposed to it, the extension should be approved. To those who argued that at least Ivan's house should be seized and used for payment, the magistracy responded that the matter was beyond its competence. It had received a copy of a legal deed of sale to the person in Moscow (Andrei Goroshkov), and what happened to the property after that was not recorded in Dmitrov and therefore did not concern the Dmitrov magistracy. As for the special family claims of the uncles, the magistracy officers pointed out that if they acceded to them, it would open the door to further demands for seizure of the house by other creditors, and they added that if the uncles were unhappy with the decision, they were welcome to appeal.[50]

Although the magistracy officers did not record their motivations, it seems clear that the morality on which their decisions rested placed class and community above other values. Tolchënov, who well understood his community and its leaders, had shrewdly engineered a series of credit operations that shifted his debt into the hands of people who had little influence on the Dmitrov magistracy. Except for his uncles, all of the creditors were either nobles, whom the magistracy had little reason to protect, or merchants from other communities. One person in the district to whom he owed money and who may have had some influence with the magistracy was Liubov Nagibina, wife of the former district police captain. In this instance, Ivan convinced his friend Afanasii Iushkov to pay the 2,000 rubles owed her before the bankruptcy trial started and then add that amount to the total Ivan owed Iushkov.[51] As for Tolchënov's home, it had been purchased at a fair price by the mayor and leading entrepreneur of the community, Ivan Tugarinov, and he had been very decent toward Tolchënov in managing the transaction. The magistracy was by no means going to deprive Tugarinov of his ownership of this valuable property, all the more since it was obvious that the 15,000 rubles Tugarinov had paid Ivan for the house was gone and would never be recovered. The key for the magistracy was that the Dmitrov urban community had not been injured by Ivan's misfortunes. The city would be able to meet its normal tax and service obligations without additional strains, and apart from Ivan's uncles, none of Dmitrov's citizens was being harmed by his fall. The magistracy officers might well have believed that the uncles should have known about the failing financial position of their nephew, for they had worked closely with Ivan and his father in commercial ventures. In short, with the exception of the debt to his uncles, Ivan's obligations were held elsewhere. This configuration of liabilities allowed the magistracy to arrange things in a way that did not disrupt their own community—while others could try as they might to pursue Ivan in other places. But inasmuch as his principal assets remained safely in the hands of citizens of Dmitrov or had been legally transferred to a son no longer under his protection and to other members of his family, there was little creditors could hope to get from him.

The judgment of the magistracy court also reflected an evolution in Russian law mapped in Michelle Marrese's recent book: the move away from collective family responsibility for debts incurred by the head of a family.[52] The bankruptcy law of 1740, for example, allowed seizure of assets held by a merchant's wife for payment of her husband's debts. The new bankruptcy code promulgated in 1800, shortly after the Tolchënov case, forbade seizure of a wife's property if she was not party to her husband's business affairs.[53] The Dmitrov court was, in essence, putting this principle of individual responsibility into action before it had been officially enacted into law. The decision could be seen as part of a larger societal shift, reflected in the new law a few years later, to protect family property from seizure by the state and to assess culpability in individual rather than collective terms. We have already discussed how this same shift in values was affecting the character of dishonor suits earlier in the century.

*   *   *

Ivan's behavior offended personal and community morality, not to mention the law, which expressed a ferocious condemnation of conscious, deceitful bankruptcy. Books of moral guidance for commercial people conveyed the normative values of the community, repeating incessantly admonitions to avoid luxury, laziness, debt, and gambling, and to conduct one's business directly and not through hired agents.[54] Ivan felt the sting of these injunctions and regretted his inattention to trade. He also admitted to dishonest conduct, noting in his summary notes for the year 1797 that in order to keep his creditors at bay after the bankruptcy trial he felt compelled to engage in "further illegal acts and deceptions."[55] But for him family trumped personal conscience. Preservation of his family and his own freedom to continue to work and to have hopes of recouping his losses overrode whatever concerns he had about his relationship to the law and to his God. And by family, he meant above all his immediate family, not the larger collective composed of uncles, cousins, and in-laws. The extended family or clan was receding in social and legal importance as the values of individual fulfillment and individual responsibility more and more shaped the thinking of educated Russians. This change in attitude and values may have caught Ivan's uncles off guard. They seemed to believe, or at least to hope, that Ivan would protect their investments or that, in the final analysis, the magistracy would interpret the law in their favor. When neither of these things happened, a rupture occurred between Ivan and his uncles that would be a long time in healing.

In his summing up of the year of the bankruptcy trial and move to Moscow, Ivan stressed the personal losses, his feelings of shame at his lowered status, and his failure to meet his responsibility to his immediate family. "In this year," he wrote, "I was compelled to leave my beloved hometown, the city of Dmitrov, in which I was born and lived for more than 42 years. I grew up there and partook fully of all earthly blessings, having inherited from my father a substantial capital. I engaged in trade there myself successfully and to good purpose for ten years and on the basis of my growing commerce built a lovely masonry home, orangeries, and had gardens and orchards, a fishery, and good servants." This report of his birth, elite status, and beautiful life constituted a sketch of the social and personal identity that he had aspired to and had crafted in the years since he began his diary. Then he filled in the other side and the descent into a new identity to which he would now have to adjust. While he was willing to accept most of the blame for his losses, he could still not refrain from deflecting some of it onto his hapless agent Stepan Tiut'kin. "I deprived myself and my innocent family of all of this through my excessive luxury and inattention to business, added to which were some losses in Petersburg, such that from the honored rank of leading merchant of the city, I fell to a contemptible station." This last refers to his descent into the status of "lesser town dweller," a social category subject to the poll tax and exposed to corporal punishment and other degrading practices. And to complete the picture, he added that "from a beautiful home I moved to the dark and noisy rooms of a Moscow apartment, where my sole occupation was the manufacture of playing cards, which in that year did not even yield a profit."[56]

Throughout the mounting crisis Ivan's behavior shifted between depression and heightened action. Sometimes he sank into despair that left him in a state of lassitude, resigned to the coming catastrophe. At other times, he sprang into action to seek out new loans or productive investments. Ultimately, he did not succumb to fatalistic acceptance and become paralyzed in his former routines and his self-identity as a civic leader and model citizen. He found the will to save what he could of his wealth, even if it had to be done by illegal means. We know that Ivan was a gambler. The sociologist Irving Goffman has pointed out that someone strongly inclined to risk-taking, such as a gambler, is better able than others to see how situations might offer opportunities for the play of chance and to take risks that could bring advantages. Perhaps this quality of Ivan's, together with his attentive self-monitoring, a prerequisite for effective planning, allowed him to salvage what was possible from his fall.

It was characteristic of Ivan, too, that he looked back on this calamity with a sense of balance. He closed this summing up of his life by writing that despite the financial ruin and humiliation of his family, "my new life in Moscow offered some consolation in a new occupation and in the abundance of new things that happened there this year [1797], not to mention that I was able to renew my acquaintance with Squire Iushkov and through him with some others as well."[57] Even so, the adjustment that Ivan had to make in his social identity and consequently also in his self-identity was eventually going to exact a price in his physical and psychic health.

7

Moscow Townsman

THE CORONATION OF TSAR PAUL

[1797, March] 17th At 8 o'clock in the morning I rode away to Moscow in the company of my cousin Grigorii Petrovich. We had dinner in Sholokhovo and arrived at my apartment in Zaikin house at 7 in the evening.

18th In the morning I strolled along Tverskaia Street up to the Triumphal Arch and had the pleasure of seeing for the first time my most august monarch riding into Moscow on horseback from the Petrovskii Palace, and the grand prince and heir was riding with him. From there I walked down to the Kremlin and viewed the changing of the guard.

19th I spent the day in the apartment. At 11 o'clock in the morning our emperor and ruler accompanied by a numerous suite came riding down Nikitskaia St. past the apartment. In the evening I visited my relative Goroshkov.

Ivan mentioned "the abundance of new things that happened" in Moscow during his first year there as helpful in distracting him from his troubles. The most important of these new things were the entry into the city and coronation of Emperor Paul. The interplay between Ivan's immediate reaction to the events of the coronation reported in the diary and his later evaluation of this ruler in his year-end summaries is instructive and tells us something more about his identity and values. His initial response recorded his instinctive respect for authority and fascination with the pomp of power. His later evaluations reflected, on the one hand, the broader societal view of this failed monarch, and on the other, Ivan's horror and revulsion for the act of regicide. First the diary.

In the excerpt starting this section Ivan reported that the very next morning after moving to Moscow he took a walk along Tverskaia Street, the main artery for arrival into the city from the northwest. He strolled up to the Triumphal Arch at the top of the street and got his first view of Paul as emperor, riding on horseback accompanied by his son and heir Alexander.[1] The following day, March 19, Ivan did not even have to leave home to see the tsar, for he passed right down Nikitskaia Street underneath Ivan's window. A few days later, after making a short trip to Dmitrov, Ivan was back in Moscow arranging for the family to view the coronation pageantry. A measure of how far Ivan's financial collapse had displaced him from proximity to power can be seen in the distance between his family's position for viewing the entry to the city of Empress Catherine and the imperial family in June of 1787 and the place they now occupied for viewing Paul's official entry. Ten years earlier they had stood at the very steps of the Dormition Cathedral inside the Kremlin. This time they viewed the entry from specially built stands opposite the Kazan Cathedral on Red Square, outside the walls of the Kremlin. The entry took place on March 28. For the next few days Ivan could not deny himself the pleasure of seeing whatever else was available to the general public of pageantry associated with the forthcoming coronation. On the twenty-ninth, a Sunday, he took the family for an evening carriage ride to see the fireworks and other illuminations at the court and along the main streets, a feature of imperial visits to Moscow that Paul had raised to a new height. The next afternoon he visited various Kremlin churches and stopped in at the Synodal Palace to see the preparation of the holy oils for the coronation. Also "out of curiosity" he went into the Kremlin's Palace of Facets and Golden Tsarina's Chamber. A day later he was at the Slobodskii Palace on the city's northeast side to see the changing of the guard in the presence of the emperor and the grand princes.

Ivan's diary entry for the day of the coronation itself, August 5, was composed in a kind of official, unctuous tone that he undoubtedly borrowed from the rhetoric and ritual of the coronation. It was saturated with religious language and compared Paul's accession to the coming of Christ.[2] Ivan wrote: "This was a joyful day for Christians, just like the day our Redeemer rose from the grave, and especially for Russia, the day in which Paul the First, who had been chosen by God to rule over her, placed on his head the wreath of the ruler and accepted the anointing of holy oils." Ivan went on to write that after hearing mass at the University Church, he and his wife went at nine in the morning to the Kremlin and found a place on the porch of the Monastery of the Miracles from which to view the procession of the new monarch and the imperial family from the Dormition Cathedral, where the coronation took place, to the Cathedral of Archangel Michael, the resting place of rulers before the eighteenth century. They also saw the military parade that accompanied the festivities. To top off an exciting day, they then invited their son Pëtr and his wife over for dinner and watched from the apartment as a long column of dignitaries moved out of the Kremlin and down Nikitskaia Street on the way to their lodgings on the outskirts of the city. More articulate and informed chroniclers of Paul's coronation pointed out that it exhibited a number of elements not before seen, such as the emperor riding on horseback and stopping to pray at the shrine of the Iberian Madonna. Prussian-style costuming was also everywhere enforced.[3] Ivan wrote nothing about these things either in the diary or in his later summary notes. Although he had seen two other imperial entries to the city, he had not been present for the coronation of Catherine II and may therefore not have been able to make comparisons of these particular events. At any rate, he did not comment on the presentation of the monarch or the parade.

Ivan seemed to be enjoying himself and indulging in the atmosphere of goodwill and hope for the future that customarily accompanied the coronation of a new ruler in Russia. He was no doubt also finding in these events a welcome, if passing, escape from the humiliation and guilt he felt at having lost his money and position. Right through the month of April Ivan continued to behave as a tourist in his new hometown and to get around to one or another post-coronation event or site of power. After another short trip to Dmitrov, he took his entire household on April 11 to the Kremlin for a stroll around the palace. A few days later they viewed the imperial family passing by their apartment on the way out of town to visit the Resurrection or "New Jerusalem" Monastery west of the city near the town of Zvenigorod. The next day Ivan went again to the Kremlin to see the imperial regalia at the Palace of Facets. The same evening he and the family watched as the new tsar again passed by their apartment on his way back from the Resurrection Monastery. Toward the end of the month Ivan reported seeing the emperor on Tverskaia Street coming back to the Kremlin palace after visiting the King of Poland at a suburban residence.

But these encounters and identifications with power and its pageantry could not serve for long as distractions from the painful reality of Ivan's position. Even before the imperial family left Moscow Ivan was visited by new humiliations. On April 25 he made a call on Countess Elizaveta Orlova, with whom he had exchanged frequent visits in the past and even assisted in her gardening projects. He reported simply in his diary, "I did not find her at home." Countess Orlova then disappears from the diary for many years. Ivan's reception at her door must have made it clear that he was no longer welcome. Another quick trip to Dmitrov on business followed, and this time when Ivan visited the new owner of his masonry house, he did not note, as he had earlier, that Tugarinov was in "my home" but instead wrote that he was "in my former home." Ivan was beginning to adjust to his new role as a formerly wealthy merchant. One week later was the date of his arrest and incarceration in Moscow and then his dispatch to Dmitrov for the settlement of his bankruptcy case.

These humiliations and losses no doubt affected and colored his later evaluation of the Tsar Paul's reign, although the capriciousness of this ruler may have been enough in itself to prompt Ivan's later evaluation of him.

While Ivan had not written anything about the exceptional character of the coronation events and symbolic presentation of the new ruler in Moscow, he had a lot to say about the disturbing practices connected with the burial of Catherine II in Petersburg and Paul's first steps in administering the country. These remarks appear in his year-end summary for 1796. It is not altogether clear when Ivan composed this summary. Possibly he made some preliminary notes soon after the events described, but he was unlikely while Paul was still alive to have written down incriminating comments in his expensive leather-bound diary books intended for preservation.[4]

He began the summary with an announcement that on November 6, 1796, Russia saw the untimely death of Catherine II and the elevation to the throne of Paul I. "Shortly thereafter," Ivan continued, "there occurred not just daily but one could say even hourly changes ordered by the new monarch in the military and the civil administration. And soon everyone learned about the fiery and unstable character of the new ruler, for just as he showered excessive bounties on some, he punished others outside the law and in defiance of legal process." Ivan then launched into a mini-history of Catherine's concerns about the succession and of Paul's belittling of her and exaltation of his father.

For a long time, coldness and hostility had existed between the most august deceased mother and her now crowned son. The deceased Catherine had intended before her death to assign the crown to her favorite grandson Alexander, for she could not see in her son the ability to govern the vast empire that she had glorified with her rule. And she had shared her intention with close and trusted persons, but she kept putting off its execution, and then her rapid and unexpected death left the plan unfulfilled. For this and other reasons, when Paul I took the throne, he showed little consideration for the one who gave him life and openly exhibited indifference to her remains and quickly altered all of her institutions and plans. This greatest among women and benefactress of millions was deprived of the gratitude owed to even ordinary people, not to mention the great, who after death are feted with laudatory speeches or odes or the like, as all the Russian poets did not dare to speak out in public, knowing the displeasure this would elicit from the severe monarch.

Ivan then expressed in sharp words his disapproval of Paul's resurrection of Peter III.

On the contrary, all the filial emotion due to his mother he devoted instead to his father Peter III, and he ordered that his decayed body, which had been buried in the Annunciation Church in the Nevskii Monastery in 1762, be removed from its rotting casket and placed in a magnificent catafalque in that church with all imperial tributes and honor guard and that on top of the casket be placed a

crown. This crown, which, Peter III did not want to place on his own head when
he was alive, was placed on his casket without his will by his attentive son. And he
took this ludicrous display of honor to such an extent that whoever of the people
might happen by Nevskii Monastery, each one was required to go into the church
and unwillingly offer praise to the remains of the former emperor.

Ivan's reverence for Catherine II and scorn for this symbolic elevation of Peter III
echoed the feelings of many educated Russians of the day, who, like Ivan, could
express their views only in private writings and unmonitored conversation.

Although Ivan mentioned briefly the transfer of Peter III's remains to the
Winter Palace and the interment of the two monarchs three days later in the
Sts. Peter and Paul Cathedral, he did not describe in detail the process of
the transfer of Peter III's remains to lie in state next to Catherine at the Winter
Palace or the public humiliation of Aleksei Orlov, a participant in the coup
of 1762 and the recent purchaser of Ivan's serf family, who was forced to follow
the funeral carriage while bearing the large new crown made for Peter III.
What he focused on instead was the unusual and disturbing behavior of Paul,
noting that "with great fanfare the new ruler showered extraordinary gifts of
villages, money, objects, and ranks on all the still-living favorite officials of
his father. Among them was my benefactor and in some ways even my friend
General-Major Prince Ivan Fëdorovich Golitsyn. On November 14, after traveling from Danilovskoe to Moscow, Golitsyn received from the monarch by
courier an edict awarding him the second highest military rank (*general-
anshef*) and the Order of St. Alexander. In contrast, the favorites of the deceased empress and in particular those who had assisted her accession to the
throne were exiled to their villages under house arrest, and many of them
moved to foreign lands." Ivan then went on to tell of the "strange ideas" of the
monarch about clothing, only certain styles of which were permitted in the
capital cities. Special attention was given to hats. If you were found wearing a
round hat, it would be immediately seized and chopped to ribbons, Ivan
pointed out. He also mentioned the dangers of appearing in the wrong type of
coat or boots.

Ivan likewise reported on the problems that Paul's monetary policies were
causing for commerce. One of the first things that Paul did was to outlaw trade
in gold and silver money, a change that was not only abrupt and unprepared
but also enforced with such strictness that it created a sudden inflation in the
circulating paper and copper currencies. As a result, Ivan wrote, people refused
to give up precious metal for the softer equivalents, and this in turn "caused
major disruptions in trade and great conflict."

Although it is difficult to believe that Ivan would have penned these critical
remarks while Paul was still in power, one passage in his summary appears to

have been recorded soon after it happened. It is out of sequence with the other comments and set off in a separate paragraph. This refers to an abortive trip that Metropolitan Platon was making to Petersburg soon after the death of Empress Catherine. Ivan was still residing in Dmitrov at the time, attending mass and receiving visits from relatives and friends, even from the abbot of the monastery. He wrote:

On the morning of December 3 Right Reverend and Metropolitan Platon passed through Dmitrov on his way from the Trinity Monastery to Petersburg for the appropriate meetings and bell-ringing, but on the 4th at 6 in the evening he returned to our city and stayed overnight at the monastery. The next morning he left for the Trinity Monastery. The reason for his turnaround was rumored to be that just before reaching Tver he received from Petersburg some papers that were distasteful to him.[5]

We learn from biographies of Platon that these papers concerned his objections to a plan by Paul to confer orders of chivalry on churchmen. Paul not only rejected Platon's intervention in this matter but also upbraided him in a sharply worded letter for his presumptuousness at questioning an imperial decision.[6] The papers included an order from the Holy Synod that Paul insisted it produce in support of his decision. Judging from the account in another source, the memoirs of Senator Ivan Lopukhin, Paul was furious that Platon, his former beloved teacher, would resist his will.[7] And, indeed, as Ivan Tolchënov's diary confirms, the conflict resonated in the public mind. People may have wondered what hope there could be for peace and stability in the country when the new sovereign could not get along with his former teacher, the metropolitan of Moscow.

Despite this incident, Platon played a role in the coronation of Paul a few months later in April of 1797, and Ivan recorded in his summary for that year that as soon as Paul arrived at the Petrovskii Palace in March, he awarded Platon the chivalric order of St. Andrew the Apostle. Ivan did not write it but may have known by this time that the award was likewise a public rebuff of Platon for his opposition to conferring chivalric orders on clergymen.

Other than this report (and what Ivan observed in the daily entries about the coronation), he offered no more information on Paul and his reign until he composed his summary notes for the year 1800. Here again we can feel Ivan's disapproval of the emperor's behavior. He noted first that "in St. Petersburg this summer the Mikhailovskii Castle was finished at the cost, according to reliable reports, of about 17 million rubles, and in November Emperor Paul I and his entire eminent family moved in with great fanfare." Ivan then went on to explain that the tsar's persecutions had intensified to an extraordinary degree this year and were driving the court elite and nobility more generally into secret opposition, "because the least error or indiscretion was enough to get them sent to Siberia." He added that this was affecting not just nobles in the capital cities but even those serving in the provinces and in the military. They were daily being arrested and exiled without the slightest legal process, purely on the say-so of the emperor. "It often happens that the tsar will give a high award to someone one day, and the next day he will have him thrown in prison or exiled to some distant place and forbidden to enter the capital cities. Among the well-known unfortunates you could find Prince Sibirskii, a general and holder of numerous imperial orders, who was accused of misconduct in his management of logistics and supplies and deprived not only of his ranks but was even ordered to go on foot to Siberia in chains like the lowest kind of criminal."[8] It is interesting to observe here Ivan's respect for legal process, something that he and other educated Russians now expected from everyone in authority, includ-ing the emperor. Ivan well understood what this meant. He and his father, and other members of the family, had spent years in service on the magistracy court, and although Ivan had skillfully bent the legal rules in the case of his own bankruptcy trial, he believed in the process and the protection it presumably afforded the accused.

Ivan rarely commented on international politics, but he did so now in mentioning the "dispute with England" that was having very marked effects on commerce. He was referring here to the agreement that Paul had made with Napoleon to embargo British trade to the continent. Ivan reported that English citizens of any rank were being detained and exiled to internal provinces of Russia and that the result was an immediate sharp rise in the price of sugar and other commodities supplied by the English. He obviously had found all this disturbing and perplexing but prudently stopped his pen, saying finally that "it would require several books to describe all the arrangements and changes made by the government in domestic and foreign affairs during this year."

The following year brought the assassination of the tsar. Ivan reported in his diary that the news of Paul's death and assumption of the throne by his son Alexander had reached Moscow on March 15 and that the populace began taking the oath to the new sovereign on the very same day in the Dormition Cathedral amid general rejoicing.[9] His subsequent year-end report was fuller, more interesting and revealing.

On the night of March 12 in the Mikhailovskii Castle in St. Petersburg the death of Emperor Paul occurred as the result of miraculous events which I will leave to posterity to describe. But I cannot neglect to say that on this day the governor-general, Count Deripalen,[10] and the Zubov brothers showed themselves to be monsters of cruelty. To the rejoicing of all of Russia Emperor Alexander ascended the throne and immediately signaled the mild character of his administration by

a number of charitable measures and, even more so, by the rapid release from
prison and from Siberia of persons of all social statuses who had been imprisoned
despite their innocence or the trivial nature of their offenses.

What a mixture of emotion! The act of regicide was shocking and repellent to
Ivan. It was after all symbolically also an act of patricide and did violence to the
patriarchal principles on which all authority in Russia rested. Political theory in
Russia as enunciated in the foundational decrees of Russian rulers for centuries
underlined that the tsar was anointed by God and that a harsh ruler was a
scourge that had to be suffered. By extension, the authority of each head of
household was sustained by the same idea and could not be questioned (unless
he or in rare cases she could be officially recognized as mentally incompetent).
The recognition that a handful of favorites and high officials could murder
the reigning ruler cut the ground out from under the established order and
invited chaos. Men who could undertake such an act had by definition to be
"monsters."

On the other hand, Ivan could not but join in the relief felt by most educated
Russians at the end of the capricious and unstable rule of Paul. Ivan disliked
many aspects of Paul's behavior, starting with his disrespectful treatment of the
memory of his mother and her achievements and his anger toward Metropolitan Platon. Paul's reign had brought not only hardships for commerce but
also humiliation and insecurity to the high officials, nobles, merchants, and
clerics with whom Ivan identified. Because he also identified with the supreme
power and the majesty of the ruler and imperial family, his response was
conflicted. He apparently resolved the matter by displacing the sin onto Count
Palen and the other conspirators, but it is unlikely that Ivan, or most other
Russians at the time, could escape feelings of guilt for rejoicing at the end of a
reign cut short by the unspeakable act of murdering the nation's father. Russians had nevertheless learned that, however terrible the crime of regicide, the
acts of a capricious monarch could also shake the foundations of the state and
invite chaos.

ADJUSTING TO LIFE IN MOSCOW, AN
EDUCATION FOR PAVEL, FEARS FOR PËTR

[1797, August] 16th I heard mass for the holy day at the lower church of the Mon-
astery of Our Savior by the Icon Shops.[11] After dinner [the architect Mikhailo]
Agafonov visited at my home, and in the evening I rode out with the younger
children to see fireworks at the amphitheater by the Tverskaia gate.

17th At noon I visited my son Pëtr Ivanovich, who was saying his confession
and taking communion because of his dangerous illness. The rest of the time I
spent at home.

18th In the morning I was at the university chancery, and the rest of the time at home.

19th In the morning I was again at the university and stopped in on a number of supervisors to enroll my son Pavel there among the self-paying students [whose parents were] people of various ranks, and after dinner my wife and I rode to the gardens of Count Stroganov by the Monastery of Our Savior and St. Andronicus to take a stroll, and we arrived at vespers.

20th In the morning I was again at the university. Then I went to the gardener Shein, and after dinner I was once again at the university to see Secretary Darnov.

21st Before dinner I was present at the transfer of my trees from the gardener Shein to Squire Iushkov, and after dinner I visited the Grezenkovs in the city.

When Ivan was complaining in his year-end notes for 1797 that he had moved to a dark and noisy apartment in Moscow where his sole occupation was the production of playing cards, he was leaving out a lot of activity. We have already seen that he was busy traveling back and forth to Dmitrov in connection with his bankruptcy trial and was active, too, in getting out to events of the coronation. The diary entries for this year reveal a number of other affairs that occupied him, including continued work with Moscow gardeners and efforts on behalf of his children.

Not surprisingly, the pattern of Ivan's life shifted significantly. His financial collapse and move to Moscow seem to have brought him closer to religion and to his wife Anna. In Dmitrov, Ivan had attended church services on Sundays and holy days and irregularly also on other days, except for the final year when he was hiding out at home and did not leave the house even to attend mass on important holy days. But after the move to Moscow, he attended church services almost daily and sometimes more than once a day. He went to different churches nearly every time, as if he were making an intra-city pilgrimage and was determined to visit every last church in Moscow before he finished. He nowhere enunciated such an objective, but the range of his wanderings and his careful notation of the name of the church attended each day suggest that he may have had this goal in mind, perhaps as a form of penance for his sins of financial legerdemain. And no longer do we find Ivan spending half or more of his evenings with Anna Obreskova. She faded from his life in 1797, and he spent his evenings at home with his family and friends or on visits to male friends in the city. More often now his references to people coming to visit are couched in the plural—"at our home" (*u nas*) rather than "at my home" (*u menia*)—although "at my home" still predominates. He had begun to use the form "at our home" as early as 1789, but its usage came and went in the diary. Its appearance may be a measure of the strength of his feeling of partnership with his wife Anna. If so, that feeling had become stronger in this new Moscow-based period of their life together. Ivan, Anna, and the children also frequently went on family outings, strolls around palace gardens, woods, and other points of interest or relaxation. Ivan's identity as a family man and devoted churchgoer will even intensify for a time from late 1799 through the early years of the new century when he loses his playing card business and suffers a severe and prolonged illness.

As for gardens, Ivan's engagement with them continued. In part this was a practical matter. Some of his remaining exotic trees were being kept by a gardener named Shein at his orangeries in Sushchëvo, a northern suburb of Moscow. Ivan went there on a number of occasions. The diary excerpt above finds Ivan in late summer at Shein's gardens to supervise the delivery of his trees being held there to Squire Afanasii Iushkov. Ivan was evidently transferring the trees in payment for a debt, although he may also have earned some additional cash from the sale, for the diary excerpt reveals that later the same day he visited the Grezenkov family, one of his creditors unwilling to defer repayment. Possibly, Ivan used the proceeds from the tree sales to pay some of his debt to the Grezenkovs. On another occasion Ivan went to Iushkov's Seliuvkino estate to check on the orangery there. Ivan's knowledge of plants had evidently earned him a reputation as an expert who could assist and advise others on horticulture. This interest and knowledge was also being cultivated in his son Aleksei, who as an adult would make a living as a horticulturalist.

Another of Ivan's sons, Pavel, had reached the age of nine in 1797, and an education for him was becoming an urgent matter. Although the diary does not include specifics, we can assume that Ivan had provided early schooling for Pavel, either at home or at the local school that had been established through the efforts of Ivan and his fellow merchants in Dmitrov in 1785. Now that the family was in Moscow the opportunities for Pavel were greater, assuming Ivan would be able to pay for them. Ivan was determined to get all his children set up as well as he could for the future. This was one purpose behind his efforts to shelter his assets and defer his debts. Undaunted by the weight of the remaining debt, he went to work in July of 1797 to get Pavel into school at the pansion attached to Moscow University. He noted that on July 7 he visited the director of Moscow University, Ivan Petrovich Turgenev. Turgenev evidently facilitated these efforts or was able to direct Ivan to someone who could. In August Ivan was back at the university for a visit to the chancery and then returned the next day to sign Pavel up as a student without stipend from the social category "people of various ranks."[12]

In the diary excerpt at the head of this section, it can be seen that at the very same time Ivan was daily going to the university to arrange for instruction for Pavel and attending to the delivery of his exotic trees to Squire Iushkov, he was also visiting his gravely ill eldest son. Pëtr was twenty-three years old with a family of his own, and although he was legally attached to the household of his father-in-law, he was helping Ivan in his new business enterprise. His parents were naturally concerned when he became very sick on the first day of August 1797 and continued to suffer right through the middle of the month. Ivan visited him on several occasions. Anna was probably there even more often. In the August 17 diary excerpt above Ivan reported on his visit to Pëtr on the day that Pëtr said his confession and received communion in hopes that these sacraments would either help him get well or prepare him for death. This measure not only failed to help but in the following days Pëtr's condition deteriorated further. After arranging things for Pavel at the university and transferring the trees to Iushkov, Ivan visited Pëtr every day for the next week. Finally, on the morning of August 26 he went to the Pauline Hospital on the southeastern outskirts of the city to consult with a military physician (*shtab lekar'*), Mr. Zhambel, and then went directly from there to Pëtr, who, Ivan wrote, "had become very dangerously ill this day." Ivan then went to mass, stopped off at home for dinner, and returned to spend the evening with Pëtr. He was back at his bedside the next morning. The following day it was decided to try religious intervention again. Ivan reported that "before the dinner hour I was with my son Pëtr Ivanovich, who at this time received the sacrament of extreme unction in hopes of God's help."

For Russians this sacrament was not only the last measure that could be taken to prepare the soul of a gravely ill person for death, but it was also considered to have a potentially curative power. It was as if this were a final shout to get God's attention and positive engagement to save a life. In Pëtr's case it had the desired effect. Ivan visited Pëtr on August 30 and September 1. The next day, after reporting on a trip he, Anna, the younger children, and a family friend from the nobility, Ivan Molchanov, made to see the interior of the Slobodskii Palace and its "magnificent dresses and attire," Ivan wrote: "From there we went to visit our son Pëtr Ivanovich, who thanks be to God from the very day on which he received extreme unction had begun to show improvement." In an act of thanksgiving, the next morning Ivan and Anna went on foot to pray before the famous miracle-working icon of the Madonna "Comfort Me in My Time of Sorrow" (*Utoli moia pechali*) in the church of St. Nicholas on Pupyshi in the Sadovniki section of Moscow. This icon was brought to Moscow by Cossacks in the mid-seventeenth century and was credited with many miracles in the late eighteenth century, especially so during the time of the plague epidemic of 1771.[13] A few days later Ivan entertained the physician Mr. Zhambel at home, showing his respects to the secular side of healing. As we have seen, Ivan believed in both approaches, religious and medical, and he would soon have occasion to try both again in an effort to restore his own failing health.

THE DEATH OF PRINCE GOLITSYN

[1797, December] 7th In the morning I was at the home of the deceased Prince Ivan Fëdorovich Golitsyn, and in the evening visited [A. P.] Iushkov.

8th In the morning I was in the city and in the evening at Iushkov's.

9th In the morning Nikolai Pavlovich Iushkov, Kvashnin, and some other persons visited me to watch from my place the funeral procession of the deceased prince. After the noon hour I rode to the Donskoi Monastery to see the military honors conducted at the burial. In the evening I visited for a short time at Iushkov's.

Although Ivan's underground life for most of 1796, followed by his bankruptcy and move to Moscow, had cut him off from many of his former friends and acquaintances in Dmitrov, he continued for some time to take an interest in their lives and to record in his year-end summary the news of their deaths. It was these people who formed the context in which Ivan had shaped his identity, and it is not surprising that he would have trouble separating from them and adjusting to new circumstances and a new identity. In 1797 quite a few of Ivan's relatives and former neighbors passed away, and some of Ivan's brief descriptions of their deaths reveal tragedies that occasionally struck the people of his hometown. For example, a member of a prominent merchant family, Il'ia Ivanov Karavaev, died in January from carbon monoxide fumes when he incautiously remained in his house while it was being reheated after freezing out its cockroaches. Another Dmitrovite suffocated himself, according to Ivan, "without any reason, except drunkenness, and even that was not excessive." Among the dead that year was one particularly close old friend, Viktor Iakovlevich Nazimov. He had been the Klin district treasurer and a noble who through state service had reached the seventh rank on the Table of Ranks. He and Ivan spent much time together in the late 1770s and 1780s. Ivan visited his villages in the Klin area for grouse hunting and, in return, entertained Nazimov frequently in Dmitrov. In noting his death late in the year, Ivan designated him as "my friend."

On the very same week that Nazimov died, another person of great importance in Ivan's life and in his role as a community leader passed away. This was Prince Ivan Golitsyn. As we know, Ivan Tolchënov had early on sought out and cultivated a connection to the prince, who at first did not appear inclined to mix with the young merchant, except for important business or civic tasks. But after the introduction of new local government institutions that fostered contacts between the leading townsmen and the district nobility, Ivan Tolchënov and Prince Ivan Golitsyn saw more of one another. Ivan Tolchënov's wide-ranging interests, reading, and personal cultivation, and his apparent charm and affability must have won over Golitsyn. For many years, Golitsyn's home on his Danilovskoe estate and his residence in Moscow were open to Ivan, and he and his wife Anna became part of the Golitsyn family's regular social circle. Although Ivan Tolchënov had perhaps been too ashamed to visit Golitsyn after the bankruptcy, he went to see him in Moscow in October of 1797, probably after having heard that the prince was ailing. He must thereafter have closely followed news of the prince's decline, for when Golitsyn died on December 6, Ivan showed up at his home the very next morning to pay his respects. The funeral took place two days later at the Monastery of the Epiphany in central Moscow, and Golitsyn was buried with full military honors in the Donskoi Monastery. The funeral cortege proceeded right past Ivan's apartment on Nikitskaia Street. As we see from the diary excerpt at the head of this section, a number of people from Dmitrov district, including two of Ivan's noble friends, Nikolai Iushkov and the District Police Captain Ivan Kvashnin, watched the procession from Ivan's home.

Prince Golitsyn, it will be recalled, had served as an adjutant for Emperor Peter III and refused to sign an oath to Catherine II when she seized the throne via a coup d'etat. For most of the rest of his life Golitsyn lived in a kind of internal exile, although he did make peace enough with the regime to serve as marshal of the Dmitrov district nobility. In return for his loyalty to Peter III, Emperor Paul gave Golitsyn decorations and raised him to the second highest military rank. Hence the splendid military display with which he was interred. Ivan noted in his year-end summary that the prince's body "was consigned to the earth with the sounding of a salute from nine cannon in accordance with a new law, and two battalions of musketeers fired their guns three times."

The social distance that separated Prince Golitsyn and Ivan Tolchënov made it difficult for Ivan to define their relationship. The two men had for many years been close enough for Ivan and his wife to be welcome at Golitsyn's table on a regular basis, and the prince appeared at Ivan's home for dinners and meetings with visiting dignitaries or on important family occasions. When Ivan was writing about the prince's elevation in rank after the accession of Emperor Paul, he was able to say that the prince was "my benefactor and in some ways even my friend." Yet when he reported sometime later on the prince's death, he wrote merely that he was "my true benefactor."[14] The word Ivan had used for "friend" (*priiatel'*) does not define an intimate relation of friendship so much as a shared position in a network of reciprocity, an insider rather than an outsider, a person for whom one does favors and receives favors in return.[15] Ivan's reduction in status to a Moscow factory manager rather than mayor and leading merchant of his town, positions that had permitted him to do favors for Golitsyn, must have increased his mental distance from the prince and made it hard for him, when he was later composing his yearly summaries, to suggest that they had once been friends.[16]

CONSOLATION OF WORK, FRIENDS, AND
ATTRACTIONS OF THE CITY

[1798, July] 7th In the morning I visited Mikhail Lavrent'ev L'vov, and after din-
ner was at [Afanasii] Iushkov's and then rode with him to stroll in the garden of
Count Orlov.

8th I heard mass at the Monastery of the Cross. After 2 in the afternoon I went
with my wife, father-in-law, and younger children to Kuskovo [the estate of
Count Sheremetev] and strolled there until dusk.

9th In the morning I visited Chobotov, and after dinner was at Iushkov's and
went with him to stroll in the garden of Choikin.

10th I heard mass at the Dormition Cathedral. Later I was in the city, and I
attended the vespers vigil in the Church of Metropolitan Aleksei, which is between
Tverskaia and Dmitrovka.

11th I heard mass at the Presentation Church in Barashki. After dinner I vis-
ited Iushkov and rode with him to stroll in Demidov's garden.

12th I did not go anywhere.

13th In the morning I went to the orangeries of Iakovlev, which are in Basman-
naia. From there I went to Demidov's garden, the one in Kazach'e. I had dinner
and lingered until vespers at Iushkov's.

14th In the morning I visited Obreskova and at dusk Iushkov.

15th In the morning I visited Krasnoglasov, and later was at Iushkov's, and
spent the evening at the home of my son Pëtr Ivanovich.

16th I did not go anywhere.

The bankruptcy settlement gave Ivan a three-year extension on major debts and some breathing room. During the remainder of 1797 and through 1798, he worked at improving the quality and competitiveness of his playing cards and proudly reported at the end of the second year that the cards from his factory had begun to be recognized for their excellence. Even so, the business was not yielding a desirable monetary return. In his summary note for 1798 he explained that the scarcity and consequent high cost of good paper ate into his profits and that he was making only a modest income while spending down his remaining funds on living expenses. And because of continuing pursuit by creditors who had not accepted the bankruptcy decision, he further lamented that "I could not openly do anything." By this, he must have meant that any substantial profit he might have made for investment in other business efforts would be seized by his creditors.[17]

What he did do was settle his life into a new pattern that allowed him to enjoy some of his favorite activities. A few of his former noble friends did not desert him. In particular, Afanasii Pavlovich Iushkov and his brother Nikolai remained loyal, and, as mentioned earlier, Ivan wrote that through them he got acquainted with other people who shared his interests. The noble families of the Molchanovs and the Obreskovs and a few others, such as Nikolai Vakhromeev and his wife and Squire Vel'iaminov-Zernov, continued to visit Ivan when they were in Moscow. The Dmitrov district medical officer, Dr. Kepeng, was also a frequent guest at the Tolchënovs' in Moscow.

Contact was most frequent with Afanasii Iushkov, as the diary excerpt at the start of this section suggests. Ivan often went to his place for dinner and stayed through the evening. They regularly took strolls together, attended religious services, or visited gardens and orangeries. In September of 1797 Ivan stayed at Iushkov's Seliuvkino estate for two nights on his way to Dmitrov and then on the return trip stopped again at Seliuvkino for three days of hunting with Iushkov. The next spring he went on a week-long journey with Iushkov to his villages in the Vereia region west of Moscow. Ivan accompanied Iushkov as a friend but no doubt also acted as an adviser on horticultural matters, a service he had been providing Iushkov on his Seliuvkino estate. Ivan also mixed in some business of his own on this trip, for he spent time inspecting a paper factory outside the hamlet of Borovsk. In the fall, Ivan was again at Seliuvkino for a week of running with the hounds. Hence, for a time, Ivan was able to enjoy occasional tastes of his earlier life of hobnobbing with noble landlords and enjoying the diversions of a country squire.

By the fall of 1797, Ivan was also back to attending theater. He mentioned going to the Petrovskii Theater on November 18. Then a month later he was there again, this time in the company of Afanasii Iushkov, when they "saw the talented experiments of Chevalier Pinetti," one of the great illusionists of the age.[18] The next year Ivan attended the theater at least seven times, three before the Lenten closing and four afterward. Unfortunately, he failed to jot down what he saw, let alone his opinions of performances. Ivan was also soon back to indulging his other great passion: gardens. We have seen that the famous naturalist Peter Simon Pallas, in the 1770s, marveled at the blossoming of gardens and orangeries in Moscow that supplied not only Moscow but other Russian cities with tasty fruits and vegetables. Although Pallas later wrote that this production fell off toward the end of the century, Moscow was still a garden city. A sampling can be found in the diary, which records that in his first two years in Moscow Ivan visited by himself or together with friends and family the following orangeries and gardens: those of the Demidovs (who owned several), of the deceased Count Fëdor Orlov, of Prince Zasekin, of Count Stroganov, of gardener Shein, of gardener Krasnoglasov, of merchant Frolov, of Pëtr Ivanovich Levashov, of merchant Lebedev in Khamovniki, of gardener Choikin, of Iakovlev, of gardener Kokov in Kazach'e, plus the Volynskii gardens at Three Hills, the gardens at Kuskovo, the Invalidnyi garden, the gardens at Presnia Ponds, and the hugely popular Pashkov gardens with their attractive ponds and peacocks. Other outings included strolls around the gardens and grounds of the Golovinskii Palace and the tsarist Petrovskii and Slobodskii palaces, and excursions into the countryside to, for example, Catherinian Hermitage (*pustyn'*) and Tsaritsyno.

CHANGES IN THE PLAYING CARD BUSINESS

[1799, February] 9th . . . In the morning a supervisor from the foundling home, Olofson, visited me.

10th I heard mass for the feast of the Martyr Kharlampii at the Dormition Church in Kozhevniki. From there I rode to the Post Office. Afterward Mr. Kvashnin visited me, and in the evening I was at Vakhromeev's.

11th In the morning I was at home and then had dinner at Iushkov's and stayed until evening.

12th I heard mass at the Monastery of the Miracles and spent the rest of the time at home, and in the evening the Dmitrov police commissioner Sal'kov and [Squire] Vakhromeev visited me.

13th I heard [Sunday] mass at Our Savior on Stremenka. After dinner the card factory owners Gum and Pemchere visited me.

14th In the morning I visited [Mrs.] Obreskova. In the evening I was visited by Sal'kov, Vakhromeev, and [Dr.] Kepeng, and I went with them to the theater.

15th I was at home during the day, and after dinner Afanasii Pavlovich Iushkov visited me, and in the evening I rode with him over to see his brother Nikolai Pavlovich.

16th I spent the day at home and the evening at Iushkov's.

17th In the morning I visited Chobotov, and spent the rest of the time at home. Kepeng ate dinner at my house, and in the evening [the card manufacturer] Mal'e and [the architect] Agafonov visited me.

18th I did not go anywhere.

19th In the morning I was in the city, and I ate dinner and lingered at Iushkov's.

20th I heard [Sunday] mass in my parish, and in the evening visited Mal'e.

21st In the morning I was at home, and I had dinner and stayed until evening at Vakhromeev's.

22nd In the morning I visited Iushkov and Pëtr Orlov. In the evening the supervisor Olofson visited at my house.

23rd I did not go anywhere.

24th In the morning I was at home. I had dinner at Iushkov's, and in the evening was at home again.

25th In the morning I visited my brother-in-law Kaftannikov, and the rest of the time was at home.

26th Our son Pëtr Ivanovich and his wife came for dinner at our house, and in the evening I visited my relative Goroshkov.

27th I attended [Sunday] mass at the Monastery of Our Savior by the Icon Shops. From there I visited my son Pëtr Ivanovich, and the rest of the time was at home.

28th In the morning I was at the card franchisee Karmolin's, and in the city, and after dinner I once again visited Karmolin. Then I went to the Post Office and to Mal'e's.

The diary excerpt above contains hints of changes in the playing card business that were about to undermine Ivan's new enterprise and stymie his attempts to settle into a comfortable routine and familiar neighborhood. In the late 1790s the trustees of the imperial foundling homes decided that their monopoly on playing cards was failing to yield anything close to anticipated revenues. The foundling homes had initially operated their own factory under the supervision of what must have been a transplanted west European named Zhan Mat'e. He had been contracted not only to produce cards but to train twenty foundlings from the Moscow Foundling Home in the arts of card manufacturing. Other factories, as we have seen, were nevertheless allowed to operate as well but were required to pay a stamp tax on their products, the proceeds of which went to the foundling homes. Unfortunately for the trustees of the charity, the factory run by Mat'e produced cards of inferior quality at high cost, while the competing private manufacturers found ways to evade the stamp tax and undersell the foundling home factory. Revenue was accordingly proving to be anemic, despite repeated efforts to police the private firms. After trying various strategies, including the firing of Zhan Mat'e, the foundling home trustees decided to follow the example of the central government, which had farmed out the liquor tax earlier in the century. Accordingly, they turned the playing card business into a franchise that would go to the highest bidder for a period of four years.[19] The decision was announced in March of 1798 and scheduled to take effect one year later.

In the diary excerpt at the head of this section we see a couple of things. On the one hand, it reveals again Ivan's success in retaining the comradeship of a number of nobles and officials from Dmitrov, including his close friends the Iushkovs, plus Nikolai Vakhromeev, Anna Obreskova, the Dmitrov police commissioner Pavel Sal'kov, and the district physician, Dr. Kepeng. They stopped by when in the city, and some of them even joined Ivan for a trip to the theater. On the other hand, we also see something new. Ivan was meeting regularly with other card manufacturers and with the accountant from the Moscow Foundling Home, Mr. Olovson (Ivan used the variant spelling Olofson and called him a supervisor).

Indeed, right after the official announcement in early March of 1798 of the coming sale of the card monopoly, Ivan began meeting with other card factory owners. He invited two of them, Messrs. Lesazh and Lui, to his home as early as March 11, and the next day he visited another by the name of Mal'e. Judging by the names, these three, like Mat'e mentioned earlier, were transplanted Francophone Europeans. These meetings that, as Ivan noted, were "for consulting on the franchising," continued off and on through the year. Ivan also met several times with a man named Nakazin, an official of the foundling homes who supervised the card factories. These activities, which included stops at the offices of the foundling home trustees, intensified toward the end of the year and into the first months of 1799. Ivan was also meeting at this time with some other card factory owners: Messrs. Ivanov, Gum, and Pemchere. It is unclear if he was trying to organize some sort of consortium to win the franchise for local manufacturers. Given Ivan's financial straits, it seems doubtful that he would have enjoyed the trust required for such an effort. In any event, the franchise ultimately went to a group headed by a wealthy Riazan merchant by the name of Riumin and included four Petersburg merchants: Cholokov, Kusovnikov, Ol'khin, and Inferov.[20] The Riumin in question was probably Gavrila Vasil'evich Riumin, the wealthiest of a number of Riazan merchants of the same family.[21] The group's agent in Moscow was a merchant named Karmolin, who operated the playing card store there, the only outlet that now was permitted to sell cards in the city. Karmolin evidently likewise contracted for the manufacture of cards. Ivan began meeting with him in late February of 1799 (see again the diary excerpt above) and continued through March to see him frequently. It was apparently at these meetings that Ivan negotiated a contract to produce in the next year, from paper supplied by the franchisees, 20,000 dozen sets of playing cards. In addition, Ivan was able to work out an arrangement for his son Aleksei to be assigned as an employee of the card store. Aleksei was nineteen years old and needed to gain entry into the Moscow business community now that the family grain trade for which he had been trained no longer was an option.

Although Ivan was pleased to win this contract, it was only a short-term arrangement with no guarantee of renewal. And, inopportunely, the change in the playing card business came at just the time Ivan had succeeded in mastering the manufacturing operations. It will be recalled that in his summary for the year 1798, he mentioned that his cards had begun to be recognized for their excellence. In summing up the next year, he crowed that his factory "had reached a state of perfection and the quality of the cards was being compared to those made at the very best factories."[22] This success no doubt helped him win the contract with the franchisees. But the agreement to deliver such a large consignment also disrupted his living arrangements. He had to give up the lodgings the family had occupied on Nikitskaia Street for several years and find new space where he and his partner Nikolai Mal'tsov would have sufficient room to produce the huge order. He eventually found the space needed in a building on Piatnitskaia Street in the heart of the old merchant quarter across the Moscow River and spent most of the spring preparing the factory and adjoining rooms for a residence. In June the whole family picked up and moved from Nikitskaia to the new lodgings. Ivan and his partner employed between forty and sixty persons in an enterprise that Ivan described as a big success "both in the praise accorded to the cards and in the benefits to us." When they finished up the order in May of the following year, Ivan reported that it fetched "a very handsome profit." Unfortunately, he also had to report that "the franchisees did not permit us to continue such work, and our factory along with all the others [working for the franchisees] was dismantled."[23]

Ivan had to find another means of support, and he had to do so under especially trying circumstances: while fighting off a prolonged and debilitating illness.

ILLNESS STRIKES

[1799, November]

4th The pain in my stomach got worse again.

8th I began to feel better.

11th At noon Afanasii Pavlovich Iushkov visited me.

13th I heard [Sunday] mass at Pope Clement Church.

16th I heard mass at the Monastery of the Miracles.

18th In the morning my son Pëtr Ivanovich visited me and after dinner Dmitrii Zherebin.

21st I heard mass at Pope Clement Church.

23rd In the morning [the physician Mr.] Zhambel visited me, and I took an emetic.

26th Because Zhambel himself fell ill, I summoned military physician Leiman to treat me.

27th I began to take his prescription of strong medicine.

30th Not feeling any improvement and growing weak from the strong medicine and dietary regimen, I took to my bed and began to mistrust all physicians and to get angry and melancholy, which made me feel even worse.

December 1st At dawn I was privileged to host in my apartment the miracle-working icon of the Holy Iberian Madonna, and [priests] performed prayer chants and sprayed holy water. From noon onward, by God's goodness and thanks to all the prayers of his mother, I was feeling better and my spirits lifted.

2nd In the evening Andrei Fëdorovich [Makarov] came to us from Dmitrov and stayed overnight at our place.

I spent the following days nearly entirely in bed, and although I took plenty of medicines, I did not feel the slightest improvement.

The illness that Ivan referred to in this diary excerpt from November and early December of 1799 first struck more than two months earlier. On August 16 he wrote that "I did not go anywhere, because since the 10th I had begun to feel weak, lost my appetite and suffered other attacks, and I had been trying to overcome the sickness. However, today it got worse." Ivan's first resort was to medical advice, which he had learned to value through his reading and his association with the district doctors in Dmitrov. The very next day, August 17, he rode over to the Pauline Hospital to consult again with the military physician Mr. Zhambel, whom he had gotten to know two years earlier when his son Pëtr was gravely ill. The physician prescribed medicine that may have worsened Ivan's condition; a favorite curative agent of the time contained arsenic. As soon as he began to take the medicine the next morning, he suffered an acute episode in which "bile poured through my whole body and colored me yellow every-where, even in my eyes. On top of that, my fever started to rise, and I took to my bed." Ivan penned very short diary entries for the next two days and then ceased to write again for almost two weeks. On September 2 he returned to the diary to report that "I took an emetic, which drove out a lot of the bile and phlegm, and things got better." We learn what happened in the intervening period from a note he inserted between his August 20 and September 2 diary entries. Here he explained that "in the next days my condition was very dangerous, and for several days I lay unconscious in an intense fever and without any food, so that Mr. Zhambel doubted that I would survive, and he visited me twice each day. But owing to the kindness of almighty God, the last few days have brought a break in the illness, and I began to feel a bit better."[24]

Whatever bug or medicine had attacked Ivan, it was obviously something that obstructed his liver functioning and threw him into intense and nearly fatal fevers. Because of the complicated interactions of diseases and therapies of the time, it is hard to know what the underlying pathogens might have been. Yellow fever appeared in northerly locales at the end of the eighteenth century and caused jaundice but most often occurred in large epidemics and did not recur in its victim. Ivan's case was different. Ivan suffered recurrent bouts, and it took a year for him to get back to an even attenuated pattern of work and socializing. It is not clear that he ever fully recovered from the illness. This course would be more consistent with a diagnosis of malaria. But retrospective diagnosis is unlikely to yield a definition of the disease, nor is one needed. What is interesting is how Ivan coped with the illness and what this can tell us about him and his situation.[25]

Another indication of the severity of Ivan's illness, if one is needed, can be seen in his diary keeping. As just mentioned, when an acute phase of the disease struck, he went for nearly two weeks without penning a single diary entry, whereas in the past he had written something each day, even if only to record "I did not go anywhere." The diary excerpt at the start of this section shows regular gaps in his writing of one or more days, and this pattern continued throughout the long course of the illness to the end of the following year, 1800. On many days he apparently did not have the strength to sit up and write even the briefest of notes.

After the first devastating bout of illness in August and early September, Ivan gradually began to feel better. He stopped his medicine, was able to walk in his room and receive occasional guests. By the middle of September he even took a carriage over to the Pauline Hospital to talk with Mr. Zhambel about a schedule of exercise (*matsion*), an important component of healing arts of the time. A few days later Ivan was walking the short distance to the card factory or taking rides in a droshky to the Donskoi Monastery on the southern outskirts of the city. But the reprieve was brief. On October 6 his stomach pains, which had not entirely gone away, returned with new severity and were not relieved by laxatives or "London drops." A few days later on Zhambel's advice Ivan started taking magnesium. Still the pain continued until we find him, as described in the diary excerpt at the start of this section, in the midst of a second acute attack. At that time, because Zhambel was himself laid up, Ivan saw another military physician, a man by the name of Leiman, who prescribed stronger medicine. After finding this treatment useless and even debilitating, Ivan got angry, discouraged, and mistrustful of doctors, and he turned to religious practices and the aid of miracle-working icons, as he had in the past when he or family members were sick.

On December 1 he asked that the icon of the Iberian Madonna be brought to him. This icon, based on a Greek original and brought to Moscow from Mount Athos in 1648, occupied its own special chapel at the Resurrection Gate that opened onto Red Square. It was associated with many miracles and was frequently brought into the homes of ailing Muscovites to assist in their cure.[26] This visit of the icon, Ivan reported, lifted his spirits and made him feel better, but it did not bring any lasting improvement in his condition, for he could scarcely get out of bed in the following days. The next week he again tried religion. "For the easing of my conscience and healing of my spirit that were suffering together with my body from this sinful illness," he wrote, "I made my confession to God before my confessor, the priest Terentii Konstantinovich from the Dormition Church on Vrazhek."[27] But this, too, had no effect. "My illness continued in the following days to the most intense degree and from the 19th I began to despair for my life." Again, he made his confession to Father Terentii on December 21 and the next day took communion in his apartment, in this case couching his report in a Church Slavonic idiom. Despite his turn to

Icon of Iberian Madonna.

religious assistance and religious language, Ivan had not given up on the doctors. While rejecting Leiman, whose efforts Ivan deemed worthless, he began again to consult with Zhambel. Socializing also seemed to bring some temporary relief. Visits on Christmas day from his family and friends lifted his spirits, and he was able to get out of bed and walk about his room. Still, he lamented that "in the following days my illness did not lessen and as time went on got worse because of my troubled spirits and extreme doubt." Finally, he decided to try yet another physician, and one with better credentials than Zhambel or Leiman. On the last day of the year he summoned not a physician but a practitioner with advanced degrees in medicine, Doctor and Collegiate Councilor Matvei Khristianovich Peken.[28]

Peken was a name well known among educated Russians. Matvei's father, also a doctor, was author of a popular *Home Medical Manual* published in 1765 in 2,400 copies and then again the next year in a run of 6,000 copies to meet the unexpected demand. Matvei continued his father's work and updated the book, calling it the *New Home Medical Manual,* editions appearing in 1796 and 1797. These books were intended for use by young inexperienced physicians and by people without medical training. They did not therefore include the most radical or heroic treatments. But in line with the established notions that fevers were caused by unclean blood and that many diseases stemmed from overmuch blood, bleeding was a recommended therapy; in the case of inner inflammations the books recommended the extraction of three or four cups of blood immediately.[29] The Pekens were still practicing on the basis of the theory of the four humors, and for the kind of yellow fever that Ivan had presented, Matvei Peken advised disgorging yellow bile from the body through vomiting, diarrhea, or abundant urination.[30] For strengthening life forces, wrote Matvei Peken, best of all was the application of Spanish fly (crushed wings of a green beetle), which was used in plasters on sensitive areas of the skin or apparently also in tinctures to stimulate expansion of the bladder for release of fluids.[31] Ideas about personality and mental or spiritual influences likewise played a central role in the healing practices of the period. These ideas were especially pronounced in Matvei's many writings. He dilated on the ill effects of anger, fear, and foreboding, writing that they make any illness much worse and can even cause death. Likewise, according to him, feelings of shame, sadness, grief, and despair could have harmful, even fatal effects, such as unresolved constipation of the liver and intestines.[32]

A few days after Ivan called in Matvei Peken, medics came to his home to apply leeches to his hemorrhoids and draw out four cups of blood, but neither this procedure nor the medicines Peken prescribed brought relief. In fact, right afterward, from January 7 to 13, 1800, Ivan was too weak to write in the diary. When he returned to it, he placed a note after the January 6 entry, saying that "in the following days my illness increased despite many changes in medicines tried by Doctor Peken. Not only did I not feel any better but I experienced great distress and could get out of bed only with difficulty." On the fourteenth Peken placed Spanish fly on Ivan's sore spot (presumably his stomach, which seemed to be his main source of pain), and Ivan reported it as having "worked properly," and so it was removed later the same day. Plasters made from Spanish fly produced strong blistering and were accordingly believed to have powerful effects. But either this prescription, if ingested in some form, or the other medicines Ivan was taking produced such "fierce constipation" that he soon had to give up all but the most gentle of them.

While these ministrations continued, Ivan had not abandoned his intensified religious practices. In this same month, on January 5, he had brought to his apartment an icon cover and nail of Christ the Savior from the Dormition Cathedral, items believed to have curative powers. A week later, as he sank further, he again asked to say his confession to Father Terentii and beg for repentance, and he followed this with the rite of extreme unction performed by three priests. "From this time," he wrote, "my conscience eased somewhat." But if his mind was calmer, his bodily illness remained, and Ivan continued to make an explicit link between his spiritual and physical health. "During the last days of January," he wrote, "I was very sick and could only get out of bed two or three times and walk about the room, and although Doctor Peken and military physician Zhambel visited regularly and administered gentle medicines, I did not see any improvement, for my soul was very troubled."

February brought a turn for the better. Ivan was finally able to get out for some fresh air. He went to the factory on a few occasions and even rode a sledge down to the Great Stone Bridge at the end of street and took a stroll there. On March 1, he went still farther; he rode across the Moscow River and past the Kremlin to the chapel of the Iberian Madonna, where he prayed without leaving his sled. But even as he took this short trip, the disease was regaining strength and soon caused another acute episode. Despite the deep misgivings Ivan now harbored toward doctors generally, he decided to call in a Russian physician by the name of Gavril Efimov and took the medicine he prescribed for this new attack.

Ivan was remarkably self-aware and capable of relating in his diary how these recurrent bouts of intense pain were affecting his state of mind. He wrote that although he took the medicine prescribed by his doctors, "from my imaginings and mistrustfulness at the same time my thoughts kept vacillating and I would have regrets, and this mental disturbance made me feel the bodily pain even more. Powerful hypochondria took hold of me and insomnia, and these weakened me still more." Probably strongly influenced by his doctors' beliefs about the effects of emotions on illness, Ivan began by the middle of March 1800 to understand his disorder as mental or spiritual as much as it was physical, and efforts seemed to be directed toward getting him in a more positive frame of mind. For example, Ivan penned the following diary entry on March 14:

Again I went to confession at home with my confessor. However, still having disturbing thoughts, I was daily in fear of death, although, thanks to the kindness of God, there was not the slightest danger, except for a powerful internal pain. At noon, on the advice of Peken, I rode again for exercise to the chapel of the Iberian Madonna and made a visit to the Kazan Cathedral and there had the privilege of kissing the icon of the Blessed Virgin.

Then, in his continuing mix of religious practices, outdoor activities, and medical intervention, Ivan was the next day again bled with leeches and treated with Spanish fly overnight. But, as happened before following Peken's vigorous interventions, the treatments merely weakened Ivan and plunged him into further depression. Ivan wrote on March 18 that these treatments so sapped his energy that he felt hopeless and suffered "almost a kind of insanity." For two weeks he could not write in the diary. When he returned to it, he noted that "the entire end of March I was in a bad state, for the disease would give me no rest and weakened me both in body and spirit, and I began to have absolutely no faith in medicines."[33]

April and May were not much better. During Passion Week at the start of April he lay gaunt and exhausted, unable to write his diary. On Easter Sunday, April 8, he recorded that "I did not feel much spiritual joy, for the illness continued with the same intensity, and my profound weakness did not allow me to fight off my affliction." As the weather improved, Ivan would struggle out of doors for brief exposures to sunshine and fresh air, one day reporting with pride that he had been able to sit by the gate of the house for half an hour. He received guests from time to time, took cool baths in the morning, and by April 24 managed to walk to a nearby church. But during the next days his pain increased, "why, no one knows," he sighed. The gaps in Ivan's diary continue, and it is clear that he was not seeing any substantial improvement. After a week-long interruption in his entries in mid-May, he reported that "my illness continued in the strongest degree and my insides hurt uninterruptedly." Curiously, we no longer see references to Dr. Peken or indeed any physician, except for one visit from Zhambel in early May. Ivan seems now to have been avoiding doctors in preference to a mix of religious practices, fresh air, and exercise. He had the icon of St. Artemii the Miracle Worker brought to him from the nearby Piatnitskaia Church on May 18. A few days later he rode "with God's help" to the Alekseevskii Convent to pray before the icon of Madonna the Healer of the Sick. At the end of the month, he reported that "I again did repentance to God before my confessor for my countless sins."[34]

Despite continuing to complain about his health and his pain, Ivan was

Nail of Our Lord (*Gvozd Gospoden*) housed in the Kremlin Dormition Cathedral.

getting out of doors more often, if in some cases merely to lie on a bed in the yard. On other occasions he took walks to the local church. By June he began walking all the way to the Kommissariat building on the banks of the Moscow River and riding to the Kremlin and to one or another monastery for strolls on their grounds. About this time he found another physician, Dr. Frez, who prescribed some "pills" that Ivan was willing to try. The next month he acquired yet another medical adviser, the military physician Grave from the Catherinian Hospital, who was recommended for his skill in the healing arts. (This may have been the son of Dr. Christian Grave, who had played an important role in fighting the plague in Russia in the early 1770s.)[35] During June and July Ivan continued to get out for strolls and to attend religious services, even though his health, by his own account, did not show much improvement. At the end of July he noted in the diary that the whole month "I did not feel much of a turn for the better in my illness, and frustration and spiritual qualms weighed on my mind and sapped my strength."[36] Even so, he continued his excursions. On August 4 "my wife and I rode to Simonov Monastery and heard the minor vespers and prayed, after which we took a stroll, and returned home toward 8 o'clock with God's help." On August 9 "I went with my wife and younger children to the Taganka outskirts through the village of Dubrovka to the woods and took a stroll, returning safely toward 8 o'clock." Ivan was also regularly getting out to mass or to part of a vigil at nearby churches. A visit to a cathedral in the Kremlin on August 24 proved especially beneficial. "I heard mass at the Dormition Cathedral conducted by Right Reverend Serafim, Bishop of Dmitrov. Afterward I prayed before the miracle-working icon of the Jerusalem Madonna, and later was privileged to touch the icon cover of Christ the Savior with holy water and to kiss the nail of our Lord and the cross of St. Konstantin the Ruler. I also kissed the miracle-working icons and the relics of the

Table 7.1. Diary entries per month for the year 1800

January	8
February	7
March	7
April	9
May	12
June	17
July	16
August	20
September	25
October	24
November	27
December	26

saints. . . . I stood during the entire service and had a distinct feeling of relief from my illness."[37]

Indeed, this experience, which occurred almost exactly one year after the onset of the disease, seemed to mark the beginning of the end. A strong sign was Ivan's resumption of nearly daily entries in his diary. These had been increasing gradually from a low point early in the year. By September he was penning notes for twenty-five of the thirty days of the month. Table 7.1 records the number of days he made diary entries during each month in 1800 and can be taken as a measure of the severity of his illness through the year. Although he was feeling stronger by September, he was far from cured and continued to suffer debility and occasional severe pain. For example, on December 22 he recorded that in the evening he "felt a ferocious pain in my left side." The next day was the same. "All day I suffered from the pain in my side." The hurt was scary enough that Ivan decided to summon Dr. Peken again, despite his misery from this doctor's earlier heroic ministrations. This time things turned out better. By December 27 Ivan could happily report that the pain had gone away.

Still, right through the next year Ivan was not his old self. Although he fully resumed his diary writing at the start of 1801, no longer missing a single day (had he made a New Year's resolution to do so?), occasional references indicate the continuing delicacy of his health. For example, as late as September of 1801, when the new ruler Alexander I and imperial family were in the city for the coronation, Ivan went to a number of events where he could view tsarist dignitaries and the pageantry he loved. But on the coronation day itself he chose not to go to the Kremlin, he explained, "because of the huge crowd and [my] weakness." Whatever the weakness—perhaps a temporary relapse or a fear of contracting something in the crush of people—it did not inhibit his strolls, including a longish one just two days later, when he and his wife walked from the governor-general's house on Tverskaia Street down into the Kremlin, then out the Tainitskie Gates on the Moscow River embankment, which in those days were open to pedestrians, and then proceeded along the embankment to the Pashkov House at the southwest corner of the Kremlin, past the trading stalls on Mokhovaia Street and back through narrow lanes to Tverskaia.[38] Though continuing to be concerned about his health and probably subject to spells of weakness and fears of relapses, Ivan was getting back into action socially and professionally during 1801 and seems to have put the worst of the illness behind him.

RECONCILIATION WITH HIS UNCLES

[1800, January]
28th Visiting with me was my cousin Dmitrii Ivanovich, who had arrived urgently from Dmitrov on behalf of my uncles in response to a letter from me.

What was the meaning of this brief diary entry, the first one since January 17, and written at a time Ivan could scarcely get out of bed? Ivan referred to a letter he had sent to his uncles in Dmitrov, which he must have dispatched not long before, perhaps in the middle of the month when he believed he was at death's door and had received the last rites. Although Ivan's letter is not available, it probably was an effort to reach out to his uncles and to heal the rift in the family that Ivan had opened by borrowing large sums of money from his uncles and then selling the assets with which he could have paid off the loan. When Russians felt that death was approaching, they usually would try to patch up differences with those close to them. Indeed, this notion is embedded in the language of farewell, which in Russian means both to say goodbye and to ask for forgiveness. The word even carries the meaning, especially appropriate in Ivan's case, of forgiving a monetary debt.

Ever since Ivan's bankruptcy trial and the failure of his uncles to receive any satisfaction of their demands for repayment or their claim on Ivan's real property in Dmitrov, there had been no contact between Ivan and the uncles, save for a brief visit by Uncle Mikhaila in June 1797 and another by Uncle Dmitrii in the summer of 1798. The family, it will be recalled, had been very close before that time. The uncles had been partners in the family grain trade and guided Ivan in his commercial and civic work when his father died. The families had spent much time socializing together, sharing dinners, evenings, and holidays. The bankruptcy brought this to a sudden halt. Even under the best of circumstances the family contacts would have become less frequent as a result of the move of Ivan and his immediate family to Moscow. But a complete cut-off of personal contact would not have occurred had Ivan not betrayed his uncles' trust. Even the younger generation, the children of the uncles, seem to have cut Ivan off. Until the arrival of Uncle Ivan's son Dmitrii Ivanovich in response to Ivan's letter to his uncles in January 1800, none of the children of the three living uncles had visited Ivan.[39] The only cousins who continued to see Ivan and his family on a regular basis were the children of deceased Uncle Pëtr: Aleksandr, Grigorii, and Praskov'ia. Uncle Pëtr, it will be recalled, had died long before, in the mid 1760s, and had not lost money to Ivan; his children, too, were evidently unaffected by the losses of the other uncles.

Exactly how matters developed between Ivan and his uncles after his letter to them in January 1800 and the arrival of his cousin Dmitrii Ivanovich is not altogether clear. At the end of April, when Ivan was getting outdoors more often and feeling a bit stronger, he had a visit from some prominent citizens of Dmitrov, including the former mayor Ivan Tugarinov, close family friend and in-law Fëdor Loshkin (the husband of Uncle Ivan's daughter), and a church deacon, Ivan Rodionov. These men may well have been acting as go-betweens to bring peace between the uncles and Ivan. Rodionov returned a month later, possibly to follow up on the earlier contact. Clerics, as we saw in chapter 2, sometimes served as arbitrators in personal disputes. In October, the Dmitrov police commissioner, Sal'kov, spent time with Ivan as did the Dmitrov cathedral archpriest. It is possible that they, too, were helping prepare the ground for what happened the following month when, as Ivan's diary entry for November 15 records, "after dinner Uncles Mikhaila and Dmitrii Il'ichi visited me." This meeting apparently included discussion of the terms for composing the dispute and ended with an invitation to the uncles to return the next day for dinner. And on that day, Ivan wrote in his diary: "I heard mass at the parish church. My dear little uncles dined with us. With God's help I was reconciled with them." The diary entry on the first meeting referred to the uncles in a standard form of the time as *diad'ia* (in modern Russian it would be *diadi*). The second entry, recording the reconciliation, used the diminutive term of endearment: *diadiushki*. And Ivan used this term again when his "dear little uncles" spent another afternoon with him two days later.[40]

This peace in the larger family came none too soon. Ivan's uncles were getting up in years and would not be around much longer. Uncle Mikhaila suffered a mental breakdown just one year later and died six months afterward in early June of 1802. Uncle Ivan, who had been ill continuously from about the time of the reconciliation (this no doubt explains his absence when the other two uncles visited Ivan), died late in the year 1802 at the age of seventy-five. Ivan at least had an opportunity to visit with him one last time in September of that same year when he, with his wife Anna and son Iakov, made a pilgrimage to the Trinity Monastery, Vedernitsy, and the Pesnoshskii Monastery, stopping in Dmitrov along the way. The lone surviving uncle, Dmitrii Il'ich, lived on until 1817 when he died at the age of seventy-six.[41] The diary reveals that he continued to visit with Ivan and Anna when he came to Moscow.

A NEW BUSINESS ENTERPRISE

[1801, January]

20th I heard [Sunday] mass at the Grebnevsk Mother of God Church on Lubianka.

21st I heard mass at the Intercession Cathedral.

22nd I heard mass at the Presentation of the Lord [Sretensk] Monastery.

23rd I heard mass at the Joy for All Grieving Church on Ordynka.

24th I was at home. At noon Ivan Iakimov from Wallpaper Lane visited me.

25th I heard mass at the Feast of the Virgin Comforting Our Sorrow, which is in Pupyshi.

26th I heard mass in my parish church.

27th I heard mass at the Church of Nikita the Martyr in Basmannaia. I had dinner at my son Pëtr Ivan[ovich]'s and returned home before 5 in the evening.

28th I heard mass at Archangel Michael Church in Ovchinniki.

29th I heard mass at the Church of St. Nicholas the Miracle Worker in Pupyshi.

30th I attended the hours in my parish church. In the evening Ivan Iakimov visited me.

31st I stayed at home. Having dinner with us were our son Pëtr and his wife.

These diary entries from the second half of January 1801, despite their brevity, reveal two features of Ivan's life at this stage. First, and most obvious, he was attending mass nearly every day, and doing so at a different church each time. Just as when he first moved to Moscow and was doing penance for his sins of financial manipulation by frequent and varied church attendance, he now seemed to be fulfilling some pledge, perhaps a vow to God in return for sparing his life, to visit all the many hundreds of churches of Moscow. He had begun the practice of attending services each day as soon as he began to feel stronger in the last quarter of the previous year, 1800, and would continue this steady church-going through the following years of convalescence, and even add a series of pilgrimages.

The second thing that appears in the excerpt above is two visits from a man from Wallpaper Lane in the Kitaigorod commercial district, Ivan Iakimov. Ivan's contacts with Iakimov and other people in the business of wallpaper manufacturing and sales had begun as early as November of the previous year when he was just getting back on his feet and also coming to the reconciliation with his uncles. In the days surrounding his uncles' visit Ivan had met four times with a paper manufacturer by the name of Kuznetsov from the Volga town of Uglich. The reason for these contacts was the need for Ivan and his partner in the playing card business, Nikolai Mal'tsov, to find a new occupation. As mentioned earlier, they had completed the big order of 20,000 dozen playing cards that they had won from the franchisees the previous year. The work was finished in May of 1800 (primarily under Mal'tsov's supervision because of Ivan's crippling illness) and yielded a good profit. But the franchisees refused to renew the contract and ordered the dismantling of Ivan's factory and others that might compete with their own.

Ivan and his partner, who by now had acquired know-how and contacts in the paper business, decided to start up a factory for producing wallpaper. Ivan's meetings with the paper manufacturer from Uglich, Kuznetsov, were part of this project, which got up and running toward the end of the year 1800 at the same Piatnitskaia Street locale as the previous card factory.[42] Not surprisingly, things did not go as smoothly at first as they might have hoped, and when the enterprise suffered early losses, Mal'tsov decided to withdraw, and he and Ivan went their separate ways. Ivan chose to continue the business and accordingly had to find a new place to house his operations. He found the building he needed in late April of 1801 in the northwest Moscow settlement known as the Novaia Dmitrovskaia sloboda or commonly simply as Novaia Sloboda (just southwest of Sushchëvo, where his former collaborators, the gardeners Beliaev and Shein, had their orangeries).[43] He set up his factory there and ran the operation with thirteen to eighteen workers. Adjoining rented rooms served as an apartment for his family, and in mid-May 1801 they moved across the city from Piatnitskaia Street on the south side to their new home in Novaia Sloboda on the north side. The apartment was duly blessed with holy water by the parish clergy three days later, and the Tolchënovs settled in.[44]

Ivan demonstrated his commercial acumen by turning the wallpaper business around. He reported in his year-end summary for 1801 that after setting up on his own, he worked on perfecting the production and also on making the acquaintance of people on Wallpaper Lane, presumably to learn better ways to market his product. In the diary we see him regularly meeting with such people. Ivan Iakimov is mentioned in the excerpt at the head of this section, and several more people in the wallpaper trade appear in the diary as the year progresses.[45] Ivan was evidently using his charm and ease with people to find skilled workers to improve his product and to win the cooperation of the people who sold it on Wallpaper Lane. As a result, he was able to report in his year-end summary that he had not only recouped the losses during his partnership with Mal'tsov but even turned a modest profit in his first full year as a wallpaper manufacturer.

*   *   *

These fateful years of readjustment for Ivan reveal a number of things about his frame of reference and his self-identity. The first thing that strikes one is how internal to Russia his entire perspective on the world was. Events outside of the country scarcely impinged on his consciousness. Occasionally, he mentioned victory in a war the country was fighting. But the French Revolution, to take the most remarkable example, had simply passed by without the slightest remark from Ivan. His retrospective notes for the year of the revolution, 1789, include mention of a victory over the Turks in the Second Turkish War, but otherwise record merely local events such as the contribution by parishioners of silver icon covers for the parish church, high water that allowed ships to sail for the first time in memory into Dmitrov, and, tragically, the death of two girl cousins who drowned after falling from a pond float. Ivan responded to international events only indirectly, for example, in his comments about internal political or economic changes, as he did in his remarks about Emperor Paul's decrees on clothing, monetary, and trade policy.

He did not shrink, however, from commenting favorably and unfavorably on national figures, including rulers. In this period we can see his fascination and respect for Catherine II, expressed in his remarks about her death and burial. He was initially, too, taken with the figure of Paul and the brilliant pageantry of his coronation. But at the same time he began to hear disturbing reports about the new emperor's behavior and decisions, matters about which he considered it safe to write in his journal only after the death of Paul. The assassination of Paul itself revealed ambivalence in Ivan that must have been shared by many people of his time. A religious reverence for the figure of the ruler continued to be a feature of Russian life at this time, and it was especially marked among the commercial groups. Not only Ivan's journal but the memoirs and diaries of other merchants express their eagerness to view the imperial family at every opportunity and to be in as close a proximity to the ruler and the imperial family as possible.[46] Merchants, at least the most prominent of them, had played a part in coronations and other ceremonials of the ruler since the time of Peter the Great. They were participants in what Richard Wortman has called the "scenarios of power," and they seemed to derive a magical sensation from the experience. Belief in the sacred character of the ruler continued to exercise a hold. To murder the person of the tsar could only be a "monstrous" act, to Ivan's way of thinking. Yet he apparently shared in the feelings of joy and relief with which the new ruler was greeted.

Apart from his bankruptcy and exile from his home and hometown, the most fateful moment for Ivan came in the collapse of his playing card business in Moscow. The card factory, which he had acquired in 1793, had eased his transition to Moscow, for this enterprise and its associated lodgings provided him with a home and a recognized status in his new city. Once he recovered from the initial shock of bankruptcy and began to devote himself to the card factory he improved the quality of the product and took pride in this achievement. But just as he received this affirmation and appeared to be regaining his confidence, the decision to turn the card business into a government franchise cut the ground out from under him. It was probably no coincidence that this change was followed by Ivan's devastating and prolonged illness. During the illness, what was remarkable about this man caught between the inherited practices of his habitus and his desire to live a cultivated, modern life was not so much his vacillating faith in medical doctors, resorting to them initially, then rejecting them, then returning to them, but his intense, reflexive monitoring of both his physical and mental states and his awareness that his inner life, his feelings of guilt and shame, were affecting his ability to get well.

We see him reaching out in a number of ways. He pursued a variety of medical options, from the use of ordinary hospital military physicians, to the highly credentialed doctor of medicine Matvei Peken, to a native Russian practitioner, Gavril Efimov, and from heroic to gentle methods of treatment. He drew on the counsel and confessional of Father Terentii, who may in turn have guided Ivan to particular icons and holy places for healing. Possibly, too, Father Terentii and others encouraged Ivan to initiate a reconciliation with his uncles and to heal what must have been a distressing emotional rift, as it cut him off from the people who had been closest to him and to his father, whose memory Ivan respected deeply. Tellingly, Ivan did not cease looking for solutions. Even at his lowest points, when he thought he was losing his mind, he rallied and tried to find some new means for conquering his "sinful illness." He demonstrated the resilience to continue and, with breaks when he was flat on his back, the ability to keep his narrative of the self going.

8

A New Equilibrium

THE NEXT GENERATION

[1802, July]

30th I heard mass for the feast of St. John the Warrior in the Church of the Life-Giving Trinity, the one in Kapel'ki.

31st I heard mass in my parish church. After dinner our son Aleksei Ivan[ovich] returned to us from Letovo, having left [Squire] Bibikov.

August

1st I heard mass at the Monastery of the Miracles. Then I viewed the procession from the cathedral to the Moscow River, which was led by Right Reverend Serafim.

2nd I heard mass at the Church of St. Basil the Blessed on his feast day.

3rd I heard [Sunday] mass at the Church of the Tikhvin Madonna in Krasnoe Selo.

4th I heard mass at the New Virgin Convent.

5th I spent the day at home and heard the evening vigil at my parish church.

6th I heard mass there too. This evening my son Pëtr and his wife returned to Moscow from the Markar'ev Fair.

7th I heard mass in my parish church. Our son Pëtr Ivanovich had dinner with us.

In the excerpt above from 1802 we find Ivan continuing his daily mass attendance at a wide variety of churches, a practice that he had begun in penance for the financial manipulations associated with his bankruptcy and which he had intensified in response to his devastating illness. Scattered in this schedule of faithful religious practice we see references to the activities of his children and their associates that can help us sketch the personal trajectories of these offspring of a provincial merchant of the eighteenth and early nineteenth centuries.

The children of Ivan and Anna were growing up and finding their place in the world. Each of their four surviving children, all males, would eventually settle into a commercial or professional life that would justify Ivan's strategy to salvage what opportunities he could from the wreckage caused by his own improvidence. Curiously, though perhaps not surprisingly, the mix of professions chosen by the children reflected interests that Ivan had cultivated in his own life. The fortunes of his step-uncle and ward, a kind of fifth child, Andrei Fëdorovich Makarov, also are of interest.

Of the couple's biological children, the eldest child, Pëtr, began with the greatest advantages. He received an excellent education at two private schools in Moscow. He had been married in 1794 to the daughter of a Moscow merchant family and had since 1796 been legally registered in the Moscow merchant guild as a member of the family of his father-in-law, Andrei Goroshkov. This move, it will be recalled, had been part of Ivan's strategy to shelter his assets from his creditors. It also allowed Pëtr to continue to enjoy the privileges and exemptions of a guild merchant. In the meantime Pëtr had acquired on-the-job training in the grain business, which familiarized him with long-distance travel and trade that extended from south Russia and the middle Volga up to Petersburg. Even though he was unable to continue in the grain business after the family's crash, Pëtr had education and professional experience that would allow him to succeed at other commercial enterprises.

Like his father, Pëtr suffered some serious bouts of illness after the move to Moscow. We saw that in 1797 the family feared for his life when he lay ill for over a month in late summer. This illness apparently did some damage to his lungs, for in the summer of 1799 he moved on his doctor's advice to a home in Sokol'niki on the wooded northeast side of Moscow, where the air was fresh. He experienced another serious bout of illness the following year while on a trip to Petersburg. But thereafter we see no further references in the diary to health crises for Pëtr.

Although Pëtr assisted his father for a time in the playing card business and he and Ivan may have continued to help one another from time to time, Pëtr's professional life developed primarily within the sphere of his wife's family. Curiously, too, Pëtr seemed to have an exceptionally close relationship to his wife, Anna Andreevna. She not only accompanied him on almost all of his visits to his parents but was also his companion on long business trips. In the diary excerpt at the start of this section we see her returning with Pëtr in 1802 from a trip to the famous Makar'ev Fair, the largest annual market in Russia. This fair had begun in the sixteenth century and met every year throughout the month of July under the walls of the Makar'ev Monastery, eighty-eight kilometers down the Volga River from the city of Nizhnii Novgorod. It attracted merchants and manufacturers from as far away as Central Asia, the Transcaucasus, Persia, and India as well as from virtually every region of Russia.[1] Pëtr and Anna had also traveled to the Markar'ev Fair two years earlier. Soon after returning to Moscow from the 1800 trip to the fair, Pëtr and Anna were together again on the road, this time to Petersburg on a trip that lasted nearly two months. Possibly, the Petersburg trip was for the purpose of peddling wares they had purchased at the Makar'ev Fair. Although Ivan did not record in the diary the type of commerce that Pëtr was engaged in, it most likely involved the cloth trade, as it was something he was developing in cooperation with a member of his wife's family and the Goroshkovs made their money as cloth merchants. Accompanying Pëtr and his wife Anna on the Petersburg trip was the husband of Anna's sister Katerina, a second-guild cloth merchant by the name of Pëtr Gorbunov. It can also be observed in the diary that Pëtr Tolchënov was in frequent contact with Gorbunov or his agent Artemii Deviatov, a third-guild cloth merchant.[2]

The following year, 1801, Pëtr, his wife, and Gorbunov traveled to Kiev together during late May and June. Then in July Pëtr again went to the Makar'ev Fair, this time in the company of his younger brother Aleksei, then twenty-one years of age. Pëtr's wife Anna stayed behind in Moscow, and she dropped in on occasion to visit Ivan and Anna Tolchënov during the month her husband was away. Late in the year Pëtr traveled to Petersburg for a month, again without his wife. He made another quick trip there in June of the next year, being gone for only two and a half weeks. These increasingly frequent trips to Petersburg prefigured a major change that was about to occur for Pëtr and his family. Back in Moscow at the end of June 1802, he picked up his wife, Anna, and they headed out once more for the Makar'ev Fair on the trip recorded in the diary excerpt above. Then, at the end of September, they changed apartments in Moscow from the outskirts of the city to a building near the center. A few days later, we learn from the diary, Pëtr and Anna Andreevna left for Petersburg to take up permanent residence there. They even left behind in Moscow their son, Vladimir, now seven years old, with his nanny. Probably the last-minute move to an apartment in the center of Moscow was to place Vladimir in closer proximity to his grandparents and other relatives who could look in on him from time to time, as, indeed, Ivan and Anna Alekseevna would do in the next few months. In March 1803 they moved Vladimir and his nanny to their apartment to prepare them for a journey to Petersburg to join the parents one month later.

The move to Petersburg ended regular visits between Pëtr and his parents, although they seem to have kept in contact through correspondence, business agents, and friends traveling between the two capital cities. Pëtr came to Moscow for three weeks in 1804 and again in April and May of 1805, just before Ivan and Anna took an extended trip to Petersburg and stayed with Pëtr and his wife at their apartment in a fashionable section of Vasilevskii Island. They spent six weeks in the city on this trip, residing the entire time in the apartment of Pëtr and Anna Andreevna. They also visited with their son Iakov (age fifteen), who was living in Petersburg across the Neva River not far from Kazan Cathedral and working for a member of the large Sitnikov merchant family.[3] They were able to spend time, too, with their grandson Vladimir, who at age ten was already studying and boarding at the Commercial School founded by Catherine II, which had recently been relocated to Petersburg from its original site in Moscow.[4] Pëtr had evidently succeeded in his commercial efforts in Petersburg; he was doing well enough to live in an attractive location and send his son to a good school. He was also sufficiently well placed among the local merchant society to be invited, together with other merchants, to dine at the Taurida Palace with the emperor and the entire imperial family, an event that occurred during the visit by his parents.

The diary contains no further references to meetings between Pëtr and his parents. Although their daughter-in-law Anna Andreevna later appears in the diary on a number of occasions when she came to Moscow to visit family and friends in the following years, we hear nothing more of visits from Pëtr. He had done what was expected of a merchant son. He had followed his father's footsteps into the society of guild merchants and also followed his example in providing a formal education for his own son. But Pëtr's life was going to be lived elsewhere.

It would be interesting to know more about the relationship between Pëtr and his wife, Anna. She does not fit the stereotype of the reserved, stay-at-home merchant wife. This suggests again that Pëtr may have had a role in finding her himself and that possibly she was another product of a Moscow private-school education and compatible with Pëtr in his values and outlook. What is more, we find no reference to children of the couple other than Vladimir. In view of Anna's travels with Pëtr, it is unlikely that she was pregnant continually and had lost a whole series of children to an early death, as had happened to Pëtr's mother and grandmother. It may well have been that Anna Andreevna shared with Pëtr an aspiration to live more openly and freely than was the norm among merchants at the time. It represented a choice that was becoming available to educated members of merchant families in the large urban centers who were in frequent contact with the Westernizing nobility and were acquiring many of the same tastes.[5]

Ivan's second surviving son, Aleksei, did not enjoy the advantages of a private-school education or the material assets that Ivan had transferred to Pëtr after Pëtr's separation from his natal household. It therefore took Aleksei a while to settle into a profession that would provide him with an independent living. We first saw him in an adult role when he was barely seventeen years old and had to go to court to speak for his father at the opening of the bankruptcy trial in September of 1796. Ivan was feigning illness at the time, and Aleksei, as the eldest son still registered with the family, had to appear in his father's place. The diary does not tell us about what Aleksei was doing in the two years after the family moved to Moscow, apart from his inclusion in some family outings to palaces, gardens, and menageries in the city and surrounding area. We can discern only that he was still living at home and presumably assisting Ivan at the playing card factory. When the card business was franchised in April of 1799, Ivan negotiated a position for Aleksei in the Moscow store of the franchisees and "released" him into the service of the card store, where Ivan himself frequently visited and, it seems, even worked at times (or filled in for Aleksei) while he and his partner were manufacturing the large order of cards for the franchisees.

At the end of the following year, after the contract with the card franchisees ended, Aleksei was working at a pomade factory. Ivan even called it "the factory of my son Aleksei," a hint that he may have used some of the proceeds from his card contract to set Aleksei up in the pomade business. Then a couple of months later, in early 1801, Ivan recorded that he "released" Aleksei to go to a fair at the city of Rostov, a two-and-a-half-week trip. Ivan's use of the term "released" in these instances indicates that Aleksei was still living at his parents' home and under their authority.[6] We hear of Aleksei next in July of the same year, 1801, when Ivan mentioned that "my children Pëtr and Aleksei Ivan. departed for the Makar'ev Fair." Unfortunately, Ivan did not mention what the two brothers were buying or selling at the fair or whether they were cooperating on a venture, assisting Ivan, or operating separately.

The next year, 1802, we see Aleksei getting started on what would finally be his adult profession, a field that he had no doubt learned directly from his father and at home. Aleksei's youth from age five to sixteen took place in the gardens and orangeries of his parents' homes in Dmitrov, and he apparently acquired an expert knowledge of horticulture in assisting his father in his gardening projects, purchase and cultivation, grafting and propagation of exotic trees and other plants. Ivan, who had become respected for his knowledge of such matters, may have helped Aleksei to find work in this field. The first job began in mid-March of 1802. Ivan recorded in the diary, "my son Aleksei Ivan. departed for the village of Letovo to manage the orangeries of Mr. Bibikov." P. I. Bibikov was a noble landowner in Dmitrov district. In this job and in subsequent ones, Ivan appeared to be working in cooperation with his son, serving as an adviser and sometimes purchaser in Moscow of trees and flowers to be used in the orangeries and gardens that Aleksei was managing. Soon after Aleksei went to Letovo we find Ivan purchasing saplings in Moscow.[7]

Aleksei's job for Squire Bibikov lasted only a few months (the diary excerpt at the head of this section shows him returning home at the end of July 1802 after finishing his stint at Bibikov's estate). He spent late summer and fall in Moscow and then at the end of the year landed another job of the same kind, this time with Ivan's close friend from the Dmitrov landed nobility, Afanasii Iushkov. At the beginning of December he left to live on Iushkov's Seliuvkino estate and continued there until mid-May of the following year, when he evidently left Iushkov's employ to take another job father north on the Kashin district estate of a Mr. Shishkov, a job that lasted into the autumn of the next year, 1804. The Shishkov in question may well have been the famous Admiral Aleksandr Semënovich Shishkov, who was a native of Kashin district and owned a number of properties there.[8] He had long been serving at sea or in Petersburg, but just at this time he took leave from service and retired to his estates. Later he would become the president of the Russian Academy and leading conservative intellectual.

Another role that Aleksei seemed to be playing in the family was friend and mentor to his two younger brothers. During the time he was working for Iushkov, he took Iakov, and then on a separate occasion Pavel (they were ages fourteen and fifteen at the time), to Seliuvkino for a week or two of vacation from the city.

Then at the start of 1805 Aleksei won a job in south Russia, far from the familiar terrain of Dmitrov and Kashin districts, where his father may have played a role in finding him his first employment as a horticulturalist. His new position was in the village estate of General I. A. Pozniakov near the city of Elets. Again we see cooperation between Aleksei and his father, as Ivan in the next months visited in Moscow with Pozniakov and with the general's steward, probably to consult on plants that could be introduced to the estate gardens. This job on the Pozniakov estate very soon led to another for Aleksei, a position that proved to be lasting. In February of 1806 he left Pozniakov's service and moved to new employment on an estate in Slobodsko-Ukraina known as Terny and owned by Prince A. A. Shcherbatov. This time, cooperation between Aleksei, Ivan, and Prince Shcherbatov was remarkably close. Ivan met frequently with Shcherbatov and took him to orangeries, gardens, and plant sellers throughout Moscow. These shopping tours occupied much time during the first spring and summer of Aleksei's employment with Shcherbatov and then continued less intensively in following years. Ivan seemed to enjoy his role as consulting horticulturalist, and Aleksei had obviously found his professional niche. He settled into his new home at Terny and rarely came to Moscow. His employment with Shcherbatov continued through to the end of the diary when we lose sight of him.

The next brother, Pavel, was nine years younger than Aleksei and still growing up when Aleksei was out establishing himself as an expert gardener. Apart from the information already noted about Ivan arranging for Pavel to take classes at the university school in August of 1797 and mention of him at family outings and his visit to Seliuvkino during Aleksei's employment there, we see nothing of Pavel in the diary until October of 1803 when Ivan recorded that "this morning with the help of God I released my son Pavel to live in service to Lukhmanov." The employer was probably Dmitrii Aleksandrovich Lukhmanov, a wealthy first-guild merchant and later "honored citizen" who owned a number of stores and antique shops in the center of Moscow.[9] Pavel was fifteen years old at this time, an appropriate, not to say late, age for a young merchant to get on-the-job training by working for another business. In the first half of the eighteenth century townspeople reported that they started their children in such positions from age ten to fifteen. The age must, however, have been advancing, especially for families like the Tolchënovs that had educational aspirations for their children.[10] This may have been a difficult time emotionally for the family, as Aleksei was away at work in Kashin district and the youngest brother Iakov was preparing to leave to work in Petersburg. The departure from home of Iakov and Pavel at the same time would be the last time that Ivan and Anna would have their own children at home. Possibly, too, Ivan had mixed feelings about releasing Pavel into a commercial apprenticeship. Ivan understood that Pavel was different. He had received more formal education than Aleksei or Iakov and, as it turned out, was nourishing a taste for a different type of life than buying and selling wares.

Pavel continued to apprentice at Lukhmanov's shop in Moscow for the next several years, coming home to be taken care of by his parents on only a couple of occasions when he fell seriously ill. Ivan stopped by periodically at the shop where Pavel worked to see how he was faring. Then in May 1809 Pavel went on the road for a while. He hired on as an agent for a shawl manufacturer by the name of Lazar Kozmin and left Moscow to visit fairs first in Kolomna and then beyond, covering a circuit that ended four months later in the southern city of Khar'kov. What happened after that is not entirely clear. Pavel may have stayed with Kozmin or gone back to Lukhmanov for a while. But at the same time he must have been working to get access to another career, for by 1811 he was in service as an actor with the Imperial Moscow Theater troupe. This information comes not from the diary but from an archival file containing Pavel's later requests to escape the category of poll-tax payer.[11] From the diary we learn merely that in 1811 Pavel was sharing an apartment with his brother Iakov in the center of Moscow on Dmitrovka (Iakov had recently returned from Petersburg). From this time Pavel went on to a successful career as an actor of tragedies, first in Moscow and then from 1814 with the Petersburg Imperial Theater troupe. He enjoyed a good reputation, even if Aleksandr Pushkin in a youthful essay criticized his acting. Pavel lived into the 1860s.[12] His son, Aleksandr Pavlovich Tolchënov, continued in his father's footsteps, studying at the

Petersburg Theatrical Academy and becoming an actor and playwright at the Alexandrine Theater in the 1850s.[13]

The youngest son of the Tolchënovs, Iakov, has already been mentioned a few times. He followed his older brother Pëtr into the merchant life. Indeed, he moved to Petersburg just one year after Pëtr, Anna, and their son Vladimir had moved there. Iakov was only fourteen years old at the time but not too young, as we have seen, for a merchant son to get practical training in commercial affairs. Iakov worked for and lived in Petersburg with members of the Sitnikov family, one of the senior and rooted merchant clans in Moscow. He remained in Petersburg for more than eight years, from 1803 until his return to Moscow early in 1811. During this time Ivan would check in from time to time with Luka Timofeevich Sitnikov in Moscow, presumably in regard to Iakov and his position with the Sitnikov firm. When Iakov finally returned to Moscow he was running a shop on Tverskaia Street and, as we saw, sharing an apartment with his brother Pavel. The references in the diary to Ivan stopping by to see Iakov at this shop unfortunately do not reveal whether Iakov owned the shop or was merely managing it.[14] Iakov did not live a long life. He is listed in the Dmitrov census records as having died in 1826 when he was only thirty-six or thirty-seven years of age.[15]

Andrei Fëdorovich Makarov, Ivan's young step-uncle and ward, could in a sense also be considered a child of Tolchënovs. He was reared from a very young age in their household, and Ivan and Anna arranged his marriage to Fëdora Timofeevna Shemiakina. Inheriting the capital left by his father (and managed until his marriage by the Tolchënovs), Andrei escaped the crash of Ivan's household and was for a time able to set up on his own in the grain business for which he had been trained. Although he and his family continued to live as third-guild merchants in Dmitrov, Andrei did not enjoy sufficient financial strength to survive the ups and downs of the grain trade, and by 1804 he could no longer meet the rising capital requirements for guild merchant status. Together with his seventeen-year-old son, Gavrila, he had to relinquish this privileged position and enter the ranks of the lesser townspeople subject to the poll tax.[16] Andrei and Fëdora Timofeevna remained close to the Tolchënovs. Andrei often stayed overnight at the Tolchënovs' apartment when in Moscow, and Fëdora visited them when she was in the city to see her natal family.

As their own children dispersed into their adult occupations, Ivan and Anna seemed to derive some pleasure from playing a grandparental role for the children of their servants and also for foundlings they took from the Moscow Foundling Home for "upbringing and training" (and probably, as was customary, also for use as servants). They first had a foundling named Avdot'ia, who left them in 1803 when she no doubt had reached the age to be inscribed independently in the urban population and could take a paying job. Toward the end of the decade they had a male foundling name Evsei Mikhailov, for whom they hosted a wedding when he had come of age. Ivan also served as godfather for the children of his servant Anton, who had been with them from at least 1797, after Ivan had sold his serf families. Again, in the case of Anton's children, we can get a measure of the emotional attachment that Ivan formed with children of particular ages. Anton's first child, a son named Nikolai, born in 1803, died within a week of birth. The death did not seem to affect Ivan, who simply recorded that "by the will of God Anton's son Nikolai died." A year later Anton's wife gave birth to another boy, this time named Nika, who apparently survived childhood. But it was a different story two years later when Anton's wife gave birth to a girl, Mar'ia. Ivan again served as godfather, as he had for the two boys, and as Mar'ia grew into her second year, Ivan became strongly attached to her. Then heartbreak. In late May 1807 she became sick with the measles and a high fever, and twelve days later Ivan wrote: "At four-thirty this afternoon my darling goddaughter Mar'ia Antonovna died, having lived on the earth for 1 year 5 months and several hours." The next day he continued, this time using the affectionate diminutive: "At 5 in the afternoon we carried the body of my darling Mashen'ka to the parish church at vespers and afterward following prayers for the dead took her to Lazarus Cemetery for burial."[17]

It was no doubt satisfying for Ivan that his biological children, his four sons, were able to establish themselves in independent circumstances and, moreover, to express in their professional lives three features of Ivan's own life: commerce, horticulture, and theater. Pëtr was able to maintain throughout this time his privileged position as a guild merchant and exemption from the poll and soul tax. As for Pavel, even though his life could not have been easy (Richard Stites has pointed out that educated people in this period often held actors in contempt), he was able within a few years to escape the poll tax and achieve the privileges and exemptions of an accomplished professional.[18] In contrast, Iakov, like Andrei Makarov, had to enter the ranks of lesser townspeople. I have found no record of Aleksei's subsequent status.

THE PILGRIM

[1804, February] 8th Calling on the help of our all-beneficent God, Anna Alek-seevna and I departed for the monastery of St. Nil Stolbenskii the Miracle Worker to pray. We left the apartment at 11 in the morning. We stayed overnight in the village of Chashnikovo after having traveled 39 verstas.

9th We ate dinner in the village of Davydkovo. Continuing on our way, we passed through Klin at 2 in the afternoon. We stayed overnight at the village of Golovkovo.

10th We ate dinner in Gorodok and at 5 in the evening arrived in Tver and took a walk to the bazaar.

11th In the morning we rode to the Zhëltikov Monastery and after hearing the prayers to St. Arsenii we were privileged to touch his sanctified relics. Then we rode back to Tver directly to the cathedral, where the mass was letting out, and after having heard the prayers to St. Prince Mikhail, we were privileged to press his relics to our heads. We left Tver at noon and stayed overnight in Mednoe, having crossed the Tvertsa [River].

12th We arrived in Torzhok at 8 in the morning and going to the Boris and Gleb Monastery, we heard the early mass at the cathedral church and afterward prayed and were privileged to press to our heads the sanctified relics of St. Efrem and his brother, who lie together in a single casket. We did likewise to the icon of his disciple, the righteous Arkadii, who reposes out of sight there. Afterward we strolled through the trading lanes and walked to the cathedral to pray. After having dinner we left at 1 in the afternoon on the Ostashkov Road and after 33 verstas stayed overnight in the village of Kuznetskaia.

13th In the morning, having covered 23 verstas, we had dinner in the village of Sokolovaia. Continuing on our way, in 17 verstas we passed the Mogilevskaia Hermitage and stayed overnight in the village of Zhdanovo after having traveled another 15 verstas.

14th At 8 in the morning we reached the Monastery of St. Nil and stayed in the merchant bazaar. Then, having dressed, we attended early mass in the Cathedral Church of the Epiphany and late mass in the heated Church of the Annunciation, conducted by the abbot Pavel, and afterward the communal prayers to the saint according to the rules there. We ate dinner in our apartment, but everything was fish and dairy items brought from the monastery kitchen and following its rules. Afterward we strolled around the island and monastery, attended vespers, and stayed overnight.

15th We attended matins and prayed and then went to early mass at the cathedral church and also to a portion of the late mass, and after eating dinner we departed at 1 in the afternoon into a big snowstorm and after having covered 13 verstas with difficulty and at a walking pace, we stayed overnight at the village of Lopotsy.

16th Because the snowstorm continued, we did not depart from the inn until past 7 in the morning and had to dig our way out of the village with shovels before we got moving. Having traveled 13 verstas at a walking pace to the village of Kukarevo, we ate dinner. We went 20 more verstas and stayed overnight at the inn at the monastery in Mogilevskaia Hermitage.

17th In the morning we traveled 27 verstas to the village of Kachanovo and ate dinner there. We went 22 more verstas to the village of Rudnikovo and stayed overnight.

18th We arrived in Torzhok at 8 in the morning, having covered 24 verstas, and we strolled through the trading lanes. We were in the Resurrection Convent to hear mass, and after dinner, continuing on our way, we stayed overnight in Mednoe.

19th We arrived in Tver at 7 in the morning and had dinner there. We stayed overnight in Gorodok.

20th We had dinner at [the village of] Spas v Zaulki.¹⁹ We passed through Klin before 4 in the afternoon. We stayed overnight in the village of Kos'kovo.

21st We ate dinner in the village of Rzhavki, and before 6 in the evening by the grace of God we arrived safely to our apartment in Moscow.

Here we see Ivan and Anna on a winter trip to one of the favorite destinations for Russian pilgrims, the retreat of the early-sixteenth-century hermit St. Nil Stolbenskii, a monk of the Krypetskii Monastery who withdrew from the world to an island in a lake near the city of Ostashkov in Tver province. His name is associated with a series of miracles and legends that make him beloved to Russian Orthodox believers. I included the diary account of the entire journey to show again how carefully Ivan was recording his religious duties and to note that he had given up his earlier practice of keeping exact horological time. While he may have jettisoned his pocket watch with his other valuable possessions at the time of the bankruptcy, Ivan had in any case begun to focus more on the spiritual than on the material after his financial collapse and prolonged illness. We have seen his turn to almost daily church-going. Pilgrimages now also figured importantly in his life. This pilgrimage to the monastery of Nil Stolbenskii was one of a series that Ivan went on during the five years following recovery from his illness, completing at least one a year. This period could almost be considered a time of monkish withdrawal for Ivan himself. He had apparently suspended his theater-going in Moscow, and even information on his business affairs appears rarely in the diary. Although Ivan continued to mention meetings with friends, neighbors, and business associates, the diary in this period becomes a record primarily of religious duty.

Pilgrimages were a central feature of life in Russia before the Soviet era. They began at the very earliest days of Christianity in the Kievan period, although for several centuries only clerics and princely personages undertook them, and the principal destinations were the Holy Land, Constantinople, Athens, or Mount Athos. As Mongol rule and the dwindling size and eventual fall of the Byzantine empire reduced Russians' contacts with the Levant, Russian religious leaders placed greater emphasis on pilgrimages to holy places within Russia. This attitude was strengthened by the subsequent ideological assertion, prompted by the end of Byzantine rule, that Russia was the only true Orthodox Christian realm, and pilgrims flooded across Holy Russia to visit the many sites that

boasted miracle-working relics and icons. Most Russians believed that the relics
brought them into direct communication with the saints or that the essence of
the saint inhered in the relic or icon, and so it was important to be present at the
site and if possible to touch or kiss the object. A very common stimulus to
pilgrimage was a serious illness or deep grief and feelings of despair. Russians
often took a vow to go on pilgrimages if God would grant them relief.[20] Although Ivan did not state explicitly in his diary that he had taken such a vow, his
actions strongly suggest that he had. Just as in the case of his earlier wide-
ranging visits to Moscow churches when he first moved to the city, he probably
had made a pledge this time that if spared from his terrible illness, he would
undertake a series of pilgrimages over the next five years.

The pilgrimages began with a very short trip in May of 1802 to the village of
Bogorodskoe northeast of Moscow on the left bank of the Iauza River.[21] Anna
Alekseevna's father had died unexpectedly earlier that month, and the trip may
have had a connection with this event, as Ivan and Anna took Anna's sister
Mar'ia Alekseevna and their servant Duniasha along with them. The trip undoubtedly also was a step in Ivan's convalescence. He had been confined to
central Moscow during the previous two years of illness and slow recovery,
his physical exercise consisting of walks in his neighborhood or around the
grounds of monasteries and parks. And, indeed, the trip to Bogorodskoe included physical as well as spiritual enrichment. On the first day the party
strolled through the "surrounding pleasant places until nightfall." The primary
object was reached the second day when Ivan and the others prayed before the
icon of the Kazan Madonna housed in the church there (Bogorodskoe refers to
Mother of God). They then invited the priest for tea and later stopped on
the way home at the Nikolo-Ugreshskii Monastery to pray before the icon of
St. Nikolai, one of those that was thought to have appeared miraculously and
not by the hand of man.[22]

In September of the same year, 1802, Ivan struck out farther, taking Anna
and their son Iakov with him on a pilgrimage along the heavily trodden circuit
to the Trinity Monastery, through Dmitrov to the Nikolo-Pesnoshskii Monastery and the church at Vedernitsy, and then back to Moscow. This was the trip
on which Ivan met for the last time with his ailing Uncle Ivan Il'ich, who died
less than three months later. It was also the first time he had been back to
Dmitrov since 1798, and he accordingly took time to visit other close relatives
and the grave of his father. Prayers at the Vedernitsy shrine were likewise of
great importance, as the icon of Our Savior there was thought to have played a
role in Ivan's recovery from his near-fatal illness in 1777.

The following year, 1803, the pilgrimage, which again included Anna and
Iakov, took the family to Zvenigorod and two beloved destinations for Russian
pilgrims. The first was the Savvino-Storzhevskii Monastery, founded at the end

of the fourteenth century and containing two limestone churches that were jewels of early Muscovite architecture.[23] The second was the Resurrection–New Jerusalem Monastery, founded by Patriarch Nikon in the seventeenth century and where the family had been at least twice before when they were still living in Dmitrov. It was a short trip. They arrived on June 13 in Zvenigorod, an attractive town in the hilly country along the Moscow River, a ten-hour carriage drive west of Moscow. They attended evening vigil and prayers, went to bed, and thanks no doubt to the early morning light of mid-summer were up shortly after three in the morning to continue through beautiful weather to the Resurrection Monastery. There they examined the magnificent church and curiosities, attended late mass, ate dinner and strolled—before returning to Moscow late the same evening.[24]

Ivan and Anna took no more trips that summer, as they were busy arranging the marriage and hosting the wedding of Anna's younger sister Mar'ia Osorgina. Because Anna's father had died the previous summer and her elder brother was a merchant far away in the north, Ivan and Anna were expected to fill the role of parents and matchmaker for Mar'ia. And so Mar'ia (in fact, the second or younger Mar'ia in the Osorgin family; a first Mar'ia, whose married name was Kaftannikova, had died twenty years before, in 1783, of an illness contracted after giving birth prematurely) was married to a Moscow merchant named Savelii Timofeevich Kulikov.[25] With this task complete, Ivan began planning the next pilgrimage, which took place early the following year.

Each year the pilgrimages extended farther from Moscow. The one in 1804 was to the Tver province town of Ostashkov and the nearby hermitage of St. Nil Stolbenskii. This winter trip is described in full in the diary entries at the start of this section and need not be recounted here, except to point out that the daunting struggle through blinding snowstorms that accompanied the travelers' return journey may have dampened their interest in winter excursions; the diary contains no further travels in that season.

The couple's pilgrimage in 1805 was exceptional. They combined it with a trip to St. Petersburg that included a long stay with Pëtr and his family as well as a business matter: a legal action for recovery of a debt. The pilgrimage destination was the Tikhvin Monastery, which lay along the northerly route to Petersburg on a highway begun in the 1770s to connect the northern capital to Nizhnii Novgorod. In May, the month of departure, Ivan asked to have the icon of the Iberian Madonna brought into the apartment for prayers during its annual May procession through the city. He and Anna then took off a few days later, following the route through Sergiev Posad and the Trinity Monastery and then north to Uglich. The journey was recorded almost village by village, and Ivan's descriptions of the sights were fuller and more literary than usual; he painted detailed portrayals of the shape and decorations of palaces and churches. He also commented on the life of the people and was especially impressed with the region north out of Uglich with its frequent and attractive settlements. "The construction was everywhere good and the inhabitants enjoyed a life of abundance, especially on a festival day when the women were dressed spotlessly and in every settlement they participated in singing and dancing."[26] At one overnight stop they stayed with a Karelian peasant woman who astonished them with stories of her many pilgrimages. "She had been to Tikhvin 12 times, to Moscow five, once to Tot'ma and once to the Nil Stolbenskii Hermitage, for the most part on foot." Her stories of the remote northern town of Tot'ma may have inspired Ivan and Anna to choose this as their next pilgrimage destination. Another thing that caught Ivan's eye along the road was a village containing "a rather nice townhouse with gardens and orangeries," evidence that aspirations akin to Ivan's own were reaching people and places far off the main routes.

North of the city of Ustiuzhna, which Ivan noticed had been rebuilt on a regular plan with broad streets just like Dmitrov, he encountered something unexpected: nobles scarcely worthy of the name. "A large number of smallholding nobility live in the vicinity. Some of them not only do not have an education proper to their station but they fail even to perform service. Among them are three brothers by the name of Rozhitnyi who have 7 souls between them. They run the post station and themselves ride around on coachman's boxes wearing gray Russian kaftans and full peasant attire and, to boot, all three are young."[27] A few days later, after an inspiring visit to the monastery at Tikhvin, Ivan and Anna stopped for dinner at the village of Savinka, where "we dined at the place of a poor nobleman Obernibesov, who runs an inn and has a few acres of land, and by such means he earns his living."[28] Whether observed with bafflement, compassion, or dismay (hard to tell from Ivan's flat description), these encounters underscored the importance of display and style in confirming and creating social status. The position of these nobles made quite a contrast not only with the life Ivan and Anna had enjoyed in Dmitrov but even with the life they were currently living in Moscow and would participate in a few days later in Petersburg.

The stop at Tikhvin was preceded by a visit to the nearby Antoniev Dymskii Monastery, in part for personal reasons. Ivan had a letter from a friend of his in Moscow, Nikita Gaidukov, whose brother had been contracted to rebuild the monastery complex after it had recently burned down. After taking a soul-cleansing dip in the adjacent holy lake, as was the custom, and attending late mass, Ivan and Anna were invited to dine with the abbot, Gerasim, a sign that Ivan's personal contacts and status were allowing him back into some of the spheres where he had once enjoyed entree as a matter of course.[29] Later in the day they arrived at the principal objective, the Holy Mother of Tikhvin Monastery, a large complex with a huge five-domed Church of the Dormition. They

Tikhvin Monastery of the Dormition. Photograph by William C. Brumfield.

prayed and attended mass. Ivan described the location, accessibility, and orna-
mentation of its miracle-working icon of our Holy Mother. The town, too, was
large but, curiously, mainly populated by Old Believers and therefore devoid of
the usual complement of Orthodox churches. But the monastery was enough
for Ivan; it made a lasting impression. He wrote: "In the Tikhvin Monastery the
rules and song are extraordinarily good and reverential, of a quality that I have
not seen either at the Trinity or the Aleksandr Nevskii Monasteries. After
dinner we walked again to the monastery to pray to our Holy Mother, and there
I could not stop my tears from flowing out of joy and out of the sorrow of
knowing that I had no hope of ever again being in this blessed place."[30] Deeply
touched and pained at leaving, he and Anna set off that day for Petersburg.

The pilgrimage completed, Ivan and Anna devoted their first days in Petersburg to sightseeing, which they did largely on foot and by canal boat (*elbot*),
starting from the apartment of their son Pëtr on Vasilevskii Island. Anna had
not been to Petersburg before, and Ivan was undoubtedly eager to show her the

offices, palaces, churches, and markets that defined the city and that had played
a role in opening the world to him. The first two days they went to the commodity exchange and government offices near Pëtr's home on Vasilevskii Island. They then rode to the Petersburg Quarter, the Winter Palace and the
Marble Palace, St. Isaac Cathedral, the Resurrection Church, Haymarket Street,
the Great Bazaar, Kazan Cathedral, and along the way visited their son Iakov at
his lodgings. The third day they went to the Bol'shoi Theater (*Bol'shoi Kamennyi Teatr*) and saw the comic opera *Lesta, the Dnepr River Siren*, part 2 (*Lesta,
Dneprovskaia Rusalka*), by the prodigious composer and director at the imperial theaters, Caterino Cavos.[31] This was just one of a number of evenings he
and Anna spent at the theater. They also went out to the St. Aleksandr Nevskii
Monastery to pray before the relics of the saint and walk in the cemetery, the
burial place of Ivan's mother. On the same outing they stopped at the Commercial School to visit their grandson Vladimir.

But the trip had other purposes. Ivan went to the Senate Surveying Office to
get a document for a new friend and neighbor of his in Moscow. He also visited
his friend and former police commissioner in Dmitrov, Anton Letstsano, who
had lost his job for delaying the reordering of streets in Dmitrov. But most
critical for Ivan was his effort to recover a long overdue debt. Much of July was
taken up with his pursuit of Mrs. Karpova, the widow of a contractor who had
evidently cheated Ivan out of a substantial sum of money for goods delivered to
Petersburg. It will be recalled that Ivan's trips to Petersburg in 1789 and 1791
included efforts to recover this debt. In the meantime Mr. Karpov had died, and
Ivan now had to pursue the case with his widow, which proved difficult. He first
went for negotiations on the case to the nearby country estate of a secretary of
the Civil Court. When after this he tried on two occasions to contact Karpova
directly at her home, she was either not there or refused to receive him. Failing
to work matters out personally, he hired a legal adviser. Although Ivan spent a
lot of time with this expert and at least thirteen days at the district court, it is
unclear if he was ever able to win compensation for his loss. He did not
mention in the diary a resolution of any kind before, or indeed after, his
departure from the city.

Interspersed with this effort was more sightseeing, including trips by Ivan
and Anna to the Taurida Palace and Smolnyi Convent and School for Noble
Women, the Arsenal, the Tapestry Factory, the Admiralty, the Academy of Arts,
the Academy of Sciences bookstore, the Senate, the first home of Peter the
Great, the Summer Gardens, and Mars Field. They also saw the flight of the
Englishman Robertson in a hot air balloon. On a few occasions they ran into
the emperor and imperial family at ceremonial events. One was at the laying of
the cornerstone of the new commodity exchange building. Another time the
imperial family was in attendance when Ivan and Anna went to the theater, in

this case seeing another Cavos opera, *The Invisible Prince* (*Kniaz' Nevidimka*), which was in its first season. They encountered Alexander I again on a particularly pleasant outing into the archipelago northwest of the city.

Anna Alekseevna and I left after 10 in the morning from the Tuchkov Bridge in a canal boat and passing Krestovskii and Aptekarskii islands went to Kamennyi Island to the court church there for mass. The emperor and his august spouse were in attendance. Afterward we were invited to lunch with [Commerce Councilor] Kusov [at his dacha]. We then went to the dacha of Count Stroganov and strolled in his gardens, returning by water to our apartment after 3 in the afternoon. In the evening we went to the Bol'shoi Theater.[32]

Ivan was enjoying these meetings, and may well have sought them out, as he was powerfully affected by proximity to the high and mighty and flattered even to be included in socializing with people of rank such as the Commerce Councilor. He was no doubt also proud to write in the diary that their son Pëtr at this time was privileged to attend a dinner at the Taurida Palace with the emperor. These incidences of recognition were personally gratifying but also signified that the governing elite, if not the nobility as a whole, had come to appreciate the importance of the commercial groups to the wealth and strength of the state. Accompanying this appreciation was an increasing sense of pride among merchants themselves about their role in the society and state.

In Ivan's touring of the capital with his wife it is hard to imagine that he did not pick up on the heavy symbolism of Roman and Greek classicism inscribed in the architecture of the city and imbibe through his conversation and reading the spirit of imperial striving that have been described in the works of Richard Wortman and Andrei Zorin.[33] If Ivan shared these feelings, however, he did not write about them in his journal. He was a patriot, no question about that. He hailed Russia's victories over the Turks. He deeply admired Empress Catherine, who had expanded Russia's southern territories and fostered plans for the destruction of Turkey and rebirth of Greek sovereignty in Constantinople. But to these larger aspirations and the symbolism that accompanied them Ivan made no reference. His early education may have been too limited and practical to have instilled in him an understanding of classical symbols and references.

One intriguing aspect of the stay in Petersburg was the visit by Ivan and Anna not just once but three times to a Roman Catholic church. Although Ivan had quite purposefully gone to a Catholic church "out of curiosity" during his 1789 trip to Petersburg, and even earlier, when he was a young grain trader, had visited a Protestant church there, again "out of curiosity," in the current instance he and Anna seemed at first to do so almost accidentally. They could not find an Orthodox service in progress and so decided to go to the nearby Catholic church on Nevskii Prospect. Yet just a few days later they made a point of going again to the Catholic church to attend mass. Then, a third time, not long before their departure for Moscow, they made another visit to the Catholic church. Unfortunately, Ivan did not record what fascinated them so about this church. It may just have been, as he wrote, his curiosity about the world and perhaps a need to understand what was going on in the wider world, as the Catholic nation of France under Napoleon was going about conquering Europe. But Ivan's interest in the religious buildings and practices extended to other confessions and may have been part of his aspiration to be an enlightened man, a person of broad interests and tolerant disposition. We find him on later occasions visiting a Lutheran church again, this time in Moscow in 1807, and he and Anna even went to the Moscow Rogoshkoe center of Old Believers in 1809 and heard vespers at the chapel, again, he explained in the diary, "out of curiosity." At these times Ivan appears as a very pale reflection of the Freemasons described most recently by Raffaella Faggionato and Douglas Smith.[34] The era of tolerance that Empress Catherine had fostered until the 1790s and that resumed for a time in the reign of Alexander permitted people to indulge their curiosity about other religions. Just as Ivan's interests in scientific instruments, his practice of scientific plant management and fish cultivation, and his consultation with medical experts expressed his modern enlightened attitudes, so too did his curiosity about other religions indicate his adoption of certain elite values of the time, though, to judge by his journal, without any intellectual depth or intense engagement. These interests did not seem to have shaken his Orthodox faith or religious practices or led him to Masonic texts (although, to be sure, Ivan revealed virtually nothing about his reading).

One further pilgrimage in the following year, 1806, brought to an end the series of annual religious journeys that Ivan had set out on in 1802 and suggests again that he had taken a vow to complete a round of five years of pilgrimages if God would relieve his suffering and spare his life. This final pilgrimage took him and Anna on an arduous journey to the far north of Russia. The objective was the Spaso Sumorin Monastery in the town of Tot'ma, in the northeast of Vologda province. Why such a remote destination? It was almost as if Ivan had decided that each pilgrimage in succession would be more challenging than the last, its completion at once proof of his devotion and of his improving health. But other reasons could have prompted the choice of Tot'ma. Though little known today, Tot'ma was in the eighteenth century a prosperous center of salt production, as well the site of a number of beautiful churches and a monastery established in the sixteenth century by the miracle worker St. Feodosii. Moreover, it was the home of courageous merchant explorers of the Aleutian Islands and Alaska (one of whom founded Fort Ross on the California coast a few years after Ivan's visit to Tot'ma). The city had likewise been a regular stop for Peter the Great on his trips to the White Sea. In short, it was known to eighteenth-

Spaso Sumorin Monastery in Tot'ma. Photograph by William C. Brumfield
from his book *Vologodskii al'bom* (Moscow: Tri Kvadrata, 2005).

century Russians as a romantic and storied locale. Possibly, too, tales about
Tot'ma told by the Karelian woman and avid pilgrim with whom Ivan and Anna
had stayed on their recent trip to Petersburg inspired them to choose this
destination.[35]

The trip took Ivan and Anna along a familiar route to Sergiev Posad and the
Trinity Monastery, then to Pereslavl and the Danilov Monastery, and on the
third day to Rostov and a whole string of monasteries there. Next was Iaroslavl,

where they made a stop at the Tolgskii (or what Ivan called the Tolchskoi) Monastery that had been an important pilgrimage destination and part of a rite of passage into his young manhood. The road north from there to Vologda and beyond had not been traveled by Ivan or Anna before. In Vologda they shopped for provisions and then visited the principal churches and monasteries, praying in the presence of the relics of the local saints. Pushing on, Ivan remarked in his diary on how flat and low the terrain was and how much of it was swampland that they had to traverse on corduroy roads. After crossing the Vologda and Sukhona Rivers in a landscape dotted with monasteries, they continued on the corduroy roads and seemingly endless log causeways over marshes and sur-rounded by great forests. Occasional good stretches of road in dryer places, which were heavily populated, would be followed by difficult, lonely, even scary travel. One morning, Ivan recorded, "we rode through great forests without a single house on a horrible road and on the way had to go 10 verstas on a rotting causeway, expecting every second that our coach would crack up." Once they arrived, however, they were not disappointed. Very soon after putting up in the monastery guest house, they received a visit from the most important figure in town, the mayor and guardian of the monastery, Ivan Kuznetsov, who was accompanied by his sister. Kuznetsov was a man who had attained collegiate assessor rank, the eighth step on the Table of Ranks introduced by Peter the Great, and an achievement that at this time conferred hereditary nobility. The arrival to this remote destination of a former mayor and a man bearing the title of "distinguished citizen" attracted the attention and deference of the leading citizen of Tot'ma, which must have been flattering to Ivan. He and Anna made all the expected visits to religious ceremonies and the relics of St. Feodosii, and in the afternoon they were guests at the home of Kuznetsov. Another day in the town and they were on their way back, stopping along the way in Iaroslavl once again to honor the icon of the Tolgskaia Madonna, which was being moved that day in a procession from the cathedral to the monastery.[36]

THE PLAYING CARD MANUFACTURER, AGAIN

[1806, July] 26th In the morning I visited Vasil'ev and [Mrs.] Faleeva in the city.

27th I heard early mass at my parish church, and after vespers I was in the city at Vasil'ev's, and he and I rode to Syromiatniki to consider whether to rent the building of the merchant Prokof'ev for the card factory. I returned home after 9 o'clock.

28th I attended mass and the evening vigil at my parish church. After dinner Mal'tsov and his wife visited us.

29th I heard [Sunday] mass at my parish church again. In the evening Kondrat'ev visited me.

30th From morning until vespers I stayed home, and then I rode to the Pashkov house, which is on Chistyi Prud. From there I went to Vasil'ev's in the city.

31st In the morning I visited Vasil'ev and went with him to see Ensign Kampioni, and from there I went to the shop on Kupavenskaia St.

August

1st I heard early mass at my parish church.

2nd I spent the entire day at home.

3rd I heard early mass at my parish church, and after vespers visited Chernov and Vasil'ev in the city.

4th In the morning I visited Kampioni, and then I was at Vasil'ev's and we were in the city and rode to various places to consider buildings for the card factory. I attended the evening vigil at my parish church.

5th I heard mass and the evening vigil there again.

6th Mass as well. Today my brother-in-law Aleksei Alekseevich returned from Petersburg and stayed overnight with us.

7th Before dinner I was at Faleeva's and in the city. After 6 in the evening my brother-in-law left for Kotel'nich [in Viatka province].

8th I heard early mass at my parish church.

9th In the morning Kondrat'ev visited me. Later I was at the shop on Kupavenskaia St. and in the city.

10th After dinner I visited Vasil'ev.

11th In the morning Dmitrii Zherebin visited me. I attended mass and the evening vigil at my parish church.

12th I heard [Sunday] mass there too. After dinner and until dusk I was at Chernov's.

13th Before noon I visited Prince Sergei Ivanovich Odoevskii.

14th In the morning I was in the city and at Vasil'ev's, and he and I rode to Ostozhenka [Street] to look over a building. I heard the evening vigil at my parish church.

15th I heard mass at my parish church too.

16th Early mass there too.

17th I heard early mass again at my parish church, and after dinner I was at Kampioni's, and then at the shop on Kupavenskaia St., and then I visited Vasil'ev and was in the city, and at Vasilii Kotel'nikov's. In the evening Mar'ia Vasil'evna Obreskova visited us while traveling from the village and [Miss] Khodneva was with her.

18th I spent the day at home and attended the evening vigil at my parish church.

19th I heard early [Sunday] mass there too. Afterward and before dinner I was at Kondrat'ev's and in the city. From there I visited Faleeva and Obreskova. After dinner Chernov came to my place, and I rode with him out to the village of Svirlovo and strolled until dusk.

This diary passage captures a look at Ivan's life very soon after his return from the pilgrimage to Tot'ma and reveals a number of things that have suddenly changed. First, where are all the different churches he had been methodically visiting? Without explanation he was back to the normal practice of regularly attending his parish church. This reinforces the notion that Ivan had made a vow of extraordinary religious practice over a five-year period that was brought to a close with the pilgrimage to Tot'ma. Ivan's attendance at mass and other services returned to the expected forms, and he undertook no further pilgrimages in the six final years of the diary record. Second, we see that a member of the Obreskov family is back in the picture. This is the daughter of Anna Obreskova with whom Ivan had once enjoyed such a close relationship. Anna had died in 1800, but this encounter with her daughter Mar'ia in Moscow prefigured a reconnection with the younger generation of Obreskovs, including Nikolai Vasil'evich Obreskov, who was marshal of the Dmitrov nobility and would rise to the post of civil governor of Moscow and Moscow province in 1810. Finally, we see Ivan riding around looking for a building in which to set up a card factory. He had not been making playing cards since he and Nikolai Mal'tsov finished a special order in 1800 and then, like other Moscow manufacturers, were forced out of the business by the new franchisees. Why was he now looking to set up a new factory?

The answer is that the end of Ivan's round of pilgrimages had been accompanied not only by a restoration of his health but also by an invitation to return to the card business. It is not altogether clear how this happened, but within a few days of his and Anna's return from the Tot'ma pilgrimage, Ivan was meeting with a man named Iakov Vasil'ev and a woman named Faleeva (and soon after with Mr. Faleev as well), people who had not earlier appeared in the diary. A short time later, Ivan and Iakov Vasil'ev began scouring Moscow to find a building in which to install a playing card factory. Another new acquaintance, identified as Ensign Kampioni, may also have had something to do with organizing the project. About this time Ivan's former partner in the business, Nikokai Mal'tsov, showed up, either with his wife on a social occasion (as in the excerpt above) or alone to meet with Ivan. Mal'tsov seems to have been acting as a consultant, for he did not appear consistently in the diary in connection Ivan's new work. What the diary entries soon make clear is that Ivan has been hired to be the manager of a new playing card factory in Moscow, the rights for which had been won in the third or fourth franchise auction by Mr. Faleev and Mr. Obolenskii. The first person was probably Dmitrii Fëdorovich Faleev, a merchant who moved to Moscow from Kaluga in 1780, and then married into the Moscow family of S. P. Vasil'ev. Faleev had become mayor of Moscow in 1804, which may have given him a leg up in getting the playing card rights.[37] Iakov Vasil'ev was probably from the family of Faleev's wife. The second owner,

Mr. Obolenskii, may have been a grandson of Ivan's former friend Ivan Petrovich Obolenskii, the district judge in Dmitrov after the 1775 local government reforms. His son, Mikhail Ivanovich, died in 1794, and his estate was divided between his three sons, Andrei, Sergei, and Ivan (there was also a daughter Praskov'ia).[38] Iakov Vasil'ev seemed to be acting as an agent for the two owners and was working closely with Ivan in finding a site for the factory and in providing the resources for outfitting the facility.

Ivan set to work right away. In a short time, he had arranged to rent a building in Syromiatniki on the east side of Moscow. He then scurried about to various lumber yards and other suppliers to get the materials needed for the factory and for his family's residence, and we see him meeting frequently with contractors as he gets everything prepared. The work went remarkably fast. On October 11, Ivan recorded that "in the morning I left forever our Novaia Sloboda apartment and moved to Syromiatniki to the playing card factory established by Mssrs. Obolenskii and Faleev in the building rented from the merchant Prokof'ev, where rooms were assigned to me." The next day he reported that "Anna Alekseevna, our son Pavel, and our people moved here to join me." A feeling of sadness is apparent in his report of the departure from Novaia Sloboda. The Tolchënovs had lived there since 1800, and their neighbors and landladies had shared in their holiday celebrations and family rituals (one of the women served regularly with Ivan as godparent for the children of the servant Anton, for example) and had assisted the family when Ivan was convalescing from his prolonged illness. Indeed, these friendships continued long after the Tolchënovs moved to the other side of town. We find his neighbors from Novaia Sloboda showing up again and again in visits recorded in the diary.

Ivan threw himself into the new work and was evidently happy to have gained not only this new source of income but also an affirmation of his skill as a manufacturer of playing cards. Just one week after his move to the Syromiatniki building, he reported with pride that "today at noon the first work at the card factory began under my supervision." About the same time, Ivan was also testifying for the state in a case against people who had cheated the system by selling playing cards without permission and without paying the tax due on them.[39] Unfortunately, we do not learn much about the new business from the diary. Ivan had stopped giving year-end summary reports on his commercial activities after 1801, when he shifted from card manufacturing to wallpaper production. The practice of reporting on his finances did not resume with his return to the card business. The diary entries themselves nevertheless indicate that the factory was operating profitably and well. Ivan worked diligently at the factory and on its accounts, regularly entertained the staff, and can be seen busily seeking out building materials and supplies for the work. Evidence of the success of the enterprise can also be found in diary entries that tell of an expansion of the factory in 1808.[40]

Despite this new and demanding work, Ivan also continued his job as a consultant on gardening projects for Prince Aleksandr Shcherbatov, cooperating with his son Aleksei, who continued to serve as the gardener at Shchebatov's country estate of Terny. In the diary excerpt at the start of this section we see a new aristocratic personage, Sergei Ivanovich Odoevskii. Although Odoevskii does not appear in entries directly connected with trips to orangeries or plant purchases, we can assume that he was standing in for Shcherbatov, as he was Shcherbatov's father-in-law. Not long after meeting with Odoevskii and while Ivan was heavily occupied with setting up the new card factory, he took a large portion of one day to go out to orangeries near the Donskoi Monastery (these must have been the ones built by Prokofii Demidov four decades earlier) to purchase pineapple plants for Prince Shcherbatov.[41] Ivan kept at this job for Shcherbatov right through the following years until the diary ends. He met with him a few times each spring and sometimes also in the fall. They met five times in the spring of 1812, perhaps because Aleksei had made a rare appearance in Moscow during that March.

Ivan was also entrusted with a special commission for his boss Obolenskii in another matter in 1809. This task had a connection not to the card franchise but to another very lucrative government regulated tax franchise, the liquor monopoly. Although Ivan neglected to record in his diary what the substance of the mission was, we can see that it sent him urgently from Moscow to the city of Tula in the adjoining province to the south. There he first checked in with the vice governor and the liquor office and then rode seventeen verstas out to a village to meet with another man. He returned to Moscow in great haste on relays of post horses, the entire mission taking only four days, if one does not count the time spent on arrangements for the journey such as obtaining a documents and orders for post horses. This mission revealed something important about how Ivan's standing had changed since his exposure twelve years earlier as a defaulter and trickster on a grand scale. He had now somehow transcended this reputation and returned to a position of trust with people of power.

We see this, too, in another experience: a renewal of his contact with Countess Orlova and her family. The elevation of Ivan to manager of a profitable enterprise owned by leading Moscow families and his service as a consultant on gardening for aristocratic estate owners must have done much to restore his reputation and make possible a renewal of his acquaintanceship with Countess Elizaveta Fëdorovna Orlova, the widow of Ivan Orlov. It will be recalled she snubbed Ivan Tolchënov after the collapse of his fortunes when he came to her home in Moscow and was not allowed entry. Now after a thirteen-year absence from the diary, we find her name again in the entry for February 14, 1810. The person who brought them together was apparently Nikolai Obreskov, the son of Ivan's old and close friend. The diary entry reads: "Before noon I was at Countess Elizaveta Fëdorovna Orlova's and at Nikolai Vasil'evich Obreskov's, and afterward in the city." Then a month went by before Ivan again reported that "before dinner I was at Mikhail Goroshkov's [the brother of his son Pëtr's wife], and from there I went to Prince Shcherbatov's and to Countess Orlova's." April and May passed by without a meeting, and then on June 3 Ivan recorded: "In the morning I rode to Prechistenka [Street] to Countess Orlova, and from her I went out by the Donskoi [Monastery] to General Chesmenskii." A few days later, Ivan wrote, "I rode out by the Donskoi [Monastery] to the office of Countess Orlova-Chesmenskaia." He was back there again two weeks later. What could have been going on here?

First, we need to identify this General Chesmenskii. It is not well known that Aleksei Orlov, another of the five brothers who had put Catherine II on the throne and then served her government in a variety of capacities, had an illegitimate son Aleksandr Alekseevich, to whom Catherine II later gave the surname Chesmenskii at the end of the First Turkish War. In this war, Aleksei Orlov had led the Russian fleet to victory in a great naval battle at Chesme. Orlov himself was granted the honor of adding to his surname forevermore the extension Chesmenskii, and thus his legitimate daughter, Anna Alekseevna, whose office Ivan visited, was likewise known as Orlova-Chesmenskaia. The fact that Catherine II allowed Orlov's illegitimate son to bear the extension Chesmenskii without the use of Orlov was quite an honor in itself, as aristocratic bastards at that time were generally made to bear some odd abbreviation of their father's name (such as Betskoi for Trubetskoi or Pnin for Repnin). By all accounts, Chesmenskii was well liked and had a good career. He went to school in Halle in Germany, like many other highly placed Russians of the time, and later spent a year in England and learned English. He served under Field Marshal Potëmkin in the Second Turkish War and rose to the rank of general major in 1807. When his father died the same year, he became executor of the affairs of his half-sister and his father's heir, Countess Anna Alekseevna Orlova-Chesmenskaia—much to the anger and chagrin of her uncle, Vladimir Orlov, who regarded himself as the protector of his niece. But she was an independent twenty-two-year-old with an inheritance worth close to 60 million rubles and made her own decisions.[42]

Judging from the record in the diary, Ivan Tolchënov had been asked by Nikolai Obreskov, whose mother had also been a friend of Countess Elizaveta Orlova, to act as a mediator or consultant in some affair of the family's. He first met with Elizaveta Orlova and Nikolai Obreskov and subsequently contacted General Chesmenskii, and thereafter he made a few trips to the office of Coun-

tess Anna Alekseevna Orlova-Chesmenskaia, all during the summer of 1810.
The last in this series of meetings took place at the home of Countess Anna
Alekseevna, and from there Ivan went directly to Nikolai Obreskov. Whatever
the specific issue—perhaps it was related to the organization of a great carrousel
(a display of competitive horsemanship) that the countess was planning for the
following year—Ivan's role evidently ended with this meeting; we find no further references in the diary to the Orlov family. But, again, it must have been
flattering for Ivan to be called in as a consultant or mediator for this prominent
family and, in this way, to recover in some measure his former status as an
associate of people from the leading families of the country.

LAST DAYS IN MOSCOW

[1812] June

*7th In the morning I was at Vasil'ev's in the city, and in the evening I visited
and had supper with Borodin.*

*8th I was home during the day at my work, and in the evening I attended the
vigil at the parish church.*

*9th I heard mass there too. In the evening Vasil'ev, Borodin and his wife, and
Lukin came to our place for supper.*

10th I heard mass at the parish church.

11th I was at home doing my work.

12th The same.

13th The same.

*14th At noon Glushkov visited me. At 4 o'clock Anna Alekseevna and I rode to-
gether with Lukin to see the Izmailovskii menagerie and there strolled until dusk.*

15th I did not go anywhere.

*16th In the morning I was in Miusy at the lumberyard, and in the evening vis-
ited and had supper with Vasil'ev.*

By 1812 Ivan's life had settled back into a satisfying, if less impressive, pattern
than it had presented before the collapse. He had survived his loss of credit and
surmounted his personal health crisis. His period of penance and religious
devotion had passed, and he returned to the normal religious practices of
Sunday mass, vigils on Saturdays and the eves of holy days, and once a year
confession and communion. His social life, which had contracted significantly
during his period of convalescence and repentance, began to pick up toward the
end of the first decade of the new century. The theater, which (except during
the visit to Petersburg) he had avoided entirely for several years either because
he could not afford it or chose to concentrate on cleansing his soul, returned to
the agenda by 1810, when he and Anna began on occasion to attend performances. Ivan's interest in the secular manifestations of the Enlightenment and

organization of knowledge likewise reappeared, as he again enjoyed trips to menageries (as noted in the diary excerpt above) and to the "cabinet of rarities" at the university. He and Anna also continued to take pleasure in the gardens of the city and surrounding countryside; they went frequently on strolls from their home in Syromiatniki to the nearby Golovin gardens and others, and Ivan even became a regular visitor to the famous Serebrianicheskie baths on the banks of the Iauza River not far from his apartment. As for his personal finan-cial affairs, diary entries tell little but do indicate that he continued to pursue his case against the widow Karpova for return of the money owed him. His Petersburg legal adviser appeared in Moscow in 1809 and met with Ivan a few times, followed by a meeting between Ivan and a secretary of the Moscow Magistracy. Whether anything ever came of this seemingly endless project is not known.

Unfortunately for Ivan, this new equilibrium in his life, his position as a respected manager of a Moscow factory and as gardening consultant to the well-born, could not avoid yet another shattering blow, this time from a source far beyond what he or other Muscovites had imagined could happen: the in-vasion of the Grande Armée of Napoleon Bonaparte. France must have seemed a million miles away. It was rarely mentioned in the diary. Even after the Napoleonic invasion of Russia started, life in Moscow went on much as it had before, as can be seen in the diary excerpt at the start of this section from the first month of the invasion. Indeed, the authorities did not issue any alerts or give cause for alarm until the very last minute.[43] The diary contains the first hint of the invasion on July 30, seven weeks after its start, when Ivan recorded that prayers were said at the parish church asking for a victory over the French. During the first half of August, Ivan seemed still to be going about life more or less normally. He met with his business colleague Iakov Vasil'ev and with the usual suppliers and contractors. However, on August 16 he visited Mar'ia Obreskova, and at that date we see what looks like a later interpolation, where he wrote: "From this day onward the residents of Moscow, especially women, together with personal property, began to depart in huge numbers. Likewise the Council of the Moscow Foundling Home ceased its operations and began to dispatch all its money, goods, and papers to Kazan because the powerful enemy, having occupied Smolensk, threatened Moscow with invasion." Ivan remained in the city during the next several days, apparently making whatever arrange-ments he could to save the assets of the card factory. On July 22 he again visited Mar'ia Obreskova, possibly to learn whatever he could about the threat to the city, as her brother was the governor and in a position to know. The news was not good. The enemy was by then converging on Borodino, site of an epic battle of the same name, just a short distance from Moscow. Three days later Ivan recorded that "today we sent from the factory a large portion of the paper and finished cards to Iaroslavl, more than 60 wagonloads, and we included with them part of our own personal property." The next two days he was at the factory or in the city. On August 28 he wrote: "I spent the entire day packing up all the remaining things in the factory and putting them in storage."[44]

With this entry the diary ends. The remainder of the third leather-bound volume is a series of blank pages.

What happened to Ivan and Anna after the tragic events of 1812 is not known. The last church records that I have found for them are from the parish lists for their church in Syromiatniki, the Church of the Trinity, in 1812.[45] Possibly, after following the factory supplies and their personal effects to Iaroslavl, they joined their children in Petersburg. But it seems more likely that they eventually returned to Moscow. The vital records of the city of Dmitrov, where Ivan continued to be registered despite his many years of living elsewhere, indicate that Ivan died in 1825. He was 71 years of age and listed in the social category of lesser town dweller, indicating that he had not succeeded in reestablishing his financial position to a point that he could recover his former standing as a guild merchant.[46]

*   *   *

During this first decade of the new century Ivan's self-identity gradually came into line with his revised social identity. The social identity that his father and grandfather had bequeathed to him along with the family businesses was as a first-guild or "first-rank" merchant. To this Ivan had added the title of "distinguished citizen" by virtue of his long service in positions of civic leadership. His move to Moscow coincided with his loss of this social identity and relegation to the category of lesser townsman. But his self-identity remained for a time what it had been: a wealthy merchant of cultivated interests who mingled with the powerful and the well-born. He seemed for a time to live in denial of the change in his circumstances and continued, when he could, to spend time with his few remaining noble friends. It may have taken the shock of losing his one remaining livelihood, the card business, that fully awakened him to his altered conditions and threw him into a protracted physical and mental breakdown that he eventually surmounted by intensifying his inherited religious practices.

The process of recovery of his health and adjustment to his new circumstances was assisted not just by the strenuous religious practices described here, but also by a number of other positive changes in his life. Above all, the success of his children in finding employment, in some cases with Ivan's assistance and connections, was undoubtedly helpful. Pëtr was established in what must have been a profitable cloth business in Petersburg early in the decade. Because of his superior education, including instruction in foreign languages, he may have been working in the import/export trade in the northern capital. Aleksei had become an experienced manager of estate gardens with steady employment at the manor of a wealthy aristocratic family. Pavel was launched into a career on the stage of the imperial theaters, and Iakov was running, if not owning, a shop on a main street in Moscow. As for Ivan himself, as he finished his five-year round of religious devotion and pilgrimages, opportunity opened for his return to the manufacturing of playing cards, a business for which he seems to have acquired a good reputation. It must also have been satisfying to him personally, and helpful in his recovery, that on his pilgrimages to Tikhvin and Tot'ma he was received by the most important figures in these locales as a man of importance and interest, a "distinguished citizen" and person of the acquaintance of leading families in the nobility and government. Finally, in his new role as manager of the Faleev and Obolenskii playing card factory, he was entrusted with important additional duties that suggested a renewed faith in his honesty and probity, and he was even enlisted by the Moscow civil governor to assist in the affairs of the celebrated Orlov family, from whose circle he had earlier been cast out. Indeed, the capacity in which we observe him and the Orlovs at this later stage provides a good illustration of his altered circumstances and dramatically changed social identity. In the 1790s his association with Countess Orlova was as a close friend of her friends in the nobility and as a dinner and soiree guest at her home (and she as a guest in his). When he reconnected with her and her family late in the first decade of the new century, he was evidently called in merely to give advice on or mediate a specific business matter and not as a person worthy of socializing with an aristocratic family.

Conclusion

The story of Ivan Tolchënov is valuable for many reasons, but perhaps especially so because of its account of the ups and downs of life in a little-known social context. The few surviving memoirs of merchant life in Russia from the early and mid-imperial period are success stories. In these accounts, authors from prosperous families looked back at the path they or their forebears had taken from poverty to wealth. The life of Aleksandr Berezin, for example, made for an inspiring tale of a man who had been born into poverty in a peasant family and worked his way to a distinguished position as mayor of Petersburg and one of the city's richest merchants.[1] Less dramatic rises were chronicled in the memoirs of Vasilii Baranshchikov, Pëtr Rychkov, G. T. Polilov, N. Vishniakov, Pëtr Medvedev, and others.[2] In such works, obstacles to success were deployed primarily as literary devices that allowed the authors to demonstrate their ability to overcome barriers on their road to prosperity. In contrast, the daily record of personal contacts, evolving interests, and triumphs and defeats that Ivan Tolchënov produced is rare, possibly unique, in Russian sources on the lives of non-nobles in the eighteenth century. We know that Russian merchant families suffered a high rate of attrition, but the available tales are almost exclusively about people who moved upward. Ivan Tolchënov's journal is one of the only accounts we have of downward mobility—and it is a particularly rich and detailed story.

Another useful aspect of Ivan's journal is its picture of Russian life in the era before the Napoleonic invasion. That event, it is generally agreed, had profound effects on the outlook and behavior of Russians and led to determined efforts on the part of privileged groups and the government to narrow social classifications and fix persons in a more clearly defined hierarchy of legal categories.[3] Because Ivan's diary ends with his departure from Moscow ahead of Napoleon (even his retrospective summaries appear to have ended before that date), the society we see through his lens is one in which social categories were somewhat more spacious and less well defined than they became in the subsequent era.[4]

But this is a matter of degree. The striving toward clearer social classifications had been evident in the middle decades of the eighteenth century when nobles and townspeople began pressing for exclusive privileges. Peter III's emancipation of the nobility from obligatory service in 1762 presented issues of social estate definition that Catherine II soon set about trying to resolve with the help of special government committees and the famous Commission on Laws. These bodies again brought to the surface demands on the part of nobles and townspeople for clearer distinctions of rights and privileges. Nobles were worried about the retention of the privileges they had acquired since the 1730s. Townsmen, fearful of falling into the degraded soul-tax paying population, sought to win exclusive commercial rights in the cities and recognition of themselves as a true social estate with enduring privileges and security of person and place, something that was impossible so long as their status depended on a yearly declaration of capital.[5]

The reforms that Catherine II instituted on the heels of the Pugachëv rebellion strengthened ties between the nobles, government officials, and urban elite. But they also created more exclusive definitions of each estate's rights and privileges and drew brighter lines around social boundaries. A striking example of this is the radical reordering of city streets and residential zones that Dmitrov and other towns suffered in the late eighteenth century. Nobles were instructed henceforth to live in their own separate section, merchants in another, and lesser townspeople in yet a third (although the extent to which these rules were actually followed remains to be studied). At the same time, merchants happily acquired privileges and exemptions they had long sought. Although they could still fall into the soul-tax paying population, as happened to Ivan when he suffered bankruptcy, the reforms furnished an opening to a more enduring status as a "distinguished citizen" through civic leadership, philanthropy, or the accumulation of substantial wealth. Continuing business success over a series of generations even promised to lift a commercial family into the nobility.[6]

How did Ivan fit into this evolving social context? Was his interest in a cultivated life and socializing with the well-born a sign that he wished to rise into the nobility? Earlier in the eighteenth century a number of plebeian families had risen into the nobility through wealth or extraordinary service to the state, and therefore it is conceivable that Ivan and other prominent merchants might have hoped to do the same.[7] Yet it seems unlikely. By the time Ivan rose to local prominence, sufficient barriers had been erected to the transgression of social boundaries that if Ivan had harbored an aspiration to rise into the nobility, it would have been a distant goal. Moreover, if this had been his ambition, he could have prepared his sons for a career in government service, which was the most common path taken by non-nobles toward entering the nobility. If Ivan did not seek ennoblement for himself or his sons, he nevertheless aspired to, and to some degree succeeded in, transcending his ascribed social position by creating a personal identity, defined by his manners, tastes, interests, and style of life, that allowed him to feel at ease among the nobility of his district and to consider them his personal friends. Even when financial difficulties foreshadowed his social descent, he contrived to maintain his posi-

tion for nearly ten years through a variety of ruses that demonstrate the importance of style, taste, and an impressive self-presentation in defining social status
at this time. Indeed, Ivan's fall into the ranks of the soul-tax paying population
did not entirely exclude him from the company of nobles and the entertainments of the elites. It was for this reason, perhaps, that he could observe with
detachment and appeared not to envy the impoverished nobility of Tver province, who wore peasant clothes and did not command sufficient knowledge and
polish to appear in polite company, even though they enjoyed, as Ivan did not,
the personal protection and stability of place that belonged to a favored social estate.

Although Ivan nowhere stated his aspirations explicitly, his life and behavior
before the bankruptcy would seem to place him among the growing number of
educated commercial people who wished not so much to become nobles as to
enjoy the protections, style of life, and respect that was accorded to nobles. This
stratum of merchants and manufacturers began to form an estate consciousness in the mid- to late eighteenth century. The emergence of this attitude can
be seen in the commerce commissions, the Commission on Laws, the papers
of local magistracies, and in the lives, education, and avocations of more and
more people like Ivan Tolchënov and his neighbors, relatives, and associates
with whom we have become acquainted through his journal.[8] A more assertive
expression of this estate consciousness appeared in the period following the
Napoleonic invasion, when members of the urban elite began to define themselves as distinct from and in some respects superior to the nobility. They came
to accentuate their differences in style and attitude from the nobility and present themselves as more genuinely Russian, in contrast to the Europeanized
nobility.[9]

This accentuation of difference had not yet appeared at the time Ivan enjoyed local prominence. As a young man and then head of his family firm, he
educated himself in gardening, theater, scientific instruments, and to some
extent medicine. He enjoyed reading, purchased books from the Academy
bookstore, and, judging from his reports of faraway events, also kept up with
national news by reading the twice-weekly publication *Moscow News* (*Moskovskie vedomosti*). He was evidently charming and affable as well as knowledgeable, the kind of provincial merchant with whom, as Nikolai Chechulin
pointed out, "nobles did not find it embarrassing or unpleasant to be acquainted."[10] He was able therefore to pull away in some measure from his given
social setting and refashion a personal or self-identity that allowed him to
occupy a valued place above that normally accorded to people of his position.
Likewise, when confronted with a crisis that shifted him outside his field of
habituated practice (and refashioned self-identity), he demonstrated an ability
to reorient and reclaim a new sense of self that accorded with his revised

circumstances. Although the change cost him in physical and psychic suffering and drove him back to an intensification of his inherited religious practices, he eventually came through this fateful turn. One cannot help but wonder if the same personal resources carried him through the next crisis, the destruction of Moscow that began just days after the diary ends. Whatever challenges that new episode may have brought, we can be grateful to Ivan for having left an unmatched record of his education, interests, achievements, and failings, and of the refashioning of his personal and social identities.

Appendix

GENEALOGICAL TABLE FOR THE
FAMILY OF BORIS TOLCHËNOV

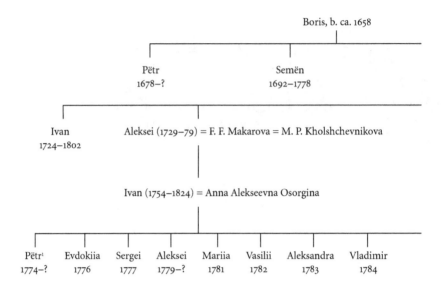

Boris, b. ca. 1658

Pëtr
1678–?

Semën
1692–1778

Ivan
1724–1802

Aleksei (1729–79) = F. F. Makarova = M. P. Kholshchevnikova

Ivan (1754–1824) = Anna Alekseevna Osorgina

Pëtr[1]
1774–?

Evdokiia
1776

Sergei
1777

Aleksei
1779–?

Mariia
1781

Vasilii
1782

Aleksandra
1783

Vladimir
1784

[1] *Married Anna Andreevna Goroshkova, their son is Vladimir*

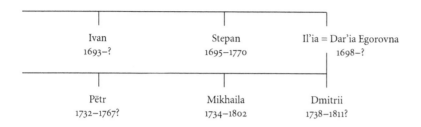

Ivan	Stepan	Il'ia = Dar'ia Egorovna
1693–?	1695–1770	1698–?
Pëtr	Mikhaila	Dmitrii
1732–1767?	1734–1802	1738–1811?

Varvara	Ekaterina	Pavel	Iakov	stillborn girl	Nikolai	Ol'ga	Aleksandr
1785–86	1786–87	1788–?	1789–1826	1790	1792	1793	1794

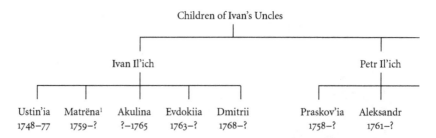

Children of Ivan's Uncles

Ivan Il'ich

Ustin'ia	Matrëna[1]	Akulina	Evdokiia	Dmitrii
1748–77	1759–?	?–1765	1763–?	1768–?

Petr Il'ich

Praskov'ia	Aleksandr
1758–?	1761–?

[1] *Married to Fëdor Loshkin*
[2] *Married to Koz'ma Bespalov*

Family of Ivan's wife Anna Alekseevna nee Osorgina

Parents: Aleksei Vasil'evich Osorgin = Saburova
Children:
    Anna = Tolchënov
    Elizaveta (d. 1787) = Vandashnikov
    Vera (d. 1783, age 23)
    Mar'ia (the elder, d. 1783) = Kaftannikov
    Ivan
    Aleksei
    Katerina (d. 1806, age 24) = Gorbunov
    Mar'ia (the younger) = Savelii Timofeev Kulikov

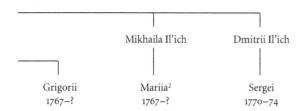

	Mikhaila Il'ich	Dmitrii Il'ich
Grigorii	Mariia[2]	Sergei
1767–?	1767–?	1770–74

Siblings of Pëtr's wife Anna Andreevna nee Goroshkova

Mikhail
Aleksandra (d. 1801 smallpox) = Kvasnikov
Vasilii (d. 1806, age 22)

Notes

INTRODUCTION

1. See examples in I. E. Barklai, ed., *Dnevniki tverskikh kuptsov* (Tver', 2002).

2. Michael Confino, "Issues and Nonissues in Russian Social History and Historiography," *Occasional Paper, Kennan Institute for Advanced Russian Studies,* no. 165.

3. A. I. Aksënov, *Genealogiia moskovskogo kupechestva XVIII v.* (Moscow, 1988), 53, 61. B. N. Mironov, *Russkii gorod v 1740–1860-e gody* (Leningrad, 1990), 151–169.

4. A brief background to the development of this approach in Italy can be found in the introduction by Edward Muir, "Observing Trifles," to the book *Microhistory & the Lost Peoples of Europe,* ed. Edward Muir and Guido Ruggiero, trans. Eren Branch (Baltimore, 1991); the essays in the book are examples of the method.

5. For Kracauer's view, see his posthumously published *History: The Last Things Before the Last,* especially chapter 5 (New York, 1969). For a recent detailed explication of Kracauer's ideas about history, see Dagmar Barnouw, *Critical Realism: History, Photography, and the Work of Siegfried Kracauer* (Baltimore, 1994).

6. Giovanni Levi, "On Microhistory," in *New Perspectives on Historical Writing,* ed. Peter Burke (University Park, PA, 1991), 93–113. Carlo Ginzburg, "Microhistory: Two or Three Things That I Know about It," *Critical Inquiry,* 20 (Autumn 1993): 10–35.

7. For his categorizations, see A. G. Tartakovskii, *Russkaia memuaristika XVIII– pervoi poloviny XIX v.* (Moscow, 1991). He develops his thoughts on this form of writing and its relationship to the development of historical consciousness in his more recent *Russkaia memuaristika i istoricheskoe soznanie XIX veka* (Moscow, 1997).

8. Peter Boerner, *Tagebuch* (Stuttgart, 1969), 11–14.

9. Rachael Langford and Russell West, eds., *Marginal Voices, Marginal Forms: Diaries in European Literature and History* (Amsterdam, 1999), 8–9.

10. Although Boerner mentions daily accounts of occurrences that the officials of some German cities began to write in the late fifteenth century as a possible model. *Tagebuch,* 40.

11. Jürgen Schlaeger, "Self-Exploration in Early Modern English Diaries," in *Marginal Voices, Marginal Forms,* ed. Langford and West (Amsterdam, 1999), 32–35.

12. Béatrice Didier, "Pour une sociologie du journal intime," in *Le journal intime et ses formes littéraires: Actes du Colloque de septembre 1975,* comp. V. Del Litto (Geneva, 1978), 245–248.

13. Didier, "Pour une sociologie du journal intime," 261.

14. Didier, "Pour une sociologie du journal intime," 250.

15. Philippe Lejeune, "Débat," in *Le journal intime,* comp. V. Del Litto, 272.

16. See more on Lejeune's researches on this theme in his essay "The Practice of the Private Journal: Chronicle of an Investigation (1986–1998)," in *Marginal Voices, Marginal Forms,* ed. Langford and West, 185–202.

17. Lejeune, "Débat," 272.

18. Anthony Giddens, *Modernity and Self-Identity: Self and Society in the Late Modern Age* (Stanford, 1991), passim.

19. *Slovar' russkogo iazyka XVIII veka*, vol. 6 (Leningrad, 1991), 146.

20. *Slovar' russkogo iazyka XVIII veka*, vol. 7 (Leningrad, 1992), 148.

21. The Russian words are *memorial'naia kniga, vsednevnaia kniga,* and *zhurnal. Kliuch kupechestva* (St. Petersburg, 1768), 3–4.

22. Tartakovskii compared Ivan Tolchënov's journal to the very famous and much longer memoir of Andrei Bolotov in their attention to changes in the weather and to observations of plant life (or "growings"). The titles of the works were also similar. Tartakovskii thought that Bolotov's title was borrowed from a popular sentimental Enlightenment work by A. Prevo, *Prikliucheniia markiza G . . . ili, zhizn' blagorodnogo cheloveka, ostavivshego svet* (in six parts, St. Petersburg, 1756–1765). Tartakovskii, *Russkaia memuaristika XVIII–pervoi poloviny XIX v.,* 70.

23. See also Tartakovskii's *Russkaia memuaristika i istoricheskoe soznanie XIX veka* for more on the development of historical consciousness. I am grateful to Orest Pelech for sharing his work with me: "Great Russian Secular Culture: the Sense of Self in Diary-Keeping," a paper delivered at the 29th National Convention of the American Association for the Advancement of Slavic Studies, Seattle, Washington, November 22, 1997.

24. On such writing as a sign of leisure, see Sara Dickinson, "The Russian Tour of Europe Before Fonvizin: Travel Writing as Literary Endeavor in Eighteenth-Century Russia," *Slavic and East European Journal,* 45:1 (2000): 15.

25. A notable exception is Thomas Newlin, *The Voice in the Garden: Andrei Bolotov and the Anxieties of Russian Pastoral, 1738–1833* (Evanston, IL, 2001), which places Bolotov's life and works at the center of his analysis of the Russian pastoral.

26. *The Travel Diary of Peter Tolstoi: A Muscovite in Early Modern Europe,* trans. Max J. Okenfuss (DeKalb, IL, 1987); *Time of Troubles: The Diary of Iurii Vladimirovich Got'e,* trans., ed., and intro. Terence Emmons (Princeton, 1988). Gary Marker and Rachel May have done the same for the memoirs of Anna Labzina, *The Days of a Russian Noblewoman: The Memoirs of Anna Labzina 1758–1821* (DeKalb, IL, 2001). Recent Russian examples from the mid-imperial period include: *1812 god . . . voennye dnevniki,* compiled and introduction by A. G. Tartakovskii (Moscow, 1990), and *Rasskazy babushki: Iz vospominanii piati pokolenii zapisannye i sobrannye ee vnukom D. Blagovo,* ed. T. I. Ornatskaia (Leningrad, 1989).

27. Arne Jarrick, *Back to Modern Reason: Johan Hjerpe and Other Petit Bourgeois in Stockholm in the Age of Enlightenment* (Liverpool, 1999; first published in 1992 as *Mot det moderna förnuftet*); Laurel Thatcher Ulrich, *A Midwife's Tale: The Life of Martha Ballard, Based on Her Diary, 1785–1812* (New York, 1990).

28. Natalie Zemon Davis found in her studies of early modern France a process similar to this, in which the very embeddedness in a web of social bonds and common experience may have been key to imparting a sense of one's distinctive history. "Boundaries and the Sense of Self in Sixteenth-Century France," in *Reconstructing Individualism: Autonomy, Individuality, and the Self in Western Thought,* ed. Thomas C. Heller et al. (Stanford, 1986), 53–63.

29. For a summary of the concept, see Pierre Bourdieu, *Outline of a Theory of Practice,* trans. Richard Nice (Cambridge, 1989), chapter 2, "Structures and the habitus." I have also used here the discussion in Matthew Adams, "Hybridising habitus & reflexivity: towards an understanding of contemporary identity?" *Sociology* 40 (3): 511–528 (quotation from page 514 in Adams).

30. See Adams's discussion of Bourdieu's effort to give the notion flexibility by arguing that certain fields such as academia "generate reflexivity as a habitus-field requirement."

31. Italics in the original. Charles Taylor, *Sources of the Self: The Making of the Modern Identity* (Cambridge, Mass., 1989), 47.

32. Giddens, *Modernity and Self-Identity*, 54.

33. The Russian word is *urod.*

34. See, for example, the information from government inventories cited in Akademiia Nauk, *Istoriia Moskvy*, vol. 2 (Moscow, 1953), 565–567.

35. O. V. Fomina, "Imushchestvenno-demograficheskaia kharakteristika moskovskoi kupecheskoi sem'i poslednei treti XVIII veka," (PhD diss., Moscow State University, 2003), 50–55.

36. N. D. Chechulin, *Russkoe provintsial'noe obshchestvo vo vtoroi polovine XVIII v.* (St. Petersburg, 1889), 84. Chechulin did add that the nobility regarded the majority of merchants and lesser townspeople as coarse and dirty, but in the case of Tolchënov and others like him we are identifying the top rank of this social category.

37. Victor Terras, *A History of Russian Literature* (New Haven, 1991), 371.

38. Storozhev pointed out that "the merchant estate has its own culture and civility" but that the study of this aspect of merchant life has not even begun to be studied from a sociological point of view. V. N. Storozhev, ed., *Istoriia moskovskogo kupecheskogo obshchestva, 1863–1813*, (Moscow, 1913–1916), 1:20–21.

39. A. I. Kopanov, "Arkheograficheskoe vvedenie," *Zhurnal ili zapiska zhizni i prikliuchenii Ivana Alekseevicha Tolchënova*, ed. N. I. Pavlenko (Moscow, 1974), 19–28. The observations that follow are from my own de visu examination of the source, which is located in Rukopisnyi otdel Biblioteki Akademii Nauk Rossii, shifr 34.8.15, in the Osnovnoe sobranie.

40. Kopanev for some reason thought the paper for all three volumes was acquired at the same time, but this seems wrong.

1. THE SETTING, EDUCATION, YOUTH, AND MARRIAGE

1. The monastery, though first mentioned in the will of Prince Iurii Vasil'evich in 1472, contained a memorial suggesting an earlier origin. M. N. Tikhomirov, *Gorod Dmitrov ot osnovaniia goroda do poloviny XIX veka, s planami, kartami i diagrammami* (Dmitrov, 2006), 22–23, 54.

2. N. S. Vsévolojsky, *Dictionnaire géographique-historique de l'empire de Russie* (Moscow, 1813), 163–164. *Dmitrovskii krai: Istoriia, priroda, chelovek . . . Rasskazy, ocherki, vospominaniia* (Dmitrov, 1993), 24–29. M. N. Tikhomirov, *Rossiiskoe gosudarstvo XV–XVII vekov*, 269, 273–275, cited in *Goroda podmoskov'ia v trekh knigakh*, kn. 2 (Moscow, 1980), 83.

3. *Dmitrovskii krai*, 28.

4. Unfortunately, Ivan Tolchënov left the city for the family's northern mills and for barge buying along the Volga on the very day Miller arrived. Ivan records nothing about the visit in his diary.

5. Tikhomirov, *Gorod Dmitrov.* See tables at the end of the book.

6. *Istoricheskoe i topograficheskoe opisanie gorodov Moskovskoi gubernii s uezdami* (Moscow, 1787), 202–206.

7. Tikhomirov cites a description of Dmitrov from as early as 1624, which tells of one or more orchards connected with each urban household. *Gorod Dmitrov*, 48.

8. G. F. Miller, *Sochineniia po istorii Rossii* (Moscow, 1996), 304–307. See also A. A. Kizevetter, *Posadskaia obshchina v Rossii XVIII st.* (Moscow, 1903), 643, who reports that Dmitrov merchants were selling garden and forest crops all the way up to Petersburg and along the Volga.

9. Miller, *Sochineniia*, 310–311. A report produced eight years after Miller's visit confirms and expands on his observations, noting that the city had a population of 3,000, 4 cloth manufactories, 3 galloon makers (braiding for uniforms), 6 malt houses, 8 tanneries, and 5 tallow works. The nearby countryside boasted 9 cloth factories, 2 sail-cloth shops, 100 galloon makers, 4 brick works, 12 tanneries, and several other manu-factories. See excerpt from F. I. Tokmakov, *Istoriko-statisticheskoe i arkheograficheskoe opisanie goroda Dmitrova*, ch. 2 (Moscow, 1893), 9, cited in *Dmitrovskii krai*, 50–51; figures also given in N. I. Pavlenko, "I. A. Tolchënov i ego 'Zhurnal'," an essay attached to the rotoprint edition of a portion of the diary, *Zhurnal*, ed. N. I. Pavlenko (Moscow, 1974), 6.

10. Miller, *Sochineniia*, 307.

11. *Zhurnal*, 1: 1–2

12. Tikhomirov tells of a Grigorii Tolchënov who owned a shop and tavern there in 1624. *Gorod Dmitrov*, 34.

13. *Delovoi mir Rossii: istoriko-biograficheskii spravochnik* (St. Petersburg, 1998), 119–120.

14. A. I. Aksënov, *Ocherki genealogii uezdnogo kupechestva XVIII v.* (Moscow, 1993), 64–65. Mironov, *Russkii gorod v 1740–1860-e gody*, 166–169. On the difficulty of moving more than one son into the first guild from a family of several sons, see A. K. Sorokin, ed., *Predprinimatel'stvo i predprinimateli Rossii ot istokov do nachala XX veka* (Moscow, 1997), 156.

15. This protocol was still in effect in 1762 when Makarov made attestation for tax purposes that Aleksei Il'ich had moved into his household in 1750 and was heir to his daughter's movable and immovable property. RGADA, f. 724, op. 1, d. 3867.

16. The protocols were found in the archives by V. Kh. Bodisko and are reported in Pavlenko, "I. A. Tolchënov," 7.

17. *Zhurnal*, 1: 2–3.

18. Aksënov, *Ocherki genealogii uezdnogo kupechestva*, 77.

19. In 1774, he declared a capital of over 35,000 rubles. The next wealthiest merchant (not counting the combined declaration of Aleksei Tolchënov's brothers) was Stepan Loshkin, with declared capital of 10,000 rubles. *Zhurnal*, 1:49.

20. *Zhurnal*, 1:32.

21. Pavlenko, "I. A. Tolchënov," 7–8.

22. A suggestion made by Aksënov, *Ocherki genealogii uezdnogo kupechestva*, 11, 91, who could find no evidence in the archival documents of Aleksei's control of the assets. My own researches, however, turned up evidence that the diarist owned a number of shop stalls in Dmitrov, most likely those given to his father by Makarov and inherited by the diarist. He sold them in 1795. See below chapter 6.

23. O. V. Fomina, "Imushchestvenno-demograficheskaia kharakterisktika moskov-skoi kupecheskoi sem'i," 41–42. I. G. Kusova, *Riazanskoe kupechestvo: Ocherki istorii XVI–nachala XX veka* (Riazan', 1966), 111. Elise Kimerling Wirtschafter references a few cases in the late eighteenth and early nineteenth century in which courts were still affirming the right of particular merchants to hold serfs (members of families acquired

before the ban on non-noble serf ownership). *The Structures of Society: Imperial Russia's "People of Various Ranks"* (DeKalb, IL, 1994), 78–79.

24. *Zhurnal*, 2: 164, 177.

25. *Zhurnal*, 1:2.

26. On the announcement and scholarship offer, see RGADA, f. 724, op. 1, d. 5182.

27. P. M. Maikov, *Ivan Ivanovich Betskoi: Opyt ego biografii* (St. Petersburg, 1904), 412–415. N. V. Kozlova, "Rossiiskii absoliutizm i kupechestvo (20-e–nach. 60-kh godov XVIII v.)" (PhD diss., Moscow State University, 1994), 536. On the changing definitions of the social category "people of various ranks" (*raznochintsy* in Russian), see the Wirtschafter's detailed study *Structures of Society*. It is worth noting that Ivan Tolchënov's grandson, Vladimir, would attend this very same Commercial School, in its St. Petersburg incarnation, during the first decade of the nineteenth century. See chapter 8 below.

28. A few extraordinary exceptions existed. For example, Fëdor Karzhavin, son of an educated Old Believer, studied in France in the 1750s and 1760s. John T. Alexander, "Adventures of a Russian-American Citizen of the Universe: Fëdor Vasil'evich Karzhavin (1745–1812)," *Eighteenth-Century Russia: Society, Culture, Economy*, ed. Rogert Bartlett and Gabriela Lehmann-Carli (Berlin, 2007), 459–471; See also RVB.ru (Russkaia virtual'naia biblioteka), "Pis'ma russkikh pisatelei XVIII veka," at http://www.rvb.ru/18vek/letters_rus_writers/02comm/introcomm_korzhavin.htm (accessed January 15, 2008).

29. *Ocherki Moskovskoi zhizni* (Moscow, 1842), 162–163, cited in M V. Briantsev, *Kul'tura russkogo kupechestva: Vospitanie i obrazovanie* (Briansk, 1999), 41.

30. N. V. Kozlova, "Nekotorye cherty lichnostnogo obraztsa kuptsa XVIII veka," *Mentalitet i kul'tura predprinimatelei Rossii XVII–XIX vv.*, (Moscow, 1996), 48.

31. Briantsev, *Kul'tura russkogo kupechestva*, 45–48. See also comments by a nineteenth-century merchant about his elders' view of too much education and its effects: N. Vishniakov, *Svedeniia o kupecheskom rode Vishniakovykh (1636–1762 gg.)*, 2:92.

32. RGADA, f. 724, op. 1, d. 4100.

33. Inventories of the property of fourteen Moscow merchants in 1739 showed that only four had no books; the rest had from eleven to seventy books each. Akademiia Nauk, *Istoriia Moskvy*, 2:572–573. See also from some of the same material the detailed inventories of merchant libraries in N. A. Baklanova, "O sostave bibliotek moskovskikh kuptsov vo vtoroi chetverti XVIII v.," *TODRL Institut russkoi literatury AN SSSR*, 14 (Moscow, 1958), 644–648. Later in the century very large libraries could be found among merchants in the faroff Urals. See V. Khvostov, "Zapiski Vasiliia Semënovicha Khvostova," *Russkii arkhiv* 3 (1870), 566.

34. M. G. Rabinovich, *Ocherki etnografii russkogo feodal'nogo goroda*, (Moscow, 1978), 277. See also A. A. Preobrazhenskii and V. B. Perkhavko, *Kupechestvo Rusi IX–XVII veka* (Ekaterinburg, 1997), 175–179.

35. N. V. Kozlova, "Rossiiskii absoliutizm i kupechestvo," 515–516. See specific outcomes for the trading town of Torzhok as early as 1710, in M. Ia. Volkov, "O gramotnosti posadskikh liudei Torzhka v nachale XVIII v.," in *Istoriograficheskie i istoricheski problemy russkoi kul'tury* (Moscow, 1982), 79–83.

36. N. V. Kozlova, "Rossiiskii absoliutizm i kupechestvo," 518–519. We may in some instances be observing here the kind of functional literacy discussed by Simon Franklin, namely, a working combination of orality, reading and writing, in which oral briefings and dictation played an important role. See his *Writing, Society and Culture in Early Rus, c. 950–1300* (Cambridge, UK, 2002), 2–9.

37. Evgeniia V. Komleva, *Eniseiskoe kupechestvo (posledniaia polovina XVIII–pervaia polovina XIX veka)* (Moscow: Academia, 2006), 183.

38. Kozlova, "Rossiiskii absoliutizm i kupechestvo," 517.

39. If they tried, the consequences were often dire. A contemporary writer on commerce, M. D. Chulkov, *Istoricheskoe opisanie rossiiskoi kommertsii* (St. Petersburg, 1781–1788), gives a 2½ page list of Moscow commercial families that went under because the head of the family did not maintain proper records or handed over unanticipated debt at his death. See vol. 1, bk. 1, 51–53.

40. See the many examples in N. V. Kozlova, "Rossiiskii absoliutizm i kupechestvo," chapter 10. On a prominent letter-writer edition, see also my article, "Character and Style of Patron-Client Relations in Russia," *Klientelsysteme im Europa der Frühen Neuzeit*, ed. Antoni Mączak (Munich, 1988), 211–231.

41. Gregory L. Freeze, "The Rechristianization of Russia: the Church and Popular Religion, 1750–1850," *Studia Slavica Finlandensia*, vol. 7 (Helsinki, 1990), 101–136. Freeze notes that instruction in the rules of religion was carried out by barely 10 percent of churches as late as the 1850s (p. 110).

42. Kozlova, "Rossiiskii absoliutizm i kupechestvo," 513.

43. Although he also thought that a merchant should be schooled in foreign languages. A. Fomin, "Pis'mo k priiateliu s prilozheniem opisaniia o kupecheskom zvanii voobshche i o prinadlezhashchikh kuptsam navykakh," *Novye ezhemesiachnye sochineniia*, part 24 (1788), 9–11. For similar views, see M. D. Chulkov, *Istoricheskoe opisanie rossiiskoi kommertsii*, vol. 1, part 1 (1781), 21–55; and "Vospominaniia o M. A. Makarove (razkas kaluzhskogo starozhila)," *Pamiatnaia knizhka Kaluzhskoi gubernii* (Kaluga, 1863), 105–106.

44. *Zhurnal*, 1:3. For reference to "Tolchskaia," *Zhurnal*, 3:220 (from another pilgrimage in late June, 1806). The miracle-working icon in question is properly known as the Tolgskaia Madonna, dating from the early fourteenth century and associated with the founding of a monastery on the Tolga River (which empties into the Volga just above Iaroslavl) by the bishop of Rostov and Iaroslavl, Prokhor. It is of the "umilenie" type. See *Zemnaia zhizn' presviatoi bogoroditsy i opisanie sviatikh chudotvornykh ee ikon*, comp. Sofiia Snessoreva (Iaroslavl, 1998), 261–263. The monastery is today the Tolgskii Convent of the Presentation. See *Sviato-Vvedenskii Tolgskii Zhenskii Monastyr'* (Sofrino, n.d.). The pilgrimage from Moscow to Rostov and Iaroslavl was a common and much beloved practice for Russians. Empress Catherine had taken it, partially on foot, in the second year of her reign. Richard S. Wortman, *Scenarios of Power: Myth and Ceremony in Russian Monarchy*, Vol. 1, *From Peter the Great to the Death of Nicholas I* (Princeton, 1995) 1:121.

45. *Zhurnal*, 2:53.

46. *Zhurnal*, 1:4.

47. *Zhurnal*, 1:139.

48. *Zhurnal*, 1:4.

49. A versta was a Russian measurement of length. Its use can be somewhat confusing because it varied in size at various times and for different uses. The law code of 1649 set it at 1,000 sazhens (a sazhen was usually equivalent to 2.133 meters). However, in the eighteenth century Russians used along with this 1,000 sazhen versta a "road versta" measuring 500 sazhens. This is undoubtedly the measure Ivan was referring to when he recorded his travels. A road versta of 500 sazhens is equal to 1066.781 meters (1.067

kilometers or 0.663 miles). Russian measures were not standardized until 1835. My thanks to Alexander Martin for pointing out this problem.

50. *Zhurnal,* 1:6.

51. Here and elsewhere I will be drawing in part on a detailed report on the grain traffic submitted to the government in 1781 and held in RGADA, f. 16, op. 1, d.511, ll. 1–140b.

52. *Zhurnal,* 1:8.

53. E. G. Istomina, "Vyshnevolotskii vodnyi put' vo vtoroi polovine XVIII–nachale XIX v.," in *Istoricheskaia geografiia Rossii XII–nachalo XX v.: Sbornik statei k 70-letiiu professora Liubomira Grigor'evicha Beskrovnogo* (Moscow, 1975), 193–195.

54. Istomina, "Vyshnevolotskii vodnyi put'," 197–98.

55. *Zhurnal,* 1:11.

56. Makarov was buried next to his first wife in the vestibule of the Presentation Church. *Zhurnal,* 1:9–10.

57. *Zhurnal,* 1:12.

58. *Zhurnal,* 1:12. For a detailed account of the plague in Russia, see John T. Alexander, *Bubonic Plague in Early Modern Russia: Public Health & Urban Disaster* (Baltimore, 1980).

59. *Zhurnal,* 1:13–14. The plague did reach Nizhnii Novgorod and Lyskovo in the autumn of 1771, but the loss of life was small compared to the devastation of the Moscow region. Alexander, *Bubonic Plague,* 244–245.

60. *Zhurnal,* 1:15.

61. *Zhurnal,* 1:15. On the movement of provincial merchant families to Moscow, see Aksënov, *Ocherki genealogii uezdnogo kupechestva,* 165–184.

62. *Zhurnal,* 1:15.

63. Vishniakov, *Svedeniia,* 2:50–51. A fictionalized account of a merchant marriage not merely arranged but forced, which the author claims to have based on letters and notes left by his grandfather, can be found in G. T. Polilov-Severtsev, "Divan (Dnevnik kupecheskoi devushki)," part 2 of *Nashi dedy-kuptsy: Bytovye kartiny nachala XIX stoletiia* (St. Petersburg, 1907), 103–142. The story seems too pat to be unembellished, but the central claim rings true. Another eighteenth-century account of the unemotional calculation of marriage can be found in M. V. Danilov, *Zapiski artillerii maiora M. V. Danilova, napisannye im samim v 1771 godu,* (Moscow, 1842), 90–102.

64. Aksënov, *Ocherki genealogii uezdnogo kupechestva,* 76.

65. K. A. Aver'ianov, ed., *Istoriia moskovskikh raionov, Entsiklopediia* (Moscow, 2005), 65–66.

66. *Zhurnal,* 1:15.

67. A. T. Bolotov, *Zapiski Andreia Timofeevich Bolotova 1737–1796.* Vol. 2 (Tula, 1988), 408.

68. Labzina, *The Days of a Russian Noblewoman,* (DeKalb, 2001), 23.

69. *Zhurnal,* 1:26, 36, 50, 70.

2. LOCAL POLITICS DURING IVAN'S YOUTH

1. *Zhurnal,* 1:3–4.

2. The word "citizen" in mid-eighteenth-century Russia referred simply to a town dweller who did not occupy some other established social category such as noble, cleric,

or peasant. By century's end the word began to acquire under the influences of Catherinian legislation and European literature some of the connotations of modern citizenship and the holding of specific rights and privileges. See my essay "Russian Merchants: Citizenship and Identity," in *Eighteenth-Century Russia: Society, Culture, Economy*, ed. Roger Bartlett and Gabriela Lehmann-Carli (Berlin, 2007), 417–428.

3. For the legal regime leading up to that time, see A. G. Man'kov, *Ulozhenie 1649 goda: Kodeks feodal'nogo prava Rossii* (Leningrad, 1980), 137–153.

4. See, for example, Iu. R. Klokman, *Sotsial'no-ekonomicheskaia istoriia russkogo goroda: Vtoraia polovina XVIII veka* (Moscow, 1967), 71–74, and literature cited therein.

5. The long-established practice of using such an appointment to enrich oneself had not entirely died out, despite growing norms against it. See the story in *Russkii byt po vospominaniiam sovremennikov. XVIII vek*, chast' 2, vyp. 2 (Moscow, 1922) 101–102.

6. A. A. Kizevetter, *Posadskaia obshchina v Rossii XVIII st.* (Moscow, 1903), 355–356.

7. Merchants had been petitioning for these changes throughout the century. See N. V. Kozlova, "Gil'deiskoe kupechestvo v Rossii i nekotorye cherty ego samosoznaniia v XVIII v.," in *Torgovlia i predprinimatel'stvo v feodal'noi Rossii* (Moscow, 1994), 218–219.

8. See, for example, the discussion in Iu. R. Klokman, *Sotsial'no-ekonomicheskaia istoriia russkogo goroda*, 77–89. Also N. G. Sokolov, "Nakazy riazanskogo kupechestva deputatam ulozhennoi komissii (1767–1768 gg.)," in *Rossiiskoe kupechestvo ot srednikh vekov k novomu vremeni* (Moscow, 1993), 68–71.

9. See the discussion by V. I. Sergeevich in his introduction to the town instructions in *SIRIO (Sbornik imperatorskogo russkogo istoricheskogo obshchestva)*, vol. 93: vi–vii.

10. Nothing was said about this in the brief Dmitrov town instruction, probably so as not to raise an issue that was of little concern because it was not being enforced—and could in any case be worked around, as happened elsewhere. More on the Dmitrov town instruction below.

11. A. V. Demkin, "Kupecheskie nakazy 1767 g. v Ulozhennuiu komissiiu," in *Kupechestvo v Rossii XV–pervaia polovina XIX veka* (Moscow, 1997), 224–228.

12. V. I. Sergeevich in his introduction to the town instructions in *SIRIO*, vol. 93, xi. On similar and other complaints in petitions submitted to the government at other times, see Kozlova, "Gil'deiskoe kupechestvo v Rossii," 221–224.

13. See examples in Kozlova, "Gil'deiskoe kupechestvo v Rossii," 224.

14. Sergeevich, *SIRIO*, vol. 93:x.

15. See, for example, *A Manual of Roman Law, the Ecloga*, trans. Edwin Hanson Freshfield (Cambridge, UK, 1926), 82–84; P. Ivan Žužek, *Kormčaja kniga: Studies on the Chief Code of Russian Canon Law*. Orientalia Christiana Analecta, No. 168 (Rome, 1964), 213, 239–240.

16. RGADA, f. 724, op. 1, d. 5188.

17. RGADA, f. 724, op. 1, d. 4158

18. RGADA, f. 724, op. 1, d. 4161. The accusations included charges that the people in office did not keep accounts properly and then imposed extra taxes on the citizens, including on poor widows and orphans, causing suffering and ruin. RGADA, f. 724, op. 1, d. 4158.

19. RGADA, f. 724, op. 1, d. 4488.

20. *SIRIO*, 93:91–95.

21. The Holy Governing Synod, a central government board composed of prelates and secular officers that ruled on church affairs, was invited to submit a statement of needs and desires (*nakaz*), to the Commission on Laws.

22. The role of the diarist's father at the Commission on Laws likewise suggests that he preferred to keep a low profile. His name appears only one time, among a list of people who signed on to an opinion by the deputy from Rybnaia Sloboda. *SIRIO*, 8:44, 93:91–92 (as cited in rotoprint edition of *Zhurnal*, 423).

23. Michelle Lamarche Marrese, *A Woman's Kingdom: Noblewomen and the Control of Property in Russia, 1700–1861* (Ithaca, 2002), 59–62.

24. From Ivan's year-end summary for 1772. *Zhurnal*, 1:14.

25. RGADA, f. 724, op. 1, d. 4096.

26. The diarist, who spent a lot of his time in visits with this uncle, did not mention this incident, probably because he was away from home moving barges through the northern waterways to Petersburg at the time.

27. RGADA, f. 724, op. 1, d. 4839.

28. Aleksandr Kamenskii details a particularly interesting case of this kind in the city of Bezhetsk at just this time. See his *Povsednevnost' russkikh gorodskikh obyvatelei: Istoricheskie anekdoty iz provintsial'noi zhizni XVIII veka*, (Moscow, 2006), 341–370; also the chapter on billeting, 291–299.

29. RGADA, f.482, op. 1, ch 2, d. 9973, ll. 1, 5, 9, 96–97, 109–110 (as cited in note #10 of the rotoprint edition of the diary).

30. *Zhurnal*, 1:14.

31. See note #10 in the rotoprint edition of *Zhurnal*, 424.

32. RGADA, f. 724, op. 1, d. 4966. For a detailed account of Khitrovo's antics, see L. R. Vaintraub, *Khram v chest' kazanskoi ikony Presviatoi Bogoroditsy v Podlipich'e: Istoriia khrama i prikhoda XVI–XXI vv.* (Dmitrov, 2005), 22–39.

33. RGADA, f. 724, op. 1, d. 5264.

34. RGADA, f. 724, op. 1, d. 5246.

35. RGADA, f. 724, op. 1, d. 5246.

36. RGADA, f. 724, op. 1, d. 5571, ll. 1–20.

37. RGADA, f. 724, op. 1, d. 5822.

38. Kamenskii, *Povsednevnost' russkikh gorodskikh obyvatelei* (Moscow, 2006), 116.

39. RGADA, f. 724, op. 1, d. 5535, ll. 1–5.

40. RGADA, f. 724, op. 1, d. 6144, ll. 3–11.

41. RGADA, f. 724, op. 1, d. 5261 (May 27, 1773).

42. *Zhurnal*, 1:45.

43. For confirmation of these subordinate posts and their holders, ratified in a general assembly of the merchants and lesser townspeople on December 22, 1775, see RGADA, f. 724, op. 1, d. 5517.

44. *Zhurnal*, 1:49. The legal minimum declarations in 1775 were set at 10,000 rubles for registration in the 1st Guild, 1,000 for 2nd Guild, and 500 for 3rd Guild.

45. Aksënov, *Genealogiia moskovskogo kupechestva*, 33–34.

46. I. S. Belaeva, "Kratkaia istoriia poiavleniia otechestv u vostochnykh slavian," in *Russkaia tsivilizatsiia*, at http://www.rustrana.ru/print.php?nid=9369 (accessed August 6, 2007).

47. *Zhurnal*, 1:80, 1:93.

48. RGADA, f. 724, op. 1, d. 5553, l. 1; TsIAM, f. 37, op. 1, d. 777, l. 5. A sampling of other such insult or dishonor cases, in addition to those cited in the previous section of this chapter, can be found at RGADA, f. 724, op. 1, d. 1588 and d. 5237.

49. Nancy Shields Kollmann, *By Honor Bound: State and Society in Early Modern Russia* (Ithaca, NY, 1999), 190–201.

50. Kamenskii, *Povsednevnost' russkikh gorodskikh obyvatelei*, 174–175. See also comment on p. 147 on possible continuing importance of "dishonor."

51. *Istoriia predprinimatel'stva v Rossii* (2 vols., Moscow, 2000), 1:225–228; Arcadius Kahan, *The Plow, the Hammer, and the Knout: An Economic History of Eighteenth-Century Russia*, ed. Richard Hellie, (Chicago, 1985), 311–318.

52. For a sampling of these between the years 1753 and 1780, see: RGADA, f. 724, op. 1, d. 2759; d. 2942; d. 3854; d. 3871; d. 3872; d. 4168; d. 4407; d. 4497; d. 4701; d. 4821; d. 4823; d. 4824; d. 4829; d. 4835; d. 4848; d. 4853; d. 4978; d. 5124; d. 5127; d. 5257; d.5260; d. 5417; d. 5661; d. 5767; d. 6131.

53. *Zhurnal*, 1: 119.

54. *Zhurnal*, 1:95, 1:120.

55. *Zhurnal*, 1:119.

56. RGADA, f. 724, op. 1, d. 5959, ll. 4–30.

57. *Zhurnal*, 1:17, 59, 62, 67, 70, 76, 89, 117, 122, 128.

58. *Zhurnal*, 1:152.

59. RGADA, f.724, op. 1, d. 5960, ll. 1–13; d. 5962, ll. 1–9; d. 5963, ll. 1–3.

60. Man'kov, *Ulozhenie 1649 goda*, 150.

61. For a concise summary of the issue, see L. F. Pisar'kova, "Razvitie mestnogo samoupravleniia v Rossii do velikikh reform: obychai, povinnost', pravo," in *Otechestvennaia istoriia* (2001), 2:3–17, and 3:25–39. Also, Boris Mironov, "Bureaucratic- or Self-Government: The Early Nineteenth Century Russian City," *Slavic Review*, 52:2 (Summer, 1993), 233–255.

3. JUNIOR MEMBER OF THE FAMILY FIRM

1. *Zhurnal*, 1:18–20.

2. *Zhurnal*, 1:34.

3. *Zhurnal*, 1:30.

4. Another merchant from Dmitrov, Eremei Fedotov Novoselov, who was at a fortress in the south of Russia to collect vodka taxes in 1772, was captured by Pugachëv and had to explain to the Dmitrov authorities what he was doing in Pugachëv's camp when Pugachëv captured the great fortress of Orenburg. RGADA, f. 724, op. 1, d. 5518, ll. 3–4.

5. Personal communication, September 3, 2007. On early Russian clocks and Russians' methods of counting time, see L. D. Raigrodskii, *Chasy i vremia* (St. Petersburg, 2001). I found only a few references to watches in personal sources of this period. One example is from the only personal memoir from the eighteenth century published in the author's lifetime, a tale done up as a literary work. See P. Z. Khomiakov, *Pokhozhdenie nekotorogo rossiianina, istinnaia povest', im samim pisannaia* (Moscow, 1790), part 2, 146, where he mentions checking his watch while traveling on campaign and being unable to sleep.

6. The Moscow manufactory evidently did not thrive and was shut down in 1778. "Ocherki istorii chasovogo dela," http://www.clock-history.com (accessed January 15, 2008).

7. *Zhurnal*, 1:30.

8. David S. Landes, *Revolution in Time: Clocks and the Making of the Modern World* (Cambridge, Mass., 1983), 133–134.

9. On significance of timepieces for culture and modern production, see V. N. Pipunyrov, *Istoriia chasov s drevneishikh vremen do nashikh dnei* (Moscow, 1982), 188–193.

10. Pavel Tolchënov was another Dmitrov merchant, a second cousin of the diarist and friend of Semën Korob'in. Pavel was twenty-four years older than the diarist and well established in Petersburg, where a few years later he transferred his official registration, declaring capital assets of 500 rubles. RGADA, f. 724, op. 1, d. 6333 (March 17, 1881).

11. Zhurnal, 1:29.

12. On the background, see David L. Ransel, *The Politics of Catherinian Russia: The Panin Party* (New Haven, 1975), especially chapter 9.

13. John T. Alexander, *Autocratic Politics in a National Crisis: The Imperial Russian Government and the Pugachev's Revolt, 1773–1775* (Bloomington, Ind., 1969), 152–153.

14. See Golubtsov, "Moskovskaia provintsial'naia vlast' i dvorianstvo v ozhidanii Pugacheva." *Staraia Moskva. Stat'i po istorii Moskvy v XVII–XIX v.v.* Sbornik pervyi (Moscow, 1929), 14; this summary language from Alexander, *Autocratic Politics,* 154.

15. See evidence in Golubtsov, "Moskovskaia provintsial'naia vlast'," 31–32.

16. *Zhurnal,* 1:35. For a detailed description of this process in another town, see Alexander, *Autocratic Politics,* 155–156.

17. Quoted in Alexander, *Autocratic Politics,* 152.

18. *Zhurnal,* 1:35.

19. For interesting observations and data on Russian naming practices, including this one, see Daniel H. Kaiser, "Naming Names in Early Modern Russia," *Harvard Ukrainian Studies,* 19 (1995), 271–291. Kaiser's student, Sophie Church, also wrote on naming practices, in her case in Tula province in the late eighteenth and early nineteenth centuries, and found that, as in the case of the Tolchënovs, names were chosen most often from saints whose feast days came near the time of birth. "Naming Practices in Tula: Local Influences of Family and Religion, 1780–1804," *Izvestiia tul'skogo gosudarstvennogo universiteta,* Seriia Istoriia i kul'turologiia, 5 (2006), 785–790.

20. *Zhurnal,* 1:31.

21. He was the son of General-Major Fëdor Ivanovich Golitsyn (1700–1759), whose first marriage was to a cousin of Peter the Great. She died young. Ivan was born of a second wife, Anna Petrovna nee Izmailova, in 1731. Ivan was also married twice, first to Nastas'ia Andreevna Saburova, who died in 1754, and then to Nadezhda Ivanovna Vikhliaeva (from 1787), but remained childless. *Istoriia rodov russkogo dvorianstva,* comp. P. N. Petrov (1886), 1:342–343.

22. *Zhurnal,* 1:60.

23. Although Ivan fails to mention it, the famine also touched some areas of Voronezh and Moscow provinces. See note in the rotoprint edition of *Zhurnal,* 425.

24. *Zhurnal,* 1:37.

25. *Zhurnal,* 142.

26. *Zhurnal,* 1:40.

27. *Zhurnal,* 1:42.

28. *Zhurnal,* 1:77–78.

29. *Zhurnal,* 1:77–79.

30. *Istoriko-statisticheskoe i arkheologicheskoe opisanie tserkvi vo imia spasa-istselitelia rasslablennogo v sele Vedernitsakh, Dmitrovskii uezd, Moskovskoi gubernii,* comp. I. Tokmakov (Moscow, 1895), 10–11. Description of the church in *Pamiatniki arkhitektury moskovskoi oblasti,* vol. 1 (Moscow, 1975), 75. See also V. Kholmogor and G. Kholmogor, *Istoricheskie materialy o tserkvakh i selakh XVI–XVIII vv.,* vyp. 11 (Moscow 1911), 366–367.

31. *Zhurnal,* 1:86.

32. It was only in the 1760s that the central government's Medicine Kollegium decided to station doctors, to the extent possible, in every city and district capital, but it was not until late in the 1770s that Dmitrov received one. Chechulin noted that people often complained that the services of a doctor cost too much, 10–25 rubles a visit (or even up to 100 rubles in countryside calls), rates that were beyond the means of most families. *Russkoe provintsial'noe obshchestvo*, 85.

33. *Zhurnal*, 1:109–110.

34. *Zhurnal*, 1:43. Ivan wrote of two fortresses, whereas we normally think of Petersburg as having only one, the Peter and Paul Fortress, which guards the Neva River from Petersburg Island. In the eighteenth century the Admiralty complex on the opposite side of the river was also fortified with walls and trenches, and it was no doubt this fortress that Ivan was referring to. Iu. K. Balenko et al. "Istoriia Admiralteistva," http://www.navy.ru/edu/admiralty/hist-a.htm (accessed January 15, 2008).

35. *Zhurnal*, 1:63.

36. From *S.-Peterburgskie vedomosti* no. 89, 1776, as cited in notes for the rotoprint portion of *Zhurnal*, note 27, p. 425.

37. *Zhurnal*, 1:65

38. *Zhurnal*, 1:122–123.

39. *Zhurnal*, 1:130, 134. Podlipich'e is now within the city of Dmitrov on its hilly eastern side. The church mentioned by Tolchënov, now the parish church, is named for the Icon of the Mother of Kazan.

40. For detailed discussion of theater in this period in Russia, see the recent studies: Elise Kimerling Wirtschafter, *The Play of Ideas in Russian Enlightenment Theater* (DeKalb, IL, 2003), and Richard Stites, *Serfdom, Society, and the Arts: The Pleasure and the Power* (New Haven, 2005).

41. I. N. Iurkin, *Demidovy: uchenye, inzhenery, organizatory nauki i proizvodstva* (Moscow, 2001), 136–137.

42. *1000 let russkogo predprinimatel'stva: Iz istorii kupecheskikh rodov* (Moscow, 1995), 99–100.

43. *Zhurnal*, 1:56, 1:82.

44. *Zhurnal*, 1:110.

45. D. S. Likhachëv, *Poeziia sadov: K semantike sadov-parkovykh stilei. Sad kak tekst*, 2nd ed. (St. Petersburg, 1991), passim.

46. *Zhurnal*, 1:136.

47. The profits for 1779 ran to 12,500 rubles, plus substantial additional receipts still coming in from non-contract sales in Petersburg. *Zhurnal*, 1:151. Compare the profits recorded here to the capital declarations of other families in 1775, all of which were under this amount (although it is true that families did not normally declare their full capital holdings). Capital listings are at *Zhurnal*, 1:49.

48. All the material here describing this trip and death are from *Zhurnal*, 1:136–139.

49. *Dictionnaire russe-français des termes en usage dans l'église russe* (Paris, 1980), 78.

50. *Zhurnal*, 1:138.

4. YOUNG PATERFAMILIAS

1. *Zhurnal*, 1:146–147.

2. *Zhurnal*, 1:141–142.

3. In the diary Ivan recorded that the name was taken, as was the Russian custom, from St. Aleksei Metropolitan of Moscow, whose feast day fell on October 10. The

number of feast days of saints within a couple of weeks of a birth and therefore the number of names that can be drawn on is large, and we can safely assume, even though Ivan did not make it explicit, that the name Aleksei was chosen in honor and remembrance of Ivan's father Aleksei. For studies of naming practices, see the sources in chapter 3, note 19 above.

4. *Zhurnal*, 1: 142–144.

5. From the year-end summary notes for 1778. *Zhurnal*, 1:120

6. *Zhurnal*, 1:95

7. A point made by Tartakovskii, *Russkaia memuaristika*, 70.

8. *Peterburgskoe kupechestvo v XIX veke,* ed. and comp. A. M. Konechnyi (St. Petersburg, 2003), 30–31.

9. *Zhurnal*, 1:212–213.

10. The historian G. F. Miller, who visited Dmitrov in 1778, wrote that the market days fell on Sundays and Thursdays but not every week. *Sochineniia po istorii Rossii. Izbrannoe* (Moscow, 1996), 307. Either some shift had occurred within a short time, or, more likely, Miller was poorly informed (his account of the town contains other mistakes), for Tolchënov's diary faithfully records the market days. Accurate accounts can also be found in *Istoricheskoe i topograficheskoe opisanie gorodov Moskovskoi gubernii s uezdami* (Moscow, 1787), 209; and L. I. Bakmeister, *Topograficheskie izvestiia, sluzhashchie dlia polnogo geograficheskogo opisaniia Rossiiskoi imperii,* vol. 1 (St. Petersburg, 1771), 30.

11. *Zhurnal*, 1:183.

12. *Zhurnal*, 1:285, 2:368, 1:312.

13. *Zhurnal*, 1:296.

14. *Zhurnal*, 1:310.

15. *Zhurnal*, 2:51–52.

16. *Zhurnal*, 1:154.

17. *Zhurnal*, 1:145.

18. *Zhurnal*, 1:172 (entry for Nov. 17).

19. *Istoricheskoe i topograficheskoe opisanie gorodov*, 209–215.

20. *Zhurnal*, 1:187.

21. *Dmitrovskii krai* (Dmitrov, 1993), 27.

22. Priscilla Roosevelt, *Life on the Russian Country Estate: A Social and Cultural History* (New Haven, 1995), 85, 98.

23. *Zhurnal*, 1:110.

24. See her memoirs. Or also Akademiia Nauk, *Istoriia Moskvy,* (Moscow, 1953), 2:577.

25. Information from government inventories cited in Akademiia Nauk, *Istoriia Moskvy,* 2: 565–567. In Ol'ga Fomina's sample of 58 Moscow merchants' properties in this period, she found that 23 (40 percent) contained parks with orchards and ponds. If this sample was typical, it would give strong confirmation to the picture painted (see below) by Peter Simon Pallas of Moscow in this period as a garden city that supplied not just itself but other cities with fruits and vegetables. Fomina, "Imushchestvenno-demograficheskaia kharakteristika moskovskoi kupecheskoi sem'i," 50.

26. P. S. Pallas, *Katalog rasteniiam, nakhodiashchimsia v Moskve v sadu . . . ego prevoskhoditel'stva . . . Prokopiia Akinfievicha Demidova* (St. Petersburg, 1781), xi–xxiii (final quotation on xiii). This property and some adjoining areas were purchased by Princess Orlova in the nineteenth century and turned into a natural garden that became a favorite spot for Muscovites to relax in. See L. P. Aleksandrov, *Proshloe neskuchnogo sada (istoricheskaia spravka)* (Moscow, 1923), 28–30 and passim. A portion of this woodland garden, though in poor repair, is still open today.

27. *Zhurnal*, 1:147.

28. Although measures were not standardized in Russia until the nineteenth century, a sazhen was usually equivalent to 2.133 meters. Local variations did, however, exist. If Ivan was calculating by the usual measure, this first orangery of his would have been about seventeen meters in length.

29. *Zhurnal*, 1:178.

30. *Zhurnal*, 1:169.

31. Vasilii Khvostov, "Zapiski Vasiliia Semënovicha Khvostova," *Russkii arkhiv* 3 (1870): 566.

32. Peter Simon Pallas, *Travels through the southern provinces of the Russian empire, in the years of 1793 and 1794*, 2nd ed. (London, 1812), 7–8.

33. *Zhurnal*, 1:172. Unfortunately, Ivan never tells us Beliaev's first name, but it may have been first-guild merchant Sergei Beliaev, a factory owner who had several ponds on his properties (see Fomina, "Imushchestvenno-demograficheskaia kharakteristika moskovskoi kupecheskoi sem'i," 50) or possibly third-guild merchant Fëdor Beliaev, who lived in the Zaprudnaia sloboda, not far from Sushchëvo (see *Materialy dlia istorii moskovskogo kupechestva: Obshchestvennye prigovory* (Moscow, 1892–1911), 4:339.

34. *Zhurnal*, 1:169, 1:201 (second date was November 25, 1781).

35. From year-end summary notes. *Zhurnal*, 1:262.

36. Entries for July 12 and 13, 1783. *Zhurnal*, 1:249.

37. Entries for August 8 and September 2, 1783. *Zhurnal*, 1: 250, 252.

38. *Zhurnal*, 1:257.

39. Not a lot is known about the poor in early modern Russian towns, but some valuable information and analysis can be found in Daniel H. Kaiser, "The Poor and Disabled in Early Eighteenth-Century Russian Towns," *Journal of Social History* 32 (1998–1999): 125–155.

40. *Zhurnal*, 1:152.

41. Entries for February 15–20. *Zhurnal*, 1:156.

42. This chandelier still adorns the center of Presentation Church.

43. *Zhurnal*, 1:207.

44. The contributions included nearly 3,000 rubles in 1786. He does not specify the contribution in 1787 but includes it in a record of 10,500 rubles in combined household expenses.

45. See, for example, the contributions and donations made in merchant wills and the introductory comments by the editor in N. V. Kozlova, ed., *Gorodskaia sem'ia XVIII veka: Semeino-pravovye akty kuptsov i raznochintsev Moskvy* (Moscow, 2002); also T. V. Kontseva, "Zaural'skoe kupechestvo i tserkov': Blagotvoritel'naia deiatel'nost' vo vtoroi polovine XVIII–seredine XIX vv.," *Religiia i tserkov' v Sibiri* (Tiumen', 1996) 30–31.

46. Kozlova, ed., *Gorodskaia sem'ia*, 31; see also the comments by the contemporary merchant writer and moralist, Aleksandr Fomin, "Pis'mo k priiateliu," 6.

47. Entry for November 1, 1780. *Zhurnal*, 1:171.

48. T. A. Bernshtam, *Molodezh' v obriadovoi zhizni russkoi obshchiny XIX–nachala XX v.* (Leningrad, 1988), 262–263.

49. *Zhurnal*, 1:198–199.

50. See on this Vladimir Dal', *Tolkovyi slovar'* (Moscow, 1955), 2:715, where he explains that this dinner usually occurs on the third or seventh day after the wedding but can even come much later. In the Tolchënovs' case, it fell on the third day after the wedding.

51. *Zhurnal*, 1:199–201.

52. *Zhurnal*, 1:284, 291.

53. *Zhurnal,* 1:333.

54. *Zhurnal,* 1: 195, 202.

55. Kamenskii notes this same ambivalence about public service in the city of Be-zhetsk. Merchants complained about it, yet they also wanted to be qualified for it, because such qualification was a confirmation of their status as a merchant and re-spected citizen. *Povsednevnost' russkikh gorodskikh obyvatelei,* 110–111.

56. *Zhurnal,* 1:189–190.

57. *Zhurnal,* 1:202. Ivan calls Maslova "assesorsha," which signals that the treasurer, officially known as *kaznachei,* was referred to locally as an assessor.

58. *Zhurnal,* 1:197.

59. In Elizaveta Ian'kova's memoirs, N. P. Obolenskii appears in old age as a proud and cantankerous landowner in a fight with his neighbors over cattle that wander onto adjoining properties (*Rasskazy Babushki,* 59–60), but Tolchënov seemed to get along fine with him.

60. *Zhurnal,* 1:218–219.

61. *Zhurnal,* 1:222–223.

62. "Medoks" is Russian for Maddox. Michael Maddox was an English magician, me-chanic, and set designer who moved his troupe into the new theater on Petrovka Boule-vard (near the later Bolshoi Theater). See Stites, *Serfdom, Society, and the Arts,* 131–132.

63. *Zhurnal,* 1:227–228.

64. The very next day he was on a visit to Prince Sergei Golitsyn, with whom he had business dealings.

65. *Zhurnal,* 1:271.

66. *Zhurnal,* 1:158–159, 178.

67. *Zhurnal,* 1:222.

68. *Zhurnal,* 1:240–241, 263.

69. *Zhurnal,* 1:246. The grounds of the magnificent Kuskovo estate were open for promenades by non-nobles on Sundays and Thursdays in the summer (the Tolchënovs were there on Sunday). On visiting Kuskovo, see Priscilla Roosevelt, *Life on the Russian Country Estate,* 140.

70. *Zhurnal,* 1:253, 263.

71. *Zhurnal,* 1:258. Marina Semënovna Tolchënova was a blood relative, the unmar-ried sister of Ivan's great-uncle Semën Borisovich. She died in 1802 from a gangrenous infection on her arm that, according to Ivan, turned into St. Anthony's Fire. *Zhurnal,* 3:131.

72. See, for example, the observations of one of the best merchant writers of the time, the Arkhangel'sk merchant A. Fomin, "Pis'mo k priiateliu," 9–11. Also "Vos-pominaniia o M. A. Makarove," *Pamiatnaia knizhka Kaluzhskoi gubernii na 1862 i 1863 gody* (Kaluga, 1863), 105–106; and G. P. Polilov-Severtsev, *Nashi dedy-kuptsy,* 3–4.

73. Kozlova, "Rossiiskii absoliutizm i kupechestvo" (1994), 528.

74. N. V. Kozlova and V. R. Tarlovskaia, "Torgovlia," *Ocherki russkoi kul'tury XVIII veka,* in 2 parts (Moscow, 1985), part 1, 254.

75. Maikov, *Betskoi,* 412–415.

76. Ivan Vavilov, *Besedy russkogo kuptsa o torgovle: Prakticheskii kurs kommercheskikh znanii* . . . (St. Petersburg, 1846), 1:253.

77. "General'noe uchrezhdenie o vospitanii oboego pola iunoshestva," a report that was confirmed by the empress in March 1764 and published in the collection of Russian laws. *Polnoe sobranie zakonov Rossiiskoi imperii,* 1st series, 30 volumes (St. Petersburg, 1830), No. 12103, and republished in a number of collections of Betskoi's writings.

78. Maikov, *Betskoi,* 402–406, for the exchange between the two men.

79. Some merchants evidently saw the foundling homes as inducements to immoral behavior. A merchant named Aleksei Smolin landed in Shlisselberg prison because he openly reproached Catherine for two decisions: secularizing church property and encouraging depravity by creating the foundling homes. V. A. Gol'tsev, "Zakonodatel'stvo i nravy v Rossii XVIII veka," *Iuridicheskii vestnik* (1886), 3:436.

80. *Zhurnal,* 1:271.

81. K. V. Sivkov, "Chastnye pansiony i shkoly Moskvy v 80-kh godakh XVIII v.," *Istoricheskii arkhiv* 6 (Moscow, 1951): 315, 319. Rafaella Faggionato suggested that the investigation of the schools was initiated by Catherine II because of concerns pressed on her by the Holy Synod about heretical and Masonic teaching in Moscow; *A Rosicrucian Utopia in Eighteenth-Century Russia: the Masonic circle of N. I. Novikov* (Dordrecht, The Netherlands, 2005), 196.

82. Sivkov, "Chastnye pansiony," 319.

83. The certification appears in a file containing a request in 1817 by Ivan Horn to open a pansion school in Moscow. TsGIAM, f. 418, op. 73, d. 1503, l. 7.

5. LEADING CITIZEN

1. From the year-end summary for 1785. *Zhurnal,* 1:323.

2. I could not find a record of the purchase from Sergei Voropanov that Ivan mentioned in the excerpt at the start of the chapter. Ivan's father bought land from Artemii Stepanov Tiut'kin in 1776 in the western or Koniushennaia sloboda section of the city where the new home was to be built. Ivan may have used much of the original property for his horticultural projects and purchased the additional property from Voropanov to accommodate the new townhouse. RGADA, f. 724, op. 1, d. 5662.

3. A. V. Iaganov and E. I. Ruzaeva, *Uspenskii sobor v Dmitrove* (Moscow, 2003), 143.

4. R. F. Khokhlov, director of the historical museum in Dmitrov, suggested on the basis of a single mention in the rotoprint edition of the diary that the province architect N. P. Osipov designed the home. Agafonov does not appear in the rotoprint edition; Khokhlov obviously never read the full diary. A report on the Tolchënov house in the Dmitrov archives by K. A. Solov'ev is even further from the mark in identifying the architect as Vasilii Bazhenov on the basis of the style alone. It is doubtful that the well-known Bazhenov was ever in the area, and he never once appears in the diary. On Khokhlov's mistaken views, see R. F. Khokhlov and E. V. Iakuta, "Pamiatniki arkhitektury Dmitrova," *Russkii gorod: issledovaniia i materialy* 2 (Moscow, 1979), 90.

5. Although Ivan referred to the home in his diary and in official documents as standing on Birch Street, the house itself lies very close to what was then Klin Road. The documents from 1785 signed by the police commissioner and a member of the magistracy (and also mentioning approval by the Governor Lopukhin) giving Ivan permission to erect the building on this property refer to it as on Birch Street. TsIAM, f. 37, op. 1, d. 767, ll. 24–240b, 53–540b.

6. *Zhurnal,* 1:302–303.

7. *Zhurnal,* 1:305.

8. *Zhurnal,* 1:315–316.

9. *Zhurnal,* 1:330.

10. *Zhurnal,* 1:358.

11. *Zhurnal,* 1:338.

12. *Zhurnal,* 1:344.

13. If Ivan's new home was the first masonry townhouse in Dmitrov, it was not something out of time or place. The late eighteenth century witnessed a remarkable development of masonry home building by nobles and merchants alike in central Russia. A report on the city of Riazan, for example, revealed that in 1784 merchants were rebuilding homes on stone foundations or constructing entire masonry homes. By 1794 the city boasted 14 masonry homes owned by nobles and merchants, of which 11 were newly built. The 770 remaining homes were, however, made of wood. Kusova, *Riazanskoe kupechestvo,* 108, 109.

14. *Zhurnal,* 2:27–28.

15. *Zhurnal,* 2:3–4.

16. It is interesting to observe that Ivan's account of the mass on June 29 at which Archbishop Platon was elevated to the rank of metropolitan reports only the fact of his promotion "by her majesty." We know from other sources that the empress surprised Platon with this announcement in the midst of the mass, much to the amusement and approval of those in attendance. See K. A. Papmehl, *Metropolitan Platon of Moscow (Petr Levshin, 1737–1812): The Enlightened Prelate, Scholar and Educator,* (Newtonville, Mass., 1983), 48. If Ivan had not realized this at the time (it seems he was not inside the cathedral for the mass), he may have learned about it later when he had a personal meeting with Metropolitan Platon.

17. Members evidently of the household of a district assessor, who is mentioned as a guest of the Tolchënovs elsewhere in the diary.

18. N. A. Naidenov, *Vospominaniia o vidennom, slyshannom i ispytannom,* 2 vols. (Moscow, 1903–1905), 1: 9–10.

19. *Russian Women 1698–1917: Experience & Expression, An Anthology of Sources,* comp. Robin Bisha et al. (Bloomington, Ind., 2002), 65–69.

20. *Rasskazy babushki,* 65–108 passim.

21. For a review of the debate, see Karin Calvert, *Children in the House: The Material of Early Childhood, 1600–1900* (Boston, 1992), Introduction.

22. *Zhurnal,* 1:139.

23. This point is admittedly speculative. I do not recall finding a reference in the diary to a wet nurse or a milk brother.

24. *Zhurnal,* 2:20–22.

25. *Zhurnal,* 2:23–24.

26. P. I. Rychkov, "Zapiski Petra Ivanovicha Rychkova," *Russkii Arkhiv* 11 (1905), 291–292, 306–316.

27. M. V. Danilov, *Zapiski artillerii maiora M. V. Danilova,* 107–111, 121.

28. *Russian Women, 1698–1917,* 65–66.

29. *Rasskazy babushki,* 70.

30. *Rasskazy babushki,* 78.

31. *Zhurnal,* 2:60–61.

32. *Zhurnal,* 2:43. Although it is difficult to find evidence for twentieth anniversary remembrances, merchants commonly set aside money in their wills for early after-death distributions to churches and to the poor in remembrance of their souls. In some cases these were quite substantial—for example, the 5,000 rubles left in the 1791 will of Moscow merchant Pavel Tokarev. See this and others in Kozlova, ed. *Gorodskaia sem'ia,* 67–236 (Tokarev will, 194–195).

33. Both this St. Nikita and St. Simeon, who appears later in the same set of diary

entries, were ascetics known for having made their abode on top of a pillar (*stylites* in Greek, and *stolp* in Russian).

34. *Zhurnal,* 2:57.

35. *Zhurnal,* 2:59.

36. Dmitrov's leadership in the grain trade was eroded with time by merchants in cities better positioned along the waterways to exploit this opportunity. As noted earlier, Dmitrov was not situated on a navigable stream.

37. *Zhurnal,* 2:55–56.

38. *Zhurnal,* 2:79–80, 83–84.

39. Letter of July 25, 1789, from Zhurnal Dmitrovskogo Dukhovnogo Pravleniia (ll. 168–168 ob.), reproduced in appendix no. 6 of Iaganov and Ruzaeva, *Uspenskii sobor,* 233–234.

40. *Zhurnal,* 2:93–94.

41. Iagonov and Ruzaeva, *Uspenskii sobor,* 143 (and associated documents in appendixes).

42. Quoted in Faggionato, *A Rosicrucian Utopia,* 195–196.

43. Iagonov and Ruzaeva, *Uspenskii sobor,* 144, 240–244 (for documents from Dmitrov Spiritual Administration, showing Ivan's contributions and desire to finish the work urgently).

44. Iagonov and Ruzaeva, *Uspenskii sobor,* 136, 145, 244–245.

45. *Zhurnal,* 2:194.

46. See the detailed discussion in Alexander, *Bubonic Plague,* especially chapter 3. Wirtschafter presents some of the maps for the newly designed towns to reinforce an argument about the porosity of social categories in imperial Russia and the government's aspiration to draw clearer lines between them. *Structures of Society,* chapter 5.

47. See chapter 4.

48. The new plan for the city made the Dormition Cathedral and old kremlin the central focus and aligned public buildings along a clearly expressed axis oriented to the main openings (the former gates) in the earthen wall. Three zones were designed: the kremlin and monumental buildings; the main square and ancient market reorganized as rectangular spaces; and much transformed posad and slobodas. Four roads cut through the city and were marked at the periphery by tall structures that unified the overall design; on the north the Tikhvin Church, on the south the Church of Our Savior; on the west the Presentation Church, and on the east the Trinity Church. N. F. Gulianitskii, ed. *Moskva i slozhivshiesia russkie goroda XVIII–pervoi poloviny XIX vekov,* 309–310. See the city map on page xxix of this volume.

49. Even though Governor Lopukhin had informed the city magistracy in May of 1785 of the need to prepare for the change, presumably in the very near future. When the governor visited the city in August of the same year, he asked that the citizens meet as a group and try to resolve any issues that the new city plan might present. TsIAM, f. 37, op. 1, d. 766, ll. 790b–80, 120–1200b.

50. For different views on the Novikov affair, see recent works by Douglas Smith, *Working the Rough Stone: Freemasonry and Society in Eighteenth-Century Russia* (DeKalb, Ill., 1999), 3, 173–174; and Faggionato, *A Rosicrucian Utopia,* 183–223.

51. Prozorovskii was himself unhappy with the assignment, as he yearned for a major military post at this time when two wars were in progress, but he understood that to refuse the empress meant the end of his career. N. F. Dubrovin, "General-fel'dmarshal

kniaz' Aleksandr Aleksandrovich Prozorovskii," *Voennyi sbornik* (St. Petersburg, 1868), 11:20, 21. See also B. Alekseevskii, "Kniaz' Aleksandr Aleksandrovich Prozorovskii," *Russkii biograficheskii slovar'*, (St. Petersburg, 1910), 7–8. For the memoirs of his early career and an introductory essay on his life, see A. A. Prozorovskii, *Zapiski generalfel'dmarshala kniazia Aleksandra Aleksandrovicha Prozorovskogo 1756–1776.* Introduction by A. K. Afanas'ev (Moscow, 2004).

52. TsIAM, f. 16, op. 1, d. 337, ll. 14–150b.

53. The essay was included in the summary material appended to the diary notes for the year 1792. *Zhurnal*, 2:208–209.

54. *Zhurnal*, 2:209–210.

55. *Zhurnal*, 2:210. Ivan's memory or notes failed him here but by only one day. The diary records the date of the bridge relocation as October 18, not 19.

56. Iaganov and Ruzaeva, *Uspenskii sobor*, 134.

57. *Zhurnal*, 2:224, 241.

6. EMINENT TRICKSTER

1. *Zhurnal*, 2:65.

2. From the summary for the year 1789. *Zhurnal*, 2:105.

3. *Zhurnal*, 2:139.

4. Blagovo was another Dmitrov district squire.

5. *Zhurnal*, 2:74.

6. The term for cousin in Russian is precisely "brother" or "sister" with an adjective ("second," "third," etc.) indicating the degree of relationship. Similarly, it will be recalled that Ivan referred to the cousin once removed with whom he stayed in Torzhok when he fell ill in 1777 as "uncle." The Russian term for a first cousin once removed in the generation of one's father is "second uncle."

7. Andrei Vasil'evich Goroshkov had been inscribed in the second guild of Moscow merchants in the censuses of 1775 and 1781 but rose to the first guild in 1786. O. V. Fomina, "Imushchestvenno-demograficheskaia kharakteristika moskovskoi kupecheskoi sem'i," appendix no. 1.

8. This section of Moscow was technically known as the Novaia Dmitrovskaia sloboda and lay just beyond the earthen wall as an extension of the Dmitrovka district inside the earthen wall. It was commonly referred to as Novoslobodskaia, and this was the term that Ivan always used. See Aver'ianov, ed., *Istoriia moskovskikh raionov, Entsiklopedia*, 65.

9. TsIAM, f. 27, op. 1, d. 6, l. 246 (inheritance case Oct. 1, 1804).

10. The Tolchënovs continued to use the mill through the summer of 1794 and then turned it over to the new lessee.

11. *Rasskazy babushki*, 156–157.

12. For a detailed study of this and other homes in Russia, see my book *Mothers of Misery: Child Abandonment in Russia* (Princeton, 1988).

13. Drazhusov, ed. *Materialy dlia istorii imperatorskogo moskovskogo vospitatel'nogo doma* (Moscow, 1863), vol. 1, sec. 3, 14–26.

14. *Zhurnal*, 2:236.

15. See the excellent study of this fashion by Thomas Newlin, *The Voice in the Garden*.

16. *Zhurnal*, 2: 255, 258, 265, 294.

17. A. I. Aksënov, who mentioned this episode, misread the passage about the lenders

and wrote that these men were the only two clients that Ivan had for milling. While the passage could possibly be read that way, Aksënov was almost certainly wrong. The larger context makes clear that Ivan was writing about the source of his money for obtaining and refurbishing the mill. Aksënov, *Ocherki genealogii uezdnogo kupechestva XVIII v.,* 96.

18. The nickname in Russian is "Rachok." *Zhurnal,* 2:271. On the property question, TsIAM, f. 37, op. 1, d. 799, ll. 151–154.

19. *Zhurnal,* 2:253.

20. *Zhurnal,* 2:202.

21. A. B. Chizhkov, *Podmoskovnye usad'by segodnia* (Moscow, 2000), 21.

22. *Zhurnal,* 2: 169–179.

23. During Paul's reign no organization was allowed to be called a "club." According to the memoirist Ivan Vtorov, Moscow then had two "academies," a musical academy for nobles and a dance academy for merchants and foreigners, which served the same functions as the earlier clubs. "Moskva i Kazan' v nachale XIX veka: Zapiski Ivana Alekseevicha Vtorova," *Russkaia starina,* 70 (1891), 4:6. As for the history of the English Club, an unsatisfactory hodgepodge of material was produced a few years ago by the revived Moscow English Club of post-Soviet Russia. Aleksei Butorov, *Moskovskii Angliiskii Klub, stranitsy istorii* (Moscow, 1999).

24. TsIAM, f. 16, op. 1, d. 355, l. 2.

25. *Rasskazy babushki,* 230. Other stories about Countess Orlova, including the rumor that her mother had been a lover of Ivan Orlov and then married her daughter to him, can be found in the letters of Catherine Wilmot, a friend of Princess Ekaterina Dashkova. See *Zapiski kniazhini Dashkovoi. Pis'ma sester Vil'mot iz Rossii,* 2nd ed. (Moscow: Sovetskaia Rossiia, 1991), 457–460.

26. TsIAM, f. 37, op. 1, d. 803, l. 60–600b.

27. TsIAM, f. 37, op. 1, d. 803, l. 113.

28. See, for example, Ivan's diary entry for January 24, 1794, in the excerpts that start off the section "Pëtr Gets Married."

29. See the essay by Jessica Tovrov, "Mother-Child Relationships among the Russian Nobility," in *The Family in Imperial Russia: New Lines of Historical Research,* 15–43.

30. Ivan gave us the dating himself. He wrote after his reflective comment on the year 1786: "This comment was written in what for me was the unfortunate year of 1796 at the time I was transcribing into book form the entire set of journal entries for 1786 as well as all the information on commercial matters, and it was not done in the course of those actual earlier years."

31. *Zhurnal,* 1:320.

32. *Zhurnal,* 1:352–353.

33. The sale was registered in Moscow. TsIAM, f. 37, op. 1, d. 806, ll. 73–74.

34. TsIAM, f. 37, op. 1, d. 803, l. 113.

35. Although distinguished merchants together with their wives and daughters were welcome at the Noble Assembly on certain occasions, according to Elizaveta Ian'kova, they were not allowed to mix with the nobles and had to watch from a distance. Cited in Alexander M. Martin, "Lost Arcadia: The 1812 War and Russian Images of Aristocratic Womanhood," *European History Quarterly* 37:4 (October 2007): 603–621.

36. The military code of the early eighteenth century (*Ustav Voinskii*), which served willy-nilly as Russia's law code throughout the century, recognized merchant account books as half-evidence in debt cases. Standard forms for recording debt were not intro-

duced through the College of Commerce until the 1770s and not widely distributed or insisted upon until 1807. See Kozlova, "Rossiiskii absoliutizm i kupechestvo," 530–531.

37. V. Ia. Baranshchikov, *Neshchastnyia prikliucheniia Vasil'ia Baranshchikova, meshchanina Nizhnego Novagoroda, v trekh chastiakh sveta,* 2nd ed. (St. Petersburg, 1787). At first believed to be a fabrication, this story corresponds to information later found in the archives about the life of the author. See R. A. Shtil'mark, *Povest' o strannike rossiiskom* (Moscow, 1962), 7–10. The trope of justice coming through the intervention of well-disposed higher authorities is common in Russia and appeared often in plays of this era, as Elise Kimerling Wirtschafter pointed out in her recent study *The Play of Ideas in Russian Enlightenment Theater;* see especially 129–146.

38. Fomina, "Imushchestvenno-demograficheskaia kharakteristika moskovskoi kupecheskoi sem'i," 32.

39. TsIAM, f. 37, op. 1, d. 809, ll. 670b–680b. *Zhurnal,* 2:303, 322.

40. *Zhurnal,* 2: 309, 322.

41. See her petitions for a separate passport under that category early the following year in TsIAM, f. 37, op. 1, d. 309, ll. 69–76.

42. Transcript of decisions in the bankruptcy trial. TsIAM, f. 37, op. 1, d. 808, ll. 54–55.

43. TsIAM, f. 37, op. 1, d. 806, ll. 175–1750b, 234–2340b, and passim.; d. 808, ll. 52–56. Colonel Gal'berg's surname is spelled Galborg in these documents.

44. TsIAM, f. 37, op. 1, d. 808, ll. 52–55.

45. The 1740 law, issued during a kind of interregnum, was evidently never properly defined and implemented, and various commissions continued through the rest of the century to work on it until finally in 1800 a new, well-defined law was promulgated. An excellent short review of the history can be found in N. V. Kozlova, "Nekotorye aspekty torgovoi deiatel'nosti v Rossii v XVIII veke (iz istorii razrabotki pravovykh dokumentov)," *Kupechestvo v Rossii XV–pervaia polovina XIX veka* (Moscow, 1997), 194–218. The French law is referenced in the seven-volume manual on trade compiled by M. D. Chulkov, *Istoricheskoe opisanie rossiiskoi kommertsii,* vol. 1, bk. 1, 39–40. The "Ustav o bankrotakh" of 1740 can be found in *Polnoe sobranie zakonov rossiiskoi imperii,* ser. 1 (December 15, 1740), no. 8300.

46. Kahan, *The Plow, the Hammer, and the Knout,* 312.

47. Ivan's debts to his uncles amounted to 14,558 rubles, or approximately the market price of his townhouse, which undoubtedly had been used as implied collateral.

48. The decree is in *Polnoe sobranie zakonov,* ser. 1 (November 7, 1775), no. 14,392.

49. The decision is in TsIAM, f. 37, op. 1, d. 808, ll. 52–65.

50. TsIAM, f. 37, op. 1, d. 808, ll. 63–65.

51. The loan may indeed have been mediated by Iushkov, as Ivan visited him in Moscow on the day the promissory note was signed, February 4, 1795.

52. Michelle Lamarche Marrese, *A Woman's Kingdom: Noblewomen and the Control of Property in Russia,* see especially chapter 2.

53. "Ustav o bankrotakh," *Polnoe sobranie zakonov,* ser. 1 (December 19, 1800), no. 19,692, article 111.

54. See, for example, Fomin, "Pis'mo k priiateliu," 19–20; *Druzheskie sovety molodomu cheloveku, nachinaiushchemu zhit' v svet* (Moscow, 1765); *Kliuch kupechestva* (St. Petersburg, 1768); *Sokrashchenie glavneishikh dolzhnostei koi kazhdyi Khristianin obiazan ispolniat' v tochnosti po svoemu zvaniiu i sostoianiiu.* Izd. Avg. Vitsman (St. Petersburg, 1799).

55. *Zhurnal*, 2: 358–59.

56. *Zhurnal*, 2:358–359.

57. *Zhurnal*, 2:359.

7. MOSCOW TOWNSMAN

1. This was a foretaste of the coronation entry. Paul would be the first Russian emperor to ride horseback on that occasion. Wortman, *Scenarios of Power*, 1:175.

2. Wortman, *Scenarios of Power*, 1: 176.

3. For an excellent summary and analysis, see Wortman, *Scenarios of Power*, 1: 171–174.

4. At the start of the third leather-bound volume, which begins with the diary entry for January 1, 1798, Ivan writes that "this book is begun on December 27, 1804." In other words, he was transcribing his diary notes into this impressive form for preservation with about a seven-year lag. If he was more or less consistent in this pace, he would have written the summary reports on the first year of Paul's reign in 1802, that is in the year following Paul's death.

5. *Zhurnal*, 2:331.

6. K. A. Papmehl, *Metropolitan Platon of Moscow*, 70–71.

7. I. V. Lopukhin, *Zapiski senatora I. V. Lopukhina* (London, 1859; in 1990 reprint by Nauka, Moscow), 75–76.

8. *Zhurnal*, 2:72–73. On the fate of Prince Vasilii Fedorovich Sibirskii and other highly placed victims of Paul's wrath, see M. V. Klochkov, *Ocherki pravitel'stvennoi deiatel'nosti vremeni Pavla I* (Petrograd, 1916), 117–119 and appendixes.

9. For a fuller description of the celebration, see the memoir of another merchant, Ivan Vtorov, "Moskva i Kazan' v nachale XIX veka," 11.

10. Count Petr Alekseevich Palen was sometimes known by a German name, von der Pahlen, which Ivan may have garbled in his rendering. Possibly, too, as Alexander Martin suggested to me, it could be a fusion of Palen and another recently active high official, Admiral Osip Deribas (although Deribas died in December 1800 before the assassination of Paul).

11. Known in Russian as the Zaikonospasskii Monastery, so named because it stood in Kitaigorod behind the lane where icons were sold.

12. As mentioned in a note in chapter 1, the designation "people of various ranks" (*raznochintsy* in Russian) was applied in numerous and changing ways in the eighteenth century. The government tried to classify people according to their social or economic function, but, as Elise Kimerling Wirtschafter explained in *Structures of Society: Imperial Russia's "People of Various Ranks,"* many persons had moved out of the classification applying to their parents but did not fit neatly into another social category. They were captured in the classification "people of various ranks." Ivan should now have been registered in the tax category of "lesser town dweller" (after having lost his status as a merchant), but possibly because of his position as a "distinguished citizen," he could claim admission to the category "people of various ranks."

13. Ivan refers to the icon as "Utolenie pechali." The icon is currently held in the Nikolo-Kuznetskaia church in Moscow.

14. *Zhurnal*, 2:365.

15. Compare the comments on the classical Greek concept of *philos* in Anthony

Giddens, *Modernity and Self-Identity,* 87. The mid-nineteenth-century dictionary of Vladimir Dal' indicates a range of meanings for the term *priiatel'* in the following order of preference: "a person amicable toward another, a well-wisher, a protector/benefactor, friend."

16. Although merchants and nobles mixed socially on many occasions and even intermarried in the eighteenth century, it is hard to find specific examples of friendships. On intermarriage of nobles and merchants, see the studies by N. Chulkov, "Moskovskoe kupechestvo XVIII i XIX vekov," *Russkii arkhiv* 4 (1907):9–12, 489–502, and Fomina, "Imushchestvenno-demograficheskaia kharakteristika moskovskoi kupecheskoi sem'i, 152–159. For some examples of social mixing, see V. P. Uspenskii, *Zapiska o proshlom goroda Ostashkova Tverskoi gubernii* (Tver', 1893), 45, and I. N. Iurkin, *Abram Bulygin: chudnosti, veselosti, "neponiatnaia filosofiia . . ."* (Tula, 1994), 110–117.

17. Even the playing card factory that he claimed to have owned with his partner Nikolai Mal'tsov was apparently held in Mal'tsov's or someone else's name. Russian scholars who worked with Ivan's journal could not find a record of his ownership of enterprises in Moscow. See the essay by N. I. Pavlenko in the rotoprint edition of the journal, 13.

18. *Zhurnal,* 2:357; on Pinetti, see "Sheval'e Pinetti," at http://www.avvv.ru/pinetti .htm (accessed January 15, 2008).

19. Drazhusov, ed. *Materialy dlia istorii imperatorskogo moskovskogo vospitatel'nogo doma,* 23–25.

20. Drazhusov, ed. *Materialy dlia istorii imperatorskogo moskovskogo vospitatel'nogo doma,* 25–26.

21. For more about the colorful figure Gavrila Riumin and his rise from poverty to enormous wealth, in no small measure from securing liquor franchises, see Kusova, *Riazanskoe kupechestvo,* 75–81 and passim.; and D. I. Rostislavov, *Provincial Russia in the Age of Enlightenment: The Memoir of a Priest's Son,* trans. and ed. Alexander M. Martin (DeKalb, IL, 2002), 208–218.

22. *Zhurnal,* 3:49.

23. *Zhurnal,* 3:69.

24. *Zhurnal,* 3:44–45.

25. Thanks go to my colleague Ann Carmichael for hints about the illness and also to the Kenneth F. Kiple, ed., *Cambridge World History of Human Disease* (New York, 1993).

26. *Zemnaia zhizn' presviatoi bogoroditsy i opisanie sviatykh chudotvornykh ee ikon,* comp. Sofiia Snessoreva, 104–105, 345. The chapel and icon were removed during the Soviet period but are once again in their former place at the entry into Red Square.

27. Although Ivan referred to him as Konstantinovich, Father Terentii's family name was officially listed in church records as Konstantinov. He was about thirty-three years old at this time and continued as Ivan's confessor for many years, even after Ivan moved from the parish. Father Terentii, sometimes with his wife Evdokiia, would visit the Tolchënovs socially. Basic information on Terentii from *Ispovednaia vedomost', Uspeniia tserkov' na Vrazhke, Nikitskogo soroka g. Moskvy,* 1803. TsIAM, f. 2124, op. 1, d. 2591.

28. *Zhurnal,* 3:48–49.

29. Kh. Peken, *Domashnii lechebnik* (St. Petersburg, 1765), 85–88.

30. Matvei Khristianovich Peken, *Novyi domashnii lechebnik* (Moscow, 1796), 136–142.

31. M. Peken, *Novyi domashnii lechebnik,* 69–70.

32. M. Peken, *Novyi domashnii lechebnik,* 49–50; Matvei Peken, *Fiziologiia ili nauka o estestve chelovecheskom* (St. Petersburg, 1788), 147, 249–249; Matvei Peken, *O sokhranenii zdraviia i zhizni,* 2nd ed. (Moscow, 1812), 97–109.

33. *Zhurnal,* 3:56.

34. *Zhurnal,* 56–57.

35. Alexander, *Bubonic Plague,* 141–142 and passim.

36. This and preceding quotes from *Zhurnal,* 3:56–61.

37. *Zhurnal,* 3:61–62.

38. *Zhurnal,* 3:92.

39. If one leaves aside the presence of Dmitrii Ivanovich at the brief meeting with Uncle Mikhaila in June 1797.

40. *Zhurnal,* 3:66.

41. Dmitrov revision lists 1815–1833, TsIAM, f. 1633, op. 1, d. 32, ll. 137–138.

42. *Zhurnal,* 3:69, 98.

43. The Novaia Dmitrovskaia sloboda was located just beyond the Zemliannoi val section of the city as an extension of Dmitrovka district. Aver'ianov, ed., *Istoriia moskovskikh raionov, Entsiklopedia,* 65.

44. *Zhurnal,* 3:83–84.

45. Ivan later identified Ivan Iakimov as Ivan Iakimov Suslov. *Zhurnal,* 3:96.

46. See, for example, V. Kolosov, ed., *Letopis' o sobytiiakh v g. Tveri tverskogo kuptsa Mikhaila Tiul'pina 1762–1823 gg.,* 26–28; Vishniakov, *Svedeniia,* 2:82.

8. A NEW EQUILIBRIUM

1. By the end of the eighteenth century the turnover at the fair had reached thirty million rubles. A fire in 1816 destroyed many of the buildings housing the fair at Makar'ev Monastery, and it was moved closer to Nizhnii Novgorod and henceforth known as the Nizhnii Novgorod Fair. It continued to meet right up to the Russian Revolution of 1917 and into the Soviet period, ending only in 1929. From the *Bol'shaia sovetskaia entsiklopediia,* by way of Yandex online at http://slovari.yandex.ru/art .xml?art=bse/00044/75200.htm&encpage=bse&mrkp (accessed January 15, 2008). For colorful descriptions of life at the fair around the time the Tolchënovs were going there, see the reminiscences of a doctor to the imperial family, G. Reman, "Makar'evskaia iarmonka," *Severnyi arkhiv* (1822), 8:138–156, and 9: 199–242.

2. Information on occupations of these merchants in *Materialy dlia istorii moskovskogo kupechestva,* 4: 21, 52, 54.

3. Most likely the Sitnikov in Petersburg was a relative who was cooperating with the Moscow Sitnikovs in business or operating the Petersburg branch, where Iakov was working. *Zhurnal,* 3: 180, 192–197. On the Sitnikov Moscow family see, Aksënov, *Genealogiia moskovskogo kupechestva,* passim.

4. The decision to move the school was made in 1799, and student recruitment then ended in Moscow. After a few years, however, a new commercial school opened in Moscow. The entire vol. 4 of Storozhev, ed., *Istoriia moskovskogo kupecheskogo obshchestva, 1863–1813,* is devoted to the history of the school.

5. Briantsev, *Kul'tura russkogo kupechestva,* 40–41, and the sources, memoirs, and foreigners' accounts cited there.

6. Such "releases" had tax implications and were by no means a mere formality. City officials kept careful records of people released on passport to work for others, for

travel on business, and the like (and those allowed passports to visit relatives in other towns, to go on pilgrimages, or to represent city institutions before other government bodies), because taxes had to be paid by the community (*mir*) as a whole, and they had to know the whereabouts of each obligated member. A. V. Demkin, *Kupechestvo v Rossii XVIII vek: Formirovanie gorodskikh kupecheskikh soobshchestv i torgovo-promyshlennyi otkhod. Ocherki* (Moscow, 1996), 13–14.

7. *Zhurnal*, 3:110.

8. Shishkov was not born wealthy. He claimed his family had only fifteen "souls." But he received a number of villages in Kashin district from Emperor Paul in 1797 for his service to the state. Alexander M. Martin was kind enough to provide an archival reference to Shishkov's last will and testament, in which these properties are listed. See: Rossiiskii Gosudarstvennyi Istoricheskii Arkhiv, f. 1673, op. 1, d. 5, ll. 1, 12.

9. He was later well known to Moscow citizens for having supplied militias to fight against the Napoleonic army in 1812 and for his cultural interests in Russian antiquities. D. V. Monaev, "Vydaiushchiesia kuptsy Rossii," Kurskii gosudarstvennyi tekhnicheskii universitet, at http://vm71.narod.ru/works/063/kupech.doc (accessed July 26, 2007). See also Aksënov, *Genealogiia moskovskogo kupechestva*, 67. The title "honored citizen" (*pochetnyi grazhdanin*) was established in 1832 by Emperor Nicholas I. It was bestowed on non-noble government officials who had higher education, the upper echelon of merchants and industrialists, and legitimate children of personal (as distinguished from hereditary) nobles. It was different from the honor of "distinguished citizen" that Ivan Tolchenov held. The distinguished citizen category was created by the Charter to the Towns of 1785. It was abolished with the introduction of the honored citizen designation.

10. On the earlier reports, N. V. Kozlova, "Organizatsiia kommercheskogo obrazovaniia v Rossii v XVIII v.," *Istoricheskie zapiski* 117 (1989), 289.

11. His initial attempt, at first approved, was then rejected on the grounds that he had insufficient capital to qualify as a guild merchant. He was soon after able to parlay his achievements as an actor into an exemption on the basis of the provisions in the Charter on Towns for meritorious artists. TsIAM, f. 2, op. 1, d. 430 and 780 (March 30, 1816, and April 30, 1819), and f. 1633, op. 1, d. 32, l. 148 ob.

12. Pavel died in 1862. Fragments about him can by found in the index of M. N. Laskina, *P. S. Mochalov: letopis' zhizni i tvorchestva* (Moscow, 2000). My thanks to Richard Stites for this reference.

13. His best known plays were "Gubernskie spletni" and "Kuter'ma 1 aprelia." After the 1850s Aleksandr's career moved to the provinces. He died in 1888. Bol'shoi Russkii Biograficheskii Slovar', available at http://www.rulex.ru/01190362.htm (accessed January 15, 2008).

14. The phrase Ivan used in noting his visits was: "byl v lavke u syna Iakova."

15. TsIAM, f. 1633, op. 1, d. 32, l. 148 ob.

16. The Makarovs had at least two more sons. Aksënov mentions one, Nikolai, who died in childhood. Aksënov, *Ocherki genealogii uezdnogo kupechestva*, 11, 78. The other was Ivan, born about 1803. On this and the family's descent to lesser townspeople, see 1811 census, TsIAM, f. 1633, op. 1, d. 14, ll. 3 and 105ob.

17. *Zhurnal*, 3:239–240.

18. Stites, *Serfdom, Society, and the Arts*, 148–152.

19. Today known as Spas-Zaulok.

20. For survey of early times, see S. V. Kornilov, *Drevnerusskoe palomnichestvo* (Kaliningrad, 1995).

21. The area is now in Moscow just east of Sokol'niki Park where a street named Bogorodskii Val runs. The property had belonged to the Monastery of the Miracles until the 1760s when church property was secularized.

22. *Zhurnal,* 3:114–115. Ivan called the monastery simply Ugreshskii.

23. For more on the churches, see William Craft Brumfield, *Gold in Azure: One Thousand Years of Russian Architecture* (Boston, 1983), 128–133.

24. *Zhurnal,* 3:140–141.

25. *Zhurnal,* 3:144.

26. *Zhurnal,* 3:187.

27. *Zhurnal,* 3:188.

28. Although Ivan had apparently been unaware of it, this area of Russia was heavily populated by poor nobles who lived in much the same way as the peasants. See Isabel de Madariaga, *Russia in the Age of Catherine the Great* (New Haven, 1981), 81 (and the sources cited there).

29. The noble writer and traveler Petr Chelishchev described the facility, which he called the Antonievskaia Dymskaia pustynka, as it was in 1791. It served then as a parish church, albeit without parishioners because of the predominance of Old Believers in the district. Petr Ivanovich Chelishchev, *Puteshestvie po Severu Rossii v 1791 godu: Dnevnik* (St. Petersburg, 1886), 255–256.

30. *Zhurnal,* 3:190. Tikhvin enjoyed great prosperity in this period, perhaps because of the presence of Old Believers. According to Chelishchev, of the 3,451 citizens, merchants far outnumbered lesser town dwellers, an unusual proportion. Chelishchev, like Ivan, also remarked on the extraordinarily good order of the monastery. *Puteshestvie po Severu Rossii,* 259–263.

31. Ivan called it simply "Dneprovskaia rusalka." The opera was a reworking of "Das Donauweibchen," done by Cavos with the collaboration of another composer, Stepan Davydov. See *Bol'shoi russkii biograficheskii slovar'* at http://www.rulex.ru/01119389.htm (accessed January 15, 2008).

32. Entry for July 16. *Zhurnal,* 3:196.

33. Wortman, *Scenarios of Power,* 137–138; Andrei Zorin, *Kormia dvuglavogo orla . . . Literatura i gosudarstvennaia ideologiia v Rossii v poslednei treti XVIII–pervoi treti XIX veka* (Moscow, 2001), passim.

34. Faggionato, *A Rosicrucian Utopia;* Smith, *Working the Rough Stone.*

35. *Zhurnal,* 3:185. Petr Chelishchev described the city and its lucrative Siberian trade in great detail during his trip in 1791. They ran a three-way commercial circuit, selling metal goods to the Aleuts in return for furs, which they then traded in China for finished products that they sold in central Russia at a handsome profit. The city sometimes suffered, however, when abuses of the Aleuts or a break in the China trade disrupted the circuit. Chelishchev, *Puteshestvie po Severu Rossii v 1791 godu,* 190–201.

36. The trip lasted from June 9 until July 4. *Zhurnal,* 3:216–220.

37. Information drawn from Aksënov, *Genealogiia moskovskogo kupechestva,* 79, 80, 86; and *Materialy dlia istorii moskovskogo kupechestva,* 4:203, 7:208.

38. L. R. Vaintraub and I. A. Levakov, "Novye materialy po istorii usad'by Muranovo v XVII-XIX vv." *Materialy tvorcheskogo otcheta tresta "Mosoblstroirestavratsiia"* (Moscow, 1984), accessed through the website Portal arkheologia.ru, at http://www.archeo logia.ru/Library/Book/0b75a5b685d1/Info (accessed January 15, 2008), 40.

39. TsIAM, f. 127, op. 2, t. 1, d. 99, ll. 1–17.

40. We learn explicitly about the addition to the factory only in the entry for October 1, 1809, when Ivan reports on a fire that damaged a portion of it. But we can date the construction of the addition to early 1808 by Ivan's intensive activity in purchasing at lumberyards and working with artisans and contractors.

41. *Zhurnal*, 3:224.

42. Oleg Ivanov, *Graf Aleksei Grigor'evich Orlov-Chesmenskii v Moskve*, (Moscow, 2002), 364–380; O. Ivanov, "Syn Alekseia Grigor'evicha Orlova," *Moskovskii zhurnal* (Pravoslavnoe informatsionnoe agentstvo, Russkaia liniia), April 1, 2001, available at http://www.rusk.ru/st.php?idar=800477 (accessed January 15, 2008).

43. This failure to warn citizens and to give them time to organize their goods for departure caused quite a bit of anger later, which is reflected in a number of memoirs by commercial people. See, for example, Vishniakov, *Svedeniia*, 2:37–48; and G. N. Kol'chugin, "Zapiski G. N. Kol'chugina," *Russkii arkhiv* 9 (1879): 46. Also see the angry comments by Vasilii Popov and others cited in Alexander M. Martin, "The Response of the Population of Moscow to the Napoleonic Occupation of 1812," in *The Military and Society in Russia 1450–1917*, ed. Eric Lohr and Marshall Poe (Leiden, 2002), 469–489.

44. *Zhurnal*, 3:329–330. The road to Iaroslavl and the evacuees at this time are described in the memoirs of another merchant, Nikolai Fedorovich Kotov. See the collection *Kupecheskie dnevniki i memuary kontsa XVIII–pervoi polviny XIX veka* (Moscow, 2007), 36–44.

45. TsIAM, f. 203, op. 747, d. 841, l. 46.

46. TsIAM, f. 1633, op. 1, d. 32, ll. 120–121.

CONCLUSION

1. A. P. Berezin, "Sokrashchennaia zhizn' pokoinogo Sanktpeterburgskogo kuptsa pervoi gil'dii Aleksandra Petrovicha Berezina," *Russkii arkhiv* (1879), kn. 1, vyp. 2, 227–235; on his charitable contributions to churches, see A. G. Mel'nik essay "Unikal'naia ikona Dmitriia Rostovskogo" and notes at: http://nature.web.ru/db/msg.html?mid=1186522&s= (accessed January 15, 2008).

2. Rychkov, "Zapiski"; Polilov, *Nashi dedy-kuptsy*; Vishniakov, *Svedeniia*; Preobrazhenskii, "'Pamiatnaia kniga' moskovskogo kuptsa"; Baranshchikov, *Neshchastnyia prikliucheniia Vasil'ia Baranshchikova*.

3. Gregory L. Freeze, "The *Soslovie* (Estate) Paradigm in Russian Social History," *American Historical Review* 91:1 (February, 1986), 11–36, especially 19–25.

4. On the changes that followed the invasion, see the review of memoir literature on this in A. G. Tartakovskii, *Russkaia memuaristika i istoricheskoe soznanie XIX veka* (Moscow, 1997); and on memoirs, petitions, and other sources in Alexander M. Martin, "The Response of the Population of Moscow," esp. 485–489.

5. Kozlova, "Rossiiskii absoliutizm i kupechestvo," 545–547. On the general problem of the crisis of the urban estate, see Manfred Hildermeier, *Bürgertum und Stadt in Russland 1760–1870: rechtliche Lage und soziale Struktur* (Cologne, 1986), 152–153 and passim. Also see questions asked about Hildermeier's conception in S. K. Lebedev and B. N. Mironov, "Novaia kontseptsiia russkogo doindustrial'nogo goroda: Manfred Khil'dermaier o russkom doreformennom gorode," in *Gosudarstvennye instituty i obshchestvennye otnosheniia v Rossii XVIII–XX vv. v zarubezhnoi istoriografii* (St. Petersburg, 1994)," 32–50.

6. Although this provision was abolished and replaced in 1832 with another means of achieving enduring rights without being ennobled, the position of "honored citizen." See note 9 in chapter 8 above.

7. Unfortunately, as Natal'ia Kozlova has pointed out, no sufficiently detailed study has been made that would allow comparisons of the ennoblement of commoners over time and whether it was becoming more or less common as the century wore on. "Gil'deiskoe kupechestvo v Rossii," 228–229.

8. Kozlova, "Rossiiskii absoliutizm," 562–565.

9. See my essay on portraits of merchants, "Neither Nobles Nor Peasants: Plain Painting and the Emergence of the Merchant Estate," in Kivelson and Neuberger, *Picturing Russia: Explorations in Visual Culture* (New Haven, 2008). Also A. V. Semë-nova, "Idei Prosveshcheniia i tret'e soslovie v Rossii," in *Mirovospriiatie i samosoznanie russkogo obshchestva (XI–XX vv.)* (Moscow, 1994), 134–137; and Kozlova, "Rossiiskii absoliutizm," 544.

10. Chechulin, *Russkoe provintsial'noe obshchestvo*, 84.

Bibliography

ARCHIVAL SOURCES

The two principal repositories of unpublished documents used for this study were the Russian State Archive of Ancient Acts (RGADA) and the Central Historical Archive of Moscow (TsIAM), both located in the city of Moscow. In RGADA the collections used included no. 16 on the grain trade to St. Petersburg, no. 304 on the investigation of the Dmitrov voevoda, and no. 724 (alternatively numbered 482), the archive of the Dmitrov voevoda chancery, 1731–1782. At TsIAM I used collections no. 2 for information on Pavel Tolchenov, no. 16 for a survey of Dmitrov city and district in the 1790s and also the rules of the Moscow English Club, and especially no. 37, the archive of the Dmitrov city magistracy. I also used a number of other collections at TsIAM, including no. 418 on Moscow University and private schools in Moscow and no. 1633, the archive of the Dmitrov city duma. The staff of the archive of Dmitrov city and district provided personal assistance and guidance, plus copies of local maps from the eighteenth century.

PUBLISHED SOURCES

Adams, Matthew. "Hybridising habitus and reflexivity: towards an understanding of contemporary identity?" *Sociology* 40 (3) (2006): 511–528.

Akademiia Nauk, *Istoriia Moskvy.* 6 vols. in 7, 1952–1959. Vol. 2. Moscow, 1953.

Aksënov, A. I. *Genealogiia moskovskogo kupechestva XVIII v.* Moscow, 1988.

———. *Ocherki genealogii uezdnogo kupechestva XVIII v.* Moscow, 1993.

Aleksandrov, L. P. *Proshloe neskuchnogo sada (istoricheskaia spravka).* Moscow, 1923.

Alekseevskii, B. "Kniaz' Aleksandr Aleksandrovich Prozorovskii," *Russkii biograficheskii slovar'* 14: 4–11. St. Petersburg, 1910.

Alexander, John T. "Adventures of a Russian-American Citizen of the Universe: Fedor Vasil'evich Karzhavin (1745–1812)," in *Eighteenth-Century Russia: Society, Culture, Economy,* ed. Rogert Bartlett and Gabriela Lehmann-Carli. Berlin, 2007, 459–471.

———. *Autocratic Politics in a National Crisis: The Imperial Russian Government and Pugachev's Revolt, 1773–1775.* Bloomington, 1969.

———. *Bubonic Plague in Early Modern Russia: Public Health and Urban Disaster.* Baltimore, 1980.

Artynov, Aleksandr. *Vospominaniia kres'tianina sela Ugodich, Iaroslavskoi gubernii Rostovskogo uezda.* Introduction by A. A. Titov. Moscow, 1882.

Aseev, B. N. *Russkii dramaticheskii teatr ot ego istokov do kontsa XVIII veka.* 2nd ed. Moscow, 1977.

Aver'ianov, K. A., ed. *Istoriia moskovskikh raionov, Entsiklopediia.* Moscow, 2005.

Baklanova, N. A. "O sostave bibliotek moskovskikh kuptsov vo vtoroi chetverti XVIII v." *TODRL Instituta russkoi literatury AN SSSR* 14:644–648. Moscow, 1958.

Bakmeister, L. I. *Topograficheskie izvestiia, sluzhashchie dlia polnogo geograficheskogo opisaniia Rossiiskoi imperii.* Vol. 1, parts 1–4. St. Petersburg, 1771–1774.

Baranshchikov, V. Ia. *Neshchastnyia prikliucheniia Vasil'ia Baranshchikova, meshchanina Nizhnego Novagoroda v trekh chastiakh sveta: v Amerike, Azii i Evrope, s 1780 po 1787 god.* St. Petersburg, 1787.

Barklai, Irina Evgen'evna, ed. *Dnevniki tverskikh kuptsov,* Tver': Tverskoi gosudarstvennyi tekhnicheskii universitet, 2002.

Barnouw, Dagmar. *Critical Realism: History, Photography, and the Work of Siegfried Kracauer.* Baltimore, 1994.

Baryshnikov, M. N. *Delovoi mir Rossii. Istoriko-biograficheskii spravochnik.* St. Petersburg, 1998.

Belaeva, I. S. "Kratkaia istoriia poiavleniia otechestv u vostochnykh slavian." Russkaia tsivilizatsiia, at http://www.rustrana.ru/print.php?nid=9369 (accessed August 6, 2007). To display the page in Cyrillic, go to the View menu (Windows; for Mac users, the Page menu) and choose Character EncodingCyrillic.

Berezin, A. P. "Sokrashchennaia zhizn' pokoinogo Sanktpeterburgskogo kuptsa pervoi gil'dii Aleksandra Petrovicha Berezina," *Russkii arkhiv* 1: 2 (1879): 227–235.

Bernshtam, T. A. *Molodezh' v obriadovoi zhizni russkoi obshchiny XIX–nachala XX v.* Leningrad, 1988.

Bernshtein-Kogan, S. V. *Vyshnevolotskii put'.* Moscow, 1946.

Bernstein, Lina. "Russian Eighteenth-Century Merchant Portraits in Words and Oil." *Slavic and East European Journal* 49 (3) (Fall 2005), 407–429.

Bochkarev, V. N. *Kul'turnye zaprosy russkogo obshchestva nachala tsarstvovaniia Ekateriny II: Po materialam zakonodatel'noi komissii 1767 g.* Petrograd, 1915.

Boerner, Peter. *Tagebuch.* Stuttgart, 1969.

Bogdanov, A. I. *Opisanie Sanktpeterburga* [reprint of 18th century work]. St. Petersburg, 1997.

Bolotov, A. T. *Zapiski Andreia Timofeevicha Bolotova, 1737–1796.* 2 vols. Tula, 1988.

Borovoi, S. Ia. "Voprosy kreditovaniia torgovli i promyshlennosti v ekonomicheskoi politike Rossii XVIII veka." *Istoricheskie zapiski,* no. 33 (1950): 92–122.

Bourdieu, Pierre. *Outline of a Theory of Practice.* Trans. Richard Nice. Cambridge, 1989.

Briantsev, M. V. *Kul'tura russkogo kupechestva: Vospitanie i obrazovanie.* Briansk, 1999.

Brumfield, William Craft. *Gold in Azure: One Thousand Years of Russian Architecture.* Boston, 1983.

Buckler, Julie A. *Mapping St. Petersburg: Imperial Text and Cityscape.* Princeton, 2005.

Buryshkin, P. A. *Moskva kupecheskaia.* New York, 1954.

Bushkovitch, Paul. *The Merchants of Moscow 1580–1650.* Cambridge, UK, 1980.

Butorov, Aleksei. *Moskovskii Angliiskii Klub, stranitsy istorii.* Moscow, 1999.

Buturlin, M. D. "Zapiski grafa Mikhaila Dmitrievicha Buturlina. Vospominaniia . . ." *Russkii arkhiv* 35:2 (1897): 213–247; 35:7 (1897): 337–439.

Calvert, Karin. *Children in the House: The Material of Early Childhood, 1600–1900.* Boston, 1992.

Chelishchev, Petr Ivanovich. *Puteshestvie po Severu Rossii v 1791 godu: Dnevnik.* St. Petersburg, 1886.

Chechulin, N. D. *Memuary, ikh znachenie i mesto v riadu istoricheskikh istochnikov.* St. Petersburg, 1891.

——. "Otvet retsenzentu 'Russkoi Mysli.'" Offprint of essay published in *Zhurnal Ministerstva Narodnogo Prosveshcheniia* (May, 1890).

——. *Russkoe provintsial'noe obshchestvo vo vtoroi polovine XVIII v.* St. Petersburg, 1889.

Chizhkov, A. B. *Podmoskovnye usad'by segodnia.* Moscow, 2000.

Chulkov, M. D. *Istoricheskoe opisanie rossiiskoi kommertsii*. Vols. 1–7, St. Petersburg, 1781–1788.

Chulkov, N. "Moskovskoe kupechestvo XVIII i XIX vekov," *Russkii arkhiv* 4: 9–12 (1907): 489–502.

Church, Sophie. "Naming Practices in Tula: Local Influences of Family and Religion, 1780–1804." *Izvestiia tul'skogo gosudarstvennogo universiteta*, Seriia Istoriia i kul'turologiia 5 (2006): 785–790.

Confino, Michael. "Issues and Nonissues in Russian Social History and Historiography." *Occasional Paper, Kennan Institute for Advanced Russian Studies*, no. 165.

Dal', Vladimir. *Tolkovyi slovar'*. 4 vols. Moscow, 1955.

Danilov, M. V. *Zapiski artillerii maiora M. V. Danilova, napisannye im samim v 1771 godu*. Introduction by Paval Stroev. Moscow, 1842.

Davis, Natalie Zemon. "Boundaries and Sense of Self in Sixteenth-Century France." In *Reconstructing Individualism: Autonomy, Individuality, and the Self in Western Thought*, ed. Thomas C. Heller, Morton Sosna, and David E. Wellbery. Stanford, 1986, 53–63.

Delovoi mir Rossii: istoriko-biograficheskii spravochnik. St. Petersburg, 1998.

Demkin, A. V. *Gorodskoe predprinimatel'stvo na rubezhe XVII–XVIII vekov*. Moscow, 2000.

——. "Kupecheskie nakazy 1767 g. v Ulozhennuiu komissiiu," *Kupechestvo v Rossii XV–pervaia polovina XIX veka* (Moscow, 1997), 219–231.

——. *Kupechestvo i gorodskoi rynok v Rossii vo vtoroi chetverti XVIII veka*. Moscow, 1999.

——. *Kupechestvo v Rossii XVIII vek: Formirovanie gorodskikh kupecheskikh soobshchestv i torgovo-promyshlennyi otkhod. Ocherki*. Moscow, 1996 [an offprint of three essays].

——. *Russkoe kupechestvo XVII–XVIII vv: Goroda Verkhnevolzh'ia*. Moscow, 1990.

Dickinson, Sara. "The Russian Tour of Europe Before Fonvizin: Travel Writing as Literary Endeavor in Eighteenth-Century Russia." *Slavic and East European Journal* 45 (1) (2000): 1–29.

Dictionnaire russe-français des termes en usage dans l'église russe. Paris, 1980.

Didier, Béatrice. *Le journal intime*. Paris, 1976.

——. "Pour une sociologie du journal intime." In *Le journal intime et ses formes littéraires: Actes du Colloque de septembre 1975*, comp. V. Del Litto (Geneva, 1978), 245–248.

Dil'tei, F. G. *Sobranie nuzhnykh veshchei dlia sochineniia novoi geografii o Rossiiskoi imperii*. St. Petersburg, 1781.

Ditiatin, I. *Ustroistvo i upravlenie gorodov Rossii*. Vol. 1, St. Petersburg, 1875. Vol. 2, Iaroslavl', 1877.

Dmitrovskii krai: Istoriia, priroda, chelovek . . . Rasskazy, ocherki, vospominaniia. Dmitrov, 1993.

"Dnevnik Et'ena Diumona o prebyvanii ego v Rossii v 1803," *Golos minuvshego* (1913), 3: 80–108.

Dobriakov, T. S. "Skazanie o moskovskom I-i gil'dii kuptse Semene Prokof'eviche Vasil'eve (Soobshcheno sviashchennikom I. A. Blagoveshchenskim)," *Dushepoleznoe chtenie* (Moscow, 1860) 8: 473–480.

Dobrynin, Gavriil. *Istinnoe povestvovanie, ili Zhizn' Gavriila Dobrynina . . . im samim pisannaia v Mogileve i v Vitebske*. St. Petersburg, 1872.

Dolgorukov, I. M. *Kapishche moego sertsa ili slovar' vsekh tekh lits, s koimi ia byl v raznykh otnosheniiakh v techenie moei zhizni*. Moscow, 1997.

——. *Povest' o rozhdenii moem, proiskhozhdenii i vsei zhizni, pisannaia mnoi samim.* Petrograd, 1916.

Drazhusov, ed. *Materialy dlia istorii imperatorskogo moskovskogo vospitatel'nogo doma.* Vol. 1. Moscow, 1863.

Druzheskie sovety molodomu cheloveku, nachinaiushchemu zhit' v svet. 2nd ed. Moscow:, 1765.

Dubrovin, N. F. "General-fel'dmarshal kniaz' Aleksandr Aleksandrovich Prozorovskii." *Voennyi sbornik,* otdel neofitsial'nyi (St. Petersburg, 1868) 7:3–36, 8:171–204, 9:3–40, 11:19–48.

Efremova, N. N. *Sudoustroistvo Rossii v XVIII–pervoi polovine XIX vv. (istoriko-pravovoe issledovanie).* Moscow, 1993.

Engel'gardt, L. N. "Zapiski L'va Nikolaevicha Engel'garda, 1766–1836." *Russkii arkhiv* (1867).

1812 god v vospominaniiakh sovremennikov. Moscow, 1995.

Faggionato, Rafaella. *A Rosicrucian Utopia in Eighteenth-Century Russia: The Masonic Circle of N. I. Novikov* (Dordrecht, The Netherlands, 2005).

Farrow, Lee A. *Between Clan and Crown: The Struggle to Define Noble Property Rights in Imperial Russia.* Newark, 2004.

Fomin, A. "Pis'mo k priiateliu s prilozheniem opisaniia o kupecheskom zvanii voobshche i o prinadlezhashchikh kuptsam navykakh." *Novye ezhemesiachnye sochineniia,* Part 24 (1788), 3–34.

Fomina, O. V. "Demograficheskoe povedenie moskovskikh kuptsov v 60-e gg. XVIII veka." In *Torgovlia, kupechestvo i tamozhennoe delo v Rossii v XVI–XVIII vv.,* ed. A. P. Pavlov, 145–150. St. Petersburg, 2001.

Fomina, Ol'ga Vasil'evna. "Imushchestvenno-demograficheskaia kharakteristika moskovskoi kupecheskoi sem'i poslednei treti XVIII veka." Aftoreferat dissertatsii. Moscow, 2003.

——. "Imushchestvenno-demograficheskaia kharakteristika moskovskoi kupecheskoi sem'i poslednei treti XVIII veka." Dissertation, Moscow State University, 2003.

Franklin, Simon. *Writing, Society and Culture in Early Rus, c. 950–1300.* Cambridge, UK, 2002.

Freeze, Gregory L. "The Rechristianization of Russia: the Church and Popular Religion, 1750–1850." *Studia Slavica Finlandensia 7* (Helsinki, 1990): 101–136.

——. "The *Soslovie* (Estate) Paradigm and Russian Social History." *American Historical Review* 91:1 (February 1986): 11–36.

Galiani, Ferdinando. *Razgovory o khlebnom torge.* Trans. from French by Petr Kiuvil'e. St. Petersburg, 1776.

Georgi, I. G. *Opisanie rossiisko-imperatorskogo stolichnogo goroda SANKT-PETERBURGA i dostopomiatnostei v okrestnostiakh onogo, s planom.* St. Petersburg, 1996.

Giddens, Anthony. *Modernity and Self-Identity: Self and Society in the Late Modern Age.* Stanford, 1991.

Ginzburg, Carlo. "Microhistory: Two or Three Things That I Know about It." *Critical Inquiry* 20 (Autumn, 1993): 10–35.

Glagolev, A. G. *Zapiski russkogo puteshestvennika: Chast' 1 Rossiia, Avstriia.* 2nd ed. St. Petersburg, 1845.

Glagoleva, O. E. "Predprinimatel'stvo i kul'tura v provintsii v kontse XVIII–pervoi polovine XIX veka." In *Rossiiskoe kupechestvo ot srednikh vekov k novomu vremeni.* Moscow, 1993.

Glukhov, I. A. "Aftobiografiia I. A. Glukhova," *Shchukinskii sbornik*. Vol. 6, 202–268. Moscow, 1907.

Golikova, N. B. "Kredit i ego rol' v deiatel'nosti russkogo kupechestva v nachale XVIII v." *Russkii gorod: issledovaniia i materialy* 2 (Moscow, 1979): 161–197.

——. "O meste i roli kreditnykh operatsii v deiatel'nosti russkogo kupechestva." In *Rossiia i Finliandiia: torgovlia, promysli, krupnaia promyshlennost': Materialy*, 54–55. Leningrad, 1981.

——. *Privilegirovanye kupecheskie korporatsii Rossii XVI–pervoi chetverti XVIII v.* Vol. 1. Moscow, 1998.

Gol'tsev, V. A. "Zakonodatel'stvo i nravy v Rossii XVIII veka." *Iuridicheskii vestnik* (1886), 3:421–459.

Golubtsov, S. A. "Moskovskaia provintsial'naia vlast' i dvorianstvo v ozhidanii Pugacheva." *Staraia Moskva: Stat'i po istorii Moskvy v XVII–XIX vv.* Sbornik pervyi (Moscow, 1929), 7–50.

Goncharova, N. N. "Kupecheskii portret kontsa XVIII–pervoi poloviny XIX." In *"Dlia pamiati potomstvu svoemu . . . " Narodnyi bytovoi portret v Rossii*, 11–24. Moscow, 1993.

Gordon, Daniel. *Citizens without Sovereignty: Equality and Sociability in French Thought, 1670–1789*. Princeton, 1994.

Goroda podmoskov'ia v trekh knigakh. Kn. 2. Moscow, 1980.

Got'e, Iurii Vladimirovich. *Time of Troubles: The Diary of Iurii Vladimirovich Got'e*. Ed., trans., and intro. Terence Emmons. Princeton, 1988.

Griaznov, I. M. "Zapisnaia kniga I. M. Griaznova, 1730–1753." *Shchukinskii sbornik* 6 (Moscow, 1907), 14–37.

Gulianitskii, N. F., ed. *Moskva i slozhivshiesia russkie goroda XVIII–pervoi poloviny XIX vekov*. Moscow, 1998.

Hildermeier, Manfred. *Bürgertum und Stadt in Russland 1760–1870: rechtliche Lage und soziale Struktur*. Cologne, 1986.

Iaganov, A. V., and E. I. Ruzaeva. *Uspenskii sobor v Dmitrove*. Moscow, 2003.

Il'in, M. A. "Tver' v XVIII stoletii." In *Iz istorii Kalininskoi oblasti: stat'i i dokumenty* (Kalinin, 1960), 41–77.

Ilizarova, S. S., et al., eds. *Akademik G. F. Miller—pervoi issledovatel' Moskvy i moskovskoi provintsii*. Moscow, 1996.

Istomina, E. G., ed. *Staryi Rybinsk: Istoriia goroda v opisaniiakh sovremennikov XIX–XX vv.* Mikhailov Posad, 1993.

——. *Vodnyi transport Rossii v doreformennyi period*. Moscow, 1991.

——. "Vyshnevolotskii vodnyi put' vo vtoroi polvine XVIII–nachala XIX v." In *Istoricheskaia geografiia Rossii VII-nachalo XIX v.: Sbornik statei k 70-letiiu Professora Liubomira Grigor'evicha Beskrovnogo*, 193–206. Moscow, 1975.

Istoricheskoe i topograficheskoe opisanie gorodov Moskovskoi gubernii s uezdami. Moscow, 1787.

Istoriia predprinimatel'stva v Rossii. 2 vols. Moscow, 2000.

Istoriia rodov russkogo dvorianstva. Comp. P. N. Petrov. 2 vols. St. Petersburg, 1886.

Istoriko-statisticheskoe i arkheologicheskoe opisanie tserkvi vo imia spasa-istselitelia rasslablennogo v sele Vedernitsakh, Dmitrovskii uezd, Moskovskoi gubernii. Comp. I. Tokmakov. Moscow, 1895.

Iurkin, I. N. *Abram Bulygin: chudnosti, veselosti, "neponiatnaia filosofiia" . . .* Tula, 1994.

—— *Demidovy: uchenye, inzhenery, organizatory nauku i proizvodstva*. Moscow, 2001.

"Ivan Petrovich Kulibin 1735–1818," *Russkaia starina* 4 (November 1873): 734–737.

Ivanov, Oleg. *Graf Aleksei Grigor'evich Orlov-Chesmenskii v Moskve.* Moscow, 2002.

Ivanov, O. "Syn Alekseia Grigor'evicha Orlova," *Moskovskii zhurnal* (Pravoslavnoe infor-matesionnoe agenstvo, Russkaia liniia), April 1, 2001. http://www.rusk.ru/st.php?idar=800477 (accessed January 15, 2008).

Jarrick, Arne. *Back to Modern Reason: Johan Hjerpe and Other Petit Bourgeois in Stock-holm in the Age of Enlightenment.* Liverpool, 1999.

Jones, Robert E. *Provincial Development in Russia: Catherine II and Jakob Sievers.* New Brunswick, NJ, 1984.

——. "Ukrainian Grain and the St. Petersburg Market." In *Russia and the World of the Eighteenth Century*, ed. R. P. Bartlett, A. G. Cross, and Karen Rasmussen, 565–576. Columbus, OH, 1986.

——. "Urban Planning and the Development of Provincial Towns in Russia during the Reign of Catherine II." In *The Eighteenth Century in Russia*, ed. J. G. Garrard, 321–344. Oxford, 1973.

Le journal intime et ses formes littéraires: Actes du Colloque de septembre 1975, comp. V. Del Litto. Geneva, 1978.

Joyce, Patrick. *Democratic Subjects: The Self and the Social in Nineteenth–Century En-gland.* Cambridge, UK, 1994.

Kahan, Arcadius. *The Plow, the Hammer, and the Knout: An Economic History of Eighteenth-Century Russia*, ed. Richard Hellie. Chicago, 1985.

Kaiser, Daniel H. "Naming Names in Early Modern Russia." *Harvard Ukrainian Studies* 19 (1995): 271–291.

——. "The Poor and Disabled in Early Eighteenth-Century Russian Towns." *Journal of Social History* 32 (1998–1999): 125–155.

Kalinin, V. D. *Iz istorii gorodskogo samoupravleniia v Rossii (XVII–nachalo XX vv.)* Mos-cow, 1994.

Kamenskii, A. B. *Povsednevnost' russkikh gorodskikh obyvatelei: Istoricheskie anekdoty iz provintsial'noi zhizni XVIII veka.* Moscow, 2006.

Kantor, A. M. *Dukhovnyi mir russkogo gorozhanina: Vtoraia polovina XVII veka. Ocherki.* Moscow, 1999.

Karmannaia knizhka chestnogo cheloveka, ili nuzhnye pravila vo vsiakom meste i vo vsia-koe vremia. St. Petersburg, 1794.

Karzhavin, Fedor Vasil'evich. "Zapiska F. V. Karzhavina o svoei zhizni (1782 g)," ed. N. P. Durov. *Russkaia starina*, Vol. 12 (1875), 2:272–297.

Kavolis, Vytautas. "Histories of Selfhood, Maps of Sociability." In *Designs of Selfhood*, ed. Vytautas Kavolis, 15–103. London, 1984.

Kelly, Catriona. *Refining Russia: Advice Literature, Polite Culture, and Gender from Cath-erine to Yeltsin.* Oxford, 2001.

Khokhlov, R. F., and E. V. Iakuta. "Pamiatniki arkhitektury Dmitrova." *Russkii gorod: issledovaniia i materialy* 2 (Moscow, 1979): 71–94.

Kholmogor, V., and G. Kholmogor, *Istoricheskie materialy o tserkvakh i selakh XVI–XVIII vv.* Vyp. 11. Moscow, 1911.

[Khomiakov, P. Z.] *Pokhozhdenie nekotorogo rossianina, istinnaia povest', im samim pisannaia . . .* Part 2. Moscow, 1790.

Khvostov, Vasilii. "Zapiski Vasiliia Semenovicha Khvostova: Opisanie zhizni tainogo sovetnika, senatora i kavalera Vasiliia Khvostova, pisany, v 1823 godu, samim im dlia detei svoikh." *Russkii arkhiv* 3 (1870): 551–610.

Kenneth F. Kiple, ed. *Cambridge World History of Human Disease*. New York, 1993.

Kirichenko, Oleg Viktorovich. *Traditsii pravoslavnoi religioznosti u russkikh dvorian XVIII stoletiia*. Avtoreferat dissertatsii Instituta etnologii i antropologii RAN. Moscow, 1997.

Kirichenko, P. N. "Rozhdenie gorodskoi sem'i (po materialam g. Brianska v kontse XVIII v.)." In *Iz istorii Brianskogo kraia*, 130–138. Briansk, 1995.

"K istorii moskovskogo angliiskogo kluba," ed P. B., *Russkii arkhiv*, vol. 27, 5 (1889): 85–98.

Kitanina, T. M. *Khlebnaia torgovlia Rossii v 1875–1914 gg. (ocherki pravitel'stvennoi politiki)*. Leningrad, 1978.

Kizevetter, A. A. *Gil'diia moskovskogo kupechestva*. Moscow, 1915.

———. *Gorodovoe polozhenie Ekateriny II 1785 g: Opyt istoricheskogo kommentariia*. Moscow, 1909.

———. *Mestnoe samoupravlenie v Rossii IX–XIX st.: Istoricheskii ocherk*. Moscow, 1910.

———. *Posadskaia obshchina v Rossii XVIII st.* Moscow, 1903 [1978 reprint by Oriental Research Partners, with introduction by Gilbert Rozman].

———. *Russkoe obshchestvo v vosemnadtsatom stoletii*. 2nd ed. Rostov-on-Don, 1905.

———. "Shkol'nye voprosy nashego vremeni v dokumentakh proshlogo veka," *Obrazovanie: Pedagogicheskii i nauchno-populiarnyi zhurnal*, February (St. Petersburg, 1899): 98–119.

Kliuch kupechestva. St. Petersburg, 1768.

Klochkov, M. V. *Ocherki pravitel'stvennoi deiatel'nosti vremeni Pavla I*. Petrograd, 1916.

Klokman, Iu. R. *Ocherki sotsial'no-ekonomicheskoi istorii gorodov Severo-Zapada Rossii v seredine XVIII v*. Moscow, 1960.

———. *Sotsial'no-ekonomicheskaia istoriia russkogo goroda: Vtoraia polovina XVIII veka* Moscow, 1967.

Kniaz'kov, S. A. "Byt dvorianskoi Moskvy kontsa XVIII i nachala XIX vekov." *Moskva v ee proshlom i nastoiashchem*, vyp. 8 (Moscow, 1911), 21–64.

Kol'chugin, G. N. "Zapiska G. N. Kol'chugina." *Russkii arkhiv* 9 (1879): 45–62.

Kollmann, Nancy Shields. *By Honor Bound: State and Society in Early Modern Russia*. Ithaca, NY, 1999.

Kolosov, V. ed. *Letopis' o sobytiiakh v g. Tveri tverskogo kuptsa Mikhaila Tiul'pina 1762–1823 gg*. Tver', 1902.

Komleva, Evgeniia V. *Eniseiskoe kupechestvo (posledniaia polovina XVIII–pervaia polovina XIX veka)*. Moscow, 2006.

Kontseva, T. V. "Zaural'skoe kupechestvo i tserkov': Blagotvoritel'naia deiatel'nost' vo vtoroi polovine XVIII–seredine XIX vv." *Religiia i tserkov' v Sibiri* (Tiumen', 1996), 29–32.

Kopanov, A. I. "Arkheograficheskoe vvedenie." In *Zhurnal ili zapiska zhizni i prikliuchenii Ivana Alekseevicha Tolchenova*, ed. N. I. Pavlenko, 19–28. Moscow, 1974.

Kornilov, S. V. *Drevnerusskoe palomnichestvo*. Kaliningrad, 1995.

Korsh, E. "Byt kupechestva i meshchanstva." In *Iz epokhi krepostnogo khoziaistva XVIII i XIX vv: Stat'i i putevoditel' po vystavke*, ed. Iu. V. Got'e and N. B. Baklanov, 23–34. Moscow, 1926.

Kosheleva, Ol'ga. *Liudi Sankt-Peterburgskogo ostrova Petrovskogo vremeni*. Moscow, 2004.

Koshman, L. V. "Russkaia doreformennaia burzhuaziia: Postanovka voprosa i istoriografiia problemy." *Istoriia SSSR* 6 (1974): 77–94.

Kozlova, N. V. "Gil'deiskoe kupechestvo v Rossii i nekotorye cherty ego samosoznaniia v XVIII v." In *Torgovlia i predprinimatel'stvo v feodal'noi Rossii*, 214–229. Moscow, 1994.

——, ed. *Gorodskaia sem'ia XVIII veka. Semeino-pravovye akty kuptsov i raznochintsev Moskvy.* Moscow, 2002.

——. "Khoziaistvennaia aktivnost' i predprinimatel'skaia deiatel'nost' kupecheskikh zhen i vdov Moskvy v XVIII v." In *Torgovlia, kupechestvo i tamozhennoe delo v Rossii v XVI–XVIII vv*, ed. A. P. Pavlov, 139–144. St. Petersburg, 2001.

——. "Nekotorye aspekty torgovoi deiatel'nosti v Rossii v XVIII veke (iz istorii razrabotki pravovykh dokumentov)." In *Kupechestvo v Rossii XV–pervaia polovina XIX veka*, 194–218. Moscow, 1997.

——. "Nekotorye cherty lichnostnogo obratsa kuptsa XVIII veka." In *Mentalitet i kul'tura predprinimatelei Rossii XVII–XIX vv.*, 43–57. Moscow, 1996.

——. "Organizatsiia kommercheskogo obrazovaniia v Rossii v XVIII v." In *Istoricheskie zapiski* 117 (1989): 288–314.

——. *Rossiikii absoliutizm i kupechestvo v XVIII veke (20-e–nachalo 60-kh godov).* Moscow, 1999.

——. "Rossiiskii absoliutizm i kupechestvo (20–nach. 60-kh godov XVIII v.)," 2 vols. PhD dissertation, Moscow State University, 1994.

Kozlova, N. V., and V. R. Tarlovskaia. "Torgovlia." In *Ocherki russkoi kul'tury XVIII veka* (2 parts), part 1, 213–256. Moscow, 1985.

Kracauer, Siegfried. *History: The Last Things Before the Last.* New York, 1969.

Kulisher, I. M. *Ocherki istorii russkoi torgovli.* Petrograd, 1923.

Kupecheskie dnevniki i memuary kontsa XVIII–pervoi polviny XIX veka. Moscow, 2007.

Kupriianov, A. I. "Predstavleniia o trude i bogatstve russkogo kupechestva doreformennoi epokhi." In *Mentalitet i kul'tura predprinimatelei Rossii XVII–XIX vv.*, 83–107. Moscow, 1996.

—— "Russkii gorozhanin v poiskakh sotsial'noi identichnosti (pervaia polovina XIX v.)." *Odissei* (1998): 56–72.

Kurochkina, Irina Nikolaevna. *Formirovanie i razvitie rossiiskogo etiketa vo vtoroi polovine XVIII veka: Uchebnoe posobie.* Moscow, 1999.

Kuzmina, Ol'ga Vladimirovna. "Osobennosti transformatsii russkoi zemledel'cheskoi svadebnoi traditsii v usloviiakh gorodskoi kupecheskoi sredy (seredina XVIII-konets XIX vv.) Avtoreferat dissertatsii kandidata kul'turologii. Kemerovo: Kemerovskaia gosudarstvennaia akademiia kul'tury i iskusstv, 2004

Kusova, I. G. *Riazanskoe kupechestvo: Ocherki istorii XVI–nachala XX veka.* Riazan', 1996.

Labzina, A. E. *The Days of a Russian Noblewoman: The Memoirs of Anna Labzina 1758–1821.* Trans. and ed. Gary Marker and Rachel May. DeKalb, 2001.

Landes, David S. *Revolution in Time: Clocks and the Making of the Modern World.* Cambridge, 1983.

Langford, Rachael, and Russell West, eds. *Marginal Voices, Marginal Forms: Diaries in European Literature and History.* Amsterdam, 1999.

Laskina, M. N. *P. S. Mochalov: letopis' zhizni i tvorchestva.* Moscow, 2000.

Leach, Robert, and Victor Borovsky, eds. *A History of Russian Theatre.* Cambridge, UK, 1999.

Lebedev, S. K., and B. N. Mironov, "Novaia kontseptsiia russkogo doindustrial'nogo goroda: Manfred Khil'dermaier o russkom doreformennom gorode." In *Gosudarst-*

vennye instituty i obshchestvennye otnosheniia v Rossii XVIII–XX vv. v zarubezhnoi istoriografii, 32–50. St. Petersburg, 1994.

Lejeune, Philippe. "Débat." In *Le journal intime et ses formes littéraires: Actes du Colloque de septembre 1975,* comp. V. Del Litto (Geneva, 1978).

———. "The Practice of the Private Journal: Chronicle of an Investigation (1986–1998)." In *Marginal Voices, Marginal Forms: Diaries in European Literature and History,* ed. Rachael Langford and Russell West, 185–202. Amsterdam, 1999.

Lepekhin, Ivan. *Dnevnye zapiski.* 3 vols. St. Petersburg, 1771.

Levi, Giovanni. "On Microhistory." In *New Perspectives on Historical Writing,* ed. Peter Burke, 93–113. University Park, PA, 1991.

Levshin, N. G. "Domashnii pamiatnik." *Russkaia starina* 4 (St. Petersburg, 1873): 823–852.

Likhachev, D. S. *Poeziia sadov: K semantike sadov-parkovykh stilei. Sad kak tekst.* 2nd ed. St. Petersburg, 1991.

Lincoln, W. Bruce. "N. A. Miliutin and the St. Petersburg Municipal Act of 1846: A Study in Reform Under Nicholas I." *Slavic Review* 33: 1 (March, 1974): 55–68.

Liubetskii, S. N. "Guliane v Kuskove, pri imperatritse Ekaterine II, vo vremia prazdno-vaniia 25-letiia ee tsarstvovaniia." *Sovremennaia letopis'* 27 (1866).

Lopukhin, I. V. *Zapiski senatora I. V. Lopukhina.* London, 1859; reprint, Moscow, 1990.

Madariaga, Isabel de. *Russia in the Age of Catherine the Great.* New Haven, 1981.

Maikov, P. M. *Ivan Ivanovich Betskoi: Opyt ego biografii.* St. Petersburg, 1904.

Man'kov, A. G. *Ulozhenie 1649 goda: Kodeks feodal'nogo prava Rossii.* Leningrad, 1980.

A Manual of Roman Law, the Ecloga. Trans. Edwin Hanson Freshfield. Cambridge, UK, 1926.

Marker, Gary. *Publishing, Printing, and the Origins of Intellectual Life in Russia, 1700–1800.* Princeton, 1985.

Marrese, Michelle Lamarche. *A Woman's Kingdom: Noblewomen and the Control of Property in Russia, 1700–1861.* Ithaca, NY, 2002.

Martin, Alexander M., "Lost Arcadia: The 1812 War and Russian Images of Aristocratic Womanhood." *European History Quarterly* 37:4 (October 2007): 603–621.

———. "The Response of the Population of Moscow to the Napoleonic Occupation of 1812." In *The Military and Society in Russia 1450–1917,* ed. Eric Lohr and Marshall Poe, 469–489. Leiden, 2002.

Materialy dlia istorii moskovskogo kupechestva: Obshchestvennye prigovory. Vols. 1–11. Moscow, 1892–1911.

Ménétra, Jacques-Louis. *Journal of My Life.* Introduction and commentary by Daniel Roche. Trans. Arthur Goldhammer. New York, 1986.

Muir, Edward, and Guido Ruggiero, eds., *Microhistory and the Lost Peoples of Europe.* Trans. Eren Branch. Baltimore, 1991.

Mil'china, V. A. "Maskarad v russkoi kul'ture kontsa XVIII–nachala XIX v." In *Kul'turo-logicheskie aspekty teorii i istorii russkoi literatury,* 40–50. Moscow, 1978.

Miller, G. F. *Sochineniia po istorii Rossii: Izbrannoe.* Moscow, 1996.

Minenko, N. A. "Gorodskaia sem'ia Zapadnoi Sibiri na rubezhe XVII–XVIII vv." In *Istoriia Sibiri dosovetskogo perioda,* 175–195. Novosibirsk, 1977.

Mironov, Boris "Bureaucratic- or Self-Government: The Early Nineteenth Century Rus-sian City." *Slavic Review* 52:2 (Summer, 1993): 233–255.

Mironov, B[oris] N. *Russkii gorod v 1740–1860-e gody.* Leningrad, 1990.

Monaev, D. V. "Vydaiushchiesia kuptsy Rossii." Kurskii gosudarstvennyi tekhnicheskii
    universitet. http://vm71.narod.ru/works/063/kupech.doc (accessed July 26, 2007).

Moskva v opisaniiakh XVIII veka. Moscow, 1997.

Mudrov, N. A., ed. *Knizhnye sobraniia rossiiskoi provintsii: Problemy rekonstruktsii. Sbor-
    nik nauchnykh trudov*. Ekaterinburg, 1994.

Naidenov, N. A. *Vospominaniia o vidennom, slyshannom i ispytannom*. 2 vols. Moscow,
    1903–1905.

Nauka byt' uchtivym. Trans. from French. St. Petersburg, 1774.

Newlin, Thomas. *The Voice in the Garden: Andrei Bolotov and the Anxieties of Russian
    Pastoral, 1738–1833*. Evanston, IL, 2001.

Nilova, O. E. "Otnoshenie k obrazovaniiu v srede moskovskogo kupechestva kontsa
    XVIII–pervoi chetverti XIX v." In *Mirovospriiatie i samosoznanie russkogo ob-
    shchestva (XI–XX vv.): Sbornik statei*, 113–133. Moscow, 1994.

Ogorodnikov, S. F. *Ocherk istorii goroda Arkhangel'ska v torgovo-promyshlennom ot-
    noshenii*. St. Petersburg, 1890.

Omel'chenko, O. A. *"Zakonnaia monarkhiia" Ekateriny II: Prosveshchennyi absoliutizm v
    Rossii*. Moscow, 1993.

1000 let russkogo predprinimatel'stva: Iz istorii kupecheskikh rodov. Moscow, 1995.

Pallas, P. S. *Katalog rasteniiam nakhodiashchimsia v Moskve v sadu . . . ego prevoskho-
    ditel'stva . . . Prokopiia Akinfievicha Demidova*. St. Petersburg, 1781.

Pallas, Peter Simon. *Travels through the southern provinces of the Russian empire, in the
    years of 1793 and 1794*. 2nd ed. Trans. from German by F. W. Blagdon. 2 vols.
    London, 1812.

Pamiatniki arkhitektury moskovskoi oblasti. Vol. 1. Moscow, 1975.

Pavlenko, Ivan Antonovich. *Nravy russkogo obshchestva v ekaterinninskuiu epokhu*. Arch-
    angel, 1912.

Pavlenko, N. I. "I. A. Tolchenov i ego 'Zhurnal.'" In *Zhurnal ili zapiska zhizni i pri-
    kliuchenii Ivana Alekseevicha Tolchenova*, ed. N. I. Pavlenko, 3–18. Moscow, 1974.

Papmehl, K. A. *Metropolitan Platon of Moscow (Petr Levshin, 1737–1812): The Enlightened
    Prelate, Scholar and Educator*. Newtonville, Mass., 1983.

Pecherin, F. P. "Zapiski o moikh predkakh i o sebe, na pamiat' detiam v 1816 sdelannye."
    Russkaia starina 12 (1891): 587–616.

Pekarskii, P. P. "Russkie memuary XVIII v." *Sovremennik* 4 (1855): 53–90.

Peken, Khristian. *Domashnii lechebnik*. St. Petersburg, 1765.

Peken, Matvei [Khristianovich]. *Fiziologiia ili nauka o estestve chelovecheskom*. St. Peters-
    burg, 1788.

——. *Novyi domashnii lechebnik*. Moscow, 1796.

——. *O sokhranenii zdraviia i zhizni*. 2nd ed. Moscow, 1812.

Pelech, Orest. "Great Russian Secular Culture: the Sense of Self in Diary-Keeping." Paper
    delivered at the 29th National Convention of the American Association for the
    Advancement of Slavic Studies. Seattle, Washington (November 22, 1997).

"Perepiska mezhdu dvumia priiateliami o komertsii." *Ezhemesiachnye sochineniia k
    pol'ze i uveseleniiu sluzhashchiia* (January, 1755): 105–122. "Prodolzhenie perepiski"
    (April, 1755).

Peterburgskoe kupechestvo v XIX veke. Ed. and comp. A. M. Konechnyi. St. Petersburg,
    2003.

Petrovskii, M. P. *Zabytye memuary P. Z. Khomiakova* [Offprint from *Zhurnal Minis-
    terstva Narodnogo Prosveshcheniia* (no. 8, 1901). 62 pp.]

Pipunyrov, V. N. *Istoriia chasov s drevneishikh vremen do nashikh dnei.* Moscow, 1982.

Pisemskii, V. A. and Iu. N. Kalashnov, "Pravoslavie i dukhovnyi tip rossiiskogo pred-prinimatelia." In *Iz istorii ekonomicheskoi mysli i narodnogo khoziaistva Rossii.* Vyp. 1, Part 2 (Moscow, 1993), 342–350.

Pisar'kova, L. F. "Razvitie mestnogo samoupravleniia v Rossii do velikikh reform: oby-chai, povinnost', pravo." *Otechestvennaia istoriia* 2 (2001): 3–17

Polilov-Severtsev, G. T. *Nashi dedy-kuptsy: Bytovye kartiny nachala XIX stoletiia.* St. Petersburg, 1907.

Politicheskoe namerenie o komertsii. Trans. from French. St. Petersburg, 1765, 1771.

Polunin, F., and G. Miller. *Geograficheskii leksikon Rossiiskogo gosudarstva.* Moscow, 1773.

Polnoe sobranie zakonov Rossiiskoi imperii. 1st series, 30 volumes (St. Petersburg, 1830).

Preobrazhenskii, A. A. " 'Pamiatnaia kniga' moskovskogo kuptsa serediny XIX veka." In *Rossiiskoe kupechestvo ot srednykh vekov k novomu vremeni,* 140–143. Moscow, 1993.

Preobrazhenskii, A. A., and V. B. Perkhavko. *Kupechestvo Rusi IX–XVII veka.* Ekaterin-burg, 1997.

Prozorovskii, A. A. *Zapiski general-fel'dmarshala kniazia Aleksandra Aleksandrovicha Prozorovskogo 1756–1776.* Introduction by A. K. Afanas'ev. Moscow, 2004.

Rabinovich, M. G. *Ocherki etnografii russkogo feodal'nogo goroda.* Moscow, 1978.

Raigrodskii, L. D. *Chasy i vremia.* St. Petersburg, 2001.

Ransel, David L. "Character and Style of Patron-Client Relations in Russia." In *Klien-telsysteme im Europa der Frühen Neuzeit,* ed. Antoni Mączak, 211–231. Munich, 1988.

——, ed. *The Family in Imperial Russia: New Lines of Historical Research.* Urbana, Ill., 1978.

——. *Mothers of Misery: Child Abandonment in Russia.* Princeton, 1988.

——. "Neither Nobles Nor Peasants: Plain Painting and the Emergence of the Merchant Estate." In *Picturing Russia: Explorations in Visual Culture,* ed. Valerie Kivelson and Joan Neuberger, 76–80. New Haven, 2008.

——. *The Politics of Catherinian Russia: The Panin Party.* New Haven, 1975.

——. "Russian Merchants: Citizenship and Identity." In *Eighteenth-Century Russia: So-ciety, Culture, Economy,* ed. Roger Bartlett and Gabriela Lehmann-Carli. Berlin, 2007.

Rasskazy babushki: Iz vospominanii piati pokolenii zapisannye i sobrannye ee vnukom D. Blagovo, ed. T. I. Ornatskaia. Leningrad, 1989.

Reman, G. "Makar'evskaia iarmonka: Vypiska iz neizdannogo puteshestviia po vostoch-noi Rossii, Sibiri i Kitaiskoi Mungalii." *Severnyi arkhiv* (1822), 8: 138–156, 9: 199–242.

Richardson, William. *Anecdotes of the Russian Empire.* First edition 1784. Reprinted London, 1968.

Roosevelt, Priscilla. *Life on the Russian Country Estate: A Social and Cultural History.* New Haven, 1995.

Rostislavov, Dmitrii Ivanovich. *Provincial Russia in the Age of Enlightenment: The Mem-oir of a Priest's Son.* Trans. and ed. Alexander M. Martin. DeKalb, IL, 2002.

Ruane, Christine. "Caftan to Business Suit: The Semiotics of Russian Merchant Dress." In *Merchant Moscow: Images of Russia's Vanished Bourgeoisie,* ed. James L. West and Iurii A. Petrov, 55–60. (Princeton, 1998).

Ruban, V. G. *Opisanie imperatorskogo stolichnogo goroda Moskvy.* St. Petersburg, 1782.

Russian Women 1698–1917: Experience and Expression, An Anthology of Sources. Comp. Robin Bisha et al. Bloomington, 2002.

Russkii byt po vospominaniiam sovremennikov: XVIII vek. Four books. Moscow, 1918– 1923.

RVB.ru (Russkaia virtual'naia biblioteka), "Pis'ma russkikh pisatelei XVIII veka," at http://www.rvb.ru/18vek/letters—rus—writers/02comm/introcomm—korzhavin .htm (accessed January 15, 2008).

Rychkov, P. I. "Zapiski Petra Ivanovicha Rychkova." *Russkii arkhiv* 11 (1905): 289–340.

Sbornik imperatorskogo russkogo istoricheskogo obshchestva. 148 vols. St. Petersburg, 1867– 1916.

Schlaeger, Jürgen. "Self-Exploration in Early Modern English Diaries." In *Marginal Voices, Marginal Forms: Diaries in European Literature and History,* ed. Rachael Langford and Russell West, 32–35. Amsterdam, 1999.

Schneider, Robert A. *The Ceremonial City: Toulouse Observed 1738–1780.* Princeton, 1995.

Selivanovskii, N. S. "Zapiski N. S. Selivanovskogo." *Bibliograficheskie zapiski* 17 (1858): 515–527.

Semenova, A. V. "Idei Prosveshcheniia i tret'e soslovie v Rossii." In *Mirovospriiatie i samosoznanie russkogo obshchestva (XI–XX vv.),* 134–141. Moscow, 1994.

———. "National'no-pravoslavnye traditsii v mentalitete kupechestva v periode stanov- leniia rossiiskogo predprinimatel'stva." In *Kupechestvo v Rossii XV–pervaia polvina XIX veka,* 96–111. Moscow, 1997.

Shtil'mark, R. A. *Povest' o strannike rossiiskom.* Moscow, 1962.

Shubinskii, Sergei Nikolaevich. *Ocherki iz zhizni i byta proshlogo vremeni.* St. Petersburg, 1888.

Sivkov, K. V. "Chastnye pansiony i shkoly Moskvy v 80-kh godakh XVIII v." *Istoricheskii arkhiv* 6 (Moscow, 1951): 315–323.

Skitskii, B. V. "Ocherki byta russkoi provintsii vo vtoruiu polovinu XVIII veka," *Izvestiia: Gorskii pedagogicheskii institut* 4 (1) (Vladikavkaz, 1927).

Slovar' russkogo iazyka XVIII veka, (Leningrad-St. Petersburg, 1991–).

Smith, Douglas. *Working the Rough Stone: Freemasonry and Society in Eighteenth- Century Russia.* DeKalb, Ill., 1999.

Smith, Rogers M. *Civic Ideals: Conflicting Visions of Citizenship in U. S. History.* New Haven, 1997.

Sokolov, N. G. "Nakazy riazanskogo kupechestva deputatam ulozhennoi komissii (1767–1768 gg.)." In *Rossiiskoe kupechestvo ot srednikh vekov k novomu vremeni,* 68– 71. Moscow, 1993.

Sokrashchenie glavneishikh dolzhnostei koi kazhdyi Khristianin obiazan ispolniat' v toch- nosti po svoemu zvaniiu i sostoianiiu. St. Petersburg, 1799.

Sorina, Kh. D. "K voprosu o protsesse sotsial'nogo rassloeniia goroda v sviazi s for- mirovaniem kapitalisticheskikh otnoshenii v Rossii v XVIII–nachale XIX v (g. Tver')." In *Uchenye zapiski Kalininskogo gosudarstvennogo pedagogicheskogo insti- tuta* Vol. 38, 281–300. Kalinin, 1964.

Sorina, Kh. D. "Mesto Tveri i drugikh gorodov Tverskoi gubernii v volzhskoi vodnoi sisteme vo vtoroi polovine XVIII veka." In *Iz istorii Kalininskoi oblasti: stat'i i dokumenty,* 78–104. Kalinin, 1960.

Sorokin, A. K., ed. *Predprinimatel'stvo i predprinimateli Rossii ot istokov do nachala XX veka.* Moscow, 1997.

Staraia Moskva glazami sovremennikov (Moskva pered Otechestvennoi voinoi 1812 goda). Comp. N. N. Skorniakova. Moscow, 1996.

Startsev, A. I. "F. V. Karzhavin i ego amerikanskoe puteshestvie." *Istoriia SSSR* 3 (1960): 132–139.

Stites, Richard. *Serfdom, Society, and the Arts: The Pleasure and the Power.* New Haven, 2005.

Storch, Heinrich Friedrich von. *The Picture of Petersburg.* London, 1801.

Storozhev, V. N., ed. *Istoriia moskovskogo kupechestvogo obshchestva 1863–1913.* 5 vols. Moscow, 1913.

——. *Voina i moskovskoe kupechestvo: Istoricheskii etiud.* Moscow, 1914.

Sverbeev, D. N. *Zapiski.* Vol. 1 (1799–1826). Moscow, 1899.

Sviato-Vvedenskii Tolgskii Zhenskii Monastyr'. Sofrino, n.d.

Tartakovskii, A. G. *Russkaia memuaristika i istoricheskoe soznanie XIX veka.* Moscow, 1997.

——. comp. *1812 god . . . voennye dnevniki,* Moscow, 1990.

——. *Russkaia memuaristika XVIII–pervoi poloviny XIX v.* Moscow, 1991.

Taylor, Charles. *Sources of the Self: The Making of the Modern Identity.* Cambridge, 1989.

Terras, Victor. *A History of Russian Literature.* New Haven, 1991.

Tikhomirov, M. N. *Gorod Dmitrov ot osnovaniia goroda do poloviny XIX veka, s planami, kartami i diagrammami.* Dmitrov, 2006.

Tolstoi, Peter. *The Travel Diary of Peter Tolstoi: A Muscovite in Early Modern Europe,* trans. Max J. Okenfuss. DeKalb, IL, 1987.

Tovrov, Jessica. "Mother-Child Relationships among the Russian Nobility." *The Family in Imperial Russia: New Lines of Historical Research,* ed. David L. Ransel, 15–43. Urbana, IL, 1978.

Travin, L. A. *Zapiski (1807–1808): Trudy Pskovskogo arkheologicheskogo obshchestva.* Vyp. 10. Pskov, 1914.

Tregubov, N. Ia. "Opisanie zhizni moei, detiam moim, byv pod arestom (1799 goda, dekabria 25 dnia)." *Russkaia starina* (1908), 10: 97–108; 11: 311–327.

Tsentry torgovli Evropeiskoi Rossii v pervoi chetverti XVIII veka. Comp. M. Ia. Volkov. Moscow, 1986.

Ul'ianova, Galina. "Autobiographishche Texte russischer Kaufleute und ihre kulturelle Dimension." In *Autobiographical Practices in Russia/Autobiographische Praktiken in Russland,* ed. Johch Hellbeck and Klaus Heller, 155–177. Göttingen, 2004.

Ul'ianova, Galina, and Mikhail Zoloterev. "Azartnaia nedvizhimost'." *Novyi Inostranets–Nedvizhimost' za rubezhom i v Rossii,* no. 4 (39) (2003), 89–93.

Ulrich, Laurel Thatcher. *A Midwife's Tale: The Life of Martha Ballard, Based on Her Diary, 1785–1812.* New York, 1990.

Uspenskii, V. P. *Zapiski o proshlom goroda Ostashkova Tverskoi gubernii.* Tver', 1893.

Vaintraub, L. R. *Khram v chest' kazanskoi ikony Presviatoi Bogoroditsy v Podlipich'e: Istoriia khrama i prikhoda XVI–XXI vv.* Dmitrov, 2005.

Vaintraub, L. R., and I. A. Levakov. "Novye materialy po istorii usad'by Muranovo v XVII–XIX vv." In *Materialy tvorcheskogo otcheta tresta "Mosoblstroirestavratsiia"* (Moscow, 1984), accessed through the website Portal arkheologia.ru, http://www.archeologia.ru/Library/Book/0b75a5b685d1/Info (accessed January 15, 2008).

Varentsov, N. A. *Slyshannoe. Vidennoe. Peredumannoe. Perezhitoe.* Moscow, 1999.

Vasil'ev, Poruchik [Lieutenant]. *Dnevnik poruchika Vasil'eva*. Intro. E. Shepkina (Pamiatniki drevnei pis'mennosti cxix). St. Petersburg, 1896.

Vavilov, Ivan. *Besedy russkogo kuptsa o torgovle: Prakticheskii kurs kommercheskikh znanii, izlagaemykh v S.-Peterburge publichno po porucheniiu imp. Vol'nogo ekonomicheskogo obshchestva . . .* Parts 1 and 2. St. Petersburg, 1846.

Vistengof, P. F. "Ocherki moskovskoi zhizni." *Russkii ocherk: 40–50-e gody XIX veka*, ed. Vasilii Ivanovich Kuleshov, 103–128. Moscow, 1986.

Vishniakov, N. *Svedeniia o kupecheskom rode Vishniakovykh (1636–1762 gg.)* Part 1, Moscow, 1903; Part 2 (1762–1847), Moscow 1905; Part 3 (1848–1854), Moscow, 1911.

Volkov, M. Ia. "O gramotnosti posadskikh liudei Torzhka v nachale XVIII v." In *Istoriograficheskie i istoricheskie problemy russkoi kul'tury*, 79–84. Moscow, 1982.

"Vospominaniia o M. A. Makarove (razkas kaluzhskogo starozhila)." In *Pamiatnaia knizhka Kaluzhskoi gubernii*, 105–108. Kaluga, 1863.

Voznesenskii, S. V. "Gorodskie deputatskie nakazy v Ekaterininskuiu komissiiu 1767 g." *Zhurnal Ministerstva Narodnogo Prosveshcheniia* (St. Petersburg, 1909), 11: 89–119; 12: 241–284.

Vsévolojsky, N. S. *Dictionnaire géographique-historique de l'empire de Russie*. Moscow, 1813.

Vtorov, Ivan Alekseevich. "Moskva i Kazan' v nachale XIX veka: Zapiski Ivana Alekseevicha Vtorova." *Russkaia starina* 70 (4) (1891): 1–22.

Walker, Mack. *German Home Towns: Community, State and General Estate, 1648–1871*. Ithaca, NY, 1971.

West, James, and Iurii A. Petrov, eds. *Merchant Moscow: Images of Russia's Vanished Bourgeosie*. Princeton, 1998.

Wirtschafter, Elise Kimerling. *The Play of Ideas in Russian Enlightenment Theater*. DeKalb, IL, 2003.

——. *Social Identity in Imperial Russia*. DeKalb, IL, 1997.

——. *The Structures of Society: Imperial Russia's "People of Various Ranks."* DeKalb, Ill., 1994.

Wortman, Richard S. *Scenarios of Power: Myth and Ceremony in Russian Monarchy*. Vol. 1, *From Peter the Great to the Death of Nicholas I*. Princeton, 1995.

Zagoskin, M. N. *Sochineniia*. Vol. 5, *Moskva i moskvichi: Zapiski Bogdana Il'icha Bel'skogo*. St. Petersburg, 1889.

"Zapiska, naidennaia v bumagakh pokoinogo kuptsa S-va," In *Permskii sbornik*, book 2, appendix 2, xxvii–xxx. Moscow, 1860..

Zapiski kniagini Dashkovoi: Pis'ma sester Vil'mot iz Rossii. 2nd ed. Moscow, 1991.

Zemnaia zhizn' presviatoi bogoroditsy i opisanie sviatikh chudotvornykh ee ikon. Comp. Sofiia Snessoreva. Iaroslavl', 1998.

Zorin, Andrei. *Kormia dvuglavogo orla . . . Literatura i gosudarstvennaia ideologiia v Rossii v poslednei treti XVIII–pervoi treti XIX veka*. Moscow, 2001.

Žužek, P. Ivan. *Kormčaja kniga: Studies on the Chief Code of Russian Canon Law*. Orientalia Christiana Analecta, No. 168. Rome, 1964.

Zviagintsev, E. A. "Moskovskii kupets-promyshlennik Mikhaila Gusiatnikov i ego rod." *Moskovskii krai v ego proshlom*, 61–74. Moscow, 1928.

Index

Page numbers in italics refer to figures

Borovichi rapids, 16, 17, 46, 47–48

Borovichi town, 46, 47

Botovo estate, 132, 171

Boundaries, social, 144, 150, 253. *See also* Ranks; Status, social

Bourdieu, Pierre, xxi, xxiii

Bribery, 33–34

Bruis, Count Iakov Aleksandrovich (Moscow military governor and Petersburg governor-general), 105, 112–113, 144, 156

Burgomasters, 25, 77, 91, 93, 95, 98

Burkhardt, Jakob, xx

Bykov, Ivan Petrov (stepmother's second husband), 88, 89

Camporezi, Francesco (architect), 171

Canals, 14; Ladoga, 17, 18

Cathedral Church of the Epiphany, 232

Cathedral of Archangel Michael, 191

Catherine II (the Great), 7, 26, 31, 38, 51–52, 56, 81, 98, 118, 119, 191, 240; attitudes toward, 193–194, 221, 239; burial of, 193, 194; coronation of, 192; coup of, 54, 172, 202, 247; death of, 176, 183; and education, 9, 103, 104, 105; and freemasonry, 145; reforms of, 44, 92, 98, 110, 112, 113, 134, 136, 252–253

Catherinian Hermitage, 205

Catholic Church, 239–240

Cavos, Caterino (composer), 238, 239

Celebrations, 54, 64–65, 71, 118. *See also* Weddings

Census (1763), 2

Ceremonies, 118–119, 169, 190–191, 221, 238; for new government offices, 98, 99. *See also* Coronations; Imperial family

Charitable initiatives, *see* Philanthropy

Charter to the Towns, 136, 287n9

Chechulin, Nikolai, xxiv, 254

Chernyshëv, Count Zakhar (Moscow governor-general), 96–97, 144, 149

Chesmenskii, General Aleksandr Alekseevich, 247

Chief Magistracy, Moscow, 25, 35, 43, 44, 90, 95, 97

Child mortality, 14, 101, 122–130, 231

Childbirth, 101–102, 140, 162, 176

Children, 224; emotional attachment to, 123, 125–130, 231; illegitimate, 247. *See also* Child mortality

China factory, Verbilki, 4, 94, 99, 174

Chivalric orders, 194, 195

Chobotov, 157, 158, 163, 203, 205

Choikin gardens, 203, 204

Christ the Savior icon, 215

Christ the Savior nail (Nail of Our Lord), 213, *215*

Christenings, *see* Baptisms

Church Administration, 140, 141, 149

Church of Basil the Blessed, Intercession Cathedral, Moscow, 157, 223

Church of Metropolitan Aleksei, 203

Church of Nikita the Martyr, 219

Church of St. Nicholas the Miracle Worker, 158, 170, 219

Church of the Annunciation, St. Nil Monastery, 232

Church of the Kazan Madonna, Sushchëvo, 21

Church of the Life-Giving Trinity, Kapel'ki, 223

Church of the Presentation of the Virgin at the Temple, *see* Presentation Church, Dmitrov

Church of the Resurrection of Christ, Goncharsk region, 90

Church of the Tikhvin Madonna, Krasnoe Selo, 223

Church of the Trinity, Syromiatniki, 250

Churches: construction of, 83, 138–139; use of, 141. *See also names of individual churches*

City assembly (*skhod*), 24, 39

Civil Court, 238

Classicism, 239

Clergy, 30, 75, 84, 138, 149; and dispute resolution, 37, 218, 222. *See also individual names of clergy*

Clock manufacturing, 50

Cloth trade, 225, 250

Commerce, 2, 4, 180, 194, 196, 197; literature on, 44, 103. *See also* Grain trade

Commerce Collegium, 103

Commercial School, 9, 44, 103, 104, 226, 238

Krasnoglasov gardens, 203, 204
Kremlin, Moscow, 118, 119, 190, 191, 192, 216
Krypetskii Monastery, 233
Kuchumov, Ivan (merchant and mayor of Iaroslavl), *135*
Kulikov, Savelii Timofeevich (wife's brother-in-law), 235
Kulikov, Stepan (merchant), 183, 184
Kunstkamera, Petersburg, 64, 152, 154, 249
Kurakin, Boris, xvii, xviii
Kurmanaleev, Captain Vasilii Nikitich, 98, 99
Kuskovo, 102, 203
Kuskovo gardens, 204
Kusov (commerce councilor), 239
Kusova, Irina, 9
Kuznetsov (Uglich paper manufacturer), 220
Kuznetsov, Ivan (collegiate assessor), 242
Kvashnin, Ivan (district police captain), 131, 132, 134, 201, 202, 205; estate of, *see* Lar'kovo estate
Kvasnikov, Ivan (merchant), 159

L'vov, Mikhail Lavrent'ev, 169, 170, 203
Labor disputes, 57
Labzina, Anna (diarist), 22
Lake Ilmen, 17, 47, 48
Lake Ladoga, 17
Lake Mstino, 47
Language, 198, 202; and family relations, 161; of farewell, 217; religious, 191, 212
Lar'kovo estate, 132, 134
Larionova, Mar'ia (serf), 90
Law Code (1649), 43
Laws, 27, 187. *See also* Bankruptcy, laws on; Commission on Laws; Local Governance Law
Lazarus Church, Aleksandr Nevskii Monastery, 152; cemetery of, 231
Lebedev gardens, 204
Legal system, 180, 196. *See also* Courts; Laws; Magistracy Court
Leiman (physician), 208, 210
Leisure activities, *see* Entertainments
Lejeune, Philippe, xvi
Lent, 77, 113, 155

Letovo village, 223, 227
Letstsano, Anton (Dmitrov police commissioner), 43, 98, 132, 144, 145, 146, 147, 149, 153, 238
Levashov, Pëtr Ivanovich, 204
Levi, Giovanni, xiv
Likhachëv, Dmitrii, 67
Likharev, Ivan (cousin of Elizaveta Orlova), 173
Liquor franchise, 33, 114, 141, 164, 206, 246
Literacy, 11. *See also* Education
Local Governance Law (1775), 92, 186
Local government administration, 30, 41–44, 77, 91, 95–96, 106; elections for, *see* Elections; reforms of, 37, 38–39, 44, 92–93, 97–98, 99, 110, 112, 143–144, 252–253; structure of, 24–25, 43–44, 92–93, 112, 137, 170. *See also* Burgomasters; Commission on Laws; Councilors; Magistracy, Dmitrov; Voevoda office; Urban reorganization
Lomonosov, Mikhail, 64
Lopukhin, Pëtr Vasil'evich (Moscow civil governor), 112, 120, 131, 144–145, 147, 160, 171
Lopukhin, Senator Ivan, 195
Loshkin, Aleksandr Vasil'ev (Dmitrov merchant), 38
Loshkin, Fëdor Semënovich (Dmitrov burgomaster), 35–36, 37, 89, 90, 93, 96, 112, 122, 124, 218
Loshkin, Pëtr Sergeev (Dmitrov burgomaster), 29, 38
Loshkin, Stepan Segeev (Dmitrov merchant), 38
Loshkin family, 41
Loshkina, Matrëna Ivanovna (cousin, daughter of Ivan Il'ich), 93, 131
Lukhmanov, Dmitrii Aleksandrovich (Moscow merchant), 229
Lutheran Church, 63, 71, 240
Luzhin, Fëdor Sergeevich, 163, 165, 173; estate of, *see* Grigorovo
Lyskovo, 15, 19, 50, 73, 155

Madonna "Comfort Me in My Time of Sorrow" icon, 200
Madonna the Healer of the Sick icon, 214

DAVID L. RANSEL is Robert F. Byrnes Professor of History and Director of the Russian and East European Institute at Indiana University. His major monographs include *The Politics of Catherinian Russia: The Panin Party; Mothers of Misery: Child Abandonment in Russia;* and *Village Mothers: Three Generations of Change in Russia and Tataria* (Indiana University Press, 2000). He is co-editor of *Imperial Russia: New Histories for the Empire* (Indiana University Press, 1998) and *Polish Encounters, Russian Identity* (Indiana University Press, 2005), and editor and translator of *Village Life in Late Tsarist Russia* (Indiana University Press, 1993).

CPSIA information can be obtained
at www.ICGtesting.com
Printed in the USA
JSHW051743051120
9376JS00003B/45

9 780253 220202